Physics
in a Mad World

Houtermans · Golfand

Physics
in a Mad World

Houtermans · Golfand

Editor

M. Shifman
University of Minnesota

Translated from Russian by
James Manteith

NEW JERSEY · LONDON · SINGAPORE · BEIJING · SHANGHAI · HONG KONG · TAIPEI · CHENNAI · TOKYO

Published by

World Scientific Publishing Co. Pte. Ltd.

5 Toh Tuck Link, Singapore 596224

USA office: 27 Warren Street, Suite 401-402, Hackensack, NJ 07601

UK office: 57 Shelton Street, Covent Garden, London WC2H 9HE

British Library Cataloguing-in-Publication Data
A catalogue record for this book is available from the British Library.

Translation from Russian by James Manteith
Cover design by Anna Lovsky

PHYSICS IN A MAD WORLD

ISBN 978-981-4619-28-8
ISBN 978-981-4619-29-5 (pbk)

Printed in Singapore

CONTENTS

Preface   ix
    M. Shifman
Introduction: Information and Musings   1
    M. Shifman

Part I. Houtermans

Professor Friedrich Houtermans. Works, Life, Fate   91
    Victor Frenkel

1. Introduction   93

2. Beginnings   95

3. Göttingen   99

4. Berlin   107

5. 1933   119

6. London   125

7. Impressions of Kharkov   129

8. Kharkov: 1935-1937   141

9. Arrests   151

10. Last Months in the USSR
    (From Charlotte Houtermans' Diary)   157

11. Descent into the Prisons: 1937-39   172

12. From Desperation to Hope
    (Continuation of Charlotte Houtermans' Diary)   180

13. Fighting for Freedom   194

14. Descent into the Prisons: 1939-40   205

15. The Bridge over the River Bug   210

16. On the Other Shore   214

17. Back in Berlin   218

18. The Plutonium Report   227

19. "They should Accelerate!"   238

20. Back in Kharkov   248

21. Kharkov Trace
    (What Happened at the Session of the Academy of Sciences) 261

22. Who are Beck and Godin?   267

23. War's End   289

24. The Age of the Earth   293

25. Friends on Houtermans   303

26. Chronology   309

Appendices   313
(Compiled by the Editor)

  I. Last diary   315
     Charlotte Houtermans

  II. Odessa 1930   347
     Boris Diakov, G. Nikolaev, and Olga Cherneva

  III. Chronological Report of my Life in Russian Prisons   357
     Friedrich Georg Houtermans

  IV. Letter to Friends (Circa 1946)   369
     Alexander Weissberg

  V. After the war   379
     Edoardo Amaldi

Part II. Golfand

The Life and Fate of Yuri Golfand 391
  Boris Eskin

In Memory of Yuri Abramovich Golfand 463
  Boris Bolotovsky

Index 537

PREFACE

M. SHIFMAN

William I. Fine Theoretical Physics Institute
University of Minnesota, Minneapolis MN 55455, USA
shifman@umn.edu

When destination becomes destiny...

Five decades – from the 1920s till 1970s – were the golden age of physics. Never before have developments in physics played such an important role in the history of civilization, and they probably never will again. This was an exhilarating time for physicists.

The same five decades also witnessed terrible atrocities, cruelty and degradation of humanity on an unprecedented scale. The rise of dictatorships (e.g., in Europe, German national socialism and the communist Soviet Union) brought misery to millions. *El sueño de la razón produce monstruos...*

In 2012, when I was working on the book *Under the Spell of Landau* I thought this would be my last book on the history of theoretical physics and the fate of physicists under totalitarian regimes (in the USSR in an extreme form as mass terror in the 1930s and 40s, and in a milder but still onerous and humiliating form in the Brezhnev era). I thought that modern Russia was finally rid of its dictatorial past and on the way to civility. Unfortunately, my hopes remain fragile: recent events show that the past holds its grip. We are currently witnessing recurrent (and even dangerously growing) symptoms of authoritarian rule: with political opponents of the supreme leader forced into exile or intimidated, with virtually no deterrence from legislators or independent media, the nation's future depends on decisions made singlehandedly. Observing current events in Russia, I better understand how Nazi Germany or the Stalin-Brezhnev Soviet Union could have happened. The future of Russia at large, and of the Russian intelligentsia in particular, is rather unpredictable at the moment. Alas... it seems that lessons from the past are never obsolete.

Recently I came across a number of remarkable essays written in Russian about the lives of two theoretical physicists in the USSR. Although they did not know each other, they both spent some time in Kharkov (now in Ukraine), and there are many other commonalities in their destinies. These essays can be read as highly instructive detective stories, and I decided that it would be important to familiarize Western readers with them. Thus I returned to the task I had set myself previously and which I had left when I finished *Under the Spell of Landau*.

This collection will tell the captivating stories of the misadventures of two renowned physicists. Part I of the book presents the English translation of Victor Yakovlevich Frenkel's monograph *Professor Friedrich Houtermans: Works, Life, Fate*. It was published in 1997 by the St. Petersburg Institute of Nuclear Physics and went largely unnoticed by the general public.[1]

This part is devoted to Friedrich (Fritz) Houtermans, an outstanding physicist who was the first to suggest that the source of stars' energy is thermonuclear fusion, and who made a number of other important contributions to astrochemistry and geochemistry. In 1935 Houtermans, who was a German communist, fled to the Soviet Union in an attempt to save his life from Hitler's Gestapo. Houtermans took an appointment at the Ukrainian Physico-Technical Institute (also known as Kharkov Fiztech) and worked there for three years with the Russian physicist Valentin P. Fomin. In the Great Purge of 1937, Houtermans was arrested by the NKVD (the Soviet Secret Police, the KGB's

---

[1] An excellent book by Edoardo Amaldi about Houtermans' misadventures, which was in the making for about 20 years and complements Frenkel's work, was recently published by Springer Verlag.

predecessor[2]) in December 1937. He was tortured and confessed to being a Trotskyist plotter and German spy, out of fear from threats against his wife Charlotte.[3] However, by that time Charlotte had already escaped from the Soviet Union to Denmark, after which she went to England and finally the USA. After the Hitler-Stalin Pact of 1939, Houtermans was turned over to the Gestapo in May 1940 and imprisoned in Berlin.

The second part consists of two essays written by Boris Eskin and Boris Bolotovsky, respectively, narrating the life story of Yuri Golfand, one of the co-discoverers of supersymmetry, a revolutionary concept in theoretical physics in the twentieth century. In 1973, just two years after the publication of his seminal paper, he was fired from the Lebedev Physics Institute in Moscow. Because of his Jewish origins he could find no job. Under these circumstances, he applied for an exit visa to Israel, but his application was denied. Yuri Golfand became a *refusenik*[4] and joined the human rights movement, collaborating in this with other prominent physicists, including Andrei Sakharov and Yuri Orlov. Throughout the 1970s, to earn his living he had to do manual casual work, while facing repeated harassment from

---

[2]In 1917, shortly after the Bolshevik coup d'état, the Council of People's Commissars created a secret political police, the Cheka, led by Felix Dzerzhinsky. The Cheka was reorganized in 1922 as the Main Political Directorate, or GPU. In 1934 GPU in its turn was reorganized and became the NKVD. In 1946, all Soviet Commissariats were renamed "ministries." Accordingly, the NKVD was renamed as the Ministry of State Security (MGB) which in 1954 became the USSR Committee for State Security (KGB).

[3]Née Charlotte Riefenstahl (1899-1993), received her doctorate in physics at the University of Göttingen in 1927. In 1930, she left her teaching position at Vassar College (Poughkeepsie, NY, USA) and returned to Germany. After a physics conference in Odessa, USSR, in August 1930 during a trip in the Caucasus organized for the participants, Riefenstahl and Houtermans married, with Wolfgang Pauli and Rudolf Peierls as witnesses to the ceremony.

[4]A group of people treated as political enemies in the USSR in the 1970s and 80s. The only "crime" committed by these people was that they had applied for and been denied exit visas to Israel. Yet, they were treated essentially as criminals: fired from jobs and blacklisted, with no access to work (with the exception of low-paid manual labor), constantly intimidated by the KGB with the threat of arrest or other reprisals. In fact, the most active of them, those who tried to organize and defend their rights, were imprisoned.

the KGB. Only 18 years after applying for his exit visa did he obtain permission to leave the country, emigrating to Israel in 1990, shortly before the demise of the Soviet Union.

Many background events that may be sufficiently well-known to the Russian reader but may remain relatively obscure to the Western reader needed accounting for. Accordingly, I have added numerous footnotes scattered throughout the text which hopefully fill the gap and introduce intriguing layers of additional research.

When I started working on these supplementary notes, I realized that I had to dig deeper. In recent years, new archival documents had become available. I met and communicated with many people who knew Houtermans or Golfand, or had some new information about the *personae* mentioned in this collection. Suffice to mention Natasha Koretz (Yuri Golfand's widow), Giovanna Fjelstad (Houtermans' daughter), Jean Richards (Éva Striker's daughter), Mica Nava (Konrad Weisselberg's niece), Artjom Kharlamov (Konrad Weisselberg's grandson), and Michael Koretz (Moisei Koretz's grandson). I obtained from them a large number of relevant photographs which have never been published previously, and I found some others in various archives and online.

Soon I realized that I had much more to say than the footnotes could accommodate. In the case of a few chapters I decided to extend the writers' texts with "Editor's Addenda" placed after each given chapter's conclusion, drawing on recently acquired knowledge to shed light on events narrated by the authors. Moreover, I collected other findings in a rather lengthy Introduction. The reader less interested in background details may skip this Introduction, or return to it later, after reading Parts I and II.

I also included in this book five Appendices. One of them is a remarkable "Last Diary" of Charlotte Houtermans which was kindly provided to me by her daughter Giovanna Fjeldstad. Only some parts of this diary have previously been publicly available. Another Appendix which is not less remarkable is a letter written by Alexander Weissberg and sent to Marcel and Anna Weisselberg [5] and their close friend Gertrude Wagner (undated, circa 1946). This letter is from Mica Nava's personal archive and has similarly never been published.

If not stated to the contrary, footnotes in this collection belong to the Editor.

General Acknowledgments

First and foremost I am grateful to James Manteith. Not only did he masterfully translate Frenkel's, Eskin's and Bolotovsky's essays in this book from Russian, in many instances he acted as my invaluable adviser both on the style of presentation and the relevance of various excerpts from other sources.

I would like to thank Giovanna, Lars and Annika Fjelstad for providing me with Charlotte's papers, as well as for their inspiring conversations and correspondence, and generous assistance. I want to say thank you to Olga Cherneva, Boris Eskin and Boris Bolotovsky for their kind permission for publication of English translations of their writing.

James Manteith.

I am grateful to Anna Lovsky for the cover design and to Leigh Simmons, who handled other aspects of the graphic design. I acknowledge kind permission from the editors of Edoardo Amaldi's book – Saverio Braccini, Antonio Ereditato, and Paola Scampoli – to quote an excerpt from Amaldi (see Appendix V).

I am indebted to Professor Ugo Amaldi (Edoardo Amaldi's son) for a useful and enjoyable conversation. I am grateful to the Niels Bohr Archive, the Council for At-Risk Academics (formerly the Society for the Protection of Science

---

[5] Marcel Weisselberg was Konrad Weisselberg's brother.

and Learning) Archive, ARAN, and the Bodleian Library of Oxford University for making available to me some of the documents mentioned in Frenkel's book.

I would like to say thank you to Meghan Murray, who was in charge of my grant funds and served as this project's translation business coordinator. I am grateful to Natasha Koretz for invaluable assistance, advice and encouragement. Generous assistance of Rajesh Babu, Ben Bayman, Evelina Beketova, RaeAnna Buchholz, Anya Dashevsky, Solomon Endlich, Ilja Feldstein, Mica Nava, and Katy Ziffer is appreciated. Helpful correspondence with Olga Cherneva, Gennady Chepovetsky, Boris Diakov, Colin Harris, Leonid and Elena Glozmans, Heiri Leutwyler, Artjom Kharlamov, A. Khodjamirian, Michael Koretz, E. Nash, Mica Nava, Yuri Raniuk, Jean Richards, Igor Starostin, Judith Szapor, Taisa Tschetschik, N. Tserevitinova, Igor Verba, Alexander Vikman, Vyacheslav Vlasov, Ina Wagner, Stephan Wordsworth, and Lakshmi Narayanan, my friend and World Scientific contact, is gratefully acknowledged. If not stated to the contrary, the photographs in this book are taken from family archives (with kind permission of the owners), from my personal archive, and from Frenkel's book. Some pictures were kindly forwarded to me by Professor Dieter Hoffmann from the Max Planck Institute for the History of Science in Berlin, Germany, who published the German translation of the Frenkel's book in 2011, with a number of additional photographs absent from the book's original Russian edition. I obtained a few other photographs from Saverio Braccini, with kind permission of the University of Bern.

June 2015
Minneapolis

Disclaimer: This book is not an academic monograph on the history of science. The Editor made only a limited attempt at checking facts presented by the writers of the essays included in this collection. The opinions expressed by the writers do not necessarily coincide with the opinion of the Editor.

INTRODUCTION: INFORMATION AND MUSINGS

M. SHIFMAN

William I. Fine Theoretical Physics Institute
University of Minnesota, Minneapolis MN 55455, USA
shifman@umn.edu

1. Victor Frenkel

Professor Victor Frenkel (1930-1997), a son of the famous Russian physicist Yakov Ilyich Frenkel,[1] was an acclaimed historian of Soviet physics, and the author of two academic treatises: one devoted to his father, Yakov Frenkel [1], and another on Matvei Petrovich Bronshtein (1906-1938), a Soviet theoretical physicist who did pioneering work in quantum gravity and cosmology, and who tragically perished during the Great Purge [2]. In working on the Houtermans book Victor Frenkel extensively used archival materials from many countries, including secret documents released in the early 1990s (after the collapse of the Soviet Union) by the FSB, the KGB's successor as modern-day Russia's state security service. This archive was accessible for a while. During a 1989 trip to the USA, Victor Frenkel interviewed Charlotte Houtermans, Friedrich Houtermans' widow, who at that time was still alive and resided in the small town of Northfield, Minnesota. Charlotte provided him with extensive excerpts from her unpublished diaries covering 1937-1938, the

---

[1]Yakov Ilyich Frenkel (1894-1952) is known for his outstanding contributions in condensed matter physics. He was the first to propose the notion of "holes," to be interpreted as positively charged quasiparticles. In semiconductor and insulator physics he proposed a theory (1938) which is now referred to as the Poole-Frenkel effect. In the theory of plastic deformations he laid the foundation of what is currently known as the Frenkel-Kontorova-Tomlinson model.

1

last months of the Houtermans' ordeal in Kharkov, and Charlotte's escape from the USSR. The atmosphere of everyday fear permeates each page of these memoirs, which strikingly convey the tone of life in Kharkov in the time of the Great Purge. Later I will say a few words about the dramatic events at the Ukrainian Physico-Technical Institute: the devastation of its theory group and experimental laboratories, and arrests, arrests, arrests...

Victor Frenkel died with work on his manuscript almost completed but a few gaps still needing to be filled. The book's completion was carried out by his assistant, Dr. Boris Diakov, whose generous advice on certain issues I was happy to use. He supplemented Victor Frenkel's manuscript with excerpts from talks delivered by Frenkel in Denmark, the USA, Germany and Russia. He also compiled a chronology of Friedrich Houtermans' life.

Copyright to Frenkel's book belongs to his widow, Olga Vladimirovna Cherneva. She kindly agreed to give permission for its English translation. Several chapters in this book are long quotations from the diaries of Charlotte Houtermans. In Frenkel's book they are presented in Russian translation. Of course, it was senseless to translate them back into English.

The English originals of the notes which were provided to Victor Frenkel by Charlotte, as well as the rest of his scientific archive, are buried somewhere in the Ioffe Physico-Technical Institute in St. Petersburg. Despite numerous attempts, I failed to obtain copies of any of these documents from there.

Accordingly, in the beginning of 2014 I set out to find Charlotte's daughter, Giovanna, hoping that she might still have the diaries' originals in her possession. I will tell of this expedition's results later in this Introduction.

2. Background

The reader may now find it helpful to have a sketch of the setting for the events to be narrated in the Soviet chapter of drama of Friedrich Houtermans, as well as of its key players.

The Kharkov Fiztech (formerly the Ukrainian Physico-

Victor Frenkel.

Technical Institute, UPTI) was founded by Academician Abram
Ioffe in 1928. In the early 1930s and until the Great Purge in
1937-38, it was the leading physics research center in the USSR.

In 1932 Lev Landau became the head of the Theory Department at the institute, and by 1937, when Landau had to flee Kharkov, his department had become a top-level group. UPTI was the site of the first Soviet experimental splitting of an atomic nucleus (so-called induced fission). In 1940, just a year before the German invasion of the USSR, a memo written in this institute by Friedrich Lange, Vladimir Shpinel and Victor Maslov proposed making an A-bomb based on nuclear fission. In fact, these authors invented the concept of the atomic bomb, as well as a method of separation of the Uranium-235 isotope from uranium ore. Who knows what turns history might have taken if their proposal, "The Use of Uranium as an Explosive," had been adopted at the time

The scientific organization of UPTI was described by László Tisza [3]:

There was an experimental low-temperature group under Lev Shubnikov, Boris Lazarev, and Abram Kikoin; there was also a low-temperature group with Martin and Barbara Ruhemann oriented toward industrial application. By the way, the Ruhemanns wrote a fine book on low-temperature physics, one of the first along this line. It was intended that this group should become an independent institute. The idea of this institute was conceived by Alexander Weissberg, a Viennese engineer and a communist. He joined the UPTI in the early 1930s. He convinced the Commissariat of Heavy Industry of the soundness of applied cryogenics, and he was commissioned to build the new institute. During my May 1934 visit I was enormously impressed by his story, and during my entire stay there beginning in January 1935 he acted as a contractor. I considered it impressive that the apparently rigid system could act with such flexibility. However, all ended differently... Furthermore, an electronics group was working on secret radar problems, and a successful neutron-physics group was established by Fritz Houtermans, a German communist. Last but not least, there was the theory group, headed by Landau.

Landau reviewed the physics journals each week. There was an excellent research library, and he assigned papers to be reported on in the seminars, three-to-four papers for each session... His judgment was accepted without any questions.

The UPTI campus was at the edge of the city. It contained a dormitory, cafeteria, three-room apartments for the senior staff, and a tennis court, apart from the laboratories and workshops.

There were occasional parties of dancing and singing, involving both the scientists and the technicians of the UPTI.

UPTI's first director, appointed in 1929, was Ivan Obreimov. When Obreimov was charged with the task of turning UPTI into a world-class research center, he came up with a brilliant idea: to invite to Kharkov eminent German and Austrian physicists whose situation under Hitler was critical because they were either communist sympathizers, or Jews (sometimes both inconvenient qualities coincided in one person). The first Western physicist hired by Obreimov was Walter Elsasser.[2] In a memoir [4], Elsasser described his conversation with Obreimov and his reasons for accepting the offer:

> Sometime late in 1929 the telephone rang: "This is Obreimov. I am in Berlin and would like to see you." Obreimov was an experimental physicist who had been in Leiden at the same time as I; and since we stayed at the same rooming house, we had become well acquainted. He told me that he had been made director of the Ukrainian Physico-Technical Institute in Kharkov, a large indus-

---

[2]Walter Maurice Elsasser (1904-1991), a German-American physicist, a "father" of the presently accepted dynamo theory explaining the Earth's magnetism. He proposed that the Earth's magnetic field resulted from electric currents induced in the fluid outer core of the Earth.

Alexander Leipunsky with his UPTI colleagues in September 1934 at the entrance to the Main building of UPTI. In the first row from left to right: Lev Shubnikov, Alexander Leipunsky, Lev Landau, and Pyotr Kapitsa.

trial town in Ukraine. Would I be interested in coming to Kharkov for a year as a "technical specialist" under a suitable contract?.. Half of my salary would be paid in rubles that could be not taken out of Russia, the other half in marks or any other currency convertible on the world market. The sum he mentioned would have been generous for a reasonably experienced practical engineer; for me it was princely.

He also informed me that I was the first non-Russian to be associated with the Institute, so it was a thoroughly experimental and challenging undertaking. After a short hesitation I agreed. Although it might not be beneficial to my career as a scientist – and ultimately it wasn't – it offered both a new possibility of escaping from Germany and a great adventure.

Elsasser found UPTI little more than a glorified construction site and cut short his stay [5].

Alexander Ilyich Leipunsky with his wife Antonina Prikhotko.

Later Obreimov's idea was fully implemented by Alexander Leipunsky,[3] who succeeded Obreimov as UPTI's director in 1933.

3. The Accused

I hold in my hands a book by Alexander Weissberg, entitled *The Accused* [6]. It was published in 1951 in New York and, in fact, was one of the first testimonies of a living witness and a victim of the Soviet Great Terror published in the West. I stress, the year of publication was 1951, long before Solzhenitsyn's *Gulag Archipelago*. Let us remember this name, Alexander Weissberg: we will encounter it more than once in the pages of this collection. The foreword to Weissberg's book was written by Arthur Koestler, the famous author of *Darkness at Noon* [7].

Weissberg writes in Chapter 1:

> The aim of this book is to describe happenings without precedent in modern history. From the middle of 1936 to the end of 1938 the totalitarian state took on its final form in the Soviet Union. In this period approximately 8 million people were arrested in town and country by

---

[3] Alexander Ilyich Leipunsky (1903-1972), was born in Poland (although in 1903 his native village was a part of the Russian Empire) into a Jewish family and received his education in Leningrad under Academician Abram Ioffe. In 1937 he was purged from the Communist Party "for aiding the enemies of the people" and removed from his post as UPTI Director. Arrested in Kharkov, Leipunsky was kept in a Kiev prison for two months. Neither A. Weissberg nor F. Houtermans gave any incriminating evidence against him. Leipunsky's case was closed and he was released, an incredibly rare – almost unheard of – occurrence in judicial practice in the Soviet Union.

the secret police (NKVD at that time). The arrested men were charged with high treason, espionage, sabotage, preparations for armed insurrection and the planning of attempts on the lives of Soviet leaders. ... All these men, with very few exceptions, pleaded guilty. They were all innocent...

Alexander Weissberg. Kharkov, 1933. Courtesy of Yuri Raniuk.

Then he continues, with bitterness: "I know that I shall be fiercely assailed by those [in the West] who have made it their business to defend the system of totalitarian lies. I know that like all others who have come forward in the past I shall be ruthlessly slandered. I cannot prevent that..."

4. Alexander Leipunsky

Alexander Leipunsky was a charismatic person. People at the Institute not only respected but loved him.   Edna Cooper (K. Sinelnikov's[4] wife), whom we will meet in the pages of this book, writes [8]: "Alexander Leipunsky, was, as always, charming, it seems that all women in the Institute were in love with him. I'm trying to be an exception." Charlotte Houtermans notes in her diary: "He was *sympatico*, gentle, entertaining, pleasant and intelligent."

In Chapter 2, Weissberg writes:

Communist Leipunsky was appointed as "Red Director." ... His way of life was extremely modest. In 1931 I went

---

[4]Kirill Dmitrievich Sinelnikov (1901-1966), an experimental physicist who was the first to carry out lithium fission in 1932. At UPTI from 1930. Edna Cooper (1904-1967) and Kirill Sinelnikov were married in Cambridge, UK, in 1930, shortly before Sinelnikov's return to the USSR.

with him to Moscow to obtain permission for the publication of a journal of physics. I had been in the Soviet Union only a few weeks, but he and I already got on excellently... Before we went, I noticed the state of Leipunsky's boots. All my Western ideas of propriety revolted at appearing with broken boots for an interview with a high government official.

"Alexander Ilyich," I declared reproachfully, "you can't possibly go to see the People's Commissar with these boots. After all, you're Director of the Institute."

"So what?" he inquired. "They are the only ones I've got and I can't afford to buy any more, with things the prices they are now."[5]

The journal mentioned above was *Physikalische Zeitschrift der Sowjetunion*, which during the six years of its existence – from 1932 till 1938 – played a very important role in connecting physicists from the East and the West. Papers by major players on the theoretical scene, including such titans as P. Dirac, L. Landau, and M. Bronshtein, were published in Russian, German and English in this journal.

The last issue released was the February issue of 1938 (Vol. 13, №2). Although subsequent issues were advertised there, they never appeared. At its peak *Physikalische Zeitschrift der Sowjetunion*'s circulation reached 1,700. After UPTI's fall, such multilingual publications resumed in Russia only after the collapse of the Soviet Union in 1991.

On June 14, 1938, Alexander Leipunsky was arrested by NKVD as a Polish spy. He spent exactly eight weeks in prison under almost continuous interrogation, and left NKVD custody on August 9 a different man, completely broken. The NKVD extorted the following confession [9] from Leipunsky:

My work as Director of UPTI was extremely detrimental

---

[5]According to Weissberg, Leipunsky's monthly salary at that time was 280 rubles. The price of a pair of shoes was 100-120 rubles.

The title page of a volume of *Physikalische Zeitschrift der Sowjetunion* in 1936. This journal was published by the People's Commissariat of Heavy Machine Building. That's where Weissberg and Leipunsky were heading.

to the development of Soviet science. Although I was subjectively not associated with enemy operatives at the Institute, my activity objectively aided the enemy. Only through my assistance and support was the enemy able to sabotage UPTI so prolongedly. My support of the enemy consisted of the following:

1. I brought the spy Houtermans to the USSR and created favorable conditions for his espionage work.

2. I covered up signs of the spy Weissberg's hostile intentions, provided him with various forms of assistance,

and tried to keep him at the institute; I temporarily hid from the NKVD the fact of his obtaining information through espionage, and gave him a positive employee appraisal at his dismissal from the institute.

3. I covered up signs of the hostile intentions of the counterrevolutionaries Landau and Shubnikov, and tried my best to keep them at the institute. I created conditions at the institute for their engagement in sabotage and espionage work. All this happened because I, as a result of my total political recklessness and rotten liberalism, overestimated the importance of connections with Western European science, played lackey to the West, and made conditions at the institute exceptionally favorable for the enemy.

Leipunsky

5. Alexander Weissberg

Since both Leipunsky and Weissberg played such a fateful role in the life of F. Houtermans, I'd also like to acquaint the reader further with Alexander Weissberg. In 1931 Weissberg (or Weissberg-Cybulski, as he is referred to in some documents) became the first senior foreign physicist hired to work at UPTI on a permanent basis. This was a relatively good time in the USSR. Alexander quickly made friends, who started calling him Alexander Semyonovich, following traditional Russian usage of a first name and patronymic. He knew many Western physicists, and he was supposed to entice to Kharkov the most prominent of those who potentially might accept. Here is what Koestler writes in his preface to *The Accused* (see also [10]):

Alex Weissberg was born in 1901 in Krakow, which then belonged to Austria. His father was a prosperous Jewish merchant. In 1906 his family moved to Vienna... He studied physics and engineering in Vienna, where he was graduated in 1926. In 1927 he joined the Austrian Communist Party. Shortly afterwards, he moved to Berlin as an assistant professor at the *Technische Hochschule*.

In 1931 he received an offer from the UPTI in Kharkov and decided to move to the Soviet Union for good... In Kharkov I stayed in the Weissbergs' flat. It was a small but by Russian standards luxurious flat in the vicinity of the Institute. The flat consisted of three rooms, shared by Alex, Éva and Éva's mother.[6]

The Institute was one of the largest and the best-equipped experimental laboratories in Europe. During my stay with Alex and his wife, I met most of the scientists who appear as *dramatic personae* in this book. Among them were Leipunsky and Landau, the infant prodigy of Russian physics... I remember a long discussion with Landau, who argued with great conviction that the works of all the philosophers from the beginning of time up to and excluding Marx are not worth the paper on which they are printed.

Among other things, Koestler also tells the story of Alexander Weissberg's personal life. Before emigrating to the USSR Alexander Weissberg was engaged to Éva Striker, an artist and ceramics designer of Jewish-Hungarian descent.[7] Weissberg arrived in Kharkov in 1931 with a firm intention to establish himself as part of a paradise state of workers and peasants. Éva later joined him in Kharkov, where they were married. Their marriage lasted only a few years, ending in sep-

---

[6]According to Éva Striker's recollections [11], "Alex had a neat apartment in a modern building block of two stories attached to the Ukrainian Physical Technical Institute where he worked. I think it consisted of three rooms and a kitchen. The food situation for somebody like Alex, who had been invited as a foreign expert, was quite good. That meant that he had the right to shop in the stores established for foreigners."

[7]In 1938 after her second marriage in England Éva Striker (also spelled as Éva Stricker and Eva Striker) became Eva Zeisel. After subsequent emigration to the US she eventually made her way to the summit of the artistic Olympus and became an internationally acclaimed designer. Eva Zeisel received many distinguished awards, e.g. the 2002 Living Legend Award from the Pratt Institute, the Middle Cross of the Order of Merit award of the Republic of Hungary (2004), the 2005 Cooper-Hewitt National Design Award for Lifetime Achievements. Eva Zeisel died in 2011 at the age of 105.

aration in 1934 when she left Kharkov for Moscow. On May 26, 1936, Éva was arrested by the NKVD. One of the charges brought against her was her alleged participation in a plot to assassinate Stalin. After a few days of imprisonment in Moscow's *Butyrki*, she was transferred to a Leningrad prison where she was held for 16 months, 12 of them in solitary confinement.

Learning of Éva's arrest, Alexander Weissberg at once realized the probability of his own. Koestler writes that because Weissberg had an Austrian passport, and it was only 1936 on the calendar, he could have gotten an exit visa from the USSR had he acted quickly and, in particular, appealed for help to the Austrian Embassy (still two years before the Anschlüss!). Instead,

Alexander and Éva. Reproduction by courtesy of Jean Richards.

Alexander rushed to Moscow to solicit for Éva. He appealed to higher authorities with whom he had dealt previously in connection with a high-profile gas liquefying facility which he oversaw at UPTI. He even managed to get an audience with USSR Prosecutor General Andrei Vyshinsky. In September of 1937 Éva was deported to Poland. But for Weissberg himself it was too late.

An NKVD prison photograph of Éva Striker.

The story of Weissberg's arrest by the NKVD and imprisonment is described in Frenkel's book and, in more detail, in [6]. In 1940, after the Hitler-Stalin pact, the NKVD handed over to the German Gestapo a group of Austrian and German communists and Jews.

Weissberg was in this group. His subsequent life is no less remarkable [12] (see also Appendix IV, p. 369). The Germans sent the former NKVD prisoners first to a prison in Biała Podlaska, then moved them to Warsaw's Pawiak prison, where they conducted racial selection.[8] Five Jews, including Weissberg, were transferred to the prison at Lublin Castle; others were transported to concentration camps in the Reich. After a two-month stay in the Lublin prison Weissberg was sent to the Krakow ghetto. "This sealed my fate as a physicist. After many years on the run I could not go back to my former vocation," he would later write.

After finding out that he was on a German list of the ghetto dwellers singled out for execution, on March 18, 1942, Weissberg escaped from Krakow and stayed in the ghettos in Bochnia and Tarnow until September 1942. At the beginning of the mass extermination of the Polish Jews he went underground and moved to the "Aryan side" of Warsaw. Here he met Zofia Cybulska, his future wife. On March 4, 1943, Weissberg was arrested by Gestapo agents in the apartment of her mother. Zofia Cybulska had to go into hiding immediately. Weissberg was sent to the Pawiak prison again, and then to a concentration camp in Kaweczyn. He escaped from there with the help of a German foreman. In Warsaw, Zofia Cybulska again took care of him. They survived the Warsaw uprising (April 19-May 16, 1944), in which Weissberg took an active part. After the defeat of the uprising Austrian soldiers saved him from the Pruszków camp. Weissberg spent the last months of the German occupation in hiding in Włochach near Warsaw. When he married Zofia Cybulska he added his wife's name to his, seeking to conceal his identity in anticipation of persecution by the NKVD, which came to Poland with the Red Army. In mid-1946 he managed to escape from Poland to Sweden, where he was soon joined by his wife. Later the couple settled in Paris. In a private letter, Éva's daughter Jean Richards wrote [13]: "I visited Alex

---

[8]Victor Frenkel's version is slightly different, see p. 216.

and Zosia in Paris in 1957. I think he went into real estate.
He was an incredibly gifted businessman, which is ironical for a
communist..."

In the 1950s Michael Polanyi enlisted Weissberg as a participant in the work of the Congress for Cultural Freedom, an
anti-communist advocacy group founded in 1950. He died on
April 4, 1964, in Paris.

6. Holodomor

In 1932 a man-made disaster known as *Holodomor*, or Extermination by Hunger, struck Ukraine. It was caused by Stalin's
ruthless campaign of so-called farm *collectivization*. The property of the best farmers (considered to be enemies of socialism)
was expropriated, and they themselves were exiled to Siberia
with no means of survival. The famine that ensued in Ukraine
was so severe that in 1932 and 1933 several million people died
from starvation. Orders were given to shoot starving people
should they try to escape the zone of famine.

Arthur Koestler witnessed the beginning of *Holodomor* while
traveling in Ukraine in 1932 [10]:

> The train puffed slowly across the Ukrainian steppe. It
> stopped frequently. At every station there was a crowd
> of peasants in rags, offering ikons and linen in exchange
> against a loaf of bread. The women were lifting up their
> infants to the compartment windows – infants pitiful and
> terrifying with limbs like sticks, puffed bellies, big cadav-
> erous heads lolling on thin necks. I had arrived, unsus-
> pecting, at the peak of the famine of 1932-33 ... The
> scenes at the railway stations all along our journey gave
> me an inkling of the disaster, but no understanding of its
> causes and extent.
>
> The Kharkov bazaar was a permanent market held in
> a huge, empty square. Those who had something to sell
> squatted in the dust with their goods spread out before
> them on a handkerchief or scarf. The goods ranged from

The corpses of the starved in the streets of Kharkov at first aroused sympathy. (This and two subsequent photographs are from Alexander Wienerberg's collection).

a handful of rusty nails to a tattered quilt, or a pot of sour milk sold by the spoon, flies included. You could see an old woman sitting for hours with one painted Easter egg or one small piece of dried-up goat's cheese before her. Or an old man, his bare feet covered with sores, trying to barter his torn boots for a kilo of black bread ... Hemp slippers, and even soles and heels torn off from boots and replaced by a bandage of rags, were frequent items for barter. Some of the women had babies lying beside them on the pavement or in their laps, feeding; the fly-ridden infant's lips were fastened to the leathery udder from which it seemed to suck bile instead of milk.

A graphic idea of life in Kharkov in these years can be inferred from snapshots made by an Austrian engineer, Alexander Wienerberg, who spent 19 years in Russia, until 1934, and who witnessed all these events. As of 1933 he was a technical director at a synthetic chemical factory in Kharkov. For me it is hard to understand how Weissberg, and other Westerners who arrived at UPTI later on, could have failed to notice this disaster.

Of course, at that time Weissberg's vision could have been blurred by an unshakable belief in the communist society's radiant future.[9] Yet it wouldn't be long before he changed his mind.

Holodomor did not have such an immediate and devastating impact on UPTI as on the area's general populace, since UPTI was considered of paramount importance to the Soviet government, with food supplies distributed among the UPTI employees. The foreign members of the group were additionally privileged because a part of their salaries was paid in hard currency, which opened them the doors of special stores closed to ordinary Soviet citizens.

7. The beginning of the Great Purge

The advent of the Great Purge was imminent. A careful and unbiased observer could feel it in the air. The first to be arrested on

---

[9]In Weissberg's book (p. 212) I found this illuminating passage: "We all knew the truth, but we were all convinced that socialism would be victorious in the end. We knew that the famine was not an act of God, but due to Stalin's false policy, and we hoped he would soon see his mistake and correct it. Not one of us even thought of overthrowing him, or calling him to account. That would have been impossible without a political revolution, and anything of the sort would have meant the victory of the White counterrevolution supported by masses of starving peasants."

Fritz Houtermans himself left us remarkable evidence of the ideological bias of leftist intellectuals at that time. In May 1945 Houtermans authored a brief report about his ordeals in Soviet prisons from 1937 to 1940 (see Appendix III, p. 357). This report ends with the following postscript:

"... I do not want any propagandistic conclusions to be drawn from my experiences... I want to emphasize again that apart from the treatment by which false confessions were forced from people in Russian prisons by the questioning officials under special order from the government, nearly no facts have been brought to my knowledge indicating sadistic or even incorrect treatment in prisons by prison officials in the execution of their duties. It is my opinion that most of the atrocity stories being told by prisoners about the executions are incorrect. I don't know any case in which a prisoner has seen the execution of another one though I have frequently met people who had been sentenced to death and had sat in a so-called 'death cell' after revision of their sentences."

The empty "Khartorg" (Kharkov Trade Cooperative) food distribution site besieged by the devastated population of Kharkov.

The windows of the empty food sites decorated only by pictures of Stalin and other Muscovite rulers.

political charges, in the spring of 1936, was Éva Striker, Alexander Weissberg's wife. In 1937, when the Great Purge was fully unleashed, UPTI was decimated, with virtually all leading researchers ending up in the Gulag, executed or deported. Among those sentenced to death were Lev Shubnikov (1901-1937), Lev Rozenkevich (1905-1937), Vadim Gorsky (1905-1937), Valentin Fomin (1909-1937), and Konrad Weisselberg (1905-1937). After the first arrests, Lev Landau, the future Nobel Prize winner, who headed the UPTI theory department, left for Moscow but was arrested there in April 1938. He spent a year in NKVD prison, and only Pyotr Kapitsa's appeal to Stalin saved his life. Moisei Koretz (we will encounter his name more than once in the second part of the book), a colleague and collaborator of Lev Landau, suffered a similar fate: arrested in 1938 as Landau's co-conspirator, Koretz spent 14 years in the Gulag. Altogether 11 UPTI employees were run down by Stalin's repression machine [14].

UPTI ceased to exist as a center of excellence for theoretical and experimental physics. Its happy golden years were gone. On September 20-26, 1937, at the Second All-Union Conference on Atomic Nuclei in Moscow, the participants in the conference addressed Comrade Stalin with these passionate words of admiration [9]:

"The successful development of Soviet physics occurs against the background of a general decline of science in capitalist countries, where science is falsified and is placed at the service of greater exploitation of man by man... Vile agents of fascism, Trotskyist-Bukharinist spies and saboteurs ... do not stop short of any abomination to undermine the power of our country ... Enemies penetrated among physicists, carrying out espionage and sabotage assignments in our research institutes ... Along with all the working people of our socialist motherland, Soviet physicists more closely unite around the Communist party and Soviet government, around our great leader Comrade Stalin ..."

A special apartment house built by UPTI in 1928 as a residence for its most distinguished members, a house which had

Participants in a meeting at UPTI in Kharkov, May 1934. Left to right: D. Ivanenko, L. Tisza (obscured), L. Rosenfeld, unknown (obscured), Yu. Rumer, Niels Bohr, J. D. Crowther, L. Landau, Milton Plesset, Yakov Frenkel, Ivar Waller, E. J. Williams, Walter Gordon, V. A. Fock, I. E. Tamm. Credit: American Institute of Physics Emilio Segrè Visual Archives, *Physics Today Collection.*

seen such guests as future Nobel laureates Niels Bohr, Werner Heisenberg, Paul Dirac, John Cockcroft, Pyotr Kapitsa, Nikolay Semenov, Irene and Frederic Joliot-Curie, and Igor Tamm, fell into disuse...

8. *Other foreigners at UPTI*

Alexander Weissberg, after his arrival to Kharkov in 1931, attracted a small constellation of other top foreign scientists. In the summer of 1931, Weissberg returned to Vienna on holiday, with a mission to find and hire experimentalists. "Friends recommended Martin Ruhemann. The British-born Ruhemann moved to Germany as a young man. His German wife, Barbara, was also a physicist... Ruhemann worked in the low-temperature laboratory and in 1935 he and Weissberg proposed a plan for a new low-temperature research station, to develop the local

Among the most notable participants of the Second All-Union conference on nuclei structure were (front row, left to right) F. Joliot, Academician A. F. Ioffe, I. Joliot-Curie, and (second row) Academician D. V. Skobeltsyn and President of the USSR Academy of Sciences S. I. Vavilov. Courtesy of ARAN [15].

A session of the USSR Academy of Sciences.

nitrogen industry and other branches of the Soviet chemical industry." [5]

Between 1935 and 1937, Ruhemann was the prospective scientific director of this large new development, with Weissberg as director and manager of the construction. Weissberg's description of Ruhemann's initial reaction to the living and working conditions in Kharkov, followed by his gradual change of heart, is illuminating [6]:

"When he first came to the Soviet Union in 1932 the country was experiencing the worst year since the end of the civil war. At first he and his wife were always on the point of leaving. All they could see was chaos, poverty and hunger. He had never thought much about the significance of social revolutions but once in the Soviet Union he grasped what was really at stake and was swept up in a new and larger movement than he had ever known before."

Another Western arrival in 1935, Hungarian László Tisza, who was trained in Göttingen and Leipzig, represented a younger generation.

Here is an excerpt from a 1965 interview [10] with Victor Weisskopf, who went on after Kharkov to serve as the head of a theoretical physics group at Los Alamos, New Mexico, during the Manhattan Project, and, later, as Director General of the European Center for Nuclear Research (CERN) at Geneva:

> I went to Russia for one-half year, from February until my Rockefeller [fellowship] started, which was October or November 1932. I was there altogether about nine months. They invited me. I had a number of friends in Kharkov; Viennese who went there, communists who moved over. It was a very bad time. A lot of people who were either communists, half-communists or non-communists who just went there because it was the only place where you could stay alive. There was a new institute in Kharkov; Landau was there, as was Alexander

---

[10]This and Tisza's interview below are quoted according to [16].

Weissberg... He is a converted man now. He is a very interesting man: mostly a politician but started off in physics. He, at that time, was a big shot in Kharkov; he invited me. Placzek[11] also came and Houtermans was there.

Houtermans was an assistant of Richard Becker during the Berlin years, and I was very much in contact with him there. At Houtermans' house in Berlin I kept up in physics, but mostly I was busy with politics and met many people of the leftist-liberal type. That was an exciting time in Berlin. At any rate, Houtermans was later in Kharkov, which was sort of a receptacle of refugees, either depression refugees or Nazi refugees... László Tisza was also there.

The group of Western expats at UPTI included, among others, Fritz Lange, Konrad Weisselberg, Ürgen Peters (Lange's assistant), etc. I will say a few words about them, starting with the Ruhemanns.

9. The Ruhemanns

When Ruhemann's friends began to disappear one by one, and his contract was not renewed, he applied for exit visas. In his unpublished book *Half a Life*, Ruhemann wrote that he did not betray the ideals of communism, but realized that even his ide-

---

[11]Georg Placzek (1905-1955) was a Czech physicist, born in Brno, Moravia to Jewish parents. Placzek studied physics in Prague and Vienna. He worked with Hans Bethe, Edward Teller, Rudolf Peierls, Werner Heisenberg, Victor Weisskopf, Enrico Fermi, Niels Bohr, Lev Landau, Edoardo Amaldi, Emilio Segré, Leon van Hove and many other prominent physicists of his time, in the areas of Raman scattering, molecular spectroscopy in gases and liquids, neutron physics and mathematical physics. Together with Otto Frisch, he suggested a direct experimental proof of nuclear fission. Together with Niels Bohr and others, he was instrumental in clarifying the role of Uranium-235 for the possibility of nuclear chain reaction. During his stay in Landau's circle in Kharkov, Placzek witnessed the brutal reality of Stalin's regime. His first-hand experience of this influenced the political opinions of his close friends, Robert Oppenheimer and Edward Teller in particular. Later, Placzek was the only Czech with a leading position in the Manhattan Project.

ological purity was no guarantee against Stalin's purges. And further:

> In 1937, we began to move away from our Kharkov environment. It was very easy, because all of our friends and colleagues had already moved away from us, treating us as dangerous foreigners.

After a six-month nerve-wracking wait, exit visas were received and the Ruhemanns family made it safely to England (see pp. 26 and 34), where husband and wife lived long lives (Martin died in 1994) doing research in things they loved – cryogenics and gas separation. Yet it's important to realize that the toxic atmosphere of a state where the government tells each and every one of its citizens what is right and what is wrong, the pressure of fear, can break even decent people. In the days preceding Weissberg's arrest, the Ruhemanns helped him considerably, both financially and morally. Yet after his arrest...

From A. Koestler's preface to *The Accused*:

> ... Professor Shubnikov was later on to testify that Alex had tried to recruit him for the Gestapo, which offer he only refused because he (Shubnikov) had allegedly been in the service of a German espionage organization since 1924. Our neighbors and most intimate friends were Martin and Barbara Ruhemanns, of whom the latter, when I asked her to help Alex, affirmed that she had always known him to be a counterrevolutionary saboteur. Every member of that happy band of scientists who used to come in after dinner to play cards or drink tea, stood up after Alex's arrest and denounced him. They were neither cowards nor inferior human beings [but] ...

It seems to me that the following two stories unambiguously illustrate the mindset of the Ruhemanns. The first dramatic (although perhaps a blessing in disguise for those of its participants who responded to the warning signs) episode – the story of Placzek – is narrated by Edoardo Amaldi [17] (pp. 40-41).

Once Martin Ruhemann, a German physicist working in low temperature, gave a reception for all physicists present in Kharkov, Russian as well as foreigners.

Not long before, Placzek had received the offer of a permanent chair, and a few of the people present asked him what was his decision. Placzek, in his typical joking mood, answered that he was ready to accept provided five conditions were fulfilled. "But what are the conditions?" his friends asked.

Martin Ruhemann, circa 1935.
Courtesy of Yuri Raniuk.

The first condition was that his salary should be larger than a certain satisfactory value, the second one that about one third of the salary had to be paid in pounds because he wanted to spend every year two or three months abroad in order not to lose contact with the international scientific community. The third condition was that at least two young people who could work with him had to be paid in some form. The fourth condition was that the economic treatment of these young people had also to be decent. Finally, the fifth condition was that the "Khozyain must go."

"Khozyain" in Russian means Boss (or Master) and at that time was a euphemism for Stalin. Everybody laughed and commented humorously.

The wife of Ruhemann, Barbara, who was a very rigid party member, reported this little story to the Communist Party in Kharkov with the result that shortly later the local newspaper started to attack the foreign physicists with gradually heavier and more explicit accusations of being German spies.

Weisskopf, Placzek and most of the others understood immediately the general trend taken by the situation and rapidly left the USSR. Weisskopf went to Zurich where he stayed three years, married Ellen Tvede in 1934, and after a short return to Copenhagen went to the USA in 1937.

UPTI, Kharkov, 1933. Barbara Ruhemann is on the right. This is the only photograph of Barbara Ruhemann I could find (courtesy of the Landau Virtual Museum). The first from the left is Lev Landau.

A colorful description of the second episode (or, rather, a chain of episodes) can be found in Alexander Weissberg's book [6] (pp. 68-71):

> Ruhemann left the Soviet Union in the spring of 1938 and went to England, where, despite everything, he joined the Communist Party...
>
> Eleven years after these events I came to England... In London I met Arthur Koestler and when I told him I was looking forward to seeing Ruhemann he was furious.
>
> "What, you want to get into touch with Martin Ruhemann! You're mad. He's an out-and-out Stalinist."
>
> "That's incredible."
>
> "Is it? Very well, I'll tell you something. When we

Éva Striker and Alexander Weissberg. Circa 1932. Courtesy of Jean Richards.

hadn't heard anything of you for two years, a few of us tried to do something about it. Albert Einstein wrote a letter on your behalf to Stalin, and so did Perrin, Joliot-Curie, and one or two others. We wanted Ruhemann's signature because he had been more or less a witness to what had happened in 1937, so I went to see them. I noticed Barbara's face harden at once when I told them what I had come for. 'We'll do nothing of the sort,' she said. 'Alex Weissberg was a counterrevolutionary.'

"I was flabbergasted. 'Perhaps I don't know what you mean by a counterrevolutionary, Barbara,' I said, 'but do you think it's decent to let Alex rot in a GPU prison without making any attempt to help him?' But she answered abruptly: 'We don't want to have anything to do with the business.'

"I turned to Ruhemann: 'What about you, Martin?' He seemed a bit uncertain of himself, but he agreed with her: 'Look, Arthur,' he said, 'perhaps I wouldn't put it quite so sharply as Barbara has done, but in the matter itself I don't think I can do anything.'

"So much for Ruhemann. You can imagine how I reacted, Alex. I got up at once and slammed the door behind me."

Then Weissberg continues:

One February evening in 1948 I knocked at Ruhemann's door.

"Alex," he stuttered. "Alex. It's you!"

"Yes," I answered cheerfully. "It's me. Have I changed so much?"

"No," he said, "you look just the same as ever."

"Alex," he said finally, "Do you remember what you said to me the night when the GPU was waiting for you down below and we said good-by?"

"No, I can't say I do."

" 'Despite everything, Martin, never forget that this country is the fatherland of the free workers and peasants.' "

"Martin, since then eleven years have passed. Eleven years of tremendous happenings in which the monstrous lie has lost its mask. If you are still fighting under the old flag then you are fighting for the oppression of the people and not for its freedom."

"Alex, what am I to do? I can't bring myself to believe that all my conscious political life was an error. There are two camps in the world today, the Soviet Union and the United States. Am I to side with the American imperialists?"

10. Tisza

László Tisza (1907-2009), already mentioned, managed to get out alive, and later became a prominent American physicist. Much has been written about him in connection with Edward Teller, with whom he was on friendly terms since the end of the

1920s. Tisza graduated from Budapest University, then studied in Göttingen. In 1932 he was arrested by the Hungarian government as a communist sympathizer and spent 14 months in prison. After his release, he moved to Kharkov and worked in the theory group of Lev Landau up to its demise in 1937. Tisza managed to escape from Kharkov to Paris. In 1938, he proposed a two-fluid model of helium-II, explaining the occurrence of superfluidity. He emigrated to the U.S. in 1941 and was a distinguished Massachusetts Institute of Technology professor until 1973. Luck was on his side, you might say ...

From the transcript of a 1987 interview with Tisza:

In Copenhagen Teller met Landau, and told Landau about me, and at that time Landau was in Kharkov in the Ukrainian Physical Technical Institute, which was at the beginning a very promising Soviet institution. Landau was a very interesting inspiration. Teller said,

"Would you take him?"

"Why not?"

Then I got the invitation in June, 1934, to visit Kharkov. There was an international meeting, with a number of British, and French physicists participating. I don't think any Americans went there, but Bohr himself went, and Solomon, who was a son-in-law of Langevin...

Landau offered me a research fellowship to be an *aspirant*, you know, the term *aspirant*, it's a doctoral candidate. Although I had my PhD, but Russia had a completely different standard. Doctor was a very high degree. The candidate degree corresponded to a PhD. In January, 1935, I arrived in Russia. In 1934, when the whole deal was struck, the atmosphere was relatively relaxed. It was after the big collectivization crisis, but in 1934 there was a good harvest, the first good harvest in many years, and the general feeling was that things are going better... By the time I came there in January, the situation was not nearly as relaxed...

About the same time Landau wrote several papers on an innovative theory of the phase transitions that Ehrenfest had recently classified as a transition of second order. By that time I already had a reading knowledge of Russian and I was asked to translate Landau's Russian manuscript into German for publication in the *Physikalische Zeitschrift der Sowjetunion*, a journal which was edited at the UPTI...

Fritz Houtermans was there. Originally a theorist in astrophysics, he worked there in nuclear physics. He started off with neutron physics. And Fritz Lange, a German from a German electric company. He had a famous work on ... aiming the lightning in the Alps and devising high tension. He developed a method of taking condensers in parallel, charging them and switching ... to get high voltage. That was a method of getting particle accelerators, and he built one in Kharkov ...

11. Lange

Friedrich (Fritz) Lange was one of the authors of the 1940 memo "The Use of Uranium as an Explosive," which was drafted and sent to the Soviet government, as previously mentioned. Born in Berlin in 1899, he worked on his thesis under the supervision of Walther Nernst at the University of Berlin, where he later received a research position. He was an active member of the German Communist Party. In 1935, fleeing from the Nazis and invited by UPTI's director, he moved to Kharkov, where he was appointed head of the laboratory of high-voltage studies. The 1937 disaster at UPTI did not touch him. I do not know why. In the summer of 1942, before the German occupation of Kharkov, Fritz was evacuated to Ufa together with the Institute. There he developed a method for the separation of uranium isotopes using centrifuges, as is still done today (Uranium-235, suitable for the A-bomb, represents a small fraction of the material in raw uranium ore, which consists mostly of Uranium-238). In 1952, Lange was allowed to return to Dnepropetrovsk Polytechnic Institute, and in 1954 was appointed head of a department of the Electrical Engineering Institute in Moscow. Lange failed in his first attempt to get permission to leave for East Germany (the now defunct GDR) in 1957, but the second attempt was a success. On March 19, 1959, Fritz Lange left the USSR for good. Lange was the only foreign scientist working in the Soviet Union under Stalin who was not subject to any reprisals. He died in 1987, two years before the fall of the Berlin Wall.

12. Weisselberg

Konrad Weisselberg. Born in 1905 in Berlad, Bukovina, into a Jewish family. His father Bernard Weisselberg was an assimilated German-speaking timber merchant. In 1907 his family fled from *pogroms* to Chernovtsy, the capital of Bukovina.[12] From there they were forced to flee again, in 1914, ahead of the invading Russian army, to Vienna. Konrad Weisselberg graduated from Vienna University and then earned there his doctorate in chemistry. By the early

Konrad Weisselberg in Kharkov. Courtesy of Mica Nava and Katerina Sajez.

1930s, his elder sister Erna and Konrad himself were members of the Communist Party. His elder brother Marcel joined their father's business.

Konrad Weisselberg arrived in Kharkov in 1934 at the invitation of Alexander Weissberg, who found him a research position at the Coal and Chemistry Institute. In 1936 he was hired by UPTI and became Weissberg's neighbor. In Weissberg's *The*

---

[12]A historical region currently divided between Romania and Ukraine, located on the northern slopes of the central Eastern Carpathians and the adjoining plains. Historically part of Moldavia, the territory of Bukovina was, from 1774 to 1918, an administrative division of the Habsburg Monarchy, the Austrian Empire, and Austria-Hungary.

Accused Konrad Weisselberg appears as Marcel.

He married a Ukrainian girl, Anna Mykalo [13] (Lena in Weissberg's *The Accused*), but this did not help him. In February 1937 Konrad Weisselberg renounced his Austrian citizenship; he was arrested on March 4, 1937. Weisselberg was indicted on charges of sabotage against the Soviet Union, establishing a criminal contact with the German intelligence agent A. Weissberg, and becoming a member of Weissberg's counterrevolutionary group. After ten months of interrogations, the Procurator General of the USSR, Vyshinsky, sentenced him to death without trial on October 28, 1937; he was executed on December 16 of the same year [9].

We can see that the Houtermans' fates were not the direst...

13. A detective story

> *Distorted shadows fell*
> *Upon the lighted ceiling:*
> *Shadows of crossed arms,*
> *Of crossed legs,*
> *Of crossed destiny.*
>
> *B. Pasternak*

Victor Frenkel was not only a skillful biographer. On certain occasions he had to act as an insightful detective investigator uncovering the truth in mystery cases – for instance, solving the

---

[13] Mica Nava recalls that Ms. Mykalo was a young woman without formal education from a village in southern Ukraine. Konrad Weisselberg fell in love with her madly. To marry Ms. Mykalo he left his Jewish girlfriend Klara in Vienna. Artjom Kharlamov, Konrad Weisselberg's grandson, in a letter to Mica Nava writes: "When Konrad first met her she was working as a waitress at UPTI's restaurant and accidentally tipped over a bowl of *borsch*, ruining Konrad's suit when he was having a lunch together with some other foreign specialists. This is how it all started... She was scared to death because she thought that she would be fired immediately, and started crying as she was trying to clean up the mess... At that time it was very hard to find even that kind of work in Kharkov, especially for a village girl. Konrad was very kind and was trying to console her the best he could... Maybe it was partially his love and partially Konrad's naïveté and genuine belief in human goodness which made him make an ultimate mistake – to adopt Soviet citizenship. By doing so he signed his death warrant..."

mystery of the genuine names of Beck and Godin (see p. 267). Once, in working on this collection, I came across a similar challenge (although on a smaller scale, of course).

In May 2015 I got a message from a reader, Igor Starostin, who wrote:

> I am haunted by the following question: in Raniuk's book [9, 14] the wife of Konrad Weisselberg is referred to as Anna Mykalo. But in my childhood I knew her as Galina, aunt Galia.[14] My mother – Gerda Bratz and Galina – were friends since 1935. My mother met her at the Weissbergs, (if I remember correctly, their apartment was on Tchaikovsky Street, 16). She used to visit them with the Ruhemanns. They – my mom and aunt Galia – kept in touch until my mom's death in 1993, though mostly only by correspondence. The last time they met in person was seemingly in 1968, when we stayed with aunt Galia in Kharkov for a short time.
>
> My mom, Gerda Charlotte Bratz, was born in 1914 in Berlin. She came in Kharkov in 1934, with Martin and Barbara Ruhemanns, as a governess for their son Stephen. In Kharkov she met Weissberg, Landau, and many others who later became *personae* in the Case of UPTI. Weissberg found a job for my mother at the UPTI Cryogenics Laboratory, seemingly in the library. She met Galina Mykalo at Weissberg's place, where Konrad Weisselberg too met his future wife. I think you know that Konrad called his son Alexander in honor of Weissberg.
>
> My mother told me that after Konrad Weisselberg's arrest, aunt Galia was allowed to bring some food for Konrad to the NKVD; in return she was given Konrad's underwear for washing. The clothes were covered with blood. Then one day, a prison official did not accept food and clean clothes from aunt Galia; she was told that it

---

[14]Galia is a diminutive form of Galina.

was no longer necessary.

Weissberg was arrested too. Landau left. Meanwhile my mother got married to a Cryogenics Laboratory employee, Vassiliy Ulanov, and gave up her German citizenship in favor of Soviet citizenship. This did not allow her to obtain permission to leave the USSR to accompany the Ruhemanns. They left for London, via Italy. Originally the Ruhemanns had planned to take my mom with them for some time since Stephen (their son) was very attached to my mother. However, the exit visa for her was refused. Until 1941, she worked at the Cryogenics Laboratory. On October 2, 1941, she was deported from Kharkov, and sent to Saratov Oblast, to the Volga German Soviet Republic. Ironically by that time the Volga German Republic had already been disbanded by Decree of the USSR Supreme Soviet of August 28, 1941, and all ethnic Germans from there had been exiled to Siberia and Kazakhstan.

My mom, naturally, did not reach Saratov; she was intercepted by authorities and sent to a village, Mezheninovka, Tomsk Oblast, which was one of the Siberian villages intended for resettlement of ethnic Germans from the Volga region. In December 1942, she was conscripted into the so-called Labor Army in Novosibirsk, where she remained until 1946. Then she was returned to a resettlement village for ethnic Germans (Moryakovsky Zaton) near Tomsk. Only in 1956 she was allowed to leave. But she stayed in the same village; there were about a dozen German families there. I was born there in 1961. In 1984 my mom moved to Kyrgyzstan's capital. She used to say that the years she had spent at UPTI were the happiest years of her life. Her memories of Alex Weissberg and Konrad Weisselberg were warm and affectionate. Soon after her discharge from the Labor Army she managed to locate and contact Galina Mykalo in Ukraine, and their friendship resumed.

Happy UPTIers, Dnepropetrovsk, May 1935. From left to right: László Tisza, Galina Mykalo, Alexander Weissberg. Standing in the second row is Gerda Bratz. If they only knew what awaited them... Courtesy of Igor Starostin.

Independently, Jean Richards, after reading a draft of my Introduction, told me that her mother Eva Striker-Zeisel used to address Weisselberg's wife as Galia Davydovna.

This small discrepancy – Anna versus Galina – inspired my curiosity, and I decided to try to solve this puzzle.

First I wrote to Kharkov-based physicist and historian of science Yuri Raniuk, an expert on the UPTI case. He replied:

I never met Mrs. Mykalo-Weisselberg in person. I talked to her son Alexander Kharlamov, asking him to help her write an autobiography, which she did. More exactly, she dictated and Alexander wrote it down. There it was explicitly stated "Anna Davydovna Mykalo."

When I was writing my book [14], I tried to make inquiries with UPTI people who might have remembered Mykalo. They all went crazy about her. Apparently, she had a reputation as a very popular woman. All the institute men crowded around her. I could spend hours talking about it. She was a lab assistant, while the crowd consisted of professors. I even asked a stupid question: "What fascinated you about her?" The reply was that she was a sorceress. Period.

Having failed with Raniuk, I continued my searches until I came across the book *Visceral Cosmopolitanism: Gender, Culture and the Normalization of Difference* [18], written by Mica Nava, a professor at the University of East London. To my great surprise, she happened to be Konrad Weisselberg's niece!

From her book I learned some facts completely or largely unknown to Russian and Ukrainian historians of science. I reproduce here an excerpt from pp. 139-141:

Meanwhile my uncle Konrad Weisselberg, my father's brother, had moved to Kharkov in the USSR, married a Ukrainian woman and taken up Soviet citizenship. After completing his PhD at the University of Vienna he was apparently offered a job at Harvard but (to the disappointment of my grandfather) preferred to go to Kharkov's Physical Technical Institute, then one of the best research institutes in the world, to which a number of Austrian and German scientists – many of them communists and Jews – had gone, hoping both to contribute to Soviet science and to escape the escalating menace of fascism.

Central among them was Alex Weissberg, Konrad's close friend, who later wrote a much-cited and translated personal account and political analysis of Soviet mass interrogations in the late 1930s. Both Alex Weissberg and my uncle were among those imprisoned, interrogated and tortured by the NKVD in 1937. Both were accused of being Trotskyists and counterrevolutionary agents of the Gestapo. Alex survived three years of incarceration to write the book (and a further five in wartime Warsaw). My uncle Konrad was executed. He left behind his wife, Galia, who was designated "a wife of an enemy of the people." She was deprived of her home and job, and their year-old child, my first cousin, also Alex. Galia, unsurprisingly, suffered a nervous breakdown, and young Alex became a feral child in war-torn Kharkov, living in cellars and begging for food from both Soviet citizens and the German occupying forces. But he too survived. He was taken in by a neighbor, studied and did well. In 1959, after Stalin died, his father was posthumously rehabilitated. Contact with the family in the West was tentatively remade and thereafter sustained, albeit infrequently, given the dangers and impediments of the cold war.

Then, fifty years after Konrad's death, in Gorbachev's more liberal regime, my cousin Alex [15] and his wife Nadia (whose Ukrainian surname, Kharlamov, he adopted to protect himself from Soviet antisemitism) met up with my brother Kiffer and his wife Alison in a Moscow hotel. With the aid of an interpreter they talked incessantly all day and most of the night.[16]

After this initial encounter we all communicated regularly and in 1991 the Ukrainian family came to visit us in the UK. They were here for the electrifying events which marked the collapse of the Soviet Union and witnessed the drama through the lens of the BBC refracted again through our minimal Russian and their limited English. Then in 1996, nearly sixty years after Konrad's death,

---

[15] Alexander Kharlamov (previously Weisselberg) was born in 1936 and died in 2008.

[16] Before he went, Kiffer asked Alex what he would like from the West. We had predicted he would ask for Levis for the kids but he chose a Geiger counter to measure the effects of radioactive fallout from Chernobyl. So much for fantasies about the hegemony of Western popular culture! -Mica Nava.

the KGB opened their archives to the relatives of those executed in the great purge and Alex, by now a middle-aged man, found a meticulously logged transcript of the ten-month interrogation of his father.[17]

This was finally what convinced him to make all efforts to "return" to Western Europe. We did our best to help track down the critical evidence of his father's Austrian citizenship, which was not easy given that all documents had been destroyed, but paradoxically the data in the NKVD interrogation record itself provided most of the information required by the Austrian government. So, in the year 2000, Konrad's direct descendants – Alex, his children and grandchildren – finally gained Austrian citizenship[18] and moved in 2001, as EU citizens, with their spouses to the UK, where they have experienced the tough uprooted lives of migrants but are now settled – indeed thriving – and are part of my complex international extended family.

A few days later Igor Starostin, who was the first to draw my attention to the Anna-Galina puzzle, found a key to its solution. In his subsequent letter I read:

Recently, in my mother's address book I found Mykalo's Kharkov address. This address book is approximately from 1990, and there she appears under the name of Anna Davydovna Mykalo. At the same time, in mom's photo album from the same time I found a caption that reads Galia Mykalo. Perhaps, she had two names, one official and another unofficial.

---

[17]"The File of Konrad Weisselberg," transcribed by Alex Kharlamov in 1997 from Interrogation Record №016138, Kharkov District, Ukraine NKVD Archive, 1937. Interestingly the transcript corroborates Alex Weissberg's claim that Konrad's and Weissberg's association with a Czech physicist named Placzek, considered by the NKVD to be a subversive Trotskyist, was the trigger for their arrests. -Mica Nava.

[18]With the help of Ina Wagner, Gerti Wagner's (ex)daughter-in-law in Vienna, and Don Flynn of the Joint Council for the Welfare of Immigrants in London. -Mica Nava.

On the very same day I received the following message from Mica Nava:

> The NKVD interrogation transcript is attached. I see in the transcript that her formal legal name seems to have been Anna but she was always known as Galia or Galina.

The file from Mica Nava's personal archive, the English translation of the NKVD-KGB file of Konrad Weisselberg (published in Russian in the last chapter of [14]), includes some documents absent in the Russian version, in particular, K. Weisselberg's rehabilitation documents from the 1950's. Most importantly, it includes a remarkable note added by Alexander Kharlamov, Konrad Weisselberg's son, in 1997:

> On 16 December 1996 I managed to see and make a copy of my father's file. It was 59 years to the day since he was shot. At the very moment I picked up the file a violent snow-storm erupted, accompanied by thunder. A thunderstorm in winter? Most unusual in our part of the world! For me it was a most eerie sensation. Reading my father's file has been a harrowing experience.
>
> I was above all impressed that he consistently denied any guilt. This was very rare. As you know, Alex Weissberg held on for a long time, then admitted his guilt (he took time out, I might venture to say) and then retracted his confession, repeating this pattern several times. And this, although the interrogators treated him more mercifully because he was a foreign citizen.
>
> I can only imagine how they tortured my father. For a long time we kept his underwear (one of the few items he was allowed to change); time after time we found it not specked, but completely soaked with his blood. And this lasted for ten long months.
>
> What is so shocking is not only the groundlessness and absurdity of the charges but the complete lack of any material evidence. Most dreadful of all is that he was given absolutely no trial. They simply sent to Moscow a

list of people to be shot, and the list was signed by the supreme executioners: Yezhov and Vyshinsky.

I just imagine my father, a defenceless and a very kind man – according to my mother he wouldn't even hurt a fly – trying to oppose this senseless, angry and merciless Bolshevik system. He stood up for his good name and for his family. He knew what life was like for the family of an enemy of the people. He never succumbed; he maintained his innocence. This is staggering.

Anna-Galina Mykalo with her son Alexander Weisselberg, May 1946.

14. Stalin's order

On July 20, 1937, a meeting of the Politbureau of the VKPb [19] was convened. Appended to the top secret minutes of this meeting was a memo written by Stalin and addressed to the meeting's participants. Its concluding part reads [19]: "All Germans

---

[19]See footnote 59 on page 155.

in our military, paramilitary and chemical plants, power plants, construction sites, in <u>all areas</u>, are to be <u>arrested</u>" (underlined by Stalin).

Public face of Iosif (Joseph) Stalin.

On July 25, five days after Stalin's directive, People's Commissar of Internal Affairs N. Yezhov issued order №00439, which was dispatched to all NKVD units. The preamble of Yezhov's order is as follows: "Agents from among the German citizens in the USSR currently realize subversive acts. Their main task is to be ready for the forthcoming war, by preparing for this purpose trained saboteurs who will focus on the organization of sabotage during the war" [20]. To put an end to these alleged activities, Yezhov ordered the NKVD "to immediately arrest *all* German citizens residing in the USSR who currently

Egil Veidemanis, *Butovo NKVD Execution Range* (near Moscow). In 1937-1938 over 20,000 "enemies of the people" were shot there by firing squads.

work or worked in the past at military or paramilitary enterprises or railway networks."

The arrests of German citizens living and working in the Soviet Union, began on the night of July 30, and by August 6 340 German nationals were arrested. By August 29 the number of prisoners reached 472. A small droplet in the flood of victims of the Stalin terror machine...

15. Yuri Raniuk

Until recently the arrest stories of the UPTI foreigners (except Weissberg and Houtermans, for obvious reasons) were scarcely known, if at all. A breakthrough occurred in 1998, already after the death of Victor Frenkel. Yuri Nikolaevich Raniuk, a famous experimental physicist from Kharkov, gained access to the Ukrainian NKVD archives and found arrest files and interrogation transcripts of those participants in the UPTI tragedy who were sentenced in Kharkov. These remarkable documents are published in [14].

It is almost impossible to read them now, and yet, they are a must-read. They cry of the insanity of the communist idea and the totalitarian state machine and give first-hand testimony of human sufferings inflicted for no reason other than ideology. I feel sorry that such a remarkable book is not yet translated into English. It would be instructive not only for physicists, but for today's Western *intelligentsia* at large.

While working on this book, I started corresponding with Yuri Nikolaevich. Sometimes we exchanged messages on a daily basis. We became friends. His thorough knowledge of the UPTI case helped me to write some footnotes, and to correct a number of discrepancies in the essays published in this collection. In fact, his advice extended much further. In one of the messages Yuri Raniuk writes: "Edoardo Amaldi died, and his unpublished manuscript about

Yuri Raniuk, 2015.

Houtermans was not moving anywhere for years. Amaldi's editors could not find a consultant for the book, especially for its Kharkov chapters, until someone told them about me. I was in Kharkov when I received a letter from Bern, along with the manuscript, with an abundance of all sorts of inaccuracies. For example, in the manuscript it was stated that Sinelnikov had been executed by firing squad. I corrected all that. My remarks are intertwined in the text of the Kharkov chapters of Amaldi's book. I became an expert and authority concerning Shteppa and Houtermans."

The Editor heard the story of Edoardo Amaldi's book [17] from his son Ugo [21]. Edoardo Amaldi met Houtermans in the

1950s; they both were on a scientific committee at CERN and occasionally saw each other at various conferences in France and Italy. Houtermans told him about his adventurous life.

Many years passed. In 1978 Italian television broadcast the 1970 film "The Confession" directed by Costa Gavras (with Yves Montand and Simone Signoret), inspired by the book by Artur London [22]. Eduardo Amaldi was struck by the similarity of the film's theme and many of its details to what Fritz Houtermans had told him in the early 1950s. And then he said to himself: "I must write this book. I owe it to him."

16. Giovanna Fjelstad

In search of Charlotte Houtermans' diaries, on one sunny Sunday in March 2014 I hit the road southbound, toward Northfield, Minnesota. Charlotte was born in Bielefeld, Germany, on May 24, 1899. In the late 1980s she settled in the house of her daughter Giovanna Fjelstad in Northfield, where she died on January 6, 1993. What a long and eventful life...

Giovanna Fjelstad, 2014.

Northfield, a tiny town (twenty thousand inhabitants) in Minnesota's heartland, is home to the College of St. Olaf and Carleton College, two reputable private academic institutions. For many years Giovanna Fjelstad, now retired, was a professor of mathematics at the College of St. Olaf.

Giovanna was born in Berlin, Germany, on April 13, 1932. Thus when brought to Kharkov she was three years old. She still remembers a little bit of Russian. In Giovanna's hospitable home we heard some stories from her past, and she found two boxes filled with yellowed pages handwritten or typed by Charlotte Houtermans long ago.

Charlotte's diaries and notes were in some disarray, with some

Fritz, Giovanna and Charlotte in Berlin, 1932.

pages unnumbered and undated. At the top of the box I saw a story entitled "Marussya" – a few pages clipped together – which was apparently prepared for publication but seemingly has never been published. It was virtually impossible to find there the parts of the diary that Charlotte had given to Victor Frenkel in the early 1990s during their encounter. Giovanna's daughter, Annika Fjelstad, generously offered her help. In a few weeks I received in the mail a typewritten manuscript tediously assembled by Annika from small pieces. Thank you, Annika!

17. Giovanna's story

Again and again, the Houtermans family had to call new places home.

1934. Fritz received a telegram from his mother, Elsa Houtermans, in which she wrote that she had made up her mind to emigrate to the United States [20] and asked her son to urgently

---

[20]Elsa Houtermans made it to the United States only in 1935, based on an invitation from one of her pupils [17].

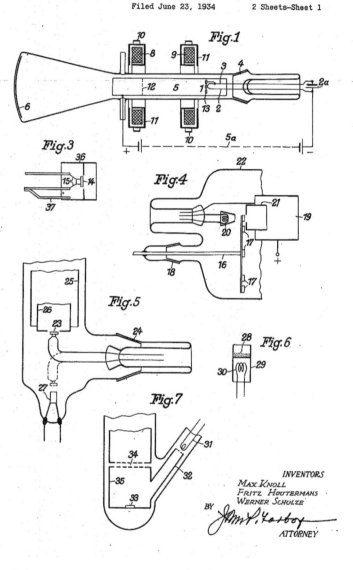

Knoll-Houtermans-Schulze patent claim (1934). Electron microscope invention.

come to see her in Vienna with Charlotte and their daughter. Fritz and Charlotte stayed at his mother's house, the word "Juden" scrawled in yellow paint on its windows. Elsa's home after the pogrom was in shambles: broken busts of Heine, Goethe, Beethoven, paintings trampled, cabinets open, family documents scattered on the floor [23].

Fritz and Charlotte helped Elsa to pack her suitcases and trunks. Little Giovanna sat quietly with her toys, huddled in a corner of the couch.

"My children," said Elsa, as her descendants tell it, "I would not want you to remain in Germany. Dark ages are approaching here. Fritz, I do not want you and our girls to risk. You have to leave before it's too late."

"Where?"

"This, my children, is up to you," replied Elsa, "but you need to decide quickly. I know what I'm saying ... I've sold my house and I'm leaving you some money. Try again in England, in Russia, but best of all, come to me in America."

1939. Charlotte and her two children, Giovanna and Jan, had to leave England, where her financial situation was dire – there was no way for foreigners to earn a living in England. Thank God, her mother-in-law, now based in the US, helped her to obtain an American visa. Charlotte managed to resume her employment with Vassar College in Poughkeepsie, New York. She was lucky to obtain a research scholarship there through old friends, Edna Carter and Monica Heaba. Only nine years before, she had left this college bound for Europe, madly in love, with high hopes for a future happy life in Germany... In 1946 she was granted American citizenship. Approximately at the same time, Maria Goeppert-Mayer [21] recommended Charlotte Houtermans for a position at Sarah Lawrence College. There

---

[21] Maria Goeppert-Mayer (1906-1972) was a German theoretical physicist. She taught mathematics at Sarah Lawrence College (Bronxville, NY) in 1941-1946. In 1963 Maria Goeppert-Mayer received the Nobel Prize for Physics for developing the nuclear shell model.

Charlotte taught physics and engaged in research. In 1953 a local newspaper published [24] the following information:

"Mrs. Charlotte Houtermans, physics professor at Sarah Lawrence College, is among 36 women who have received fellowships from the American Association of University Women for the next year. Mrs. Houtermans will study cosmic ray particles at Brookhaven National Laboratory."[22]

In addition to teaching and research, Charlotte Houtermans produced English translations of famous German textbooks, for instance, *Quantum Theory of Fields* by Gregor Wentzel [25]. Theoretical physicists of the older generation still remember this treatise.

Fritz divorced Charlotte in 1943. He had a complicated personality. As I learned from various sources – and Giovanna confirmed this – Fritz Houtermans was married four times. Charlotte was his first and third wife in four marriages. Their two children were daughter Giovanna (born in Berlin, 1932) and son Jan (born in Kharkov, 1935). A German law enacted in the Hitler era allowed simplified divorces in the absence of a spouse due to wartime separation. Fritz made use of this law in 1943. In February 1944, Fritz Houtermans married Ilse Bartz, a chemical engineer with whom he worked during the war and even published a paper. Fritz and Ilse had three children, Pieter, Elsa, and Cornelia. In August 1953, again with Pauli standing witness, Charlotte and Fritz were married anew, only to divorce again after a few months. In 1955, Fritz Houtermans married Lore Müller, a sister of his stepbrother, Hans. Lore and Fritz had a son, Hendrik, born in 1956.

---

[22]Additional details about Charlotte Houtermans' career as a physics educator can be found in Amaldi's book [17]. Amaldi mentions that after Vassar College (1939-1942) Charlotte went to Radcliffe College (1944-1945) in Cambridge, Massachusetts, where she also worked at a research laboratory of the Polaroid Company. In 1945-1946 Charlotte taught at Wells College (Aurora, New York). Sarah Lawrence College hired Charlotte in 1946, and she was on the faculty there for 22 years. After her retirement from Sarah Lawrence in 1968, Charlotte continued to lecture at Manhattanville College (Purchase, New York) from 1968 to 1972. From 1972 to 1976 she taught physics at the Summer School Courses at Sarah Lawrence College.

-i-

Brione: July 1966.

Again I am looking down onto the lake. I found a bench on the
road above the village, half hidden under a tree so that I can write in the
pleasant half-shade. Today the water is slate gray and brownish and the moun —
tains have sharp silhouettes. It is peaceful and beautiful and I am at rest.

Many things I deem to have left behind me beyond the mountains .
It may be good in this slightly detached mood, in which I find myself, remote from any interference, to take stock and to draw the final line under
my life with F., if I can. Somehow it is doubtful, that this should be possible. Too much was involved, too many invisible Threads still tie me to him in
ways which I really do not quite grasp. Our life might have been easier if I
had understood him. May be I never even knew him, never really found out a
single thing about him. I believed in him, I loved him, I invested much love
and thought to help him achieving what I thought at the time he wanted to accomplish
and what I firmly believed was a very worthwhile goal.

The last weeks in Berne were very confusing, not the fact that
Bamsi was packing up her house in Muristrasse 18 and still entertained Pit and

The front page of the last chapter of Charlotte's diary.

Giovanna met her father for the first time after Kharkov only
in 1950, when she was 18.

18. *First time in the USSR*

Fritz Houtermans came to the USSR for the first time in 1930, to
attend the All-Union Congress of Physicists in Odessa (see Appendix II, p. 347). In fact, it was a rebranded Seventh Congress
of Russian Physicists, organized by the Russian Association of
Physicists for August 19-24, 1930, in Odessa. In attendance
were over 800 delegates, with two hundred talks covering all
branches of physics. Among the foreign participants, besides
Houtermans, were Sommerfeld, Pauli, F. Simon and R. Peierls.
Charlotte Riefenstahl was there as well. For the city of Odessa
this Congress was a great event. Plenary sessions were held in
the building of the City Council, and the opening was broadcast on the radio. The city authorities took good care of the
participants of the Congress, providing them with the best hotels. Delegates could travel free on trams. All sorts of enter-

tainment were organized: tickets to theaters, cinemas, excursions, etc. However, the most popular entertainment in the free hours between the morning and evening sessions was the famous Odessa beach. R. Peierls, who came to the Soviet Union in June 1985, showed several 55-year-old pictures during his talk at the Leningrad Physico-Technical Institute. Judging from the expressions on their faces, Pauli, Frenkel, Tamm and Simon, captured in bathing suits, continued scientific debate even on the beach [2].

The Congress organizers arranged a boat trip on the ship "Georgia" to Batumi, Soviet Georgia, for the participants. Apparently, during this trip the ship made a stop in Sukhumi, where the wedding of Charlotte and Fritz may have occurred.[23] In my conversation with Giovanna Fjelstad, she said she had no memory of her mother Charlotte ever mentioning Sukhumi, but that Batumi had been mentioned many times.

19. Fisl's humor

I do not know who invented the nickname Fisl. But that's how family and friends would address Fritz Houtermans. They say that "Fisl" is a play on the German word "Wiesel," distorted by an Austrian accent. Wiesel means weasel, and in general, a nimble, fun animal, which – they say – fit Houtermans' character. Fritz-Fisl himself was good at inventing funny nicknames. Thus Giovanna became Bamsi, his wife Charlotte "Schnax" and family friend Charlotte Schlesinger "Bimbus"...

Fritz had a sharp sense of humor. One of his colleagues, Haro von Buttlar, collected anecdotal stories told by Houtermans and published them in a 40-page book [26].

Friedrich Begemann, one of his graduate students at Bern, tells the following story: when the Physical Institute was still housed in the Tellurian Observatory, Houtermans occasionally led his "boys" down into the stairwell to wobble the sandstone

---

[23]The Sukhumi version appears only in Frenkel's book. Other sources (e.g. [17]) mention Batumi as the city in which the wedding ceremony occurred.

pillar that was used as the Earth's axis in practical exercises, shouting, "Let's go and shake Switzerland a little!" Another of Houtermans' mischievous pranks was to "borrow" the fire hoses for a dousing after an evening at the pub, which brought down the wrath of the building supervisor. His excuse was that he was carrying out an emergency drill against radioactive contamination [27].

There is a legend that it was Fritz Houtermans who applied the name "Martians" to seven of the twentieth century's most outstanding Hungarian scientists, Theodore von Kármán, George de Hevesy, Michael Polanyi, Leó Szilárd, Eugene Wigner, John von Neumann, and Edward Teller, because nobody in the West could understand their language. One can find this attribution in the "pages" of Wikipedia. Unfortunately, this legend apparently has no substance. In fact, it was a fellow Martian, Leó Szilárd, who jokingly suggested that Hungary was a front for aliens from Mars [28].

20. *Houtermans and Pomeranchuk*

It is curious to note that 25 years after his arrest in the USSR in 1937 and subsequent deportation to Nazi Germany in 1940, Fritz Houtermans met one of his former UPTI colleagues. This encounter is described by S. Gershtein as follows [29]:

> In 1962, Isaak Pomeranchuk,[24] speaking of the Rochester conference held in Geneva, recalled that Fritz Houtermans approached him (that was the first and the last time in Pomeranchuk's life that he was allowed to travel abroad).
>
> "Well, and what did he tell you?" we asked.
>
> Pomeranchuk replied: "Houtermans said 'Chuk, we were idiots. We missed the Mössbauer effect!' "

---

[24]Isaak Yakovlevich Pomeranchuk (1913-1966) was an outstanding Soviet theoretical physicist, one of the best of Landau's students. The (quasi)particle "Pomeron" is named after him.

The point was that, in Kharkov, Houtermans together with Pomeranchuk considered neutron scattering in crystals and knew of the possible existence of a non-shifted line due to scattering on the entire crystalline lattice.

Left to right: Isaak Pomeranchuk, Alexander I. Akhiezer, László Tisza, and Veniamin Levich, at the UPTI campus in 1936.

Another discovery which Houtermans could have made...

21. *Choices to make*

In general, Frenkel's book is a masterpiece that succeeds as both a scientific biography and a captivating read. However, in editing the English translation of the Frenkel's book I had to make some decisions. Comparing the Russian edition with Charlotte's diaries, I noted that in a few instances V. Frenkel abbreviated the original by discarding words, sentences and even some paragraphs. On the other hand, in one or two instances Frenkel's Russian translation contains details which I could not find in those pages of Charlotte's diaries that I had in my possession. For this English edition, I decided to present Charlotte's diaries the way they had been written. Where necessary I added footnotes for explanations.

Also I decided to supplement Frenkel's book by adding five appendices. The first appendix is a slightly abridged piece of personal writing by Charlotte Houtermans, containing a wealth of hitherto unpublished material. The second appendix is a chapter, "Odessa 1930," from the book *Fisl, or the Man Who Overcame Himself* by B. Diakov et al. [23], describing F. Houtermans' first visit to the Soviet Union. The third one is Houtermans' brief "Chronological Report of my Life in Russian Prisons," which was available to Victor Frenkel. While using it extensively in his narration, Frenkel published just several quotations from this document. It seems to me that Houtermans' text in its entirety will give a fuller picture of what transpired with him in 1937-1940. The fourth appendix is an unpublished Alexander Weissberg letter (circa 1946, from the Mica Nava archive). Finally, the fifth appendix is a short excerpt from E. Amaldi [17] which covers the last years of Houtermans' life.

With some hesitation I decided to omit Diakov's brief preface to the Russian edition, as this introductory statement does not directly relate to the body of the book. I also omitted a foreword by Academician Zhores Alferov.

A list of F. Houtermans' scientific publications can be found in the above-mentioned book by E. Amaldi or in the Russian version of Frenkel's book. It is also reproduced in the German version [30] of Frenkel's book.

22. Closing gaps

Victor Frenkel was the first to gain access to the NKVD file of Friedrich Houtermans at the NKVD-KGB Archive in Moscow. It is natural that events after Houtermans' extradition to the Gestapo in 1940 are covered in lesser detail and with some gaps.

One of the gaps is hopefully closed in Appendix V on p. 379 which in this collection is added to Frenkel's book.

Some relevant German archival documents were not accessible to Frenkel in the 1990s. Since then they have been found and studied by Gerhard Rammer in his 600-page PhD thesis [31] and accompanying publications [32, 33]. These publications contain a treasure trove of relevant archival references. Here I will try to present a succinct summary. For more details and exhaustive list of references the reader is referred to [31–33].

23. *Houtermans and the Communist Party of Germany*

New research has revealed that Houtermans in 1932-33 Berlin was more actively involved with the German Communist party affairs than was previously believed. In particular, he was a part of the so-called Operation Reporting Department of the illegal Intelligence Service of the KPD,[25] also known as the "Club of Intellectual Workers." Among Houtermans' comrades in arms in this club were Felix Julius Bobek, a German physical chemist, executed by Nazis in 1938, and Fritz Eichenwald, a German politician who emigrated to the Soviet Union in 1935 and was executed by the NKVD in 1941.

24. *Houtermans and von Ardenne*

The full quotation from Manfred von Ardenne's memoirs [34] mentioned by Frenkel in passing is:

> Houtermans joined the team of the Berlin-Lichterfeld Laboratory in January 1941. He was active there until shortly before the end of WWII.[26] In these years he was full of ingenious ideas. He was one of the pillars of the Berlin-Lichterfeld Laboratory. Soon after the end of WWII this outstanding nuclear physicist, for whom

---

[25] KPD, *Kommunistische Partei Deutschlands*, the Communist Party of Germany.

[26] Seemingly, von Ardenne's dating is not quite accurate, see p. 56.

Niels Bohr had provided scientific support, accepted an offer of a professorship in Bern. He held the chair for Experimental Physics at the University of Bern until his death.

In his early works Houtermans created physical foundations for the development of a hydrogen bomb. In Berlin-Lichterfeld he estimated the energy consumption for the isotope separation. He addressed this topic right at the beginning, in view of the conjectured (and later proven) significance of uranium isotope separation for chain reactions... Also he was responsible for the measurement of cross sections for slow neutrons.

The most important results of Houtermans's activity are summarized in a secret report [27] entitled "On the question of the initiation of a nuclear chain reaction," which was dispatched to important German nuclear physicists. In this 1941 treatise Houtermans predicted the possibility of plutonium fission and potential implications. He demonstrated the superiority of this process over the production of fissionable material through isotope separation. He outlined a method which is currently used in so-called breeder reactors, as the most rational method of energy production. This path alone allows full use of the energy stored in natural uranium.

25. *Houtermans' trip to Russia in 1941*

According to Gerhard Rammer, Max von Laue and Paul Rosbaud were behind Houtermans' appointment with von Ardenne. This saved him from concentration camps. On January 1, 1941, Houtermans started working for Manfred von Ardenne's Laboratory for Electron Physics, where he researched isotope separation with his former Berlin colleague Wilhelm Walcher. In working on the above-mentioned report "On the question of the initiation of a nuclear chain reaction" he came in close con-

---

[27]See page 227.

tact with the key researchers in the Uranium Club (*Uranverein*), such as Werner Heisenberg and Carl Weizsäcker. He developed a trusting, friendly relationship with Otto Haxel, although the latter was a member of the National Socialist Party.

Houtermans left von Ardenne's laboratory in the spring of 1942 after receiving a grant from FEP III.[28] From May 15, 1942, to January 31, 1945, he worked with Carl Friedrich Weiss [29] as a guest of the Imperial Physical Technical Institute.

In the fall of 1941, shortly after the German invasion of the Soviet Union, Houtermans was assigned (at the suggestion of Robert Rompe[30]) to a three-man civilian mission charged with inspection of the captured physics institutes in Kiev and Kharkov. Houtermans' companions were Hans König [31] and Ludwig Bewilogua.[32]

Fritz Houtermans was selected by the Ministry of Aviation for this mission, because he spoke Russian and knew local conditions. On the trip to Russia he became acquainted with the SS Obersturmbannführer Theodor Cammann, with whose help he later saved the life of Marie Rausch von Traubenberg and her mother (see p. 266).

In Kiev Houtermans got in an extremely dangerous situation when an *Einsatzgruppe*[33] in action mistakenly identified him

---

[28] FEP (*Forschungen Entwicklungen, Patente*, Eng. Research, Invention, Patents) was a subdivision of the Research Office of the Imperial Naval Ministry. The group FEP III (Electromagnetic Waves) was headed by the Göttingen mathematician Helmuth Hasse Ruprecht.

[29] C. F. Weiss (1901-1981) was a German physicist in the field of radioactivity.

[30] Robert Rompe was a distinguished German physicist who worked mainly in industry, in particular for the *Studiengesellschaft für Elektrotermische Beleuchtung*.

[31] Hans König, a German physicist, Professor of Physics at Königsberg University. In 1941 he headed the Physics Department of the Aeronautical Research Institute in Munich. On behalf of Ministry of Aviation (Germ. *Reichsluftfahrtministerium*, abbr. RLM) König inspected (in addition to Kiev and Kharkov) Prague, Riga (Latvia), and Tartu (Estonia). From 1943 König conducted research in association with *II. Physikalische Institut* at Göttingen University. Houtermans knew König from their encounter in Danzig in the mid-1930s.

[32] Ludwig Bewilogua (1906-1983) was a German physicist and university professor.

[33] *Einsatzgruppen* (German for "task forces") were SS paramilitary squads that were responsible for mass executions of Jews and other "undesirable" elements in the territories

as a Jew, and was about to send him to a mass shooting range. Only intervention by König, in *Luftwaffe*[34] uniform at that time, saved his life.

Executions of Jews by a German *Einsatzgruppe* near Ivangorod, Ukraine (from Wikipedia). The photo was mailed from the Eastern Front to Germany and intercepted at a Warsaw post office by a member of the Polish resistance collecting documentation on Nazi war crimes. The original print (Tadeusz Mazur and Jerzy Tomaszewski) is now in Historical Archives in Warsaw. The original German inscription on the back of the photograph reads, "Ukraine 1942, Jewish Action, Ivangorod."

26. Why Houtermans had to flee from Berlin in 1945

Houtermans' "Tobacco Adventure" is described in detail in both Frenkel's and Amaldi's books, [1, 17]. However, its unhappy ending is known to a lesser extent. One can find some details in [31].

---

occupied by Nazi Germany during World War II.

[34]Nazi Germany's Air Force. In fact, König had the uniform and rank of Air Force staff engineer.

In the second "tobacco experiment" of Fritz Houtermans the approval letter of authority landed on the table of Abraham Esau,[35] the President of the Imperial Physical Technical Institute. Houtermans was dismissed immediately and found himself in great danger again, because Esau made a criminal complaint against him. His second wife Ilse Bartz advised Houtermans to seek help from his colleagues at the Kaiser Wilhelm Institut in Stadtilm (apparently the RFR nuclear physics experimental station in Stadtilm, Thuringia). Houtermans concocted a forged travel order (needed under wartime regulations) and visited Heisenberg,[36] who then legalized his onward journey to join Kopfermann[37] in Göttingen. Weizsäcker summarized the situation in a poetic joke:

"Heisenberg had to certify
the journey,
leaving Kopfermann to rectify
the mess."

27. Houtermans in Göttingen in the 1940's

In Göttingen Houtermans received support from both Walther Gerlach, who was also an important figure in the Reich Research Council, and Hans Kopfermann. First and foremost, Kopfermann had to procure for Houtermans an exemption from the *Wehrmacht* conscription. To this end he wrote an official report to *Wehrforschungsgemeinschaft*.[38] To ensure fast delivery of this report under wartime circumstances he immediately dispatched

---

[35]Robert Abraham Esau (1884-1955), a German physicist, head of the physics section of the newly created Reich Research Council (RFR) from 1937. From 1939, he was the president of the Imperial Physical Technical Institute. In 1942, Esau became the plenipotentiary of nuclear physics and was in control of the German uranium project. In 1944, Esau became the plenipotentiary of the high-frequency engineering and radar working group.

[36]From summer 1942 Werner Heisenberg was acting director of the Kaiser-Wilhelm-Institut für Physik (Kaiser Wilhelm Institute for Physics), in Berlin-Dahlem.

[37]Hans Kopfermann was Director of the *II. Physikalische Institut* (Second Physics Institute) at the Georg-August University of Göttingen.

[38]*Wehrmacht*'s Military Research Council.

Wolfgang Paul[39] to the local branch of *Wehrforschungsgemein-schaft* in the Harz mountains by bicycle. Thus Houtermans secured employment with the Göttingen research project on demagnetization of submarines, directed by Richard Becker.[40] Gerhard Rammer notes that Houtermans (together with Becker, Gerlach, Jensen, Kopfermann, Rosbaud, Rompe, and Haxel) succeeded in saving the "non-Aryan" physicist Richard Gans.[41] And this is despite the fact that Houtermans was under constant surveillance by the Gestapo. In the Viennese part of the Houtermans family almost no one was left alive (remember, his mother was half-Jewish), and Viennese friends were decimated in the Holocaust as well.

The Allied forces liberated Göttingen on April 8, 1945. This event opened a new chapter in Houtermans' life. An immediate danger was that he was on the Soviet list of war criminals and faced deportation to the Soviet occupation zone. However, Max Born's intervention averted this deportation.

Shortly after the capitulation of Germany on May 8, 1945, the process of denazification was launched by the occupying powers. Each employee of Göttingen University had to be cleared by a special committee appointed by the UK authority. To this end appropriate letters of reference were needed. One such letter is

---

[39]Wolfgang Paul (1913-1993), a German physicist who co-developed the non-magnetic quadrupole mass filter, which laid the foundation for what we now call an ion trap. For this work he received the 1989 Nobel Prize in Physics.

[40]Richard Becker (1887-1955), a German theoretical physicist who made contributions in thermodynamics, statistical mechanics, superconductivity, and quantum electrodynamics.

[41]Richard Martin Gans (1880-1954), a German physicist of Jewish origin mostly known for Gans theory (or Mie-Gans theory). The latter gives scattering characteristics of both oblate and prolate spheroidal particles much smaller than the excitation wavelength. For some special reason he was not sent to an extermination camp, but, instead, was ordered (in the spring of 1943) to clean up streets after Allied bombing raids. Edgar Swinne argues [35] that Gans was not murdered in the Holocaust because his friends – Gerlach, von Laue, Rosbaud, and others – protected him. Hans Jensen, Fritz Houtermans, and Heinz Schmellenmeier devised a plan that succeeded in getting Gans out of the street cleaning and into a scientific research laboratory, which was evacuated to Oberoderwitz in the fall of 1944, and liberated by the American troops on April 14, 1945.

British soldiers on Gänseliesel in Göttingen in the spring of 1945. British replaced the
Americans who liberated Götingen on April 8, 1945. Imperial War Museum, London.

The historic old town, 1945. Städtisches Museum, Göttingen.

discussed by Frenkel on p. 266. Göttingen University was the first in Germany to open its doors to students after the fall of the Third Reich.

Göttingen was in the British occupation zone; the procedure there was more lax than in the other zones. Quite soon the British realized they could not cope with the influx of applications, and introduced a self-denazification procedure.

Life in Göttingen, was not easy in the first postwar years even for world-famous physicists. Max Planck's wife Marga (Max Planck at that time was 87 years old and settled in Göttingen) wrote to Lise Meitner, on June 15, 1947: "But I can assure you of one thing: without the help of our friends abroad, my husband would very certainly not have survived the winter."

After the war, at first Houtermans continued to be Richard Becker's "guest" at the Theoretical Physics Institute in Göttingen. On September 3, 1945, Houtermans submitted a petition for an appointment as extraordinary professor "in token of compensation for the injustice done to me." His case was presented by Richard Becker. This was met with resistance from some colleagues, former members of the outlawed National Socialist German Workers' Party (commonly referred to in English as the Nazi Party) who were afraid that Houtermans would request full restitution, which would create a precedent for other similar cases. Some argued that there could be only one head of the institute at a time (at that time Hans Kopfermann), and since Houtermans' scientific achievements warranted directorship, the appropriate hierarchical order would be broken.

Kopfermann and Becker managed to convince faculty that due to Houtermans' "generally recognized scientific achievements" his admission to the faculty was justified. What also helped was Houtermans's willingness to collaborate with physicists like P. Jordan and K. H. Hellwege [42] who had been pro-Nazi

---

[42] A pioneer in quantum field theory, Ernst Pascual Jordan joined the National Socialist German Workers' Party (NSDAP) in 1933 and remained an active Nazi supporter thereafter. In 1948 Jordan asked Max Born for a testimonial that would minimize his involvement in Nazi activities and emphasize his decision to stay on in Germany "to

in the Hitler era (the latter was forbidden to teach from 1945 to 1949).

A provision was made granting Houtermans a certain degree of independence from Kopfermann's research projects. In August 1946 Houtermans was appointed assistant at the *II. Physikalische Institut* of the University of Göttingen to "undo the injustice done to him in the past." For his research he chose a scientific niche which was not yet occupied in Göttingen: nuclear physics and its application to mineralogy and geology, and in a few years, with limited financial resources, managed to build up a separate department at the *Physikalische Institut*, albeit a small one. In October 1949 he obtained a supernumerary lectureship, being recommended to the Minister of Culture of Lower Saxony as "one of the best-versed in radioactivity and the related field of nuclear transmutations."

As we see, at Göttingen University Houtermans as a physicist did not receive the recognition he deserved, to put it mildly. His scientific results were not considered to be of utmost importance, and the room he got for his research laboratory was in a god forsaken basement. According to Peter Minkowski, Houtermans was not happy in Göttingen [37]. "Once," said Minkowski, "Helmuth Faissner [43] found Houtermans completely drunk, lying on the sidewalk; he helped him to get up and took him home. During their walk, Faissner asked Houtermans whether the rumor he (Faissner) had heard, that he (Houtermans) was the inventor of the 'fast breeder' reactors, was true... Houtermans' answer was 'natürlich (of course), but who cares?' "

---

protect the Jewish contribution to physics against the racial Nazi side." Born politely declined, sending instead a list of relatives and friends who had died under the Nazis [36]. Later Wolfgang Pauli and Werner Heisenberg helped him to regain academic employment. Karl-Heinz Hellwege was a member of the NSDAP and the National Socialist Faculty League (*NS-Dozentenbund*) and was dismissed from Göttingen University as a result of denazification.

[43]Helmut Faissner (1928-2007) was a German physicist and Rector of the Rheinisch-Westfälische Technische Hochschule in Aachen.

28. Denazification

Here I want to make a digression about denazification at Göttingen University and the way it was implemented – which, frankly, surprised me.

Exact sciences at Göttingen University were hit especially hard by Nazi "reforms." Nothing remained of its unique status as a "scientific Mecca." Highly respected mathematicians, such as Richard Courant, Hermann Weyl, Edmund Landau and Emmy Noether and outstanding physicists such as Max Born, James Franck and Edward Teller – the crème de la crème of German science – were purged, mostly for racial reasons. They were replaced by scientists of much lesser caliber; many of them were members of the so-called National Socialist German Workers' Party. The hope was that the ban imposed by the Allies on this party could naturally lead to the replacement of those promoted not because of their scientific superiority, but rather because of their proximity to the Nazis, by more qualified scientists either from abroad or from Germany.

Denazification of defeated Germany was a part of a comprehensive Allied occupation policy. The primary purpose of denazification was to uproot Nazism. Initially in charge of denazification were special committees instituted by the Allies. However, before long it became clear that they could not cope with decisions affecting almost 30% of the population of Germany. The responsibility for the denazification process was delegated to the German administration. Thus, denazification turned into self-denazification.

And then something went wrong. The clear-cut criteria of scientific excellence and non-involvement in serious Nazi offenses were in fact replaced by a vague "collegial code of behavior, i.e. loyalty towards colleagues as well as to the profession and scientific establishment," "decency and honesty" [32]. Denazification committees were composed of faculty with no regard to their political orientation during the Nazi era. I do not know whether this process could have been conducted differently under the circumstances, without causing extreme tensions in the society. Gerhard Rammer writes [32] that "its purpose was to stabilize the community. In contrast, a revision according to the political standards would not have achieved stability, but would rather have put that at risk." Joint work and research projects strengthened the collegial solidarity of those involved and created alliances in which political differences no longer mattered.

As an illustration, Gerhard Rammer discusses the cases of two Nazis whose postwar careers went uninterrupted and were quite successful. This is in contradistinction to other cases in which clearly "injustice was done but never undone." One example carefully studied by Rammer is the case of Kurt Hohenemser, who before 1933 was an assistant at the Institute for Applied Mechanics of Göttingen University. In 1933 he was dismissed for racial reasons. The majority of his family did not survive the Nazi era. Hohenemser himself was a consistent opponent of Nazi ideology and viewed Nazi rule as criminal from the very beginning.

In the summer of 1945 Hohenemser returned after a twelve-year absence and requested his reinstatement as assistant at the Institute for Applied Mechanics. In his application he mentioned that the former institute director Ludwig Prandtl had been deprived of his office in 1934 for political reasons, with Max Schuler appointed in his place, also for political reasons. This remark by Hohenemser was considered offensive. He was accused of committing an "indecency." Dean Eucken wrote a clearly dismissive faculty statement defeating the reinstatement of Hohenemser on the grounds that "fertile collegial cooperation" with him would not be possible. Hohenemser's two-year battle with Göttingen University for reinstatement turned out to be to no avail, and finally he gave up and emigrated to the U.S.

The story of physics graduate student Ursula Martius is similar. She published an article in the *Deutsche Rundschau* in which she named five physicists and expressed her displeasure with the fact that they had been reinstated to university positions despite their less than "clean" past. Ursula Martius indicated that "the criticized colleagues had supported National Socialism in word and deed." The scientists named – for instance, Pascual Jordan, Herbert Stuart and Hans Kneser – were regarded as superb physicists and honorable colleagues.

As a result, she was tormented by her superiors and colleagues. In 1949, a year after successfully completing her PhD, Ursula Martius emigrated to Canada, where she became one of the most honored Canadian scientists [44] (after marriage she became Ursula Franklin).

Rammer concludes that Fritz Houtermans succeeded at postwar Göttingen University, where Hohenemser failed, not least due to his willingness to cooperate with (former) Nazis. Even so, his treatment by colleagues was not commensurate with his scientific excellence and achievements in physics. The message was that he had to be satisfied with what he was offered.

The overall scientific situation in postwar Germany was aggravated by the international isolation of German science caused by National Socialism. It was still in effect after 1945 "because the involvement of German physicists during the Nazi regime was not so easily forgotten abroad. In some cases, the resentment was quite considerable" [33]. This sentiment was spelled out, for instance, by American physicist Philip Morrison: "They worked for the cause of Himmler and Auschwitz, for the burners of books and the takers of hostages. The community of science will be long delayed in welcoming the armorers of the Nazis" [38].

No Germans attended major physics conferences in the immediate postwar period – for instance, the Conference on Elementary Particle Physics in Cambridge in 1947, the Shelter Island Conference in the same year, or the Solvay Conference in 1948.

This was probably another reason why Houtermans did not feel comfortable at Göttingen.

---

[44]Canadian metallurgist, research physicist and educator, Ursula Martius Franklin is the author of *The Real World of Technology*, and other influential books. In 2012, she was inducted into the Canadian Science and Engineering Hall of Fame.

Faculty of Exact Sciences of Bern University, Sidlerstrasse 5. Houtermans' creation.

29. Moving to Bern

In 1951 Fritz Houtermans received two offers of a professorship in experimental physics: from the University of Bern and the Free University of Berlin. The former offer was preceded by a visit from a delegation of Bern professors – André Mercier, Max Schürer and Hans König[45] – to Göttingen. At that time the Department of Physics at the University of Bern was completely and hopelessly outdated. The delegation was charged with two tasks: first, to convince themselves that Houtermans was the right person to start a vigorous research effort in modern physics from scratch, and, second, to clarify whether Houtermans' communist leanings were sufficiently harmless for conservative Switzerland. Both answers were positive. Importantly, upon their return to Bern, Mercier, Schürer and König managed to convince faculty and university authorities that Houtermans

---

[45]The latter is not likely the same Hans König who was sent on a mission with Houtermans to Kiev and Kharkov in 1941, see [32].

was the best possible candidate [39].

In 1952 Fritz Houtermans moved to Bern. He led his department to triumph. Not only did he establish the Bernese physical school as a pioneer in the area of applications of radioactivity to the geosciences, astrophysics, and cosmochemistry. He was also instrumental in the construction of a new exact sciences building, with modern laboratories. On January 16, 1958, *Gazette de Lausanne* wrote that Friedrich Houtermans, Director of the Institute of Experimental Physics in Bern, had made a very strong case for public support of revolutionary changes in experimental nuclear physics. He had explained that considerable growth was needed: the Bern physicists had to become a part of the world physics community. A special committee had approved funding at the level of SFR 10,000,000.

Since Switzerland is a direct democracy, the funding had to be approved in the cantonal referendum. Houtermans visited many local schools and met with students' parents, trying to convince them of the importance of modern physics. In certain instances he went door to door with the same mission. In the subsequent referendum the funding was approved. On April 28, 1962, *Gazette de Lausanne* wrote that F. Houtermans had inaugurated a new Faculty of Exact Sciences at Sidlerstrasse 5, with three huge underground levels for laboratories.

Heinrich Leutwyler recalls that Houtermans was an excellent lecturer. Especially memorable were his courses on general physics. For instance, to demonstrate laws of acoustics he inhaled helium, which dramatically changed his voice (the change resulting from the shortened sound wavelength).

30. *Yuri Golfand, the discoverer of supersymmetry*

Part II of this book is devoted to Yuri Abramovich Golfand (1922-1994), whom I knew personally. We were not close friends, because of the age difference, but I always felt an almost irrational attraction to him. Golfand was a frequent participant in the ITEP[46] theory seminars. I used to bump into him in the corridors of ITEP regularly. At first I did not know who this small man was, with his warm eyes and kind smile. So I asked my thesis adviser, Prof. B. L. Ioffe. Ioffe lowered his voice to a whisper and replied that this was Golfand, the discoverer of supersymmetry. Later, whenever he spoke of him, Ioffe would automatically lower his voice even if we were alone in Ioffe's office. This would wordlessly emphasize that Golfand, as a *refusenik*, was a nonperson.

Everybody who knew Golfand remembers his smile and his eyes. Usually he looked a little bit out of touch with reality, decoupled from the surrounding world, with thoughts directed within rather than without.

Yuri Golfand, circa 1940.

After Yuri Abramovich died in 1994, flashes of memory often revived his smiling face in my mind. I could not forget it. During his lifetime he had no opportunity to travel to the West, and therefore his early works – representing the inception of supersymmetric field theory – were known only to a few experts, pioneers in this subject, and his (and Evgeny Likhtman's) role in this inception was underappreciated. In 1999 I edited the anthology *The Many Faces of the Superworld* [40], dedicated to the memory of Yu. Golfand. My intention was to correct an historical injustice. Boris Bolo-

---

[46]The Institute of Theoretical and Experimental Physics in Moscow.

tovsky in his essay mentions that it was this volume's appearance which led him to write his "Memories of Golfand" (see Part II of this book). In the same year, I (with G. Kane) published the book *The Supersymmetric World* [41], which presented recollections from some of the founding fathers of supersymmetry, as well as from Golfand's widow, Natasha Koretz.

Yuri Golfand and his wife Natasha Koretz, circa 1980.

On October 13-27, 2000, the William I. Fine Theoretical Physics Institute (University of Minnesota) hosted the symposium and workshop "Thirty Years of Supersymmetry." During this event, some of the pioneers who opened the gates to supersymmetry's superworld in the early 1970s met face-to-face for the first time ever. Among the guests at the symposium were Natasha Koretz, Evgeny Likhtman, Vladimir Akulov, Vyacheslav Soroka, Pierre Ramond, Jean-Loup Gervais, Bunji Sakita, Pierre Fayet, John Iliopoulos, Lochlain O'Raifeartaigh, Sergio

Physics seminar of Moscow *refuseniks* in a private apartment. At center-right, looking toward the camera, is Kenneth Wilson, a guest from the US and a future Nobel Prize winner.

Ferrara, Martin Sohnius, John Schwarz, and others. Later the proceedings of the symposium were published [42].

Some rarely mentioned aspects of the scientific history of supersymmetry are summarized in the introductory part of *Concise Encyclopedia of Supersymmetry* [43].

31. Bolotovsky's and Eskin's essays

Several years ago I received from a Moscow friend a draft of Boris Bolotovsky's essay, which is published in Part II. This is the most detailed account written by a witness of the story of Golfand's expulsion from the Lebedev Physical Institute in Moscow and of his subsequent persecution.

I got in touch with Boris Mikhailovich, and after his essay was published in Russian in the online magazine *Sem Iskusstv* (November 2012) he gave me permission for its translation into English. I am grateful to *Sem Iskusstv* editor Evgeny Berkovich for his kind assistance and permission for publication.

Boris Eskin.

In order to clarify a few points in Bolotovsky's essay in the process of editing, I called Natasha Koretz. She kindly informed me that Golfand's biographer in Israel, Boris Eskin, had written a large essay (in Russian) covering Yuri Golfand's life from childhood to his death in 1994. It is the most detailed narrative one can currently find. He kindly agreed to the inclusion of the English version of his essay in this book. Minor abbreviations were made by the Editor.

32. *Moisei Koretz*

A digression in Eskin's essay acquaints the reader with the tragic story of Natasha Koretz's father, Moisei Abramovich Koretz (1908-1984), who was Landau's student, assistant and friend. The reader will also encounter this name more than once in Frenkel's book. An excellent essay devoted to Koretz was pub-

Boris Mikhailovich Bolotovsky.

lished by Raniuk [45]. In this essay the reader can find excerpts from Koretz's 1935 arrest files. Some other relevant documents can be found in [14].

From the 1935 arrest file we learn that Moisei Koretz was married to Eleonora Lazarevna Epstein (his second wife) and by that time had two small daughters. We also learn that his father, Abram Koretz, a watchmaker, had an apprentice. Moreover, his mother, Slava Eisurovich-Koretz, was from a relatively wealthy Jewish family and was classified as a *lishenets*.[47]

---

[47] *Lishenets, lishentsy*: these terms were used for a class of "socially alien elements" who were stripped of their voting rights from 1918 to 1936, after the Bolshevik coup d'état. Disfranchisement was applied to (i) individuals who owned private enterprises and employed hired labor; (ii) individuals whose income was not considered to be related to work (e.g. landlords); (iii) private traders and commercial brokers; (iv) clergy of all denominations; (v) former policemen and army officers in Imperial Russia, and some others. In fact, being disenfranchised meant much more than simply not being allowed to vote or be elected. *Lishentsy* could not be state employees, could not be members of cooperatives, and could not receive pensions from the state. *Lishentsy* and their children were not admitted to universities or professional schools. During the rationing

This automatically made Moisei Koretz guilty of the gravest social offense. To get an education he had to conceal his origin.

Moisei Koretz was married three times [49]. The first time, in 1928 in Moscow he married Alexandra Simonova. Their daughter Esther was born in 1929. Shortly afterward, the family moved to Leningrad. This marriage collapsed in 1932, when Koretz married Eleonora Epstein mentioned above. Later they divorced; it is not exactly known when, but certainly after 1936. During the NKVD interrogations of 1938 Koretz does not mention (surely deliberately) either of his two families. The story of Koretz's third marriage is narrated in Eskin's essay.

Moisei Koretz received his basic education at the Physics and Mechanics Faculty of the Leningrad Polytechnic Institute (1929-1934). There Koretz attended lectures by L. Landau and M. Bronshtein.

In 1935, at the invitation of Landau, he arrived in Kharkov, where he was admitted to the theoretical division of the Ukrainian Physico-Technical Institute and, concurrently, became Landau's assistant at Kharkov University.

During this period, Koretz, according to Landau, "proved himself as a capable young physicist" [46]. Soon Koretz became his "close associate and assistant" [47]. Just a half year later, Koretz was fired from UPTI, allegedly "for concealing his social origin" (remember, a watchmaker father who had an apprentice!), and two weeks later, in late November 1935, he was arrested by the NKVD on charges of "agitation that led to the failure of defense contracts." He spent eight months in a

Moisei Koretz, 1935. Courtesy of Yuri Raniuk.

system in the late 1920s and 1930s, *lishentsy* were deprived of ration cards. According to modern estimates, the number of *lishentsy* amounted to approximately 2% of the adult population of the USSR.

Kharkov prison anticipating the death penalty. In December 1935 Landau sent a letter in defense of Koretz to the head of the Ukrainian NKVD. Apparently as a result of Landau's and other similar letters from UPTI, the Ukrainian Supreme Court overturned the verdict and Koretz was released.

Natasha Koretz writes [48] of her father:

> Moisei Abramovich was not only Landau's student in Leningrad, he also became his most trusted friend, with whom Landau could talk about all the things in the world that interested him: politics, future, love and art... For example, they together invented a classification of female types, and what approach one should apply to each of them for seduction... They also worked out a general classification of human intellect, i.e. people who can create novel things, at most 2%, those who are able to accept these novel things right away 5%, those who are able to discuss problems expressing their own opinions 13%, those who can recognize a problem as such 20%, while the rest – according to this classification – create just "noise." This and much more bonded them. That's why Dau invited my dad to Kharkov, when he became the head of the Theoretical Department there. It was no accident that they wrote their notorious leaflet together when they moved to Moscow. They could easily have paid with their lives for it, had it not been for Kapitsa.

Indeed, Koretz, following Landau, moved to Moscow in February 1937 in an attempt to escape from the Kharkov NKVD. A transcript of an interrogation relevant to the second arrest of M. Koretz (on April 28, 1938) is published in [14]. Lieutenant Reznikov – the same NKVD officer who interrogated Alexander Weissberg – interrogated former UPTI employee Vladimir Gay on May 17-20, 1937:

Q: What do you know of the counter-revolutionary subversive organization existing at UPTI?

A: I worked for UPTI for five years. On the basis of the

information I acquired over these years and some personal observations I believe that there are two counter-revolutionary organizations of different political orientations acting at UPTI. At certain stages they coordinated their subversive activities.

Q: Can you identify their members?

A: The first group consists of the following individuals:

1. Lev Davydovich Landau, former Head of the UPTI Theory Department, currently employed by the Institute of Physical Problems in Moscow;

2. Koretz – I forgot his first name – former member of the UPTI Theory Department, currently resides in Moscow. He was Landau's closest friend.

3. Ivan Vasilievich Obreimov, Head of the UPTI Crystallography Laboratory;

4. Lev Vasilievich Shubnikov, Head of the UPTI Cryogenics Laboratory;

5. Olga Nikolaevna Shubnikova, Lev Shubnikov's wife, a researcher, Cryogenics Laboratory;

6. Lev Victorovich Rosenkevich, a researcher, Cryogenics Laboratory.

Lev Landau was the leader of this subversive group. To my mind, its political orientation is Trotskyist...

In Koretz's NKVD file there is an excerpt from the testimony of the UPTI physicists Shubnikov and Rozenkevich, executed in 1937 in Kharkov on charges of espionage for Nazi Germany. In this testimony they admit to their participation in a counter-revolutionary Trotskyist organization, along with both Landau and Koretz.

Thus, we see that Moisei Koretz, Landau's scientific assistant, was treated by NKVD as Landau's assistant in the alleged "subversive political activities."

Not later than on April 23, 1938, Koretz and Landau wrote a (now famous) leaflet (see p. 421):

... The country is flooded with streams of blood and filth.

Millions of innocent people have been thrown in prison, and no one can be sure when his own turn will come.

Don't you see, comrades, that the Stalinist clique has carried out a fascist coup?..

On April 27, 1938, Koretz, Landau and Rumer were arrested by the NKVD. Tortured during interrogations, Koretz entered a guilty plea, and was sentenced to ten years of hard labor for "propaganda calling to overthrow, undermine or weaken Soviet power." He served 14 years in Pechorlag (a branch of the Gulag), near the village of Mezhoga. Why 14? In 1942 he was sentenced to an extra 10 years. Among the charges was a remark allegedly made by Koretz in early 1941 about a possible German attack on the Soviet Union. In the indictment, these words were presented as "doubts about the power of the Soviet system." In 1952, after serving 14 years in the labor camp, Koretz was sent into exile to the town of Inta in the Soviet Far North until 1958 [48, 49]. There he worked as an engineer at a local coal mine.

Natasha Koretz with her parents, Inta, circa 1954.

I would like to add that Koretz's first wife, Alexandra, was a courageous woman – I would even say, a hero. She took an enormous risk by revealing to authorities her relation to Moisei in order to get permission to send food packages and letters to him in Gulag. This correspondence supported Koretz through all his Gulag years, especially when he started receiving letters from his daughter Esther-Irina. They are deeply moving... A part of their correspondence is available online [50].

33. FIAN

The scene of Bolotovsky's essay is Moscow-based FIAN, the Physical Institute of the Academy of Sciences [48] – more exactly, its Theory Department. I should say a few words about this.

FIAN was created in 1934, a few years later than UPTI. Its first director was Academician Sergei Vavilov. The Theory Department was headed by Igor Tamm, a future Nobel Prize winner (1958). He was its head until his death in 1971, with a five-year hiatus in 1938-1943 when the Theory Department was dissolved. At its inception the FIAN Theory Department consisted of nine members – among them such outstanding physicists as Matvei Bronshtein, Moisei Markov, Yuri Rumer and Vladimir Fock. We will encounter their names in the body of this book. The Great Purge exacted a heavy toll on FIAN's theory pioneers. In 1938 Matvei Bronshtein was executed, while Yuri Rumer was arrested and sentenced to 10 years as an accomplice of enemy of the people Lev Landau. After serving his term he was exiled to Siberia. Tamm himself fell under NKVD suspicion.[49] In addition to heading the FIAN Theory Department,

---

[48] Also known as the Lebedev Physical Institute.

[49] And not for the first time. In the book *Memories of Tamm* [51] Tamm's grandson tells the following story about his grandfather.

In the summer of 1920 Tamm decided to leave the Crimea, controlled by the Whites, for Elizavetgrad, which was already controlled by the Reds. Igor Tamm did not take any documents with him, because they weren't suitable for justifying departure from the territory controlled by the Whites and weren't suitable for joining the Reds, either. He successfully crossed the front line... At night, along with a casual companion, he decided

he was a professor at Moscow State University. At that time, the Dean of the Faculty of Physics at Moscow State University was Professor Boris Gessen. Tamm and Gessen had known each other since childhood. When Gessen was arrested, declared an enemy of the people and executed, the NKVD's attention turned to the Tamm family. His brother Leonid Tamm, a prominent chemical engineer, was arrested and sentenced to ten years in the Gulag, where he disappeared without a trace. In an attempt to save Igor Tamm and other theoretical physicists from Tamm's department from inevitable persecution, Vavilov dissolved the Theory Department; it was reassembled only in 1943.

Vitaly Ginzburg, the future Nobel Prize laureate (2003), became Tamm's student in 1938 and was hired by FIAN in 1940. Both Tamm and Ginzburg participated in the Soviet hydrogen bomb project. But the main player in this project was Andrei Sakharov, another member of the FIAN team.

---

to stay in an empty house at an abandoned manor, where they were detained by a Red squad.

Without documents they looked like White scouts and should have been immediately shot. Fortunately, the detachment commander was a dropout student. Tamm said that he had graduated from the Moscow University Department of Physics and Mathematics, but the commander didn't believe him. He smiled darkly and said: "So you are a mathematician! That has to be a lie, right? Let's check it out. Prove Taylor's theorem on representation of a function by its Taylor series. Don't forget the explicit formula for the remainder! If you cope with the task we will set you free. If you fail we will shoot you and your pal right away."

They gave Tamm a pencil, a piece of paper and a candle, dragged a load of fresh hay to the captives and locked them in the room. His companion quickly fell asleep. Igor Tamm was unable to sleep: there was a guard at the door and time was scarce. He was nervous... Because of this he made a mistake, which prevented him from proving the statement. Nevertheless, he correctly outlined the proof. In the morning, when the Red commander came in, the task was still unfinished, but it was clear that the unsuccessful attempt of proof was written by someone who knew math. Tamm asked the commander to show him the mistake.

"To tell the truth," he answered, "I can't. I dropped out of university three years ago and I have already forgotten everything."

His companion was released, but Tamm remained in captivity. The Whites went on the offensive and the Red squad together with their captive retreated to Kharkov instead of Elizavetgrad. In Kharkov, a soldier was delegated to hand Tamm over to the Cheka. "In the Cheka they will sort things out quickly," said the soldier.

Evgeny Likhtman, Natasha Koretz and Vladimir Akulov in Minnesota in October 2000.

In the spring of 1945 Tamm acquired a new student, Andrei Sakharov, who at that time was an engineer at the Ulyanovsk ammunition plant. He had graduated from the Faculty of Physics, Moscow State University, in 1942 as one of the best in its class. He had been offered a position at the university but had declined the offer, wishing instead to join the war effort. That's how Sakharov wound up at the munitions plant, where he authored numerous inventions. After the war's end, the desire to engage in fundamental science led Sakharov to Tamm. In 1950 Sakharov was sent to Sarov, the Soviet counterpart of Los Alamos, where he proved absolutely instrumental in the development of the first Soviet hydrogen bomb.

Starting in the late 1950s, Sakharov became concerned about the moral and political implications of his work. The turning point in Sakharov's political evolution came in 1967. Shortly after, he authored an essay, *Reflections on Progress, Peaceful*

тониане взаимодействия. Однако, при произвольной локальной плотности гамильтониана $H^{\iota}(t)$ плотность оператора $W^{\iota}(t)$ не будет, вообще говоря, локальной за счет интегрирования в (6) по времени. Поэтому, чтобы получить физические следствия, мы обобщим понятия инвариантности теории относительно алгебры (или группы) на случай, когда операторы алгебры сами могут существенным образом зависеть от взаимодействия. Мы будем требовать, чтобы пространственная плотность операторов алгебры была локальной функцией от операторов поля [1]. В результате этого требования подинтегральные выражения в (6) должны быть полными производными по времени, и соотношения (6) превращаются в уравнения для определения операторов $H^{\iota}(t)$ и $W^{\iota}(t)$.

Уравнения (6) сводятся к системе линейных однородных уравнений для постоянных коэффициентов, которые вводятся в качестве неопределенных констант связи в наиболее общий вид гамильтониача взаимодействия. Эту систему уравнений удалось решить в случае, когда $H_1(t)$ является произведением трех полей, два из которых преобразуются по представлению (2) и комплексно-сопряженному (2), а третье — по представлению (3). Система уравнений (6) в этом случае имеет единственное решение, а отличны от нуля лишь операторы $W_1(t)$, $H_1(t)$, $H_2(t)$. Зная точный вид гамильтониана в представлении взаимодействия, можно восстановить по нему лагранжиан в гейзенберговском представлении:

$$L(x) = (\partial_a \phi^* - igA_a \phi^*)(\partial_a \phi + igA_a \phi) - m^2 \phi^* \phi + (\partial_a \omega^* - igA_a \omega^*) \times$$

$$\times (\partial_a \omega + igA_a \omega) - m^2{}^* \omega + \frac{i}{2} \bar{\psi}_1 \gamma_a \overset{\leftrightarrow}{\partial}_a \psi_1 - m\bar{\psi}_1 \psi_1 - g\bar{\psi}_1 \gamma_a \psi_1 A_a +$$

$$+ \frac{i}{2} \bar{\psi}_2 \gamma_a \overset{\leftrightarrow}{\partial}_a \psi_2 - \mu \bar{\psi}_2 \psi_2 - \frac{1}{2}(\partial_\beta A_a)^2 + \frac{\mu^2}{2} A_a A_a + \frac{1}{2}(\partial_a X)^2 - \frac{\mu^2}{2} X^2 +$$

$$+ g\mu(\phi^* \phi - \omega \omega^*) X - \frac{g^2}{2}(\phi^* \phi - \omega^* \omega)^2 + \sqrt{2}g(\bar{\phi}_1 \bar{s} \psi_2 \phi + \bar{\psi}_2 s \psi_1 \phi^*) -$$

$$- \sqrt{2} g(\psi_1^c \bar{s} \psi_2 \omega^* + \bar{\psi}_2 \bar{s} \psi_1^c \omega). \tag{7}$$

Таким образом, получена модель взаимодействия квантованных полей с несохранением четности, инвариантная относительно алгебры (1).

Физический институт
им. П.Н.Лебедева
Академии наук СССР

Поступила в редакцию
10 марта 1971 г.

Литература

[1] С.Швебер. Введение в релятивистскую квантовую теорию поля . ИИЛ, 1963.

---

[1] Обоснованию этого постулата, а также сравнению его с обычной формулировкой требования инвариантности теории относительно группы преобразований будет посвящена отдельная работа.

The last page of the Golfand-Likhtman paper [44] (received by the Editorial Board on March 10, 1971) with the first-ever four-dimensional supersymmetric model presented in Equation (7). In [40] I suggested calling this model – massive supersymmetric electrodynamics – the Golfand-Likhtman model.

Coexistence, and Intellectual Freedom, which marked the beginning of his dissident career. After this essay was found in

Academician Igor Tamm.

Andrei Sakharov (center) at a physics conference (1987). To the right is Yuri Golfand, to the left is Alexei Anselm.

public circulation, Andrei Sakharov lost his security clearance and in 1969 returned from Sarov to Moscow and the FIAN Theory Department. Sakharov was arrested on January 22, 1980, following his public protests against the Soviet intervention in Afghanistan in 1979, and was sent, without any judicial procedure, into internal exile in Gorky, now Nizhny Novgorod – a city then classified as off-limits to foreigners.

Between 1980 and 1986, Sakharov was kept under tight KGB surveillance. Only after the advent of Gorbachev's *perestroika* was he allowed to return to Moscow.

34. Additional recommended literature

Iosif B. Khriplovich, "The Eventful Life of Fritz Houtermans," *Physics Today*, July 1992, p. 29;

E. Amaldi, *The Adventurous Life of Friedrich Georg Houtermans, Physicist* (Springer, Berlin, 2013), Eds. Saverio Braccini, Antonio Ereditato, and Paola Scampoli.

Friendly meeting of the editors at Bern University on June 1, 2015. Right to left: Saverio Braccini, Paola Scampoli, and myself.

References

1. Victor Frenkel, *Yakov Ilyich Frenkel*, (Nauka, Moscow-Leningrad, 1966), in Russian; *Yakov Ilyich Frenkel: His Work, Life and Letters*, (Birkhäuser, Basel-Boston-Berlin, 2001).
2. G. Gorelik and V. Frenkel, *Matvei Petrovich Bronshtein*, (Nauka, Moscow, 1990, in Russian); *Matvei Petrovich Bronstein: Soviet Theoretical Physics in the Thirties*, (Birkhäuser, 2011).
3. László Tisza, "Adventures of a Theoretical Physicist," *Phys. Perspect.*, vol. 11, pp. 46-97 (2009).
4. Walter M. Elsasser, *Memoirs of a Physicist in the Atomic Age*, (Watson Publishers, Intl., 1978), p. 106.
5. Judith Szapor, "Private Archives and Public Lives," *Jewish Culture and History*, vol. 15, pp. 93-109 (2014).
6. Alexander Weissberg-Cybulski, *Hexensabbat*, (Frankfurt, Frankfurter Hefte, 1951, in German), English translation: Alexander Weissberg, *The Accused*, (New York, Simon and Schuster, 1951) and *Conspiracy of Silence*, (Hamish Hamilton, London, 1952). A German edition was released recently in Austria under the title *Im Verhor: Ein Überlebender der Stalinistischen Sauberungen Berichtet*, (Europa Verlag, 1993).
7. Arthur Koestler, *Sonnenfinsternis*, (Atlantis-Verlag, Zürich 1946, in German), *Darkness at Noon*, translated from the German by Daphne Hardy (Cape, London 1940), Modern edition: *Darkness at Noon*, (Scribner, New York, 2006).
8. *I Married a Russian; Letters from Kharkov*, Ed. Lucie Street, (Allen and Unwin, London, 1946); The US edition: Emerson Books, Inc., New York, NY, 1947.
9. Yuri Raniuk, *Alexander Weissberg's book "The Accused": Historical Commentaries*, *http://www.sunround.com/club/22/ufti.htm* (in Russian), also in O. Weissberg, *Holodna Gora*, Ed. Yuri Ranyuk, (Prava Ludini, Kharkov, 2010), in Ukrainian.
10. A. Koestler, *The Invisible Writing*, (MacMillan, New York, 1954), pp. 51 and 55.
11. Eva Zeisel, *A Soviet Prison Memoir*, (iBook Multimedia for iPad and Amazon Kindle Edition, 2012).
12. *http://edu.gazeta.pl/edu/h/Aleksander+Weissberg-Cybulski* or *http://pl.wikipedia.org/wiki/Aleksander_ Weissberg-Cybulski*, in Polish.
13. Jean Richards, private communication, February 18, 2015.
14. Yu. Pavlenko, Yu. Raniuk, and Yu. Khramov, *The Case of UPTI, 1935-1938*, (Kiev, Feniks, 1998, in Russian).
15. http://arran.ru/?q=en/exposition15_1
16. *Oral History Transcript Program*, American Institute of Physics (AIP), http://www.aip.org/history-programs
17. E. Amaldi, *The Adventurous Life of Friedrich Georg Houtermans, Physicist* (Springer, Berlin, 2013), Eds. Saverio Braccini, Antonio Ereditato, and Paola Scampoli.

18. Mica Nava, *Visceral Cosmopolitanism: Gender, Culture and the Normalization of Difference*, (Berg Publishers, 2007).

19. N. Okhotin, A. Roginsky, "On the 'German Operation' of NKVD, 1937-1938," in the book *The Punished People* (Zvenya, Moscow, 1999), in Russian.

20. See *Butovo Execution Range. Book of Memory of Political Repressions*, (Institute of Social Sociology, Moscow, 1997), p. 348.

21. Ugo Amaldi, private communication, June 12, 2015.

22. Artur London, *L'Aveu: Dans l'engrenage du procès de Prague*, (Gallimard, 1986), in French.

23. Boris Diakov, Gennady Nikolaev, and Olga Cherneva, *Fisl, or the Man Who Overcame Himself*, in *Den i Noch*, a Literary Magazine for Family Reading, Nos. 3-4, 2005, in Russian.

24. *The Herald Statesman*, Yonkers, NY, Monday, June 15, 1953.

25. Gregor Wentzel, *Quantum Theory of Fields*, (Interscience Publishers, 1949).

26. H. von Buttlar, *Leonium und andere Anekdoten um den Physikprofessor Dr. F. G. Houtermans, 1903-1966*, (Bochum, Institut für Experimental Physik III, Ruhr-Universität, 1982, in German).

27. Ann M. Hentschel, "Peripatetic Highlights in Bern," in *The Physical Tourist. A Science Guide for the Traveler*, Eds. J. S. Rigden and R. H. Stuewer, (Birkhäuser Verlag, Basel, 2009), p. 121.

28. George Marx, *The Voice of the Martians: Hungarian Scientists who Shaped the 20th Century in the West*, (Akadémiai Kiadó, Third Edition, Budapest, 2001).

29. S. S. Gershtein, "Bruno Pontecorvo: Recollections and Reflections," in *Under the Spell of Landau: When Theoretical Physics Was Shaping Destinies*, Ed. M. Shifman (World Scientific, Singapore, 2013), p. 399.

30. Dieter Hoffmann, *Viktor J. Frenkel, Professor Friedrich Houtermans: Arbeit, Leben, Schicksal. Biographie eines Physikers des zwanzigsten Jahrhunderts Herausgegeben und ergänzt von Dieter Hoffmann, unter Mitwirkung von Mary Beer*, Report No. 414 of the Max-Planck-Institut für Wissenschaftsgeschichte, Berlin, 2011, in German; see also Dieter Hoffmann, "Ein Physiker Zwischen Hitler und Stalin," *Spektrum der Wissenschaft,* Februar 2014, p. 62.

31. Gerhard Rammer, "Die Nazifizierung und Entnazifizierung der Physik an der Universität Göttingen," PhD Thesis (Göttingen, 2004), pp 120-130, https://ediss.uni-goettingen.de/bitstream/handle/11858/00-1735-0000-0006 -B49F-4/rammer.pdf?sequence=1

32. G. Rammer, "Allied Control of Physics and the Collegial Self-Denazification of Physicists," in *Physics and Politics*, Eds. H. Trischler and M. Walker, (Franz Steiner Verlag, Stuttgart, 2010).

33. G. Rammer, "Cleanliness among our Circle of Colleagues," in *The German Physical Society in the Third Reich*, Eds. D. Hoffmann and M. Walker, (Cambridge University Press, 2012).

34. Manfred von Ardenne, *Ein glückliches Leben für Technik und Forschung. Autobiographie*, (Verlag der Nation, 1972, in German), pp. 135-136.

35. Edgar Swinne, *Richard Gans: Hochschullehrer in Deutschland und Argentinien* (ERS-Verlag, Berlin, 1992), in German.

36. Paul Lawrence Rose, *Heisenberg and the Nazi Atomic Bomb Project, 1939-1945*, (University of California Press, 1998), p. 307.
37. Peter Minkowski, private communication, June 4, 2015.
38. Philip Morrison, "Review of Samuel Goudsmit's book *ALSOS*," *Bulletin of the Atomic Scientists*, 3, 365 (1947).
39. Heinrich Leutwyler, private communication, June 9, 2015.
40. *The Many Faces of the Superworld. Yuri Golfand Memorial Volume*, Ed. M. Shifman, (World Scientific, Singapore, 2000).
41. *The Supersymmetric World: The Beginnings of the Theory*, Eds. G. Kane and M. Shifman, (World Scientific, Singapore, 2000).
42. *SUSY 30*, Eds. K. Olive, S. Rudaz, and M. Shifman, (North-Holland, Amsterdam, 2001).
43. *Concise Encyclopedia of Supersymmetry*, Eds. S. Duplij, W. Siegel, and J. Bagger, (Kluwer Academic Publishers, Dordrecht, 2004).
44. Yu. Golfand and E. Likhtman, *JETP Lett.*, v. 13, p. 452 (1971).
45. Yuri Raniuk, *Priroda*, 2008, $N^{\underline{o}}$ 1, p. 54 (in Russian).
46. L. D. Landau's letter to the Office of Military Prosecutor, 1935, see *https://sites.google.com/site/michaelkjerusalem/0143-1.jpg*.
47. L. D. Landau's letter to the Head of the Ukrainian NKVD, 1935, see *https://sites.google.com/site/michaelkjerusalem/ufti122*.
48. Natasha Koretz, private communications, 2014.
49. Michael Koretz, private communications, April 2015.
50. https://sites.google.com/site/michaelkjerusalem/ (in Russian).
51. *Memories of Tamm*, Ed. E. L. Feinberg, (Moscow, Nauka, 1986, in Russian).

PART I

Houtermans

$$W = \exp\left(-\frac{2}{\hbar}\int_R^{R_1}\sqrt{2m\left(U - E_1\right)}\,dr\right)$$

$$W = \exp\left(-\frac{\pi Z_1 Z_2 e^2}{\hbar}\sqrt{\frac{2m}{E_1}}\,D(\varphi_1)\right), \qquad W = \exp\left(-\frac{2}{\hbar}\int_R^{R_1}\sqrt{2m\left(U - E_1\right)}\,dr\right),$$

Friedrich Georg Houtermans

PROFESSOR FRIEDRICH HOUTERMANS: WORKS, LIFE, FATE

Victor Ya. Frenkel

Introduction

December 1937. At the last station before the Soviet border with Latvia, NKVD officers force a woman with two small children to disembark from the train from Moscow to Riga. On December 1, her husband was arrested in Moscow; she will not see him again for years. Ten days pass before she is allowed to cross the border and continue her journey into the unknown – she has no money, no one in Riga is waiting for her, her German passport expires in a few days, and as it is, she's afraid to use it. In Germany she'll likely be arrested and her children taken away to a ward – this is her fear as she hastily flees the Soviet Union, where she spent several years with her husband and children.

The woman and her children go on to safeguard memoirs and documents bearing vivid witness to the time's events. Graciously provided to this book's author, they are the basis for a description of the most difficult and gripping pages in the life of her husband – the German physicist Friedrich (Fritz) Georg Houtermans (1903-1966).

F. Houtermans is less known among the next generation of physicists than he deserves. The story of his life requires, in preface, at least a brief summary of his accomplishments in science. The beginning of his career coincided with formative years for the new physics, which by now is seen as classical. In the late 1920's and early 30's, he worked at its main centers, in Göttingen, Copenhagen and Berlin. Though not a theorist, he produced his two major works of that period on nuclear theory and astrophysics, in collaboration with G. Gamow [1] and R. Atkinson, [2] then continued his activities in the burgeoning science of nuclear physics at one of its leading centers – the young Ukrainian Physico-Technical Institute (UPTI) in

---

[1] George Gamow (1904-1968), an outstanding theoretical physicist and cosmologist who discovered a theoretical explanation of α decay via quantum tunneling, and published a number of breakthrough works on star formation, stellar nucleosynthesis, Big Bang nucleosynthesis, and molecular genetics.

[2] Robert d'Escourt Atkinson (1898-1982), a British astronomer, physicist and inventor. In 1929, Atkinson collaborated with Fritz Houtermans to apply Gamow's quantum tunnelling theory to the process of nuclear fusion in stars.

Kharkov, where his scientific career was interrupted.

During the war years, he worked on a problem, the atomic bomb, whose solution overturned all notions about humanity's fate – but worked for the losing side... Yet this wasn't all as simple as it might seem. That is why this book was written. F. Houtermans ought to be of interest for a wide range of people, above all, because of the circumstances of his life. They were shaped by his times, by the geography of his travels, and by his profession, so important in our age, and by the traits of his character. In the spirit of the 18th and 19th century novels, his biography could be called *The Life and Extraordinary Adventures of Friedrich Houtermans.*[3]

Milestones and turning points in his life and related events are listed at this book's end. In recounting them, we'll begin in the usual way, with our hero's birth.

---

[3]The late Eduardo Amaldi's recently published memoir is entitled *The Adventurous Life of Friedrich Georg Houtermans, Physicist* (Springer, Berlin, 2013).

Beginnings

Friedrich Houtermans was born on January 22, 1903, in the resort town of Zoppot, not far from Danzig (now Gdansk). Today it is the Polish resort of Sopot, known for its music festivals. His father, Otto Houtermans (1877-1936), a native of Holland, worked in Danzig as a representative of a Berlin-based firm. Some materials relating to his son's biography refer to him as a banker; Houtermans himself spoke of him as a lawyer. In any case, O. Houtermans was quite a wealthy man, and his son wanted for nothing.

His father's family was undoubtedly of Dutch extraction; Friedrich's grandfather, Josef, an architect by profession, was born in Holland and later moved to Germany. His business went well, and he left his son Otto a considerable estate. Fritz's mother – Elsa Houtermans (Wanek) – was born in 1875 and graduated in Vienna, where she became the first woman in the city to receive a doctorate in biology.

Little Fritz was only three years old when his parents divorced and he and his mother moved to Vienna, where he spent his childhood and youth. Perhaps the divorce occurred due to the essential difference between these people: the conservative-bourgeois father and the progressive intellectual mother. Fritz's mother influenced her son far more than did his father, who, however, always covered his expenses, including university education.[4] (Otto Houtermans remarried, and Fritz soon had a half-brother and half-sister. Yet no substantial information about them could be discovered. -V.F.)

Early 20th century Vienna was the seat of the Austro-Hungarian Empire, a pan-European capital, a center of musical culture, home to myriad fine artists and great writers who largely determined the face of literature in the first half of the century. The sciences also flourished in Vienna. Physics was represented by the great Boltz-

---

[4]Visiting his son in 1932 in Berlin, Otto Houtermans found Fritz's coat indecent and gave him a certain sum of money. His son spent the money on a trip to Switzerland to participate in a science conference. Thereafter, in order to demonstrate the "new" coat, he had borrow a newer one from friends. But because this was a different coat every time, the simple ruse was soon detected. -V.F.

mann (1844-1906) and his school, medicine and psychiatry by Sigmund Freud (1856-1939). Viennese were even somewhat offended when their hometown was called a "second Paris." They aspired, not without reason, for Paris to be called a "second Vienna." Fritz Houtermans grew up in this atmosphere of high culture and bohemia.

Elsa Houtermans, his mother, was a conspicuous figure in the the Austrian capital's cultural circles. Eminent scholars and artists frequented her home. Though feminine and attractive, she pursued purely masculine aims: she worked tirelessly, read, took notes and made annotations, kept a diary, and guided the education not only of her son but of other younger relatives.[5]

F. Houtermans studied at one of the best gymnasiums in Vienna. Its high status was underscored by its name – the Academic Gymnasium. While still within its walls, Fritz developed a deep interest in mathematics, as well as in mineralogy, gathering a rich collection of stones. He didn't neglect dabbling in psychoanalysis, either – Sigmund Freud enjoyed great renown in those years, and Houtermans even conversed with the great scientist. Yet in telling him his dreams, he crossed over into the realm of pure fantasy, the ruse was soon discovered, and Fritz stopped "assisting" the famous Viennese. Thus was revealed his penchant for tricks and jokes, refined and displayed on numerous occasions in the future.

Houtermans' friend and colleague Walter Elsasser, who met him as a student in Göttingen, recalls Fritz namely as a Viennese: "I indubitably have him to thank for my initiation into Viennese cafe life. He found a certain stand-in for the Viennese original: a five-minute walk away from the Physics Institute there was a pastry shop with a tea room. The latter contained a half-dozen marble tables and served coffee and tea. Drawing on his own wealth of experience, Fritz tried to prove a hypothesis asserting that the only food worthy of a

---

[5]Fritz once traveled from Göttingen to Italy, paying his way with odd jobs along the road. He reached Naples, where he worked as a salesman, a clerk and even a freight loader. This went on until a telegram arrived from his perturbed mother, consisting of one word: 'KommWurzDonnerMother,' which Houtermans correctly deciphered as "Come to Würzburg on Thursday. Mother," and returned (the telegram was accompanied by a money order). -V.F.

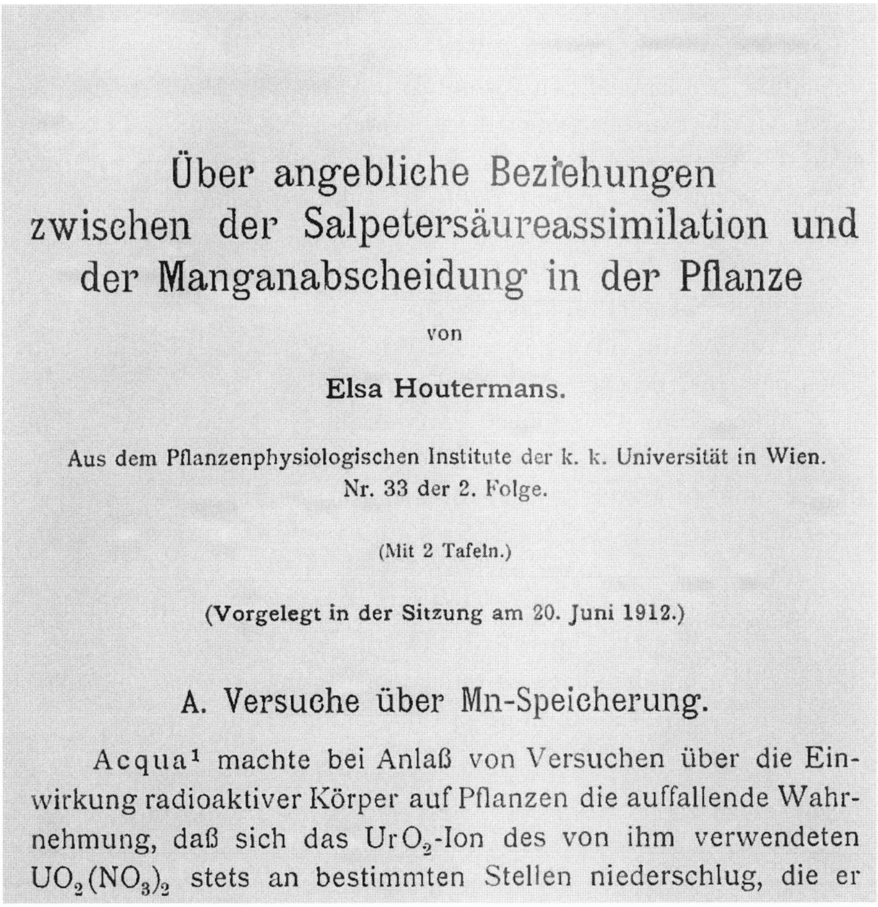

Über angebliche Beziehungen zwischen der Salpetersäureassimilation und der Manganabscheidung in der Pflanze

von

Elsa Houtermans.

Aus dem Pflanzenphysiologischen Institute der k. k. Universität in Wien.
Nr. 33 der 2. Folge.

(Mit 2 Tafeln.)

(Vorgelegt in der Sitzung am 20. Juni 1912.)

A. Versuche über Mn-Speicherung.

Acqua[1] machte bei Anlaß von Versuchen über die Einwirkung radioaktiver Körper auf Pflanzen die auffallende Wahrnehmung, daß sich das UrO_2-Ion des von ihm verwendeten $UO_2(NO_3)_2$ stets an bestimmten Stellen niederschlug, die er

Figure 1. Elsa Houtermans' PhD thesis. Elsa Houtermans (1878-1942) was the first woman in Vienna to earn a doctorate in chemistry, in 1912.

true intellectual was a pastry with strawberries and whipped cream."[6]

Houtermans was also keenly interested in politics, adhering to extreme left-wing views, which enjoyed considerable popularity in Vienna at the time. In his second-to-last year at the gymnasium, shortly before exams, he was punished for reading "The Communist

---

[6]See I. Khriplovich, *Stars and Thorns of Friedrich Houtermans*, *Priroda*, No. 7, 1991. -V.F.

Manifesto" aloud to his classmates – the reading, moreover, took place on May 1, International Workers' Solidarity Day. This was too much for the classical gymnasium to tolerate, and Houtermans was expelled. He transferred somewhere more democratic – a boarding school in Wickersdorf. In those years he formed friendships with two young men with even more radically inclinations: Alex Weissberg, a future member of the Austrian and then the German Communist Party, and Heinrich Kurella, later the editor of the communist newspaper *Rote Fahne* (Red Flag).[7]

Elsasser writes of this as well: "While in Vienna, Fritz had long been close to the extreme left; it's unclear whether he was really a member of the Communist Party or just a sympathizer, as he never mentioned this side of his life to anyone in Göttingen. When Hitler came to power, he had to leave the country immediately, as he would inevitably have been arrested for political reasons later on, and probably would never have survived."

After graduation in the summer of 1922, Friedrich Houtermans chose to enroll at the University of Göttingen, at the time considered the best German-language university, surpassing even the University of Vienna, where the tradition of Boltzmann remained alive.

---

[7]The available record indicates that H. Kurella came to Moscow as a Comintern representative in the mid-1930s. In May, 1937, Kurella was ousted from the Comintern, and in July arrested by NKVD. Under torture, he admitted to being a Gestapo agent. Sentenced to death on October 28, 1937, and executed by firing squad that same day.

Göttingen

In those years, Göttingen numbered thirty thousand inhabitants, of whom a third were students. The university buildings and laboratories were dispersed throughout the city. The students, despite the hardships of the postwar period, believed in the future and thought they owned the world. Most dined just once a day in the student cafeteria; whoever worked in the kitchen as a cook or dishwasher could eat for free. With one meal a day and no money to spare, they steadily learned and found inspiration in their studies and life in general.

The students rented rooms throughout the city, rode bikes and called on each other by whistling tunes (each circle of friends had its own) – in those days, Göttingen had neither phones nor taxis.

For all that, famous mathematicians lived there – the venerable David Hilbert and the younger Richard Courant. They attracted budding mathematicians from all over the world. Among Russian scientists who studied with them were V. K. Frederiks (Hilbert's private assistant) and N. E. Kochin. In the mid-20s, Göttingen became still more appealing to theoretical physicists thanks to the brilliant school of Max Born. Working in this school's depths, Max Born and his students forged quantum mechanics. In his autobiography, Born names physicists who belonged to the Göttingen school: W. Heisenberg, W. Heitler, L. Nordheim, W. Pauli, L. Rosenfeld (Born's assistants), Maria Goeppert-Mayer, N. Wiener, P. Dirac, O. Klein, E. Condon, N. Mott, L. Pauling, J. von Neumann, E. Teller. Russian theorists also figured in Born's list: Yu. B. Rumer, I. Ye. Tamm, V. A. Fock, Ya. I. Frenkel. How much there is in these names! Max Born himself takes care to mention that they include nine Nobel laureates in physics.

The students of that era would sit around marble tables in the "Café Cron und Lanz," with someone explaining matrix calculus or the Schrödinger equation on the tabletop. The waiters addressed the students as "Herr Doktor" and calmly wiped away the writing. They also served as bankers for the students, who frequently only paid after passing final exams, starting work and reaching their first payday.

Göttingen's experimental physicists, especially J. Franck and the renowned optician R. Pohl, were world-famous. The Soviet physicists S. I. Vavilov and V. N. Kondratiev worked under them for a long time. Memoirs recall long lines of would-be candidates for a diploma defense at Franck's institute, not least among them F. Houtermans, who also became one of J. Franck's disciples.

In this wholesome, stimulating atmosphere, Houtermans' talent grew and matured. His thesis, "On the resonance fluorescence and the photoelectric ionization of mercury vapor," [1] was a study typical of James Franck's school.

Recall that in parallel with N. Bohr's creation of the theory of atomic structure, J. Franck and G. Hertz [8] conducted experiments on mercury atom ionization, supporting the theory's assertions. Mercury vapor had long been a classic object of study.

As was customary, Houtermans published his results in *Zeitschrift für Physik*, Germany's, and the world's, leading physics journal at the time. Interestingly, the university's class of 1927 was also represented in this issue of the journal by R. Oppenheimer's [9] article on his dissertation topic, "On the quantum theory of continuous spectra." The magazine published three other doctoral dissertations that year.

The concept of "resonance fluorescence," with antecedents in works by Robert Wood (Houtermans cites them), is related to the classical (still pre-quantum) concept of resonance as the coincidence of the frequencies of an incident light and the subsequent emission from an excited atom. Mercury vapor happens to have well-defined resonance fluorescence, and an irradiated mercury atom can be ex-

---

[8]Both Franck and Hertz played a major role in F. Houtermans' future life and work. -V.F.

[9]Soon to become a famous physicist, Oppenheimer stood out among the Göttingen youth. Not constrained in means, he was very democratic and popular, particularly with the female students. In the process of passing pre-dissertation examinations it turned out that pedantic professors at Göttingen required usage of physical constants in units other than those Oppenheimer had grown accustomed to while studying at American schools. All his many friends (among them was Fritz Houtermans) worried about this. All ended well, though. -V.F.

cited not into just a single state but into a number of states. Atoms exist in these states for various spans of time (how long? – Houtermans studied namely this).

In his paper, Houtermans also established that excitation requires an energy somewhat greater than "exact" resonance energy, or, according to the new quantum concepts, a transition energy between the two states of the atom: excited and ground. He found that part of the energy is needed to dissociate the diatomic mercury molecules – that is, part of the energy goes into the relative kinetic energy of the flying atom fragments.

In the dissertation's second section, published separately in another issue of the journal, the author voices a very interesting hypothesis based on his experimental data. He has decided that the observed strengthening of mercury vapor ionization with the addition of argon, its concurrent weakening with the addition of hydrogen, and, most importantly, the ionization of mercury atoms in different excited states when colliding among themselves, indicated a new kind of mechanism at a submolecular level. Houtermans writes, "A working hypothesis may be advanced that similar collisions produce molecular positive mercury ions, which account for the measured value of the ion concentration in this process in mercury vapor." We note that molecular ion yield and study form a thoroughly modern chapter in molecular and atomic physics.

But Houtermans' talent was most vividly displayed during this period in connection with the late 1928 arrival in Göttingen of 24-year-old Leningrad University graduate student George Gamow for a two-month internship. Initially, his appearance and character attracted attention – tall (192 cm!), cheerful, a lover of jokes and pranks, and a gifted artist besides. Very soon it became clear on top of all this, Gamow was also a great physicist: at Born's seminar, he spoke on his theory explaining, from a quantum-mechanical standpoint, peculiarities of the process of α decays of heavy nuclei.

At the time, these peculiarities were pondered by many physicists, theorists and experimenters. E. Rutherford himself devoted thought to them. It had long been observed that when bombarding the nucleus of an α-radioactive element with α particles emitted by

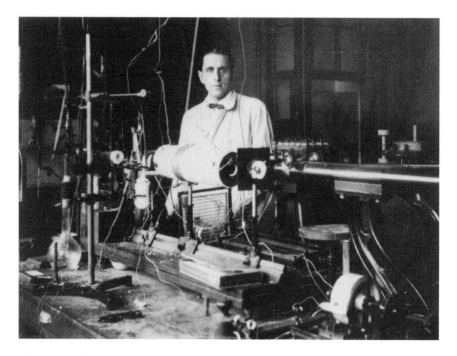

Figure 2.   Fritz Houtermans in Göttingen in 1927. Courtesy of Giovanna Fjelstad.

the same or different nuclei, they fail to penetrate the nucleus, although their energy may even exceed the energy value of the particles
emitted by these same nuclei. Some strange asymmetry was evident.
A simple mechanical example serves to describe its essence. A body
sliding with very low friction down a smooth hill acquires a certain
energy. However, this energy (and even somewhat greater energy) is
not enough to ensure the same body's climb to the top of the same
hill. The hill in this case is a Coulomb force barrier, repulsing positively charged α particles from the also positively charged nucleus.

In a 1927 article, Rutherford suggested the following image,
"super-classical" and yet far from quantum mechanics. Imagine, he
wrote, a large ship moving from a harbor into the open ocean. It's
towed by two tugs from the port.   Only when it leaves the harbor

Figure 3. Fritz Houtermans in Göttingen. At the bottom with his Soviet friends (left to right): Yuri Maslokovits, George Gamow, Natalia Lermontova-Fock, Yuri Krutkov, Fritz Houtermans, and Nikolai Andreev. August 15, 1928. Photograph by Vladimir Fock.

does the ship embark on an independent voyage, releasing its tugs. In this same way, a nucleus emits not a charged helium atom (an α particle) but a neutral one. Only after overcoming the Coulomb barrier does the atom lose two electrons, which go back to the "mother nucleus" (there was no knowledge of neutrons at the time, and the nucleus was thought to consist of protons and "intranuclear" electrons).

Gamow, according to his memoirs [2], went to the university library on his second or third day in Göttingen to see the latest physics journals, chanced upon Rutherford's article and found the answer to this paradox. It boiled down to the fact that quantum mechanics allows the particle to penetrate the region that formally corresponds to its negative kinetic energy. Such behavior of the quantum-mechanical object, similar to the phenomenon of total internal reflection known in optics, was called the tunneling effect. A particle might be said to bore a tunnel through the mountain of energy surrounding the atom.

Gamow developed a detailed theory of the tunneling effect, not only explaining a paradox that had caused considerable angst among physicists, but also developing a formula, based on his theory, that described the previously observed experimental Geiger-Nuttall law regarding the dependence of the half-life of a radioactive nucleus on the speed (equivalent to energy) of the α particles it emits. Gamow's paper, or, more precisely, the lecture he gave at Born's seminar, made a powerful impression on the audience, including Born himself. Much later, this would be recalled by several of the seminar's participants: future Nobel Prize winners E. Wigner and M. Delbrück, and Niels Bohr's assistant Léon Rosenfeld.

The lecture made just as powerful an impression on Houtermans, who although an experimenter was always deeply interested in theory (theorists, inclined to a certain snobbery, call such physicists "thoughtful experimenters"). Soon, getting to know Gamow better and forming a friendship with him, Houtermans invited him to publish a joint article that would develop and mathematically refine the theory presented in the paper.

Gamow gives the following account of this joint work's origins: "During my stay in Germany, I made friends with a jolly Austrian-born physicist, Fritz Houtermans. He had recently completed his PhD in experimental physics, but was always quite enthusiastic about theoretical problems. When I told him about my work on the theory of α decay, he insisted that it must be done with higher precision and in more detail." (See p. 62 in [2].) This was only Houtermans' fourth publication (and Gamow's sixth).[10] Its title is "On the quantum mechanics of radioactive nuclei" [3].

The significance of G. Gamow's idea was determined not only by

---

[10]The first three of Houtermans' publications presented his PhD thesis results obtained under Franck's supervision in Göttingen. -V.F.

two important factors – the use of the apparatus of Schrödinger's newly developed wave mechanics for intranuclear processes, and the creation of the vivid image of the "tunneling effect" – but also by the fairly rigorous explanation of the empirical relationship between the constant of the radioactive decay of elements, t, and the energy of the α particle, E, which they emit: $\ln t = A + B/E$ where A and B are constants.

Namely this is the experimentally observed Geiger-Nuttall law. This is the problem that Gamow and Houtermans solved in their work.

The aforementioned law followed directly from their calculations. Because their calculations defined the form of the potential nucleus barrier in terms of the nucleus radius and charge, in the comparison with experimental data, one of the isotopes from the three radioactive families of α emitters was used for normalization: Rn-222 ($RaEm$ in notation of that time) from the uranium family, Rn-220 ($ThEm$) from the thorium family, and Rn-219 ($AcEm$) from the actinium family. A comparison was provided for 23 isotopes. Assessing the margin of error and conscious of the incompleteness of the description they were using for the α particle's barrier penetration, Gamow and Houtermans discussed introducing a term with an azimuthal quantum number into the potential function and essentially stopped there, considering further refinements in the calculations to be premature, given how much remained unknown about nucleus structure.

The modern theory of α decay more rigorously accounts for the internal structure of the nucleus (recall that then-current notions saw nuclei as consisting of protons and electrons, although the authors left this unmentioned), since α-radioactive nuclei turned out to deviate significantly from spherical form. In other words, knowing just one radius isn't enough. However, this in no way diminishes the importance of G. Gamow's works. Gamow's only co-author on this topic was F. Houtermans.[11]

---

[11]The story of this work is an example of how a scientist's name can slip out of the history of science. For example, in A. S. Davydov's book *Theory of Atomic Nucleus*, (Fizmatgiz, Moscow, 1958), in Russian, the name of Houtermans is missing in the list of references. -V.F.

In the late August of 1928, Gamow left Göttingen for Copenhagen to work with Niels Bohr. Houtermans remained in Göttingen for some time and then moved to Berlin.

References

1. F. Houtermans, *Über die Bandfluoreszenz und die lichtelelektriesche Ionisierung des Quecksilberdampfes*, Inaugural Dissertation, Göttingen, 1927.
2. G. Gamow, *My World Line: An Informal Autobiography*, (Viking Press, 1970).
3. G. Gamow and F. Houtermans, *Zur Quantenmechanik des radioactiven Kerns*, Zs. f. Physik, 1928, Bd. 52, 496-509.

Berlin

The dissertation that Houtermans defended in Göttingen enabled him to secure the position of first assistant in the Physics Department at the Technische Hochschule in Berlin-Charlottenburg. He lived opposite the laboratory, in a building that had served as a barracks during the First World War. Along with him, the British astronomer Robert Atkinson, Walter Elsasser and Houtermans' school friend Alex Weissberg were conducting research there. Houtermans worked for G. Hertz,[12] advancing to the rank of *Privat-dozent* (lecturer), which gave him a chance of a professorship in the future. Concurrently, he and Max Knoll created one of the first electron microscopes (now preserved in a museum in Munich), later patenting a design for magnetic lenses.

Houtermans reported on the results of this work in February 1932 at a session of the Lower Saxony division of the Physical Society. He presented his work methodically, describing the device and its main units – especially, the cathode, the magnetic lenses and the pumping system. He examined the role of space charge in image focusing. A presentation of microphotographs, depicting a heated cathode's surface by optical and electron-optical methods, demonstrated the new device's capabilities.

Many years later, at the Eighth Congress on Electron Microscopy, held in 1974 in Canberra, Australia, one of the inventors of the electron microscope, E. Ruska, told the story of its creation. He recalled that F. Houtermans was the physicist who drew his and M. Knoll's attention to the French physicist Louis de Broglie's concept of an electron as a "wave-particle," a new and unusual idea for the time, and to the possibility of calculating electron beams as ordinary light rays in optical systems. Electron particle waves were shorter-scale than light waves, and, in accordance with the laws of optics, enabled significant image enlargement. Positing that they could obtain images of objects on an interatomic scale, the inventors even doubted

---

[12]Another of F. Houtermans' supervisors at the Technische Hochschule was Professor W. Westphal.

whether their ideas would be taken seriously. Demonstrating the first electron microscope images (at 150 times magnification) convinced them otherwise.

E. Ruska subsequently continued working in this field, and is legitimately considered the creator of the electron microscope. M. Knoll and F. Houtermans moved on to other topics, but although Knoll is mentioned in the history of electron microscopy, Houtermans' contributions are now almost forgotten. However, in the years just after the invention, he had a high reputation in this field, which helped him both in exile in England and as he sought employment in wartime Germany.

It bears emphasis that Houtermans' first papers, beginning in 1927, clearly show the application of what was then a new view of nature: the quantum-mechanical perspective. This new paradigm received definitive expression at a major scientific congress in memory of Alexander Volta, in Como, Italy, on September 16, 1927, through Niels Bohr's lecture for an audience of leading physicists. In a Russian edition of Bohr's papers,[13] the authors of the commentary to this lecture note that although the mathematical apparatus of quantum mechanics existed by 1926 and had already been applied to concrete problems, its significance for physics remained unclear. Bohr proposed the complementarity principle as the basis for interpreting quantum mechanics, maintaining that "however far the phenomena transcend the scope of classical physical explanation, the account of all evidence must be expressed in classical terms."

Accordingly, when Houtermans (and his co-authors) use the latest theoretical apparatus and also explore a proposed explanation's significance for physics – whether in dealing with alpha decay or with other puzzles described below – this not only illustrates the principle proclaimed by Niels Bohr, but also says much about Houtermans' intuition.

All this time, Houtermans never stopped thinking about the tunneling effect. What keeps two energetic protons from approaching closely enough to fuse with each other? After all, as shown by Gamow

---

[13]Niels Bohr, *Selected Scientific Papers*, (Moscow, Nauka, 1971) Vol. 2, pp. 615-616.

Zur Quantenmechanik des radioaktiven Kerns.

Von **G. Gamow** z. Z. in Kopenhagen und **F. G. Houtermans** in Berlin.

Mit 7 Abbildungen. (Eingegangen am 29. Oktober 1928.)

Auf Grund der von G. Gamow gegebenen quantenmechanischen Deutung des α-Zerfalls werden die Zerfallskonstanten der α-Strahler aus der Energie der α-Teilchen, den Atomnummern und gewissen charakteristischen Kernradien berechnet. Für je ein Element der radioaktiven Familien wird der Kernradius so berechnet, daß die Zerfallskonstante mit der Erfahrung übereinstimmt. Daraus werden — ohne spezielle Annahmen über den Potentialverlauf in unmittelbarer Nähe des Kerns — die Zerfallskonstanten der übrigen α-Strahler berechnet und in genäherter Übereinstimmung mit den experimentellen Werten gefunden. Daran schließen sich einige qualitative Betrachtungen über den Mechanismus des radioaktiven Zerfalls.

In einer kürzlich erschienenen Arbeit* hat der eine von uns (G. G.) allgemeine Gesichtspunkte für das quantenmechanische Verständnis des α-Zerfalls radioaktiver Elemente angegeben. Die angenäherte Rechnung ergab dort schon qualitativ den der Geiger-Nutallbeziehung zugrunde liegenden Zusammenhang zwischen der Energie der α-Teilchen und der Zerfallskonstante der α-Strahler, auch ließ sich danach theoretisch für den Fall des Ra C' eine experimentell gefundene** Abweichung von der Geiger-Nutallbeziehung erwarten.

Hier soll nun versucht werden, die absolute Größe der Zerfallskonstanten durch eine genauere Rechnung zu finden und mit den experimentellen Daten zu vergleichen. Dabei ergibt sich die Möglichkeit, einige weitere Folgerungen über die Struktur radioaktiver Kerne zu erhalten.

§ 1. Wir betrachten den Kern als Ausgangspunkt eines gedämpften ψ-Wellenzuges. Die ausgeschleuderten α-Partikel entsprechen der weglaufenden ψ-Welle, die Verminderung der $\psi \bar{\psi}$-Menge des α-Teilchens im Kern bedeutet den radioaktiven Zerfall.

Betrachten wir ein positives Teilchen, das sich unter dem Einfluß einer Zentralkraft um einen positiven Kern bewegt und eine positive Gesamtenergie E hat. Dann lautet die Schrödingersche Amplitudengleichung unter vorläufiger Vernachlässigung der Dämpfung

$$\frac{\partial^2 \Psi}{\partial r^2} + \frac{2}{r} \frac{\partial \Psi}{\partial r} + \frac{8 \pi^2 m}{h^2} (E - U) \Psi = 0, \tag{1}$$

---

* G. Gamow, ZS. f. Phys. **51**, 204, 1928. Vgl. auch E. Condon und J. C. Gurney (Nature **122**, 439, Sept. 1928), die genau die gleichen Gesichtspunkte wie die zitierte Arbeit zur Erklärung des α-Zerfalls heranzieht.

** J. C. Jacobsen, Phil. Mag. **47**, 23, 1924.

Figure 4. The first page of the Gamow-Houtermans paper on decays of radioactive atoms, from *Zeitschrift für Physik*, 52, 496 (1928).

(and independently by the Englishman R. Gurney and the American E. Condon),[14] protons' energy need not necessarily correspond to the height of another proton's energy barrier. Here, too, tunneling is possible. Moreover, such a fusion of two protons in a helium nucleus must be accompanied by a large energy release, since the mass of a helium nucleus is less than the sum of the masses of two protons (the atomic weights of elements were known fairly precisely by that time, thanks to the work of F. Aston and his followers). Mass difference Δm is released as energy: $E = \Delta m c^2$. This truly revolutionary idea made it possible to understand how the stars, including our Sun, have expended energy flows into the surrounding cosmos so long and so intensely. F. Houtermans and the British scientist R. Atkinson, his Technische Hochschule colleague, arrived at namely this conclusion.

Test calculations validated their theoretical considerations, and in March 1929, their article, which cited Gamow, was sent to *Zeitschrift für Physik* with the somewhat eccentric title "How to Cook a Helium Nucleus in a Pressure Cooker" (*Wie kann man einen Heliumkern in Potentialtopf kochen*). The editors replaced this title, though, with a wholly academic one, "On the Possibility of Element Synthesis in Stars" (*Zur Frage der Aufbaumglichkeit der Elemente in Sternen*).

None of this happened, though, without an interesting incident, recalled by G. Gamow in an article in memory of Houtermans, and in his autobiography.

Since Atkinson was an astronomer and Houtermans an experimental physicist, Gamow helped them with the paper's theoretical part. All three went on a ski trip to an Austrian village in the Alps. The main problem they needed Gamow's advice to solve was how to calculate the mechanism of proton energy loss through gamma-ray emission when protons penetrate the nucleus. Gamow proposed using the formula for dipole radiation (at the time, the atomic nucleus was thought to consist of oppositely charged protons and electrons). This overstated the energy output by 10,000 times. Fortunately, there was another error: the effective cross-section of a proton-nucleus collision was taken to be the geometrical nuclear

---

[14]R. W Gurney and E. Condon, *Nature*, vol. 122, p. 439, 1928.

cross-section, rather than the correct value, the square of the de Broglie wavelength of thermal neutrons. Under the given conditions, this second error understated the energy output, also by about 10,000 times. Gamow wrote in his opening note in the F. G. Houtermans Festschrift dedicated to his sixtieth birthday:[15]

> These two errors canceled out, and the figures given in the paper of Atkinson and Houtermans, published in 1929, are very close to those given by modern calculations. This event contradicts the statement that "Two wrongs do not make a right."
>
> Houtermans and Atkinson were the first to suggest in their paper, that the thermonuclear reaction taking place inside of stars results from the subsequent capture of four protons by a nucleus of some light element, with their subsequent union into an alpha particle...
>
> It was still impossible at that time to pin down the particular light nucleus which would react with protons inside of stars, and it was only ten years later that Hans Bethe in the United States and Carl von Weizsäcker in Germany showed showed that the Houtermans-Atkinson *Potentialtopf* is a carbon nucleus.

We note here that in his first articles on the subject, as in his Nobel lecture in 1967, Hans Bethe cited Houtermans and Atkinson, as well as Gamow.

Also significantly, in addition to this work, Houtermans and Atkinson published several papers, including in *Nature*, where "Transmutation of the Lighter Elements in Stars" established Houtermans as this fundamental problem's pioneer. Nonetheless, more "adventures" followed. For example, page 53 of a popular-science book by V. A. Bronshtein [16] refers to the authors as American physicists. In the chapter "How a Star Works" of William Corliss'

---

[15] *Earth Science and Meteorites*, Eds. J. Geiss and E.D. Goldberg, (North-Holland, Amsterdam, 1963), p. viii.

[16] V. A. Bronshtein, *Hypotheses about the Stars and the Universe*, (Moscow: Nauka, 1974.)

book *Mysteries of the Universe*,[17] the author speaks of Friedrich Houtermans as an Austrian physicist (which comes closer to the truth), while Atkinson, a Welshman by birth, is called an English astronomer. Page 75 of Simon Mitton's book *Daytime Star*[18] mentions only the British astronomer Atkinson...

Having mentioned the colorful personality of one of F. Houtermans' co-authors, G. Gamow, it's appropriate to say a few words about the other, Robert d'Escourt Atkinson (his name in full). He graduated from Oxford University (Hertford College) in 1922 and stayed there as a demonstrator under Professor of Experimental Philosophy Friedrich Lindemann.[19] Lindemann, using his connections, secured him a two-year internship in Germany through the Rockefeller Foundation[20] (according to V. Weisskopf, who had a scholarship from the same foundation at about the same time, the foundation paid a stipend of about 150 to 200 pounds[21] a year).

After two years as an assistant at the Technische Hochschule in Berlin, Atkinson chose not to return to his alma mater, but instead, seeking better career conditions, moved to the U.S. to work at Rutgers University in New Jersey. He stayed there until 1937. Then, returning to England, he was promoted to senior assistant at the Royal Greenwich Observatory. In the early 1960s, he reached the peak of his career, becoming president of the Royal Astronomical Society. Thus Atkinson is legitimately called an astronomer.

A brief note in *Nature* (received by the journal's editorial office on April 12, 1929) appeared in advance of the *Zeitschrift für Physik* publication. In the note, the authors, building on already completed calculations for alpha particles penetrating the nucleus, reported their calculations for penetration by protons. The latter, compared to

---

[17]William Corliss, *Mysteries of the Universe*, (Crowell, New York, 1967).

[18]Russian edition: Simon Mitton, *Dnevnaia zvevda*, (Mir, Moscow, 1984.)

[19]Frederick Alexander Lindemann, first Viscount Cherwell (1886-1957) was an English physicist and an influential scientific adviser to the British government from the early 1940s to the early '50s, particularly to Winston Churchill. He advocated the "area" bombing of German cities during World War II.

[20]Through the efforts of A. F. Ioffe, several Soviet physicists of the time, including Landau, also received Rockefeller scholarships. -V.F.

[21]Approximately $10,000 to $15,000 in today's U.S. dollars.

alpha particles, should have a significantly higher penetration factor because their electric charge is twice as small. The probability of their tunneling under the energy barrier is the largest when the speed of protons is three to four times their most probable speed, based on the Maxwell distribution. Houtermans and Atkinson suggested that the energy loss after the tunneling was due to the proton's gamma radiation at the time of fusion ("a proton will anchor itself there by radiating"). The process of fusion through tunneling becomes less probable with each new proton added to the original nucleus because of the increase of the energy barrier. If lithium Li-7 is obtained in this chain, the subsequent proton penetration leads to an isotope of beryllium Be-8, whose instability causes it to split into two helium nuclei.[22] The helium material thus undergoes constant renewal, with the entire reaction limited only by the number of available protons.

The authors examined light nuclei, including carbon, and calculated the correct order of magnitude of the energy released in such a process, which basically supports the high temperatures in stars. The final phrase of the note in *Nature* – "It would seem worthwhile to investigate the effect of the fast protons on light elements in the laboratory, and experiments along these lines are contemplated" – anticipated developments in physics [23] by a good 30 years!

F. Houtermans' reputation as a "thoughtful experimenter" grew still stronger. Gamow, who had stayed for almost half a year in Copenhagen (September 1928 to May 1929), not only ensured Houtermans' "publicity" in Copenhagen, but also an invitation to Niels Bohr's Institute for Theoretical Physics. And meeting Bohr – according to the outstanding theoretical physicist P. S. Ehrenfest – was the most important event in the young physicist's life. Houtermans felt this immediately, yet found this affirmed only considerably

---

[22] A few months later, *Nature* reported that in a number of experiments, helium had indeed been found in beryllium crystals, where it couldn't possibly have penetrated from the outside. -V.F.

[23] In popular science writing and moreover in the scientific literature one can find much more detailed descriptions and specifics regarding element synthesis in stars, as first conjectured by F. Houtermans and his co-author. Here the author limits the account to a brief statement of Houtermans' and Atkinson's idea. -V.F.

later, as we will see.

We'll finish the tale of Houtermans' "stellar" work with one more episode. It figures in Robert Jungk's *Brighter than a Thousand Suns* – one of the first books in the West to tell the history of uranium research and related events and personalities. The setting is Göttingen in 1927.

> On one hot summer day Houtermans went for a walking tour near Göttingen with Robert Atkinson. Atkinson suggested to Fritz that what had been accomplished in the Cavendish Laboratory must also be possible 'up there'. "Naturally!" Houtermans retorted, "Let's just work the thing out, shall we? How could it happen in the case of the sun?"
>
> Such was the origin of the labors of Atkinson and Houtermans on their theory of thermonuclear reactions in the sun, which later achieved such fame.
>
> Houtermans reports: "That evening, after we had finished our essay, I went for a walk with a pretty girl. As soon as it grew dark the stars came out, one after another, in all their splendor. 'Don't they sparkle beautifully?' cried my companion. But I simply stuck out my chest and said proudly: 'I've known since yesterday why it is they sparkle.' She didn't seem in the least moved by this statement. Perhaps, she didn't believe it. At that moment, probably, she felt no interest whatsoever in the matter."

The scene later made it into works on the history of the hydrogen bomb. It roamed from book to book. One of the published monographs falsely attributes the evocative remark to the aforementioned Hans Bethe. Yet the romantic young man was Houtermans, accompanied by his future wife, Charlotte Riefenstahl.

This is the very woman with two children who was forced to leave the train at the Soviet-Latvian border while fleeing the USSR. Recalling Göttingen days, Elsasser wrote,

> As the only woman in our circle, [Charlotte] automatically became the center of attention wherever she appeared, but she had mastered the art of hiding her femininity whenever this

became a stimulating element. She came from Westphalia, where her father was a newspaper editor... Her research interests were quite unusual for a woman of society. She received her doctorate under the physical chemist Tammann in Göttingen, but spent most of her time with the crowd at Franck's institute. After defending her thesis, she spent some time in the United States, where she taught at Vassar College in New York, one of the best women's schools, though apparently without much success, which came to her later. In any case, she returned to Germany and married Houtermans.

One further event must be mentioned as adding to the bond among these three young people – Fritz Houtermans, Charlotte Riefenstahl and George Gamow. This was the translation into German of G. Gamow's book *The Constitution of Atomic Nuclei and Radioactivity*,[24] done by Fritz and Charlotte and published in 1932.[25]

In 1933, after travel to the Solvay Congress on nuclear physics, Gamow became a "defector" to the West, perhaps partly out of a desire for better conditions for creative activity. For the same reason, and at about the same time, Houtermans moved in the opposite direction – to the USSR.

Houtermans' first trip to the Soviet Union took place in 1930.

In post-revolutionary Russia, beginning in 1918, physics conventions were held about once every two years. The seventh convention of Russian physicists, held in Odessa in August 1930, was the first All-Union Congress. Like its predecessors, it brought together almost all the actively working scientists in the country. Foreign guests were also invited, from the venerable – A. Sommerfeld, W. Bothe, W. Pauli, R. von Mises, C. Ramsauer – to the young – R. Peierls and F. Houtermans.[26] Houtermans received an invitation signed by A. F. Ioffe, and the recommendation to invite him undoubtedly came from Gamow.

---

[24] G. Gamow, *Constitution of Atomic Nuclei And Radioactivity*, (Oxford at the Clarendon Press, 1931).

[25] G. Gamow, *Der Bau des Atomkerns und die Radioaktivität*, (S. Hirzel, Leipzig, 1932).

[26] See Appendix II, p. 347.

Figure 5.   Odessa Opera.

Many young people gathered in Odessa. On more than one occasion, this had a side effect of yielding not only professional acquaintances, but also friendships, and even more... Yevgenia Kanegisser, a student at Leningrad University's physics and mathematics faculty and part of what was then a circle of talented young people at the university (M. P. Bronshtein, G. A. Gamow, D. D. Ivanenko, L. D. Landau), wrote a poetic address to her girlfriends:

> *Don't seize stars from the heavens,*
> *don't go searching far and wide –*
> *after all, physics conventions*
> *are a marketplace for brides!*

The verse's closing words became proverbial, with the Odessa convention offering a good illustration. The days of the congress saw the acquaintance and soon the marriage of Rudolf Peierls and Yevgenia Kanegisser herself (Lady Peierls for the rest of her life). In Odessa, Friedrich Houtermans and Charlotte Riefenstahl also decided to share their destinies. They married (with Wolfgang Pauli and Rudolf Peierls as witnesses) when a number of convention par-

Figure 6.   From left to right: Nina Kanegisser, Victor Ambartsumian, unknown, Yevgenia Kanegisser, Matvei Bronshtein, 1931.

ticipapants traveled to the Caucasus. According to family legend, the young couple, striving for originality, formalized their marriage in Sukhumi, where the convention participants had gone on their tour. On returning to Germany, they presented their marriage certificate, which no one could read, because it was in the Abkhaz language!

After Odessa the newlywed couple visited Kharkov, Moscow and Leningrad. Edna Cooper, Kirill Sinelnikov's wife, wrote[27] in a letter

---

[27] *I Married a Russian: Letters from Kharkov*, Ed. Lucie Street, (London, Allen and Unwin, 1946).

from Kharkov to her sister Marian Roger in London (dated September 5, 1930):

"The Houtermans are here and love our flat. We had a binge and spent our last ruble on wine, because they got married in the Caucasus a week ago! Nobody can read their certificate because it's in Georgian!"

Fritz and Charlotte took a great liking to the Soviet physicists, as well as to Odessa, perhaps reminiscent of Vienna (recall Odessa's opera house!). It may have been then, or somewhat later, that Houtermans received an invitation from Ioffe to visit Leningrad and lecture there at the famous physico-technical seminars, covering both theory and general physics. Houtermans' talk at the Odessa congress made a very favorable impression on the attendees. His lecture, based on then-recent research findings, was called "On the Width of Nuclear States and the Possibility of Resonant Particle Absorption by Atomic Nuclei."

The 1930 trip was followed by a visit to Leningrad in 1931 and to Kharkov two years later, in 1932.

1933

Berlin before 1933 was a completely different place for young physicists than it was soon to become. The university colloquia saw participants whose names alone were an inspiration: Einstein, von Laue, Nernst. The numerous cafés on the Kurfürstendamm were meeting places for the intelligentsia. There were new plays, films, concerts. The Houtermans' house attracted many friends: Pauli came to visit one Christmas, and frequent guests included Gamow and Landau from the USSR, Weisskopf from Vienna, Michael Polanyi,[28] whose niece, Éva Striker, later married Alex Weinberg – the same fate awaited this couple as the Houtermans. There were endless conversations on history, politics, Marxism, literature and art. Sometimes more than 30 people would gather in the small house and the tiny garden. Other physicists who visited from abroad were the Blacketts, Maria Göppert-Meyer, Tamm from Moscow, Obreimov from Kharkov. V. Weisskopf's memoirs also include warm memories of these almost weekly parties, jokingly called "Eine Kleine Nacht Physik," echoing Mozart's "Eine Kleine Nacht Musik," dear to the hearts of Germans and Viennese. Yet parallel to this, and then slowly taking over more and more of daily life, the National Socialist German Workers' Party's brown shadow stretched ever farther. The SS and Nazi students brazenly raided the apartments of the intelligentsia, and the police stopped interfering. Then came the day (this happened in April) when Jewish faculty members were no longer allowed to enter the university.[29] Houtermans, only a quarter Jewish (on his mother's side) might have felt relatively safe, but his "non-

---

[28]Michael Polanyi (1891-1976) made important theoretical contributions to physical chemistry, economics, and philosophy. His research in physical science included chemical kinetics, X ray diffraction, and absorption of gases. He pioneered the theory of fibre diffraction analysis in 1921, and the dislocation theory of plastic deformation of ductile metals and other materials in 1934. In 1933 he emigrated to England, becoming first a chemistry professor, and then a social sciences professor at the University of Manchester.
[29]It may have been in those days that Gustav Hertz left his professorship – his Jewish origin deprived him of the right to work for the government. It's also possible that the Nobel laureate's fame saved his life. He earned a living by working for an industrial company. -V.F.

Aryan" appearance, his categorical refusal to say "Heil Hitler," and above all, his known communist beliefs, made his position increasingly unstable. One dire warning was a raid on their apartment in May. Some sources also suggest that Houtermans may have been briefly arrested, underscoring the danger he faced.

Figure 7.   From left to right: W. Nernst, A. Einstein, M. Planck, R.A. Millikan and von Laue. Berlin, November 1931. From Wikipedia.

In another instance, found with both right-wing and incriminating left-wing newspapers during a Nazi police raid on his train as he returned from visiting his father, Houtermans escaped reprisal because he had accidentally picked up his father's cellar-book, with lists of wines and their impressive prices. Mistaking this book for Houtermans' own, the Nazis decided that no one with so much money to spend could be a Marxist.

Even before these events, Houtermans had made an attempt to find work in some scientific institution outside Germany. Help in finding employment abroad for Nazi-persecuted physicists was being provided by colleagues in England, the United States, Denmark and other countries. England, for instance, saw the organization of a special center, the "Society for the Protection of Science and Learning."[30] E. Rutherford and P. L. Kapitsa were among its active participants. Information about German physicists needing aid came from a variety of sources, including P. S. Ehrenfest (his extensive and extremely interesting correspondence with Kapitsa about this has been preserved). Houtermans received direct help from several colleagues who knew him well, including V. Weisskopf (who lived in Austria, which was still free then) and Patrick Blackett. Kapitsa, incidentally, also knew Houtermans, met with him during his fairly regular trips to Göttingen, and heard many good things about him from Gamow.

Weisskopf suggested looking for work in England, and on June 2, 1933, Houtermans wrote a letter to Kapitsa in Cambridge. He wrote to Kapitsa from Vienna, given the obvious risks of writing from Berlin. Kapitsa was then a consultant for a renowned electric musical device company in Hayes (Middlesex, Greater London). Its director was Isaac Shoenberg,[31] who had emigrated from Russia in 1914 and was only too eager to help.

The firm's products were very widely distributed (especially the famous gramophone records "His Master's Voice," featuring an appealing illustration of a dog listening raptly to a gramophone), and in those years its research department was developing the foundations of television technology. Kapitsa thought that Houtermans, an excellent physicist with a European reputation, who had contributed greatly to the development of electron microscopy and was thus an

---

[30]The Society for the Protection of Science and Learning was founded in 1933 as the Academic Assistance Council, by a group of academics (notably William Beveridge, Leo Szilard and Lord Rutherford). Aware of the large-scale persecution of university teachers by the Nazi regime in Germany, the council aimed to provide short-term grants for refugee lecturers, and to help them in finding new employment.

[31]Sir Isaac Shoenberg (1880-1963), an electronic engineer born in Pinsk, Imperial Russia (now Belarus), best known for his role in history of television. Isaac Shoenberg first came to Britain after the failed 1905 uprising in Russia, later returned to Russia, and finally emigrated in 1914.

expert in electronic nodes, might be of interest to the firm.

Houtermans' scientific research was interrupted at the worst possible moment.

Historians of science know that in 1932 Houtermans devised an experiment to test Einstein's ideas about forced radiation. If not for technical difficulties (Houtermans' transformer burned out, with no funds to buy a new one), the laser would have been discovered 20 years sooner! Still, the subjunctive is considered as unsound in physics as in history. A Russian study of the history of lasers, *The Emergence of Quantum Electronics*,[32] notes that much later, Houtermans himself recalled these works of his, outlining his "speculations on the possibility of generating coherent oscillations or intensifying oscillations in an optical frequency range through processes of induced radiation in systems with inverse populations."

The author of this study, I. M. Dunskaya, maintains that "the appearance of this article in 1960 deprives it of all scientific and historical value, the fundamental initial works of 1958-60 already having appeared by this time."

However, it's worth noting that this early 1930s work of Houtermans' attracted the attention of many of his friends, including W. Pauli and W. Elsasser, who mentions it in his memoirs. But above all, it was clearly an inopportune time for Houtermans to develop this major topic (with 1933 already on the horizon), and later events only further impeded its realization. One way or another, Houtermans' physics intuition suggested to him then the degree of the importance of this physics problem, basically new at the time, and now a huge sphere of research.

Editor's Addendum

Everyday life in Berlin at the dawn of Hitler's regime – a surreal intertwining of the normalcy people desperately longed for with the atmosphere of mounting oppression and terror – is chronicled in re-

---

[32]I. M. Dunskaya, *The Emergence of Quantum Electronics*, (Moscow, Nauka, 1974).

markable detail, page after page, in the diary [1] of William Edward Dodd, the US Ambassador to Germany from 1933 to 1937. For a succinct summary of Dodd's eyewitness testimony the reader is referred to the excellent book by Erik Larson [2]:

As time passed the Dodds found themselves confronting an amorphous anxiety that infiltrated their days and gradually altered the way they led their lives. The change came about slowly, arriving like a pale mist that slipped into every crevice. It was something everyone who lived in Berlin seemed to experience. You began to think differently about whom you met for lunch and for that matter what cafe or restaurant you chose, because rumors circulated about which establishments were favorite targets of Gestapo agents – the bar at the Adlon, for example. You lingered at street corners a beat or two longer to see if the faces you saw at the last corner had now turned up at this one. In the most casual of circumstances you spoke carefully and paid attention to those around you in a way you never had before. Berliners came to practice what became known as "the German glance" – der *deutsche Blick* – a quick look in all directions when encountering a friend or acquaintance on the street.

Already in September of 1933 Dodd noted in his diary that persecution of Jews continued in ever more subtle and wideranging form as the process of *Gleichschaltung* advanced. In September the German government established the Reich Chamber of Culture under the control of Goebbels, to bring musicians, actors painters, writers, reporters, and filmmakers into ideological and, especially, racial alignment. In early October the government enacted the Editorial Law which banned the Jews from employment by newspapers and publishers and was to take effect on January 1, 1934. No realm was too petty: the Ministry of Posts ruled that henceforth when trying to spell a word over the telephone a caller could no longer say "D as in David," because "David" was Jewish. The caller had to use "Dora." "Samuel" became Siegfried, and so forth. "There has been nothing in social history more implacable, more heartless and more devastating than the present policy in Germany against the Jews," US Consul General Messersmith told Undersecretary Phillips in a long letter dated September 29, 1933. He wrote: "It is definitely the aim of the German government, no matter what it may say to the outside or in Germany, to eliminate the Jews from German life."

References

1. *Ambassador Dodd's Diary, 1933-1938*, (Harcourt, Brace, 1941).
2. E. Larson, *In the Garden of Beasts*, (Crown, 2012).

London

For several weeks, the Houtermans family lived in Cambridge, enjoying the hospitality of Blackett and other Cambridge physicists before moving closer to Fritz's new workplace. In England, Houtermans began to gather signatures in defense of political prisoners. Working with fellow immigrant Fritz Lange, he began to experiment with micro-photography, successfully reproducing whole pages of the *London Times*, shrunk to the size of postage stamps – envisioned as a technique for relaying information to Germany. Despite such activism, paired with intense work at I. Shoenberg's Electrical and Musical Industries Limited, the situation apparently left Houtermans dissatisfied. He failed to publish even one scientific paper, with the possible exception of internal reports for the company's research department.

This department's work was carried out under the supervision of P. Kapitsa, who served as a scientific consultant for the company. The basic vector of the research involved developing a television system (the iconoscope). Houtermans developed his own method of image enhancement. He is known to have authored a report called "Light amplification and wavelength conversion through photoelectron acceleration." He proposed a high-voltage system where electrons hitting the fluorescent screen material would be deflected by a magnetic field.

The available record indicates that Kapitsa took a skeptical view of this idea.[33] Yet the opinion Kapitsa expressed in a letter to I. Shoenberg is quite telling : "In my own laboratory,[34] if an employee came to me with this project, I would let him try to carry it out, and also would supply him with working conditions. Research experience tells me that very often namely work in the wrong direction leads to the right choice, and sometimes it's even useful not to show a person

---

[33]The P. L. Kapitsa archives contain letters from F. Houtermans about the work he performed. The author thanks P. E. Rubinin for the opportunity to review this archive's relevant materials. -V.F.

[34]Kapitsa headed the Mond Laboratory with Rutherford in Cambridge at the time. -V.F.

his mistake but to let him figure it out on his own; in the process, he very often finds a new and unexpected result." In England, Houtermans also met with scientists working on nuclear physics. He would have found it quite natural to cross over from atomic to nuclear physics. Contact with French scientists (P. Auger,[35] F. Perrin,[36] F. Joliot-Curie[37]), who claimed an impressive roster of accomplishments by that time, reminded him of science's continuing progress.

In England, too, the Houtermans' home was again a central meeting place for physicists, especially immigrants and other foreigners. The suburb where they lived was fairly remote from London, so most guests would stay for a few days. Fritz attracted people and was full of ideas about seeing to others' futures. Charlotte Houtermans recalls visits to their home by Otto Frisch,[38] Wolfgang Pauli, and Gamow, who was just beginning his life in exile. Among their guests were Leo Szilard, who was initially seeking employment at I. Shoenberg's firm, and Fritz Lange, who stayed with them longest.

Just at this time, A. I. Leipunsky arrived in Cambridge from Kharkov, having received a two-year scholarship to work with Rutherford. Leipunsky, who already knew the Houtermans, began to spend almost every weekend with them. Leipunsky's and Houtermans' research interests coincided, and there seemed to be a wonderful opportunities at the Kharkov UPTI, an institute already familiar to Houtermans. Alexander Ilyich Leipunsky, in the opinion of all who knew him, possessed both talent and charm. He was also an excellent

---

[35]Pierre Victor Auger (1899 – 1993) a French physicist who worked mainly in the fields of atomic physics, nuclear physics, and cosmic ray physics. The process where Auger electrons are emitted from atoms is used in Auger electron spectroscopy to study the elements on the surface of materials. This method was named after him, despite the fact that Lise Meitner discovered the process a few years before, in 1922.

[36]Francis Perrin (1901 – 1992), a French physicist who in 1939 established, with Frédéric Joliot and his group, the possibility of nuclear chain reactions and nuclear energy production.

[37]Jean Frédéric Joliot-Curie (1900 – 1958), a French physicist, 1935 Nobel laureate in chemistry. The Nobel Prize was awarded to him and his wife Irène Joliot-Curie for their discovery of "artificial radioactivity."

[38]Frisch left very colorful memoirs of his time in England, which include mention of Houtermans' "laser" experiments (see O. R. Frisch, *What Little I Remember* (Cambridge University Press, Cambridge-London-New-York, 1979).

organizer, and an enthusiast of UPTI, which by 1934 had become one of the largest centers for physics in the USSR. Enjoying the support of both the Soviet and Ukrainian governments, the institute developed rapidly. Within its walls worked I. V. Obreimov (Houtermans had known him since 1929), L. V. Shubnikov and L. D. Landau.

Also influencing Houtermans' inclinations was the strain on the immigrants' monetary fund, which provided him support and had to meet the needs of an ever-greater number of new arrivals. Besides, he saw the industrial laboratory as essentially a temporary workplace. Accordingly, despite colleagues' warnings and concerns (according to Charlotte Houtermans, W. Pauli was especially adamant in this regard) about the decision, F. Houtermans accepted Leipunsky's essentially official work offer. At the very end of 1934 (that December, S. M. Kirov [39] was murdered in Leningrad), the Houtermans left England. After visiting his mother Elsa Houtermans on the way and breathing the air of his beloved Vienna, in late February 1935, F. Houtermans arrived in Kharkov and soon took charge of one of the laboratories at the Department of Nuclear Physics, headed by A. I. Leipunsky.

Had Houtermans stayed in England, his fate doubtless would have been different, perhaps similar to that of other German emigrant physicists like Otto Frisch [40] or the communist Klaus Fuchs. Otto Frisch, a nephew of the famous physicist Lise Meitner, worked jointly with her to achieve the first-ever calculation of the energy yield of a uranium fission reaction – a phenomenon discovered in Germany a few years after the events described. Frisch also introduced the term "fission" itself. After the start of the war, namely he and R. Peierls, also an immigrant German physicist, calculated the critical mass of uranium "explosives" for an atomic bomb, triggering the commence-

---

[39]Sergei Mironovich Kirov (1886 – 1934), a prominent Bolshevik leader. On December 1, 1934, Kirov was assassinated at his office in Leningrad. Many historians place the blame for his assassination at the hands of Stalin and believe that it was organized by the NKVD. This was the beginning of the Great Purge.

[40]In his memoirs, Frisch notes, in jest or in earnest, that Houtermans felt out of place in England because the poor Englishmen lived on "the residues of wool manufacture" (i.e., mutton) and can talk of nothing else but the weather. -V.F.

ment of related work in England. By an Anglo-American pact, in 1943 this research was transferred to the United States, and Frisch worked for several years at Los Alamos. Frisch's name took its rightful place in the annals of scientific discoveries of the 20th century.

Klaus Fuchs, despite his convictions, preferred staying in England to leaving for the land of communist ideals embodied in life. In 1943, he also wound up at Los Alamos, took part in the Manhattan Project, and became the most famous "atomic" spy. Who knows what turns Houtermans' fate as a physicist might have taken, had he remained in England?

Impressions of Kharkov

Interesting details are preserved in memoirs and reports by foreign scientists who worked in or visited Kharkov during F. Houtermans' years of employment there. Seen through foreigners' eyes, those years' realities may often seem amazingly familiar to people born in the Soviet Union, but sometimes these recollections' perspectives are surprising and original.

The noted German physicist Walther Meissner, a low-temperature expert and the Director of the Laboratory for Low-Temperature Research of the Berlin Physical-Technical Institute [41] who was invited to the Soviet Union, wrote in a report [42] to his supervisors:

> Just beyond the Russian border, a huge wooden arch, brightly painted and decorated with red flags, has been erected over the railroad tracks. In Poland, near the Russian border, the houses convey an impression of exceptional wretchedness. They were mostly one-story wattle-and-daub huts, poorly covered with straw. At first, the houses on the Russian side gave the same impression. The rural people we saw looked the same as the Polish populace, if not still more ragged. The farther we went into Ukraine, the homes became better and the people less ragged. The houses were now almost never made of wattle and daub. We saw wood or framed buildings with roofs of painted sheet metal (this is typical of most houses in Russia), and sometimes of slate or tile.
>
> The area along the way through Ukraine to Kharkov was mostly steppe-land. The small woods we passed through were mostly young. There were few fields in cultivation, and we rarely saw herds of livestock. At some stations there were large open areas where little peasant carts stood loaded with grain. From the train carriage windows, gasoline-powered

---

[41] Fritz Walther Meissner (1882-1974) discovered the famous Meissner effect (1933), i.e. damping of the magnetic field in superconductors.

[42] W. Meissner, *Reise nach Russland*, Oktober 1932, Archiv des Deutschen Museums München.

threshing machines could be seen harvesting wheat. Military personnel were conspicuous everywhere, their clean, quality clothing in marked contrast to that of the rest of the populace, as well as that of Polish soldiers.

Figure 8.   Kharkov Tractor Factory (XT3), circa 1933. 25,000 tractors produced!

In Kharkov, where we arrived an hour late, we were met by a German colleague employed there, Dr. M. Ruhemann, and by a young Russian physicist, Yuri Ryabinin. They brought us and our luggage in an Intourist [43] car to UPTI, about six kilometers away from the railway station on a hill in newly created part of the city, along with the associated residence buildings. The view from the hill looks out over the countryside and outlying villages and beyond to the steppe. On the horizon can be seen big factories, including a large power plant (Elektrostroy), a large turbine factory (Turbinostroy) and an even larger tractor factory (Traktorostroy). The

---

[43]Intourist, since 1929, was the only tourist agency in the USSR which was authorized to deal with foreigners.

Kharkov institute building is comparable to the main building of our Imperial Institute,[44] although with more wings and
a design allowing for possible new additions.

These memoirs' description of institute life, quite unusual from a
foreign perspective, is also very telling.

At the institute entrance hung posters urging employees to
subscribe to a domestic bond issue. A red flag also hung. In
the lobby, a bust of Lenin stood on a pedestal covered in red
cloth. In addition, many large photos on display depicted the
institute facilities and equipment.

Seminars took place from 8 p.m. to 10 p.m., with up to 50
participants. Since the conference room was then housing the
high-voltage laboratory, meetings were held on the premises
of the institute kindergarten. There was a blackboard available, but no projectors or other devices. The chalk was also
very bad, and for erasing notes, an ineffective little rag was
used, or simply paper. At the small seminar (referred to as
the "evening brigade") in the evenings about twelve people
would attend. It was held in the Theory Department. This
too had only a blackboard.

The large institute workshop is housed in basement facilities and has about 12 good lathes, milling machines and
drills, enough to build large installations. Yet there is a long
wait for order processing, with the workshop overloaded and
materials scarce. For example, in the cryogenic laboratory it
was hard to find the simplest things: copper tubing, sheet
metal, a wrench, screws, etc.

The time left after discussing presentations and touring
the institute was spent in exploring the city and its surround-
ings. We were free to do or not do whatever we wanted.
Kharkov, formerly a small provincial town, in recent years
has undergone population growth from 250,000 to 750,000.

---

[44]Berliner Physikalisch-Technische Reichsanstalt.

It is now (in 1932) the capital of Ukraine.[45] Absolutely enormous construction is under way here. Many institutes have appeared; besides the UPTI, there is an institute of silicate research, and a new high-voltage laboratory preparing to commence operations. The city has a university, but the physics program there is virtually nonexistent.

It's entirely possible that F. Houtermans first plunged into a Soviet reality much like that seen by W. Meissner.

Buildings sprout up like mushrooms after rain. All construction is carried out by modern methods and completed in a short time. Old buildings in the city are mostly modified or grafted onto neighboring buildings. The city is growing too quickly for the transport system to handle all the passengers. The streetcars on the main streets have three linked carriages, but these are overcrowded to the crushing point! Five or even more people always ride on the running board. Streetcars are boarded from the rear and exited from the front vestibule. Only women with children or invalids with special passes board from the front. The conductor sits or stands at the rear of the carriage, in the corner. Because approaching him is practically impossible, the money for the ticket (10 kopeks) is passed along the chain of tightly packed passengers – there and back – and this happens with no difficulty whatsoever. Really, despite the crushing, almost intense enough to tear the clothing off one's body, everything in the streetcar happens in peace and harmony, with no arguing.

The city's main buildings are imposing in appearance. Some, such as the government buildings, are built in a classical style, while others, such as workers' clubs and so forth, are quite modern. Particularly interesting is the new trusts building ("Gosprom"), fronted by a large public square (about a square kilometer). The large windows of this tall building (about 16 stories high) offer a view of the hilly landscape and

---

[45] In June 1934 the capital was moved to Kiev.

the smokestacks on the horizon. The trusts building houses administrative offices for a variety of industries.

Meal times in Russia resemble those in England: a morning breakfast including eggs and meat, if possible, then a one o'clock lunch with much less fare than in England. From 3 to 5 in the afternoon is the main meal, like the English dinner, and then in the evening at around 9 comes tea again, with sandwiches, cheese and so forth.

Accompanied by A. Weissberg, the German guests visited the large factories.

The streetcar ride there takes about an hour. An UPTI pass gave us easy admittance to Elektrostroy. Everything conveyed the impression of a large European factory. At the same time, it felt very cramped, apparently because of the factory's overstaffing. The most interesting visit was to Traktorostroy, where we were admitted only because Weissberg used his influence as a Communist Party member. During our two-hour visit, we saw no other visitors. This factory, with its many shops, is like a whole city. It was built and outfitted in 18 months. Given sufficient raw materials, it produces about seventy 35-horsepower tractors a day. Productivity should ultimately reach 140 tractors a day. Assembly takes place along a conveyor. One shift lasts seven hours, and there are too few qualified workers for other shifts. The factory workers looked well-fed and happy. We spoke German with some of them, and they asked about the situation in Germany. There was also a mechanic who had come from Saxony.

Political and propaganda slogans hung here and there, and names of particularly exceptional workers were displayed. Some posters about work and so on were humorous. At one point we saw a bust of Lenin, a gift from the German Red Front Fighters' League.

From what we saw personally in Kharkov and learned from the foreigners working there, particularly from Weissberg and

Figure 9.   The State Industry House (Gosprom), referred to as the "trusts building" by Walther Meissner. Kharkov, circa 1933.

his wife, we have the following idea of the economic and cultural situation in the country at the moment. Groceries are obtained by cards or stamps in so-called cooperative or state stores which sell not only groceries but also other products, albeit in limited quantities. Each category of workers has its own stores. The institute has three cooperatives: one for foreigners, another a first-category cooperative for researchers and glassblowers, and then a second-category cooperative for office staff, workers and lab technicians. The second category includes wives whose husbands receive first-category goods. This is the case, for instance, with Shubnikov's wife. The first two stores had ample bread and other products: butter, sugar, cheese, meat, sausages, canned fish, and so on. The second-category cooperative was much more poorly stocked. There was almost no meat, eggs or butter, but there was plenty of bread.

Figure 10.   Gosprom decorated. Kharkov, circa 1933. The size and form of each communist leader portrait (icon) had to strictly follow the official hierarchy.   Marx and Engels are the largest, then Lenin and Stalin, and only then all other current communist leaders, much smaller in size.

Indeed, the institute faculty themselves said that all the office staff appeared to suffer from hunger. In addition, there were shops where everything was sold without stamps, but at relatively high prices. In Kharkov, such stores are called Khartorg (in Moscow, Mostorg). In them one can buy spirits, wine, cakes, china, glassware, cigarettes, mirrors, and so on. The Khartorg shops have numbers, that is, are registered with the state. There are numerous small outdoor book kiosks, as well as several major bookstores. Books are extremely low-priced. Book sales are high, and the bookseller is always besieged by customers. There are also shops with currency-based purchasing. These stores, which deal in groceries and much else besides, are called Torgsin.[46]   Their

---

[46]Torgsin were state-run hard-currency stores that operated in the USSR between 1931 and 1936. Their name was an acronym of *torgovlia s inostrantsami*, "trade with foreigners." In fact, Soviet citizens were also allowed to buy goods in Torgsin in exchange

prices are about twice as high as in Germany.

If, like their husbands, the women work, their children attend kindergartens which are generally available at the factories and institutes. The Kharkov institute's kindergarten is spacious and furnished with all the necessities. There are also factory schools for older children (German is also studied there), and after 12 years of age, job training is also given. The state sees to children's education up to a certain grade. Apparently technical professions are preferred over intellectual or artistic ones.

As for religion, the state does not recognize it. Antireligious literature is printed in Russian and German. It cites Darwin, Mendel and others, and examines life's origins from a scientific point of view. Yet the question of the world's meaning and origins receives only weak consideration, as does the question of the infinite.

Finally, Meissner sums up his observations.

We agreed that the trip to Russia had been extremely interesting and instructive, but that it would take years before any conclusions are possible about Russia's future, that is, as to whether the dominant system can ensure well-being and order for all the people, with everything now in a phase of construction and development. Undoubtedly, these impressions, based on witnessing things obtained in such a short span of time, could change. This is why it's understandable that those who travel to Russia form such different opinions. The country already has certain achievements in different areas, and many foreigners, such as Weissberg and the Ruhemanns,

---

for Imperial Russian gold coins and golden jewelry. In 1936 Sir Walter Citrine, General Secretary of the UK Trades Union Congress, traveled to the USSR to obtain first-hand knowledge of the conditions of the working people in the Soviet Union. His report was published as *I Search for Truth in Russia*, (E. P. Dutton, New York, 1937). There he writes that goods and groceries offered by Torgsin were not available to the general populace and that prices in Torgsin were twice as high as in the UK. He also testifies that the black market exchange of hard currency in rubles was flourishing. Black marketeers offered 100 to 200 rubles for 1936 UK pound sterling.

Figure 11. The almighty Central Committee of the Communist Party of Ukraine. Kharkov, circa 1933.

feel very comfortable and materially satisfied in Russia. It is also important that the Russians themselves, in general, possess an inner sense of contentment, with life wholly focused not on appearances but on human and idealistic values.

We'll expand on this prominent German scientist's report with rather interesting data that was under discussion at about the same time in the West. In the December 11, 1937, issue of the journal *Nature*, one of the editors relates the following information [47] about the financial standing of Soviet scientists (based on purchasing power compared to the British pound relative to food products, with 1 ruble equivalent to 3 pence [48]): "The heads of university departments

---

[47] *Nature*, "Staff and Student Stipends in Soviet Union," vol. 140, p. 1007 (1937).

[48] This exchange rate was not generally accepted. It was substantiated in a response article "Salaries in Soviet Universities," L. H. Callendar, *Nature*, vol. 141, p. 290 (1938).

receive 190 pounds a year, professors 175, senior lecturers 120. First-year students are paid a monthly stipend of 130 rubles, as are the majority of unskilled workers in the USSR, which equates to 8 shillings and 4 pence weekly pay in Great Britain. The free benefits provided in addition to the salary are much less than those received by England's poorest sectors of society through welfare."

M. Ruhemann, returning to England after five years of work in the Soviet Union, provides the following commentary [49] to Callendar's *Nature* report: "The income of a Soviet family consisting of a professor husband, his working wife and two children, amounts to about 1,800 rubles a month. In Kharkov, an apartment with utilities cost 120 rubles, heating cost 20 rubles, taxes and social insurance 50 rubles. In addition, a mandatory subscription to government bonds cost 150 rubles." Beyond this, according to Ruhemann's calculations, clothing cost about 250 rubles, laundry 50 rubles, and groceries 700 rubles. This left 460 rubles for other expenses, including domestic help.[50]

It is instructive to contrast Ruhemann's report with Edna Cooper's remarks scattered in her letters to her sister Marian Roger in London.[51] The Sinelnikov couple arrived to Kharkov in June of 1930 and settled in the famous UPTI apartment building at Tchaikovsky Street, 16 – the same building in which the Houtermans resided from February 1935 to November 1937 (along with other foreigners and key UPTI employees).

It is close to that suggested by Sir Walter Citrine in *I Search for Truth in Russia*.

[49] "Salaries in Soviet Universities," *Nature*, vol. 141, p. 792 (1938).

[50] One should not forget that the Ruhemanns were ardent communists, and remained such even after Stalin's death, when Stalin's crimes and atrocities became public knowledge. Martin Ruhemann seemingly tended to adorn the story. From Weissberg we know that Leipunsky's salary was 280 rubles per month. According to Soviet sources the regular professor's monthly salary at that time was roughly 800 rubles, and that of associate professor 400-500 rubles. Ruhemann's bias could be explained in part by the fact that salaries offered to foreign scientists were higher than those of their Soviet colleagues. Charlotte Houtermans notes in her diary that Leipunsky offered to Fritz Houtermans to pay half of his salary in hard currency.

[51] Added by the Editor. Pages 120, 143-145 and 154 of the American edition of *I Married a Russian: Letters from Kharkov*, Ed. Lucie Street, (Emmerson Books, New York, 1947).

Kira and I are very happy today – we *actually got paid* – 205 rubles. We get 250 every half month, but 20 goes for income tax and 25 to the State loan. I think I begin to be a bit of a miser – we've just paid Boris for the milk – and I could have sworn that we had paid until the 17th, that is today, but Boris said only until the 13th. It's only about ten rubles different, but I hate being "done." I'd rather give 10 rubles away.

Anyway, now we owe *nobody* anything and we still have about 150 rubles, but we must live on it until the beginning of December, two weeks... We get about 900 rubles a month when Kira is lecturing.

Now I am going to make coffee. I actually bought some beans, for 24 rubles half a kilo (about one pound) and I've got lemon for tea, but they've gone up to twelve rubles each; I was fool not to buy some when they were only four rubles.

I have been invited to become co-editor, with Weissberg, a German engineer working here, of an Anglo-German Physical Magazine. That means Physical as related to science. I am to read and correct all the English articles... I suppose it will begin in the winter and there is a possibility that I shall get paid.

Professor Gerasimovich says that I must be very careful with what I write because it's quite possible to get into trouble through letters...

Wages average 190 *Roubles*

was there any belting, every machine being driven by a separate electric motor.

I had a talk about labour conditions with the Factory Committee, in the presence of the manager. Two shifts were worked, each of seven hours, with one hour for food, from 7 a.m. to 3 p.m. for the first shift, and from 3 p.m. to 11 p.m. for the second shift. There was no night shift. There was no minimum wage for piece workers, and there were only a very small number of workers who had a fixed time wage. This was 120 roubles per month. They obtained overalls free of charge. There were nine categories of workers and their average earnings were as follows :

Categories.					No. of Workers.	Roubles Monthly.
1	.	.	.	.	120	125.130
2	.	.	.	.	1050	145.50
3	.	.	.	.	1233	165.70
4	.	.	.	.	836	175
5	.	.	.	.	702	190
6	.	.	.	.	578	210
7	.	.	.	.	715	215
8	.	.	.	.	737	230
9	.	.	.	.	441	250

The number of employees in the different categories gives those for the shoe departments only. Those for the leather and other auxiliary departments were not available. This accounted for only about half those employed, but it served me as a guide. On this basis more than half the workers receive 175 roubles or less per month.

The technical director had a fixed salary of 1,300 roubles a month, and a bonus, bringing the total to about 2,000 roubles. Taking the factory as a whole, the average wage for everyone, including the technical and directive staff, was 190 roubles per month.

The monthly working hours were one hundred and seventy-five, namely twenty-five working days out of every thirty. These days are arranged so as to con-

39

Figure 12.   A page from Walter Citrine's book *I Search for Truth in Russia*, (E. P. Dutton, New York, 1937).

Kharkov: 1935-1937

Three major subsectors at the Ukrainian Physico-Technical Institute had particularly successful operations at that time. One of these was the Department of Low-Temperature Research, whose employees included I. V. Obreimov, L. A. Shubnikov, German physicist M. Ruhemann (who had received British citizenship after emigrating from Germany) and engineer-physicist Alexander (Alex) Weissberg, who had known Houtermans since his Vienna years and like him belonged to the Communist Party of Germany. Weissberg, an UPTI employee since 1931, was coordinating the establishment of the Experimental Station for Deep Cooling (ESDC), whose role was to include supporting the institute's low-temperature research program. In general, by 1935 UPTI had become the USSR's leader in this research field, with world-class projects under way there.

The UPTI Department for Nuclear Research, headed by A. I. Leipunsky, was also very strong. Its staff included such renowned physicists as K. D. Sinelnikov, A. K. Walter, G. D. Latyshev and German Communist F. Lange, a top-notch specialist in high-voltage technology. In 1932, this department achieved the complex installation of a linear accelerator, with which the Kharkov physicists successfully reproduced the remarkable experiment in which Cavendish Laboratory scientists E. Walton and J. Cockcroft had split a lithium nucleus with protons accelerated in a high-voltage tube [1]. An electrostatic Van de Graaf accelerator was also under construction.

Lastly, there was the UPTI Theory Department. Its operations dated from the inception of the institute itself. It was initially headed by D. D. Ivanenko, and then by L. B. Rozenkevich. In 1932, L. D. Landau became its head. By the time when F. Houtermans arrived, the core of Landau's Kharkov school had already formed; it included A.I. Akhiezer, E. M. Lifshitz, and several young theorists. For a long time, theoretical physicists from Germany came to work at the department. Among them were W. Elsasser and V. Weisskopf, already encountered in these pages. Other foreign employees included G. Placzek from Austria, L. Tisza from Hungary, and the American B. Podolsky.

Figure 13.   Left to right: Alexander Weissberg, unknown, Charlotte Houtermans (tentatively), Kirill Sinelnikov, Edna Cooper-Sinelnikov, and Fritz Houtermans in Kharkov. Courtesy of Jean Richards.

With his sociability and lively character, with his deep knowledge of physics, F. Houtermans fit in well this group. He became head of one of A. Leipunsky's laboratories. The Houtermans couple arrived in Kharkov with their little daughter Giovanna, and soon their son Jan was born there.

Here is an excerpt from Charlotte Houtermans' Kharkov memoirs.

The journey to Kharkov is dim in my memory. Friends in Vienna saw Bamsi and me off... Fisl met us in Prague. I remember nothing of the long, long trip, except the terrible cold icy air which greeted us in our arrival and the general mix-up at the station, the strange language, the people hustling along, not caring... When we arrived, it was the beginning of February and still the deepest, coldest of winters. The campus had two exits, both guarded by a kind of policeman with a rifle and a bayonet. Not a cozy atmosphere at all.

Supposedly the campus was to be landscaped, eventually, but at that time the buildings were not even quite finished and only a few families had made gardens. The English wife of one of the physicists [52] had planted a huge garden, which brought all kinds of surprises.

Our apartment was not ready, as we had reason to expect. We were told that the new apartment of the director, who was still abroad, would shelter us for the time being, though it too was not quite finished, but would undoubtedly do. It had to. As a matter of fact it was the strangest of the homes we ever had. The home itself has addition to the big research building and it contained six apartments, two on each floor. We would occupy the duplex, which one entered at the 3rd floor and from where an inside staircase led to the 2nd floor part, which had no exit except through the 3rd. I always felt as if I were sleeping in a cellar. Bamsi's room and the kitchen were upstairs; another room had to be given to another foreign scientist, to Fisl's extreme annoyance. Downstairs were two rooms and a bath. Our bed-living room was fairly large; the second small one was inhabited by Bimbus, who arrived shortly after us. The nightmare qualities of the first two months were never quite dispersed. Fisl and Bimbus were both dreadfully ill for many months. Bimbus almost died of the dysentery when she first became ill... They carried Bimbus off in an ambulance to the hospital and we did not see her again until months later, because visitors were not allowed. After the departure of the ambulance, a truck arrived, looking like a white van, with all kinds of hospital personnel who proceeded to fume out the whole apartment, our clothes, everything. The menus for Fisl were rice boiled in water, chicken boiled, no butter at all, nothing else but tea...

When we finally moved into our own apartment, we got a beautiful large terrace which one entered through a door from the kitchen and which extended along the whole length of the apartment and had steps leading to a small area, out

---

[52] Edna Cooper-Sinelnikov.

of which I finally made a small garden. But no particular
memories seem to be connected with either. The garden had
one beautiful tree under which there was a place to sit. Below
the terrace was one empty, cellar-like small place, presumably
for the hare, but since it had no door, he promptly escaped.
Once in August of 1937 or earlier we sat with guests on the
terrace and listened to the "Kleine Nachtmusik" which I had
brought back from England.

Our maid was beautiful. She was rather tall, big boned
with smooth dark almost ebony colored hair and enormous
brown eyes. Her name was Marussya. She appeared one day
with an older woman, who recommended her, I gathered,
very much, with a flood of words quite wasted on me. We
discussed the wages and then I asked when would she like to
start. To my astonishment she said, now, and got ready for
work. She wore a black huge kerchief over her head which
covered her down to her waist, the skirt was black too, simple gathered at the waist, the blouse was spotlessly clean,
in her hand she carried a tiny parcel, something wrapped in
another kerchief. She came in and got ready. First she took
off her black kerchief, displaying an equal large white one un-
derneath; then she took this one off too, to let me see the
beautiful hair with the heavy knot in the back. Taking off
the whole blouse and the skirt she stood there in her working
clothes – another blouse and skirt. From the parcel she took
a small kerchief to protect her hair again, then took off her
shoes and was ready for anything I might wish to be done. I
loved this girl very much...

Somewhat pedantically, W. Meissner relates his own impressions
of living conditions in the USSR.

The two residence buildings affiliated with the institute are
two-story, with four apartments on each floor. The apartments have three rooms, a bathroom, kitchen, bathroom, two
balconies, water, gas and electricity. The buildings are surrounded by green areas where trees are only now about to be

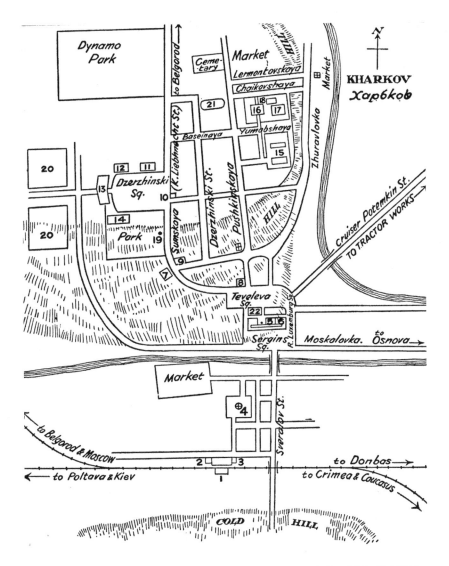

Figure 14.   A map of Kharkov sketched by Edna Cooper-Sinelnikov [2] (mid-1930s):
1. Main Railway Station; 2. Main Post Office; 5. Red Army Theater; 6. Kharkov University; 9. Bank; 15. Technological Institute; 16. UPTI, Main Building; 17. High Voltage Laboratory; 18. UPTI Housing (that's where the Houtermans lived). At the bottom of the map is a hill known as *Kholodnaya Gora* ("Cold Mountain" in Russian). This is also the name of the Kharkov Penitentiary in which F. Houtermans was imprisoned.

planted. For now, the site and buildings are in poor condition. The apartments are mainly inhabited by institute scientists, mechanics, and so on. One person is intended to have no more than one room. Room sizes are not to exceed 10 square meters, but the rooms in the institute apartments are larger – about 16 square meters.

About the institute apartments I should add that walls in residential buildings are two bricks thick and windows have double frames which don't close very well, such that in winter they are sealed with putty and never opened at all. The rooms have quite high ceilings, about three meters. The floors are boarded and the walls painted. The doors have no handles, only spring-loaded ball latches and bolts. These latches have almost no effect, so the doors stay open and are never closed, even where the bath and toilet are, which doesn't bother the apartment dwellers a bit. In front of one room's window was a small roof (above the entrance door) where numerous shards of glass, cigarettes butts and the like were lying, and no one cleaned this up for ages. The taps in the bathroom are covered with green rust, despite the building's quite recent construction. The outside stucco-work is already damaged. The same is true of the building's front door. The stairs are generally dirty, as are the apartment doors.

Houtermans always had a knack for quickly finding his bearings in new work, and starting in mid-1936 his papers began to appear in the journal *Physikalische Zeitschrift der Sowjet Union*, published in Kharkov. A few words should be said about this journal. It was launched in 1932, when it became clear that the country's existing science periodicals were not enough. In the 1920s, Soviet physicists mainly published in the physics part of *Journal of the Russian Physical and Chemical Society and in Journal of Experimental and Theoretical Physics*, the older journal's successor since 1931. Naturally, both journals were published in Russian. In those years, however, almost no one in the West knew Russian. To avoid losing precedence in important research and to inform Western colleagues of successes in

Soviet physics, Soviet physicists placed their articles in Germany's *Zeitschrift für Physik*, the most prestigious physics journal at the time. When Hitler came to power, the situation changed, with Soviet scientists ceasing to publish in this journal almost immediately (prior to this, they had accounted for 20% to 25% of the total number of articles published there). At this point, a group of Kharkov-based scientists, supported by physicists from Leningrad and Moscow, started publishing a Soviet journal in foreign languages. Articles were published predominantly in German, and then in English. Very soon, the journal became international, with other countries' physicists placing their papers there.

Among those who "pushed through" permission for the new journal's release, for printing under paper quotas, etc., was A. Weissberg (through N. I. Bukharin,[53] a high-ranking official at the People's Commissariat of Heavy Industry). The editorial board, headed by A. I. Leipunsky, also included Alexander Weissberg, D. D. Ivanenko and L. V. Rozenkevich. Two wives of foreign scientists working at UPTI, Charlotte Houtermans and Barbara Ruhemann, participated in translating Soviet physicists' articles into foreign languages.[54]

F. Houtermans' first publication in this journal's pages is dated March 15, 1936. Like most of his studies in those years, the paper dealt with the interaction of slow neutrons with different elements (in this case with tantalum). Work in this direction was begun in Rome by the group of Enrico Fermi, who in 1934 had discovered the abnormally large reaction cross section of slow neutron absorption by the nuclei of certain elements. Every physics center in the world immediately started studying this type of reaction. In the USSR, the first results were obtained by I. V. Kurchatov and his colleagues at the laboratory of the Leningrad Physico-Technical Institute.

F. Houtermans' first paper in the journal was co-authored with his

---

[53]Nikolai Ivanovich Bukharin (1888-1938) was a Bolshevik revolutionary and high level Soviet politician. Arrested in February 1937, he was charged with conspiring to overthrow the Soviet state and executed in March 1938.

[54]The magazine existed for seven years and was closed in 1938. By this time Rozenkevich had been executed and Weissberg and Leipunsky were in prison. Ivanenko was arrested in 1935 and a year later was exiled to Tomsk. -V.F.

Figure 15.   UPTI, Main Building (1930s). The upper floor was occupied by Landau and his group. The corridor which led from Landau's office to the UPTI Library on the same floor was named *Rue de Dau*. The Main Building was designed in such a way that each floor could hold the pressure of six tons per square meter. To this end, special workers had been sent to Sebastopol (Crimea). They dismantled the cruiser *Empress Maria*, which had been lying on the bottom of Sebastopol Bay. Then they cut big parts of the cruiser into smaller pieces and transported them to Kharkov. These pieces of *Empress Maria* were installed inside the walls and floors of the future building before the workers poured concrete. Even now these reinforcement structures protrude from the walls and basements in some places. Courtesy of Yuri Raniuk.

immediate colleague V. Fomin. Fomin, the son of a Soviet diplomat who worked in Germany, had received his higher education in physics there and gotten to know Houtermans while in Berlin.[55]

Less than a month after this first publication in the journal, another Houtermans paper appeared there – on the slowing of neutrons in liquid hydrogen [3]. The paper represented the combined efforts

---

[55]Fomin's fate took a tragic turn. He jumped out the window during a search raid on the laboratory. Crippled and maimed, Fomin died under arrest. Houtermans was then accused of recruiting Fomin for the "counter-revolutionary organization" which operated in Kharkov. -V.F.

of Houtermans, Leipunsky and Fomin from the Department of Nuclear Physics, along with Shubnikov from the Department of Low-Temperature Research. I. V. Kurchatov frequently came to Kharkov in the 1930s. He stayed at UPTI a long while, taking part in neutron physics research. F. Houtermans collaborated with Kurchatov to publish results [4, 5] of research on low-temperature interaction of thermal neutrons with silver.[56]

In his Kharkov years, F. Houtermans published a total of seven papers [3–9]. It's interesting to note that the most complete list of F. Houtermans' scientific papers, published in 1980 in a book dedicated to his memory [10], omits one work from this period, discovered by the author in the Ukrainian Academy of Sciences' Ukrainian-language journal [8].

In framing their research, the authors, in accordance with the ideas of the time, relied on an inversely proportional dependence between the neutron-nuclei cross section and neutron velocity v. Measurements were carried out at various temperatures, including the temperature of liquid hydrogen, at an installation with the capacity for what at the time was a record volume of liquid hydrogen – up to 50 liters. The desired $1/v$ dependence of neutron absorption was found in the range of temperatures from 20.4 °K (liquid hydrogen) to room temperature, including the temperature of boiling nitrogen (77 °K).

Based on the results of these experiments, a correct conclusion was drawn about violation of the theoretical $1/v$ dependence between the reaction cross section and neutron velocity. In neutron-nuclei interactions resonant (called "selective" at the time) neutron absorption was found to occur at certain values of energy (equivalent to certain values of v). These findings stimulated the successful development of nuclear theory (in the USSR, by Ya. I. Frenkel, and abroad, by N. Bohr and D. Wheeler), so it's entirely fair to say that in the USSR, F. Houtermans participated in research that was commensurate with

---

[56]In the list of works which Kurchatov presented in 1943 in his nomination as a candidate for full membership in the USSR Academy of Sciences, the two collaborations with Houtermans are omitted. However, in the three-volume edition of Kurchatov's selected works, they appear in the list of his published research. -V.F.

the leading laboratories in the world. In 1936, slow neutrons' role in triggering nuclear fission remained unknown, with physicists still unprepared to grasp the phenomenon. In less than three years, everything changed... Drastic change also came about in the life of Friedrich Houtermans.

References

1. *Essays on the History of the Development of Nuclear Physics in the USSR*, Ed. E.V. Inopin, (Kiev, Naukova Dumka, 1982), pp. 39-44.
2. *I Married a Russian; Letters from Kharkov*, Ed. Lucie Street, (Allen and Unwin, London, 1946); The US edition: Emerson Books, Inc., New York, NY, 1947.
3. F. Houtermans, V. Fomin, A. Leipunsky, and L. Shubnikov, *Slowing down of neutrons in liquid hydrogen*, *Phys. Zeitschr. d. Sowjetunion*, 1936, Bd. 9(6), 696-698.
4. F. Houtermans, V. Fomin, I. Kurchatov, A. Leipunsky, L. Shubnikov, and G. Shchepkin, *Absorption of thermal neutrons in silver at low temperatures*, *Nature*, 1936, v. 138, 326-327.
5. F. Houtermans, V. Fomin, I. Kurchatov, A. Leipunsky, L. Shubnikov, and G. Shchepkin, *Über der Absorption thermischer Neutronen in Silber bei niedrigen Temperaturen*, *Phys. Zeitschr. d. Sowjetunion*, 1936, Bd. 10(1), 103-105.
6. F. Houtermans, V. Fomin, *Radioaktivität in Tantal durch Neutronenbestrahlung*, *Phys. Zeitschr. d. Sowjetunion*, 1936, Bd. 9(2/3), 273-274.
7. F. Houtermans, V. Fomin, A. Leipunsky, L. Rusinov, and L. Shubnikov, *Neutron absorption of boron and cadmium at low temperatures*, *Nature*, 1936, v. 138, p. 505.
8. F. Houtermans, V. Fomin, A. Leipunsky, and L. Shubnikov, *Production of Heavy Hydrogen Nuclei from Protons and Neutrons*, *Visti AN URSR*, 1936, No. 4, p. 37.
9. F. Houtermans, A. Leipunsky, and L. Rusinov, *The absorption of group C neutrons in silver, cadmium and boron at different temperatures*, *Phys. Zeitschr. d. Sowjetunion*, 1937, Bd. 12(4), 491-492.
10. See *Publikationen von Friedrich Georg Houtermans aus den Jahren 1926-1966*, Ed. J. Geiss, Zusammengestellt im Physikalische Inst. Universität Bern, 1980.

Arrests

The UPTI situation had already grown tense when F. Houtermans arrived in Kharkov in early 1935, shortly after the assassination of S. M. Kirov. Houtermans and the fellow foreigners among his colleagues, unlike their Soviet colleagues and friends, initially watched from the side, yet with premonitions of the tragic events ahead. Foreign visitor W. Meissner evocatively relates his impressions of these events' as yet theatrical embodiment on the stage of one of Kharkov's theaters.

> The play we... saw was called *Fear* (obviously A. Afinogenov's *Fear* -V.F.). It was produced at the Theater of the Revolution, and was in Ukrainian (which none of us had any prior knowledge of). Thanks to mediation from Frau Doktor Striker, we were well able to follow the play's plot, which was quite captivating. The actors played brilliantly, just as well as one would expect of the best actors in Berlin. And the play's content was by no means superficial; the psychology was beautifully depicted and conveyed. The events in the play unfolded at an institute, where almost everyone distrusts and spies on each other, suspecting each other of connections with the old bourgeoisie, and where, because of this, everyone is afraid of being found out – except for a few who aren't hiding anything and have nothing to fear, as a character in the play, a woman made up to look like Lenin's wife, puts it. There was an ingenious scene where the supreme council questions an institute employee who had attempted to cross the border with false documents; the council also questions the instigator who later betrayed him. There was also a powerful scene where a female institute employee, one of those who has absolutely no reason to be afraid of anything, returns, along with her male companion, from studying abroad in Berlin; completely won over by the culture there, they have come back with newly modern attitudes. It was deeply moving when an old professor, also under accusation, comes

back to the institute and, despite his imperfect conduct, is entrusted with the institute keys, yet wants to return them. This professor had previously delivered a monologue about fear, to which the woman like Lenin's wife had replied in her speech about honest men having nothing to fear. Significantly, in the play, the high council condemns the instigator based not on the penal code but on inner convictions of guilt or innocence, while the professor, despite the charges against him, goes unpunished.

Later, in Moscow and Leningrad, we saw magnificent productions of *Othello* (Verdi) and *Barber of Seville* (Rossini), which, however, did not come even close to matching the impression the play *Fear* made on us.

The tradition of the "Kleine Nacht Physik" gatherings migrated from Berlin onto Kharkov's soil, where the Houtermans' apartment was often frequented by visitors. Just as often, they themselves could also be found paying visits to the Kharkovites. Yet the word "paying" hardly fits the relaxed, congenial relationships enjoyed by the UPTI employees. Weissberg's and Landau's homes were common gathering places for celebrating birthdays or other "calendar" holidays. Another appealing household was that of K. D. Sinelnikov and his wife, the Englishwoman Edna (Eddie) Alfredovna Cooper, whom he had married in the course of a prolonged business trip to Rutherford's laboratory in England. The Shubnikovs – Lev Vasilievich and his wife Olga Nikolaevna Trapeznikova, also an UPTI employee – kept an open house for visitors as well.

Such gatherings featured discussion not only of institute business but also of political events, such as the war in Spain. The memory of these meetings survives in many written accounts and oral histories. Foreigners and visitors from Leningrad also added their notes of color. A. K. Kikoin, who worked with Shubnikov in Kharkov – writes about Landau's birthday party (January 22). A game was invented: Ask any question, with points scored for correct answers. Then the points would be totaled to determine the winner. Houtermans, also born on January 22, mostly kept quiet, then went home without waiting for the game's end (Charlotte, busy with newborn son Jan, was unable to join the party). After a while, though, he phoned and asked the partygoers: which famous person, not counting Lenin, died on January 21? And with no response forthcoming from the erudite assembly, he himself supplied the answer: it was the day of the execution of Louis XVI.

The situation at the institute worsened over time, becoming especially tense as the new year of 1937 wore on. True, the clouds had begun to thicken even before this. In November 1935, theory department employee M. A. Koretz had been arrested. Soon he was released,[57] thanks to colleagues' efforts. This fueled some hope. Yet on March 1, 1937, A. Weissberg was arrested (his wife, who had risen to become the artistic director for the Soviet china and glass industry, had been arrested some time before, on allegations of participation in a plot to assassinate Stalin).

Figure 16.   Kharkov Prison (known as *Kholodnaya Gora*), mid-1930s.

On August 5, Rozenkevich and Shubnikov were arrested on the

---

[57]Only to be arrested again in 1938 in Moscow and receive a lengthy sentence. -V.F.

same day, and September saw the arrest of V. S. Gorsky, a talented experimenter who headed one of the UPTI laboratories. All three were shot in early November 1937. F. Houtermans, too, failed to escape a fate of arrest and accusations, as will be discussed in detail in later chapters.

The charges brought against the Kharkov physicists were about the same as those faced by other Soviet citizens and foreigners. A review of the case files of A. Weissberg, F. Houtermans, V. S. Gorsky, L. V. Rozenkevich, L. V. Shubnikov and L. D. Landau (the latter was arrested in Moscow in April 1938) clarifies the mechanism for formulating charges.[58]   When asked, say, whom they met with at work and outside it, the interrogated name their friends and colleagues. Then, under the pressure of the investigation, such meetings are recast as a counterrevolutionary organization's conspiratorial gatherings for planning acts of espionage, sabotage and terrorism. Or the suspects say which of the foreign specialists working in Kharkov they would invite to these meetings. Under the investigator's pen, this is portrayed as recruitment of "enemy agents." For their part, the foreign physicists, too, turn out to have been recruiters. Thus, looking ahead to the story of Houtermans' arrest, we note that his recommendation that W. Elsasser should visit Kharkov was represented as dispatching Elsasser there as an agent (Elsasser visited Kharkov in October 1930), and his 1929 meeting with I. V. Obreimov in a cafe on Berlin's Kurfurstendamm as an act of recruitment with transmission of "secret information." The same scenario was applied to the case of Houtermans' future Kharkov employee V. P. Fomin.

Here is a typical example of such interrogation statements, obtained in this instance from L. V. Rozenkevich (the interrogation protocol is from August 12-13, 1937, with its dates indicating it took place at night, following the standard practice). Rozenkevich "stated":

In conversations with me, Shubnikov, Ivanenko and Weiss-

---

[58]The author was able to study the personal case files for Gorsky, Rozenkevich and Shubnikov (see http://www.ihst.ru/projects/sohist/document/ufti/shrog.htm) through the kind assistance of Kharkov physicists A. N. Raniuk and Yu. A. Freiman. -V.F.

berg spoke at length about various political issues. Weissberg criticized the line of the Party and government in the fight against the kulaks, spoke about politics abroad, about what he saw as possible alternative policy orientations for the Party and the Soviet government, lending strength and activism to our counterrevolutionary sentiments and gradually steering them into Trotskyist channels. Weissberg spoke extensively and frequently about politics, authoritatively and categorically proving the incorrectness of the activities of the Central Committee of the CPSU [59] and the Soviet government on a series of issues.

Subsequent statements indicate Weissberg's indignation over the brutal repressions that followed the Kirov assassination. Discussions of the USSR's domestic and foreign policy were elevated to the status of anti-Soviet activities, as was contemplation of the relationship between fundamental and applied physics, or the philosophical aspects of physics theory. Characteristically, everyone arrested, later including Houtermans, concurred most consistently in their opposition to the abortion ban that had passed into law shortly before their arrests. The reason is probably that they really did consider the ban wrong and, while under investigation, said so with no coercion, thinking it impossible to see this criticism as having political overtones. Yet this too was treated as irrefutable evidence of their counterrevolutionary activities and agitation. To this were added absurd allegations of disrupting work on UPTI's defense-related projects, exaggerating the importance of nuclear physics research, harassing certain employees, and the like.

The jovial "Kleine Nacht Physik" of the first years of the Houtermans' stay in Kharkov gave way to anxious, sorrow-laden meetings among physicists fearing for their own fates and those of their comrades. Here Charlotte Houtermans writes of the atmosphere of those days in 1937.

---

[59]The Communist Party of the Soviet Union; in 1925-1952 it was called the All-Union Communist Party of Bolsheviks, or VKPb for short.

It's not likely that this was a good summer for anyone. The show trials began at the end of August, but were preceded by rumors and speculation. But at first it all seemed unconnected to our own world. The fear gradually grew as the winter approached. The political situation was becoming so uncertain that we would have been happy to leave as soon as possible. Unfortunately, we had no idea how to do it. We had no money, nor did we have jobs overseas. Most of our friends were also very worried. Éva [Weissberg's wife -V.F.] had already been arrested, and after her they took Alex. After that we made the final decision to leave...

Charlotte Houtermans so vividly describes the year's subsequent events that this book's author prefers to include her own account, describing how her husband was dismissed from the institute, arrested and parted from her in a separation that would last for many years.

Last Months in the USSR

(From Charlotte Houtermans' Diary [60])

This is not the story of our adult lives in Russia nor the story of political events of 1930s... I want to write about my last weeks in Russia, because I believe now that their extreme fears and anxieties which left me trembling and almost without spark or wish to live most of the time, must have been felt by the small children.

The character of events determined that I had to concentrate again and again on whatever step I would have to take next. It was extremely important not to take the wrong step, and so very little time remained for the children. The fear became a background. We lived in fear, and the dark curtains in the room where we lived blocked both our past and our future from view. At that time no one said much out loud about what was happening, and said even less after it was all over. I think that this kind of mysterious and threatening silence, which no one explained, and the ever-growing fear, had a huge impact on the children. It was not mentioned ever and hence probably was even more frightening or rather not understandable to them.

The fear was so intense in me that it spread and would not dispel for years to come, like a dark cloud, carving the sky from horizon to horizon.

The days I want to speak about cover events from November 30 to December 16.

Moscow seemed to be dead; one could not discover this immediately because the movement in the streets was that of a normal great city. There were more cars than 10 years ago; the cobblestones behind the Grand Hotel were replaced by smooth cement. The people hurrying along were better dressed, still wearing kerchiefs, but having already better shoes. The stores were filled with goods. Some prices were all out of proportions – usually things which were pro-

---

[60] See Appendix I, p. 315, for Charlotte Houtermans' "Last Diary" not included in the Russian edition of Frenkel's book.

duced in such small numbers that the high prices were invented to prevent their sale. Existing still were the long, long queues of men and women waiting for some stores to open or in front of newspaper stands. This at least was always a reason for me to turn away with tears almost in my eyes. Maybe they hoped to read in the *Pravda*, that life would become easier, better, happier. Only a few of the papers were available, in spite of the millions printed.

If one asked at the queues what was for sale today the answer might have been "Sugar or soap or stockings." But slowing, progressing one's position to the counter, which often took hours, the people would come away with something quite different. They would buy it anyway, since everything was scarce; the only relatively abundant article was the money itself.

I arrived from Kharkov with the two children and all the luggage which we intended to take out. The rest including the furniture had been sold during the months of waiting for the visa, most of it to Eddy[61] who had enough money to buy it and could afford to wait for it until we had actually left. All the rest of the baby things, the wool or clothing we could spare went to Olga,[62] whose little son was about 3 months old and who lived in house arrest, confined to one room which contained all her belongings. Her husband had been arrested the day before the birth of her child, and it was only the child which protected her from being taken also...

She only saw her husband once again on a visit to the prison. Some baby outfits became Marussya's[63] who had suddenly decided to get married to a man of her own faith.. He worked as an unskilled laborer and between them they owned nothing except a piece of land from which they hoped to harvest vegetables and potatoes, etc. in about 5 to 6 months. Until then bread and meat and milk had to be bought. We gave them some money as a kind of wedding present.

---

[61]Edna Cooper, Kirill Sinelnikov's wife. Kirill Dmitrievhich Sinelnikov (1901-1966), an outstanding experimentalist in nuclear physics, a participant in the Soviet nuclear bomb project. In 1928-30 he worked at the Cavendish Laboratory under E. Rutherford. He met Edna Cooper in Cambridge, and soon she became his wife. At UPTI since 1930.

[62]Olga Trapeznikova, Lev Shubnikov's wife. Lev Shubnikov was executed on November 10, 1937.

[63]Marussya was Houtermans' nanny and maid.

Marussya probably had saved some of her wages, but she was already pregnant when we left Kharkov on November 29th. To leave there was not too difficult, except the parting from Olga, who was old and almost without any hope.

The rest of the community except for Eddy and for Galla, whose husband was now in prison for almost 10 months, had no interest in me. They probably hoped I would leave soon. They did not speak to me because it was dangerous for them. Some friends came after darkness. Most of our intimate friends had already left for Moscow where the Academy Institutes offered some protection. It is difficult to understand why this could be so, except if one remembers that Stalin wanted to be a protector of the Arts and Sciences and hence shielded its personnel from his own henchmen.

But many had already been arrested. As soon as they grabbed Shubnikov, Leipunsky left for Moscow, and Fisl followed him. Éva[64] had been arrested even earlier, in Leningrad. We both lost our positions, I only as a foreign language reader and corrector in the journal *Physikalische Zeitschrift der Sowjetunion*. I meant we had no income any longer, but we were also not given an exit visa, to which as foreign citizens we were entitled within three days according to international law. Law had no meaning or validity in those days; they even broke their own laws if it suited them.

There was another gruesome and terribly sad and frightening incident that same summer. We were breakfasting when Marussya rushed in saying: "The German has jumped out of the window." He was not German, of course, only born in Berlin by Russian parents, but spoke the language fluently and hence acted as interpreter for Fisl in the first time as well as his assistant. His name was Fomin and he lived in the house next to ours, which was reserved for bachelors, and there was a club and a cafeteria there. During the vacation period he had been skiing in the Caucuses and the evening he returned he was greeted with the news that his older brother had been arrested.

---

[64]Éva Striker, Alexander Weissberg's ex-wife. In 1938 after her second marriage in England Éva Striker became Eva Zeisel. After her subsequent emigration to the US she eventually made her way to the summit of the artistic Olympus and became an internationally acclaimed designer.

The rumor had it that as a skiing teacher he became suspected to be a spy. This part is only very dim to me now.

Since a prisoner is immediately cut off from all his friends and family and cannot have a lawyer one never learns any details and since no reasons are given ever, the rumors about his guilt rise immediately out of all proportion. Fomin consequently was greatly alarmed and disturbed and though his brother was very much older and had had no contact with them for a great many years, he feared rightly that the suspicion of the court would finally involve the whole family, which really was usually the case.

He became more and more nervous, morbidly afraid of a possible arrest for himself and though nothing happened for a few days, the tension and the apprehension of coming disaster grew out of all proportions. It was typical that the anxieties for the sake of arrested members of a family were often overshadowed by the terror the next arrests seemed to foreshadow.

When at last an invitation came into his hand for him to pay a visit to the secret police, a farce no less to invite people to their own arrest, Fomin's nerves were already thoroughly shattered. His mother was visiting him in those days and he apparently tried to keep all his fears from her. Instead of following the "invitation" he went to the lab and drank sulfuric acid. It was a ghastly, also unfortunate act, since it did not kill him, but inflicted such pain and suffering that he rushed home, now thoroughly out of his mind, and jumped out of the third floor bathroom window. How unlucky was he, that even this did not kill him; he was brought to a hospital to a prisoner's ward, where a policeman probably with a bayonet stood watch. We were all certain that he was going to die. He was of course questioned, but about his end we never heard a single word.

The effect on us was almost equally disastrous. Fisl and I reacted quite differently. I seemed to freeze inside, like holding my breath, waiting for the next blow to fall. Fisl went to pieces in another way; he became restless and dreadfully loquacious as if his subconscious was trying to break through and inundate all of his mind. He walked around his room, chain-smoked and talked about ways and means of how to leave, to get us out. He did not stop talking, it became more and more fantastic, what he said; he repeated himself like a patient in a delirium, and the same images appeared again. The map of Europe with huge barbed wire fences around the country, this country, every country, and in between waste stretches of land without grass or trees, without shelters, without water, and like lost souls in the inferno, people like him and his family with no valid passports, without rights or protection, without money and food, walking this border land hopelessly, forever lost.

He went on for hours the whole night. I was so frightened, not knowing of any medical or psychological explanation or words that might calm him down, that I went the next day to a friend [65] who had brought us to the country and who being now in an official capacity had kept away from us, probably on account of his own political fear of associating with foreigners. I became very blunt and forced him to visit us and give Fisl some kind of guarantee of protection, that he was safe. This our friend did, and it did help. I was grateful, because even without this terrible worry about Fisl's mental health, the increasing number of arrests made all our lives almost unbearable.

Another incident happened shortly afterwards. One morning I came into Fisl's room trying to awaken him, but when he stirred, he opened his eyes, not quite understanding apparently where he was, like one does sometimes after a heavy sleep or after vivid dreams, and said only: "You? You're here!" It was so strange that I was frightened again, but laughed it off with a "Whom did you expect to come in?"

What had happened while I had slept deeply, not hearing a sound, was that he was woken up by a terribly loud knock at the door, which he could hear better, since his room was nearer to the entrance door. He looked at his watch. It was 2 AM. This could mean only one thing to him, so he went out to open the door, with the most frightful apprehension, and really there they were, three men, very official-looking. I cannot understand how he was at all able to speak and ask what they wanted. It is a moment when life seems to end, the brutality of knowing people out of their lives, three against one!

---

[65] Alexander Leipunsky.

They only wanted an address; I remember vaguely that it was Fomin's but am not certain about that anymore. Fisl told me he was not certain how he got back to his bed, but must have fallen asleep under the impression that they had taken him away after all.

As soon as he saw a little clearer, we decided that he was really not safe here and should go to Moscow to make an official appeal for the granting of an exit visa for us all.

Life in Kharkov was strangely inanimate, suspended between past and future, full of fear, of forebodings. Only a few moments remain clear in my memory. A visit of the Vellers [66] after dark, a meeting with Laura Mikhailovna Striker [67] who came to visit Alex in prison, hoping that he would be allowed to sign the divorce agreement with Éva. In the evening we went together to see Natasha. Grisha Veller was arrested that same afternoon; Natasha looked like death, absolutely forlorn in the large dark rooms. There was a scene at the station. A group of peasants surrounded by police, bound together by a thick rope like cattle, waiting to be herded into the train for Siberia, probably. Marussya and the maid from upstairs sitting in the children's room, crying. Their men had been taken away. They knew that they would never see them again. Olga Shubnikov's husband was arrested, the day before her son was born. When she returned from the hospital, they arrested her as well. (It was only a formal act, since with a breast-feeding baby they could not keep her in jail.) They arrested her in her apartment, left her one room into which

---

[66]Grigory Maksimovich Veller (1897-1937) was a professional musician. He was sentenced to death by an NKVD *troika* on November 19, 1937, and executed on the same day.

[67]Laura Polanyi Striker (1882-1957) was Éva's mother. Educated in the Budapest Universty, she was an early supporter of the feminist movement in Hungary and a socialist idea sympathizer. Laura Striker was politically active in the early days of the Hungarian Republic, but later focused on scholarly activities in the Austro-Hungarian history of the 17th century. Laura Striker was in Moscow when her daughter was arrested there (see Eva Zeisel, *A Soviet Prison Memoir*, (Amazon Kindle Edition, 2012)). She did everything humanly possible to help Éva. In the 1950s, Laura Striker became famous in the US for her research on Captain John Smith, the founder of Virginia, which resulted in a popular essay *Captain John Smith's Hungary and Transylvania*, see in Bradford Smith, *Captain John Smith; His Life and Legend*, (Philadelphia – New York, 1953), pp. 311-347.

all her belongings were crowded; the other two rooms were given to two other families whose husbands were in prison. Nobody except foreigners like myself and Eddy, dared to visit her. Her parents came from Leningrad with permission to stay for a short while. Should she have been arrested, the grandmother could claim the baby, otherwise the baby would have been sent to an orphanage. I only saw Eddy and Galla. I was very short of money and sold all my furniture to Eddy; she would claim it after my departure.

One day finally came a message that the visas were granted, that I should go to the department of police for foreign residents and notify them about our departure. This was the great mistake. My instinct told not to do this, but my fear paralyzed all actions and I followed Fisl's wish or order and went.

We arrived in Moscow the last day of November in 1937. Fisl met us and brought us to Landau's house, which was one of the elegant new houses for research workers belonging to Kapitsa's institute.

The evening was strange and unhappy. We were conscious of dangers and difficulties, very tired and exhausted, I physically from the long journey, Fisl from endless running around to agencies and offices negotiating with the Customs about our belongings. That was a story in itself. They had made him do a new kind of catalogue about every single book we had shipped from Kharkov. There were hundreds of books. I made a meticulous list: titles, authors, publishers. Among others, the list included 25 volumes of Shakespeare, 9 volumes of Rilke, and so on. But more difficult was the clearing of the manuscripts; it turned out to be so complicated that we decided on this our last evening that we would leave without them and trust that they would be sent later on.

It was a very unhappy, hysterical kind of night, full of tears and doubts, of fears and forebodings and prayers for escape. Nobody actually thought of anything beyond the borders. Too many friends had to be left, too many friends we would never see again. The next morning seemed almost normal. Fisl left for the Customs house.

Anya Kapitsa [68] came to visit. I believe Rumer [69] or Landau

---

[68] Anna Kapitsa, née Krylova, Pyotr Kapitsa's wife.

[69] Moscow University professor Yu. B. Rumer was arrested in 1938 in Moscow as an

called. Then came the phone call from Bimbus.[70] Fisl had been
arrested at Customs. He had been there and was just now taken back
to her and Friedel Cohn-Vossen's apartment.[71] She had pleaded for
permission to buy cigarettes and phoned me from the store.

It is too long ago to recall what I felt. A tree must experience
something like it when it is cut down. I began to act, to plan, to
phone. Anya K. came.[72] I remember that she made me swallow some
tablets; only then was I aware that I trembled and could scarcely
hold the phone. Anya took the children over to her house, to her
elegant English house with the red leather chairs from the Cavendish
Laboratory.

Fisl's friends finally answered the phone; they were astonished,
suggesting it might be a mistake, and they would inquire. Apparently
they did; the next phone call revealed that they could not even find
him.

I begged and screamed, accused them of all sorts of things, but it
was for nothing. All my words fell on deaf ears. I shook as if from a
fever when I finally put down the phone. In two minutes – just two
short minutes – I understood what the wives of the arrested felt.

R. came, saying that I was endangering L. and should move out.
K. was furious and wanted me to leave; only after long pleadings

---

accomplice of the "enemy of the people Landau" when he was going with friends to
celebrate his birthday.

[70] Bimbus was a nickname of Charlotte Schlesinger (1909-1976), a distinguished pianist
and composer. She graduated from the Berlin Hochschule für Musik (1925-1930), and
worked as an Assistant Professor at the Vienna Conservatory (1933-1934); and the
Ukrainian Conservatory, USSR (1935-1938). After her emigration to the US in the
late 1930s she taught music at Black Mountain College, North Carolina. Charlotte
Schlesinger and the Houtermans knew each other from their time in Berlin.

[71] Identification of Friedel Cohn-Vossen is ambiguous. On the one hand, Friedel Cohn-
Vossen was a brother of the famous mathematician Stephan Cohn-Vossen (1902-1936)
best known for his collaboration with David Hilbert on the 1932 book *Anschauliche
Geometrie*. Stephan emigrated to the USSR in 1934, while his brother Friedel emigrated
to the USSR in 1937. His subsequent fate is unknown. On the other hand, Stephan Cohn-
Vossen's widow Dr. Margot Maria Elfriede Cohn-Vossen was known to her friends as
Friedel. The latter identification seems more likely. After Stephan's death Mrs. Cohn-
Vossen stayed in Moscow and in 1938 married Alfred Kurella (1895-1975), a German
communist functionary in exile. She died in 1957 in Soviet Georgia.

[72] The initials K., R., and L. below stand for Kapitsa, Rumer, and Landau.

Figure 17.   Moscow, circa 1936.

from Anya did he yield and allow the children to remain. I went into town, my house-key or probably L.'s house-key with me. Fisl had my passport, which meant that I could not get anything and of course could not leave at all. I spent a day at the Metropol hotel, where every porter, every phone operator, every employee was in the service of the secret police. I did not have the addresses of either Bimbus or Laura Mikhailovna; I did not dare to go home to L.'s.

There was a trance-like moment when I stood in front of the Hotel Moskva, (trying to remember which tram in which direction I had taken months ago to Laura's house. It was not a rational thought which made me select one, standing as near to the front as possible. I suddenly got out, five streets crossing smaller streets with gardens, I went to the right, the dream confirmed, the houses seemed familiar, I went into one, up and up reading the name plates. It was right, a name I knew, the bell rang and there was Friedel Cohn-Vossen discussing with A. A. how one could find me since my phone did not answer. I drank some tea and heard that they had searched Friedel's flat. A.'s husband had been taken away a day before. She was still like ice, not knowing at all what to do. She had many friends in Moscow and knew of 70 arrests of friends only.

Later in the evening I went to Anya's to see my children, who were happy though a little bewildered. R. came again to warn me to get out.

Those mysterious friends of Fisl's phoned that they had located Fisl in the Lubianka and would or could do nothing. I exploded at the phone. I told them what I thought of their friendship, their lack of courage, their lack of character, I told them hysterically they should go to hell. I cried and swore, and pleaded and then put the receiver down. They were of course right about not being able to do anything.

My odyssey around town started again. I was hunting for an office where one could get a permit to stay the night. Bimbus came with me. I carried a tiny suitcase with a few necessary things in case of a sudden arrest. (Into the children's coats I had sewed linen plaques with their names and the address of the Blackwell's in London and their grandmother in the US.) Bimbus was practically in hysterics. The office where the permits were given was the last of a long string of rooms, all crowded with police, with desks and typewriters, secretaries, noises, talks, a clatter of machines. We held hands and went on and on. It was like a Kafka nightmare; Bimbus was sure we would be arrested and we wouldn't get out. At the end of the last room, I got a piece of paper, a permission to stay that one night. It was very late and I went back to that lonely house.

The next morning there came news from K. that he had succeeded in locating my passport and that I could call for it at 1:00 o'clock at the Lubianka window, punctually. I must have given up the key somehow, because I remember sitting in K.'s living room next to Landau's house with Friedel waiting for K.'s chauffeur. I vaguely remember that it might have happened on December 3rd, because Fisl was arrested on the 1st, but the exact date has disappeared from my memories. The huge black limousine brought me to the Lubianka at the appointed hour, the secretary-chauffeur waited in the other yard and I proceeded trembling to the window No. 2. An officer looked up. "I have been asked to call here for the passport of Charlotte Gustavovna Houtermans" ... a rustling of papers, a book appeared. "You are his sister?" I answered with my last breath: "Yes." The passport was in my hands.

Back to the Institute. K. already had arranged for a room at the Metropol. I packed; I collected the children, said good-bye with tears and thanks to Anya and drove in the black elegant car to the hotel. There were Bimbus and Friedel, and we locked the door, put the children to bed and whispered together about plans. What to do? What to do? What to do for Fisl?

I do not remember sleeping or eating. We were still under this incredible pressure. Our anxieties grew. I could not stay there; I had no home, not enough money, not a chance ever to earn anything even if I could manage to stay out of prison.

We decided finally I should leave; my passport had an exit visa. It was possible to buy a ticket to Riga, the only one without using a government travel agency. I went trembling to the German Consulate to have my passport validated. They agreed to validate my passport for 14 days and marked it "Valid only for return to Germany via Tilsit."[73] I could not change anything, and stopped thinking about it, since my main goal was to get out of there as soon as possible. By the way, in the Consulate they asked me whether I needed help for Fisl. I did not dare ask their help for Fisl and only much later was told by Fisl himself that it might have helped him. But this I did not know; I probably could not have decided between his extradition to Nazi Germany or a Russian prison, not knowing about the horrors of either but being only filled with the unknown paralyzing fear.

In the hotel, where I returned, they informed me that the passport had to be stamped by the Registration office for foreigners. This must have been December 3rd or 4th. But since the next day was a holiday, an army memorial or something, and the other day Sunday (the 6th) too, I decided to leave before they would make me give up

---

[73] Tilsit was a town in East Prussia; currently Sovetsk in the Kaliningrad Region, Russia.

the passport even for an hour.[74]

Friedel was very helpful. We went to open a bank account jointly for Fisl and me, we planned to have clothes and blankets sent to him. With the rest of the money I bought a fur coat for myself, my only fortune for the life abroad.

That last evening we went to find Veller's sister, Bimbus and I, I suppose. The city was dark and very cold and we walked along hurriedly, anxious not to draw anybody's attention. Friedel had once before been arrested, just for stopping at a square. We found the house; inside were gloomy corridors. It must have been an old aristocratic mansion, which now housed many families. The rooms were heated from the corridors, some open doors revealed kitchens, with long rows of rooms and stoves. The room we entered was dark, too, filled with furniture; I can't recollect the people; I only remember the terror. Life had stopped some time long before, one waited for the arrest, for the knocking on the door in the middle of the night. "Open up", "Pack a few things," "Go! Go!" Three men entering, confronting old women, sick men, children, young couples, helpless people who had to obey, who were driven away, separated, who would never return, who would starve, maybe, who cared. Only the knocking at the doors in the night, only the nightmares of sleep, only the trembling of hands, the terror in those tearless eyes.

We stayed a short while, we talked about the husband in a camp in Siberia, about Grisha and that he never would survive prison with its hunger and maltreatment. They gave me a precious plate, with gold border; painted with royal crowns and a precious small Cloisonné piece, blue like the sky on one side. I still have it; the plate got lost. The people, the friends are not remembered, but not forgotten is that dark room with its fear and terror and despair.

Bimbus and Friedel brought us to the station. I can still see them waving. My heart was too heavy. I did not know whether I was doing the right thing leaving Fisl in Moscow. There was no feeling left in me, none. And the children were talking and asking questions, normal children who took all the changes as the normal happenings

---

[74]In 1937 the first Sunday of December was on December 5.

of their lives; they wanted to know where their father was. "Where is Fisl? Where is he?" I did not know, but I answered, I always answered. He remained alive for them, they loved him, they thought of him, they talked of him all the time and my heart almost broke.

It was not a long trip, very few people stayed in the train after the first stop. In the "soft" (i.e. first) class there were a few people only. When we came to the border, everybody had to leave the train for passport control and customs. Including the two children I had 18 pieces to account for. Each child carried a tiny suitcase with toys, Bamsi's[75] was red, Jan's blue. My smallest case was brown; Fisl had once given it to me in London. Customs finished, some military people looked at my visa.

Later on I learned that one of them was probably a general. He declared that I could not leave but had to wait for the next train, if at all. There was all my luggage on the platform; the children were tired, hungry. I asked where I could wait for the next train, as there was no town in sight near the station, not even a village. My behavior was arrogant; I wanted to impress the general that a foreign specialist could not be treated just casually, but that we deserved some consideration.

"Where is your husband?" "He is still in Moscow and wanted to leave with the next train as soon anyway as his business was finished." "In which hotel?" "I do not know because he had to go to another one after my departure...."

All right, I might stay in the house at the end of the platform, which provided rooms for railroad personnel. Meals could be brought over from the station restaurant.

The house was clean and our room had two enormous beds. I piled the luggage, opened just enough as was necessary, found a kitchen where a disagreeable woman cooked her own meals and accepted an order for tea and milk.

The next train would come the following morning and depart for Dünaburg[76] and Riga at 10:00 AM. We slept and woke early. I

---

[75]Giovanna's nickname.
[76]Currently Daugavpils in Latvia.

dressed myself and the children in order to be ready for the train. The message from the "general" came just before it was time to go. I was not permitted to leave. Later on, in the afternoon he came to interrogate me. "Where was my husband? Where were the passport pictures for the children?"

I pointed out that I supposed my husband was on his way to Leningrad, as we had agreed. I explained that according to international law, children could be registered on the mother's passport without special photos. "How do I know that these are your children?" Then Bamsi started to cling to me. "You are my mother, you are! You must not leave me," she cried.

I tried desperately to comfort her, to reply to this monster. Would he leave his own children, to take some other entirely unknown ones?

He was adamant, he asked the same things over again; he remained entirely unmoved and finally left us. The next morning arrived, no permission was given. The meals came three times a day according to my orders, for the room I paid out of the 50 rubles which the friends in Moscow had insisted I should take along. But the meals I charged to the NKVD, and was astonished that that was possible. We had toys and a few books and I read stories to the children and played and never left them alone a single moment. [...] The days were very, very long. We did not leave the station. There was not another house, nor village, nor hills; a wide horizon, and no particular fields that I can remember – only the snow-covered plain. I had with me a volume of Balzac's *Splendors and Miseries of Courtesans*. This I read, but I remember not a word of it.

Every morning the general came, as if he were a friend paying a visit. Every morning we packed and prepared for the train. On the ninth day, he asked me whether I had any recommendations, anybody who could vouch for me. I gave him the number of those officials, those friends who had been unable to help Fisl.

The next morning, on December 16, the permission was given. Another customs checkup, then the train, no porter to help. We got in and the wheels started to roll.

We were on the way, still in a Russian train with Russian personnel, but we would get out. We did. This was the last day when my Russian exit visa was still valid. At the customs I had noticed a man and a woman who seemed to belong to some embassy. They were not Russian; neither were they German or English. It was impossible for me to place them accurately. In addition they seemed to be fakes, not genuine somewhat, but I decided to risk a talk with them, because my next problem was to get some money somehow for the first half hour at least when we would be in the station of Riga. Unfortunately it did not work out too well. Probably they did not believe that I would pay off the debt, or thought that I was an NKVD agent-provocateur...

I believe it was in Dünaburg that the Russian personnel left the train.

Descent into the Prisons: 1937-39

There exist three pieces of documentary testimony pertaining to the prison odyssey of Friedrich Ottovich Goutermans – thus the official NKVD documents designate him.[77] Chronologically, these documents form the following sequence:

1. "Case number 15844, on the charges against Goutermans Friedrich Ottovich," from the NKVD-KGB Archives. Begun on November 29, 1937. Archive number R-34938.

2. "Chronological Report of My Life in Russian Prisons," May 19, 1945, written by F. Houtermans and preserved in manuscript form.[78]

3. F. Beck, W. Godin, *Russian Purge and the Extraction of Confession*, London, 1951.

Let's consider the first two documents, saving discussion of the Beck and Godin book for later.

Thanks to the assistance of Academician Zhores Alferov, deputy of the Supreme Council of the USSR, through his request as deputy, the KGB archives provided the A. Weissberg and F. Houtermans case files for the author (Victor Frenkel) to study. The main content of the Houtermans file consists of materials from his 14 interrogations, which included three with so-called "double questionings" (also known as confrontations). Other documents supplement the interrogation reports. All this historical evidence, of course, merits publication, but reading the depositions of the arrested is very difficult. Unhappy people are forced under threat of torture to give false testimony against themselves and others. Emaciated, exhausted by many days without sleep, seeing the other in an identical state at the double questionings, each suspects he himself looks just the same. Human tragedies wind up embodied in mediocre, cookie-cutter scripts by mediocre NKVD playwrights, who deserve low marks for literacy, on top of everything else.

---

[77]The German H was traditionally transliterated in Russian as Г, i.e. G.
[78]Included in this collection; see Appendix III, p. 357.

Each interrogation report page (and sometimes also every answer to the investigator's questions) is certified by the suspect's handwritten signature. Interrogation reports in the Houtermans file conclude with the phrase "I have read the report; the written record of my words is accurate, in the Russian language, which I understand. F. Goutermans."

Figure 18.   An NKVD prison photograph of Fritz Houtermans, 1937, (the Russian caption reads: "2766. Gautermans Fritz Ottovich, 1903").

The case against Houtermans followed formal standards. A warrant for arrest and search (issued in Kharkov on November 29, three days before his arrest in Moscow), a list of seized materials (including seven folders with letters and five with photos), a short list of items that the prisoner was allowed take with him. The official charge was brought against him after his transfer from Moscow (where he spent a few hours in the Lubyanka prison before being moved to the city's Lefortovo prison) to Kharkov on January 5, 1938. The charge goes like this.

Branch 1, Division 3, UGB HOU (Office of State Security of

the Kharkov Regional Office – V.F.), Chief Drescher: Upon review of the evidence again Goutermans Friedrich Ottovich, born 1903, Jew, German citizen, accused of state crime Articles 54-6, 54-9, 54-10, 54-11 of the Criminal Code of the Ukrainian SSR,[79] found applied investigative acts to have determined that he, as a Gestapo agent, performed espionage, sabotage and subversive work on USSR territory. On the basis of Art. 126, UPK (Code of Criminal Procedure – V.F.) and following Art. 127 Code of Criminal Procedure of the USSR, I have decided to arraign citizen Goutermans Friedrich Ottovich as an accused.

This resolution bears the UGB Division 3 chief's seal of consent, with approval from the NKVD chief for the Kharkov region.

Figure 19.   Entrance to hell. Initial data for the accused were recorded (including mugshots) in this office. A modern reconstruction. Courtesy of the Karlag Museum.

---

[79] Article 54 of the Criminal Code of the Ukrainian Soviet Socialist Republic corresponds to the notorious Article 58 of the Criminal Code of the Russian Soviet Federative Socialist Republic. –V.F.

As for how it was established that Houtermans had "performed espionage and sabotage work," we learn this from his own above-mentioned account, dated May 19, 1945, as well as from one of his final interrogations, conducted in Moscow in 1939.

In his 1945 description of his first interrogation, held in Moscow on December 11, 1937 (Houtermans' description completely accords with the official interrogation record), he adds certain details not included in the filed report. Should he have confessed to the charges (note, as yet unstated) of counter-revolutionary activities on orders from the Fascist government, the Soviet authorities guaranteed his immediate expulsion from the USSR. "Of course," writes Houtermans, "I didn't give this false testimony and denied any act against the Soviet Union."

Figure 20. One of millions of NKVD dossiers compiled in 1937-1938. Courtesy of the Karlag Museum.

As a rule, charges were generally denied at first interrogations. In many cases reviewed by the author, at the first interrogation, the suspects behaved in exactly this way. But then came the work on the arrested!

On January 5, 1938, Houtermans (if he makes mistakes in dates, recalling the events of eight years past, he is never off by more than two or three days) was taken to Kharkov in a prison boxcar and placed in a cell in the prison at *Kholodnaya Gora*. On January 10 of the same year he was transferred to the central prison, located in central Kharkov, in the NKVD buildings on Chernyshevsky Street. The same day saw his preliminary interrogation, at which Houtermans was threatened with beating if he refused to confess to the crime he had committed. Houtermans writes:

> On the evening of January 11th began an uninterrupted questioning of 11 days, with only a short break of five hours the first day and about two hours the second day. No concrete charge was brought against me, as in nearly all cases of people I have seen in Russian prisons, and I was told to give all "facts" myself. The only two questions that were asked were: "Who induced you to join the counterrevolutionary organization" and "whom did you induce yourself?"
>
> Three officials questioned me in turn, for about eight hours each, the first two days I was allowed to sit on a chair, later only on the edge of a chair and from the 4th day on I was forced to stand nearly all day, I was always kept awake, and when I fell from lack of sleep I was brought to by means of fainted cold water that was poured on my face. The chief official who led the questioning was named Pogrebnoi.
>
> The night of January 22nd, shortly after midnight, Pogrebnoi showed me an order of arrest for my wife and another order to bring my children into a home of "besprisonikh"[80] under a false name so that I would not be able to find them ever again. I was of the opinion that they were all still in Moscow. I have learned since that they had left shortly after my arrest so all I was told was bluffing, but in my state of weakness after nearly ten days without sleep I fell for it.

---

[80]Orphanage, from *besprizornik*, a homeless child, waif.

Houtermans further writes in his report of 1945 that the beating wasn't very hard and was done "not with instruments" – in contrast to what his cellmates faced. As a result of many days of standing, his feet grew so swollen that it became impossible to remove his shoes, which were cut off. Physically exhausted and temporarily broken in spirit, Houtermans agreed to sign the testimony that his torturers needed. Yet he said (of course, this went unreflected in the reports) that he would recant his testimony if within three months he didn't receive a letter sent by his wife from abroad. Such a letter, written by Charlotte Houtermans from Copenhagen, was presented to him on March 17, 1938. His wife had written Houtermans repeatedly since December 1937, and copies of these letters, full of love and anxiety, are preserved in their family archives in the United States. She also sent him money, which was returned to her. (With the March 7, 1938, letter she sent a check for £1.[81])

After Houtermans signed the confession, he was fed, given tea to drink, and sent to his cell, where he slept for 36 hours straight.

In the case file, the first officially recorded Kharkov interrogation is dated January 24, 1938, and the next, January 31. After this, for a time he was left in relative peace.

But the soulless machine of repression would no longer release Houtermans. August 2 saw his transfer to a Kiev prison, where the conditions, according to Houtermans, were slightly better than in the previous ones. He is told to give information on persons of whom he has knowledge. By this time L. D. Landau (April 28, 1938) and A. I. Leipunsky (July 14, 1938) have already been arrested, and he "testifies" about them.

Why was Houtermans so quick to "confess" to committing ficti- tious crimes? In *The Accused*, his friend Alex Weissberg writes of this as follows:

> In February of 1938 I was informed of the arrest of Houter- mans I felt sorry for him. He was not physically strong and I didn't rate his chances of survival very highly. He was a chain smoker, and at the Institute he was rarely to be seen

---

[81] Approximately £60 in 2013 GBP.

without a cigarette between his lips. Coffee was another passion, and he drank one cup after another. I did my best to send him cigarettes through prisoners who were transferred to the inner prison (At this point, Weissberg has already been in prison for quite some time. –V.F.), but when I met him again in 1948 I discovered that he had received none of them.

Houtermans then faced new challenges – double questionings with other arrestees. He writes about one such event, involving himself and another UPTI colleague, Professor I. V. Obreimov. New interrogations followed – again in Kiev, where, according to Houtermans, he was held in an underground cell with no natural light. Then the interrogations ceased for several months.

Again, a few lines from Weissberg's book.

At the end of July of 1939 I was called out again for interrogation. It was a different examiner whose name was Kasin, if I remember rightly. He was a tall slim man in the uniform of an NKVD officer, and his head looked as though it were worked in bronze. He reminded me of an actor in the part of Rhadamés in Verdi's opera Aïda.

"I don't wish to intimidate you" he began. "Make your statement voluntarily, but tell us everything you've done against the Soviet Union."

I talked for about an hour. He listened attentively and made no attempt to interrupt.

"Well, what do you say to that?" he asked, and he showed me a deposition signed by Houtermans accusing himself of outrageous crimes. But there was nothing in it to compromise me.

"Hasn't he withdrawn his confession yet?" I asked.

"No, of course he hasn't."

"Citizen Examiner, I have no right to interfere in Houtermans' affairs. But I could prove to you that his confession is perfect nonsense. I know his life intimately both here and abroad. He has never done such things in reality, or anything like them."

"If that is true, why doesn't he withdraw his confession? And why did he make it in the first place?"

"Houtermans is not strong physically, and his nerves are bad. He is a brilliant physicist, but he's not a fighter. He probably got so tired and exhausted that he had to give way.

It's fitting to add a bit more about Alex (Alexander Semyonovich) Weissberg himself, given the surprising parallels between his and Houtermans' fates. Friendship at gymnasium in Vienna, membership in the German Communist Party, emigration to the USSR (Weissberg arrived a few years earlier), work at UPTI, and finally adjacent prison cells (Houtermans never learned of this!). And then, as we shall see, the same path out of the Soviet Union and into another prison. Weissberg's situation was even worse, as a Jew, facing ghettos and concentration camps, with no hope of survival. This meant that, unlike Houtermans, he could only stay alive in the Reich illegally. He survived only through active involvement in the Jewish and later Polish resistance. But this is another fascinating and tragic part of wartime history [82] which remains too little known...

---

[82]See Introduction, pp. 13-15, and Appendix IV, p. 369.

From Desperation to Hope

(Continuation of Charlotte Houtermans' Diary)

In Riga

After that it was a relatively quick trip until we reached Riga. It was late afternoon, very cold and I had no money for porters or taxis, because my attempt to borrow some money from the strangers in the train had failed. But we arrived with all our luggage and I remember sitting inside the station building on the pile of luggage right in front of an office where I could change money. I did have 100 Swiss francs and 100 French francs, which friends in Moscow had given me and which I had smuggled over the border. Each bill was rolled up tightly in the shape of a match and each was sewn into the seam of the fur bonnets of the children. So in the half-dark, dirty hall, I undid one of the seams and extricated the money and changed it into Latvian currency. Then at last I was able to engage a porter to find a café and speaking Russian gave the address of the parents of some foreigner friends in Moscow. One was an architect, his wife a Sinologist. They had met Fisl and Bimbus and suggested that I should go to her parents who would help me.

But nothing as simple as this was going to happen. The taxi driver simply said that no such address existed. "Three or four years ago, – he said, – all street names were changed." He maintained that he did not know the old names. I asked him for the names of some hotels and chose what I imagined to be a second-best one. The taxi driver deposited us, unloaded suitcases, a doorman came and lugged it all into the lobby where the proprietor came to greet us. This was a tall, squarish kind of man, who reminded me of Hindenburg and also spoke German. He advanced, half-bent down to touch Jan's head saying "Good Boy, *ein Junger Hitler.*" There was so little energy left in me that I just could not turn around and leave. The doorman was Russian and inquired from where we came. "Moscow?"

"That murderer Stalin, – was his reaction, – that beast!"

He took some suitcases and I followed him with the children to a

Figure 21. *Hotel de Rome* in Riga. Mid-1930s. Probably, one of these black taxis brought Charlotte to the German consulate.

very clean room, which had washbasins with hot and cold water. I asked for some food to be brought up, which a chambermaid brought. Then I proceeded to wash the children and put them to bed. They were of course overtired, bewildered, but finally fell asleep.

It felt good to me too to be clean; the ten days at the station, the hectic migrations through Moscow, with barely any sleep at all, had put me in a state of unnatural suspense, as if life were no longer subdivided into days with regular meals, nights in clean sheets, ordinary activities. Our clothes were in an appalling state, the children's underwear, though clean, having been rinsed in the washroom on the train, looked grey and shabbily wrinkled.

The doorman, I discovered, had been an officer in the Czar's army, had hated the Bolsheviks; he waited only for the day of their collapse, earned a small salary as a doorman and was probably one of innumerable displaced Russians who filled Riga at that time. I did not really trust him, since I did not trust anybody at that moment, but I had to get some information and I preferred him to the Nazi proprietor.

My German passport was expiring the coming Tuesday. It was

an old passport, which had been validated for two weeks in Moscow shortly before I left. The absolutely necessary visit to the German Embassy was one of the frightening incidents shortly after Fisl's arrest. The Embassy was under constant surveillance by the NKDV, of which I was only too conscious, and every visitor was noted.

Inside was my first encounter with a Nazi official. My passport was marked: "Nur gültig für Einreise via Tilsit." This would have worried me under normal circumstances, but it was a complication only in a dim future; while still in Russia my problems were the hourly ones. We had to survive, to avoid imminent arrest. What might happen in two weeks hence had meant nothing. But now in Riga it became a problem.

This was the first time I had to face the future. We had gotten out of Russia; where to go now? Both children needed rest, some normal days in which to quiet down. I was afraid we all three would get ill from sheer physical and nervous exhaustion. At least at the moment they were clean; they had slept one night at least in newly made beds, and they had a normal breakfast.

I presented our Russian doorman ex-officer with the problem of my passport, which would expire next Tuesday, December 21st. This was December the 17th. He gave me the address of the German consulate and I left the children in the charge of the maid on our corridor. It seemed better than it actually was, because she only looked in once, I believe. It was Bamsi, age $5\frac{1}{2}$, who watched over Jan, who was only two. They waved to me from the window and I hurried away.

The Embassy and the consulate were in the same building. I approached the consular official first and showed my passport, saying that I would like to apply for an extension of my passport, since we only last night had arrived from the Soviet Union. "My children, – I explained, – were very small and I had to give them a rest before resuming any more travelling." He hardly let me finish, but broke out in the clipped, official jargon of a lower-caste servant. "Did I not know that it was my *duty* to proceed to Tilsit as fast as possible? I had no business to come to Riga. I should have boarded the train to Tilsit in Dünaburg and in Tilsit I should have reported immediately

Figure 22.   The German consulate in Riga today is in the same building it occupied in 1937, Rainis Boulevard 13.

to the re-immigration official." I objected that the only ticket I was able to purchase in Moscow was to Riga and I had not known about the necessity of changing trains in Dünaburg; besides – I suddenly invented – I had no money at the moment and had to call to Sweden, to have some of my accounts conferred here before I could make any plans at all.

Again he became coldly dictatorial, treating me like a criminal almost, somebody who had broken a rule by coming here at all. "There is no necessity for you to wait for money from Sweden," he informed me. "When you will arrive in Tilsit, you will be given a ticket and food; as soon as you arrive in Berlin, you will go to Alexanderplatz [83] and apply to the general welfare."

Here I interrupted, my mind suddenly completely made up, de-

---

[83] Berlin Police Headquarters.

ciding never to go to Germany at all. I must have been white as a sheet. I certainly felt like ice and I was suddenly able to point out very haughtily that I was not accustomed to applying for "general welfare money" as long as I had my own private funds, which didn't exist – only in my imagination – and I was not going to risk my children's health, and demanded to see the Ambassador. The atmosphere upstairs was completely different. The Ambassador quite obviously belonged to the pre-Hitler diplomatic corps and, being in a minor post, had not been replaced. He was at least sympathetic. I tried to point out that I had to go to Denmark and Sweden in order to contact friends who might be able to help my husband, and I was not certain at all (since my conversation with the counselor official downstairs) whether I would be able to leave Germany once I had entered it.

He apparently was not sure either, but said I should apply at Alexanderplatz and I probably would be given permission to travel to Copenhagen, but likely would have to leave the children in Berlin. I remember breaking into tears, not having a handkerchief. The ambassador very plainly was bewildered, kind, but helpless. He could do nothing... When I left the building, my mind was made up as far as Nazi Germany was concerned. I was not going back there. When I entered the Embassy a few hours earlier it had seemed natural to me to go there after a short interval of rest in Riga – to return to my mother, my brother and sister, my family of whose love and sympathy I could be certain. This vague instinctive feeling was suddenly gone. The nasty tone of the Nazi officer at the consulate window made obvious the fact that the Third Reich was as dangerous for me as the Soviet Union.

Back at the hotel, the children were safe in our room and I had a little time to wonder what to do next. Our doorman brought up the problem of money, of contacting friends, and, learning that I had some friends in Copenhagen, urged me to cable. I can never be grateful enough that he did this, that he took the cables and dispatched them immediately.

One went to Niels Bohr. It was extremely short, saying that Fisl was arrested, and I asked for his help, also his assistance to get out of

Riga and to Copenhagen. The second went to a string of friends who I suspected to be at the Institute in Copenhagen, and I addressed all of them: the names I remember were Møller,[84] Placzek, Rosenfeld,[85] Gamow and Neugebauer.[86] This cable was longer, gave more details, asked also for money.

I went to bed early and slept until 7 when a knock woke me up. The doorman brought the answer from Copenhagen. It had arrived during the night, but he thought it would be better for me to sleep. By a lucky coincidence, the skiing weather in Norway was not very good that day and the joint ski trip of the Institute members was postponed. They all were together at the Institute when my cables arrived, and they stayed there the best part of the night too, discussing how they could help.

The telegram from Bohr said: "Go and see the Danish Ambassador for granting of entrance visa, money will be sent immediately to you via Stockholm. Niels Bohr." The reason for sending money via Stockholm was explained later. There was no possibility to send money out of Denmark, and only Neugebauer had an account in Stockholm.

This then was a Saturday morning. I dressed warmly in my black cloth coat lined with my old muskrat fur, on my head the Persian lambs hat, in my hands, so to speak, the telegram from Copenhagen,

---

[84]Christian Møller (1904-1980) was a Danish physicist and chemist who made fundamental contributions to the theory of relativity, theory of gravitation and quantum chemistry. He is known for Møller-Plesset perturbation theory.

[85]Léon Rosenfeld (1904-1974) was a Belgian physicist, a collaborator of Niels Bohr.

[86]Otto Eduard Neugebauer (1899-1990) was an Austrian mathematician best known for his research on the history of non-Greek ancient mathematics and astronomy (Babylonia and Egypt). In 1928 he carried out his famous work on the *Moscow Mathematical Papyrus* in Leningrad. In 1937 he published *Lectures on History of Mathematical Sciences in Antiquity* in Moscow. In 1931, while in Göttingen, he founded the review journal *Zentralblatt für Mathematik und ihre Grenzgebiete (Zbl)*, his most important contribution to modern mathematics. When Hitler came to power in 1933, Neugebauer was asked to sign an oath of loyalty to the new government, but he refused. From 1933 Neugebauer with the assistance of his wife edited *Zbl* in Copenhagen while it was published by Springer in Berlin. When Springer, following the Nazi racial laws, demanded the resignation of Jewish members of the Advisory Board, in particular, Tullio Levi-Civita, Neugebauer resigned, and in 1938 left Europe for the U.S.

and proceeded to the Danish Embassy. I am sure that I probably looked like a washed-out 50- or 55-year-old woman, rather neglected, with straight short hair. I was only 37, but I felt as tired and old as the mountains.

The Ambassador took one look at me – the embassy was officially closed on Saturdays – and said that he had no ways and means of ascertaining whether my story was true or not. Anybody might come and present such a telegram. Besides, there was no necessity for a German citizen to obtain a visa in order to enter Denmark. Since my passport was expiring on December 21, Tuesday, I simply would not have a valid passport and to remedy that a Danish ambassador could be of no help. It was altogether perfectly correct, he was very much the aristocrat, and he was correct and cold, but also inhuman. I was simply a nuisance and wasted his time. The only thing I achieved was to persuade him to cable to Niels Bohr for confirmation. He did not offer to phone my hotel later in the day or on Sunday, but "permitted" me to come back on Monday for a possible answer, which he doubted would be forthcoming.

In a few hours, money came from Stockholm. I paid for the room and cables and ordered tickets to Copenhagen.

I believe I spent the Sunday hunting for the missing street and the house of the parents of our Moscow friends. On Monday morning early I knocked again on the door of the Danish Embassy. The time I wore the fur coat which I had bought during the last hour before my departure in Moscow. It was a beautiful squirrel coat, dyed a lovely brownish color, very becoming though almost four sizes too large. The collar could be folded over the head to make another hood. The sleeves were very wide and the coat almost reached the floor. It was also very warm.

The Ambassador seemed to be a different person. He remarked about the coat, treated me with a certain amount of respect, which I understood when he related his activities to me. On Saturday he had cabled in code to Niels Bohr asking for information. When informed in code that he should give me a visa, he answered in code that could not do so for the same reasons he had given to me. Then Niels Bohr consulted the Minister of the Interior who advised Bohr to tell the Ambassador to give me the visa anyway. The Minister of Immigration was away for the weekend. The Danish Ambassador cabled back that he could do no such thing, that he refused to take any responsibility and would only comply with the request of the minister if it were given in the form of an order. The order arrived. He did not melt or become human, but he was polite to me and probably learned that you could not always judge the importance of people by their appearance. He put the stamp of the entrance visa into my passport and signed it.

This was the 20th of December and my passport expired the 21st. I rushed to the Latvian ministry in order to get permission to leave the country, but to Denmark, not to Germany, by sea. The ship – the only one among the ones departing that week that did not make a stop in German ports – was leaving precisely on December 21st. I bought tickets. I said "Goodbye" to the Russian ex-officer and the family of that friend of Houtermans', whose address the cab driver couldn't find but which I nevertheless found myself, who helped me get a spot on that ship.

Figure 23. The harbor of Riga, 1938. Sketch by an unknown Estonian artist. Charlotte's journey to Denmark started from here.

And we found ourselves on the Baltic Sea on the way to Denmark.

One day we docked in Memel,[87] a former German city, at that time either independent or Polish, I forgot, and I walked into it a little ways to see what it looked like. It was indescribably dreary, grey in grey, neglected, and sad.

The trip took one week. It was a small coaster with a small crew. The only other passengers were a group of circus acrobats – Germans, who were traveling from country to country. I had one cabin and in addition to the second cabin there was only a tiny galley where we could sit and where could get our meals. The captain was an obnoxious course-looking person; I did not see him often, fortunately.

The day after was Christmas Eve, which I never realized before it was almost over.

In Denmark

It was later afternoon when we docked in Copenhagen. The Fremden-Polizei, the Immigration police, swarmed over the little boat and discovered that my passport was not valid and that I had an "illegal entrance visa." Just when they started to made complications, Bohr's assistant Christian Møller appeared with some authority from Niels Bohr. A lot of Danish filled the air. The police became polite enough, but took my passport away. "In the meantime," said Møller firmly, "Bohr told me to take you to the Hotel." He must have told it also to the Police, who did not object and let us go. I never saw the passport again until weeks later when Bohr gave it back to me together with a new valid League of Nations Passport which was not only legal anywhere in the world, but also had a clause according to which the only country to which we could be returned in case of extradition was Denmark. We were safe!

Copenhagen was beautiful with the glittering snow. The Hotel-Pension to which Møller brought us seemed to me like a fairytale. While Riga had been comfort, this was luxury. Here – from one

---

[87]Memel, East Prussia, now Klaipeda in Lithuania. According to the Versaille treaty in 1919 the Memel area was separated from Germany.

minute to another – the whole world had been changed. Gone not only the tension which grew in me in Moscow like a secret cancer, gone also was the lifelessness, the stifling influence of a gloomy and closed society. Here the snow glittered, there were lights everywhere, gayness and expectation in the air.

The Pension was overwhelming. There were innumerable maids with frilly white caps, white aprons over frilly uniforms. Helping hands everywhere. The ghastly looking luggage was brought up, hot baths were drawn, supper for the children appeared. Møller stood by, ordered everything, directing everything. The children were so exhausted, they shrieked and cried, they would neither wash, nor drink, nor eat, least of all sleep. I finally calmed them down and swallowed half a sleeping pill. They were tucked in, they slept, a maid stayed with them.

Christmas 1937

Then Møller calmly announced, "Now we shall eat and talk," and brought me to a very pleasant restaurant with that subdued atmosphere of well-being all around, candles and Christmas decorations, a small table in a corner, delicious food and wine [...]

I told the story of Fisl and his arrest and the story of our friends in Moscow and Kharkov, who were all in prison, the story of those who still waited to be caught, the story of the silent terror which hung over the big city and the inhuman arm of Stalin who was the law. Møller left for a short while to telephone to Bohr and came back saying that we would all meet the next morning at the Institute.

The Institute was filled with friends, Niels Bohr came, they had brought games for the children. In his office Bohr and I, Møller and only a few others talked and they asked me many, many questions. Already before I came, Bohr had talked twice with Blackett in London by phone to have his opinion or possible advice. It was not only the case of Fisl being in prison, it was the case of many members of the scientific community being in prison, or in danger or already dead. I was the first to come from Moscow and the first to tell the story. And Bohr was deeply concerned. I suddenly had the feeling that I could relax a little now. I was not fighting any more. Here was somebody who took over who was so very human, who understood immediately and who seemed to know what to do.

He simply took over and I was so very deeply comforted and the stirring upheaval of retelling what had happened quieted down slowly. Never again did I tell it or have to tell it precisely that way. From then on we acted, we planned help for those inside, that was all. For myself there was no particular worry, no momentary anxiety or fear as far as the children and I were concerned. That same evening we were invited to the Bohrs to a family Christmas dinner. The famous Ehrenbohr opened its doors, the dining hall with the enormous square table seating three at each side, was beautiful with its red flowers and glittering silver. My children were not up to this elegance. Bohr tried to entertain them and showed them exquisite little toys and dolls he had brought back from Japan.

It did not help much. After that I brought them seldom to the house. I also asked to change to a less elegant hotel and moved into Froken where most of the guests took rooms while visiting Bohr. Every morning Møller came like the confidential attaché of a great ambassador with suggestions like: "Bohr says 'Would I like to send all my things to be dry-cleaned,' or Bohr says 'Would I like today to buy shoes for the children and myself or would I like to buy a few toys for the children.'" I never saw any money. Møller paid for everything and the money came from Bohr.

One of the hardest tasks was the cable I had to send to Fisl's mother who was in the USA. She misunderstood the situation in the beginning, probably because I myself could not quite cope with the finality of the situation. I also told her that on Bohr's advice I would stay in Copenhagen for a few weeks and then go to London in order to be better able to organize any actions for Fisl and for other friends. She herself, being an extremely active person, began to be very busy. She contacted Einstein and others and it was difficult to coordinate our efforts for a while. Bohr advised, and we all agreed, that one had to be very careful so that we would not do any harm.

In the meantime the children and I settled down to a routine. For a while they were given sleeping tablets, but this remedy was not necessary after a week or so. Every morning around 10:00 Møller came with new plans or suggestions from Bohr. We went for walks through the city, watched the Danish Army parade in the place before the Castle, three or four men only. It was like playing soldiers. Walking around Copenhagen was delightful. At the end of almost every street there is a boat on anchor and you either turn back or follow the shoreline. [...]

I spent all the days with the children and when they were tucked in safely in Frozen Havens' comfortable pension, I would often go out to dinner, mostly with Møller and Kalkar, his friend.[88] It was on these evenings that we talked about the future. Bohr had more or less decided that for the sake of Fisl and Alex Weissberg, who were in prison, I should remain in Europe and best stay in London.

---

[88]Fritz Kalkar, Bohr's student.

But England has laws which do not easily permit people to work. This problem I had to solve by myself. Møller and Kalkar suggested borrowing money from American friends. It sounded ludicrous to me. I had had no contacts with anybody there for almost 10 years. My mother in law was teaching in a private school in Massachusetts and earned only a very small salary. The person I had known best when I lived in America was Robert Oppenheimer, or rather his father, but I did not feel that the rights of friendship could stretch that far. Kalkar had been Robert's student in California and had returned only a year ago. He talked about Robert's generosity, his power of compassion and understanding. He talked so long and intensely that it finally did not seem so very strange to write to Robert. I asked Robert to send me the address of his father, because I wanted to ask his help – for help I needed so badly, until I would be able to go to America to earn my own living. It was such a warm and friendly evening when we discussed all this first. Kalkar brought me back to a world which had faded in Russia, the world of friendship.

The next morning before 10, I met Møller coming up the wide stairs terribly pale, almost trembling, "Kalkar is dead, – he said, "He died during the night. It was an embolism." It was a terrible shock to all of us. One could not believe it. He had been so very warm and alive, dark-haired, friendly and so very gifted. I sat down at the table and added at a note in the letter that namely Kalkar had convinced me to write the letter and that Kalkar had just died... This happened almost at the end of our stay in Copenhagen.

We recovered physically and emotionally and felt considerably better.

On Sundays we went to the Bohrs. One evening after dinner we sat in the living room exchanging anecdotes about Pauli, Bohr laughed and laughed. I shall never forget it. He had two studios: a small one, next to the living room and another one across the hall, which had the largest round table I had ever seen. He could work there with his assistants and leave papers and calculations spread out, and still move to the other side and continue on some different problem. [...]

The children felt quite at home. Forgotten were Christmas dinner and the tantrums. They asked for their father and were told that he was still in Moscow, but would come later on.

When finally plans for London had been finished,[89] Bohr called me one day to hand me the beautiful new passport, also some money which he said was a "left over." From what, I wondered... He also had three first class tickets to Harwich and wanted now only to know who would meet me, who would provide a place to live. I packed and said goodbye to the many kind friends: to Harald Bohr, the Neugebauers, all of them, and to Møller. Bohr with seven assistants came to the train to see us off. And the children waved frantically, "Farewell, Mr. Niels Bohr. Farewell, Mr. Niels Bohr!"

---

[89]On January 13, 1938, Pauli wrote to Weisskopf about these events: "You may consider yourself lucky that you didn't go to Kiev at that time... in this country at present reigns a totally unexampled terror which manifests itself even in mass arrests of innocent scientists." Then he mentioned the Houtermans case: "Schnax succeeded under great difficulties to travel to Copenhagen with the children where they have been since about December 25 and hope to obtain an entrance visa to England. The bad thing, however, is that Houtermans himself is in custody in Russia under some vain pretext." (See *Wolfgang Pauli. Scientific Correspondence with Bohr, Einstein, Heisenberg, et al.*, Ed. K. von Meyenn et al., (Springer Verlag, Berlin, 1985), Volume 2, page 547.

Fighting for Freedom

After Charlotte Houtermans' flight from the Soviet Union, she and Fritz Houtermans' mother began to fight for his release.[90] Elsa Houtermans first heard about her son's fate from W. Pauli while Houtermans was still free but had already lost his job at UPTI. James Franck, who also received a letter from Pauli, comforted "Frau Dr. Houtermans" with reassurance that Houtermans faced no immediate danger. If only that were true! In the United States, energetic Elsa Houtermans appealed to Albert Einstein through James Franck, and on January 5, 1938, the famous scientist signed a letter in support of F. Houtermans, addressed to the USSR's ambassador to the U.S., A. A. Troyanovsky.[91]

In the U.S., the National Coordinating Committee for Assistance to Refugees and Immigrants from Germany sent a request to E. P. Peshkova,[92] head of the "Political Red Cross." No answer followed.

Among scientists who spoke out in support of Houtermans were Niels Bohr, his brother, mathematician Harald Bohr, and Patrick

---

[90] At the time of writing of his book Victor Frenkel was apparently not fully aware of the scale of international effort aimed at procuring a release of F. Houtermans and A. Weissberg from the imprisonment in the USSR. Judith Szapor writes in her recent article [1]: "In September 1937, upon her release from prison and the Soviet Union, Éva Striker joined her brothers and mother in Vienna. A few months later, in March 1938 she escaped from Nazi Vienna and met up with Koestler in London. ... Reciprocating Weissberg's courageous attempts to free her, she mobilized her uncle, Michael Polanyi, to activate the physicists' network, including Albert Einstein, to vouch for Weissberg's and Houtermans' innocence and ask for their release [2]. In Paris, Georg Placzek and Koestler prepared a telegram signed by three French Nobel laureates, Joliot-Curie, Irene Curie, and Jean Perrin, which was sent to Stalin, protesting the two physicists' arrest [3]... This is not to say that everyone was prepared or able to help: Felix Bloch, the Nobel laureate by then settled at Stanford, was at pains to explain to Éva how his American colleagues, upon learning that the two physicists were Communist Party members, declined all assistance [4]."

[91] See Victor Frenkel, "Einstein's Letters to Stalin and Soviet Diplomats," *Zvezda*, № 12, 1994.

[92] Ekaterina Pavlovna Peshkova (1876-1965), a public figure in Russia and the Soviet Union known for using her reputation (she was the first wife of the great proletarian writer Maxim Gorky) for defending human rights under the Bolshevik regime.

Blackett. A letter from Jean Perrin and Frederic and Irene Joliot-Curie to Attorney General Vyshinsky caused a great stir in the post-war years when it was published. (This letter and their similar telegram to Stalin are presented at the end of the chapter as documents 1 and 2.)

Did these efforts have any effect? Apparently not, although sometimes letters reached their addressees. In December 1941, after the U.S. entered the war against Germany, M. Litvinov, the Soviet Ambassador to the United States, replied to Einstein, but only to the general latter part of Einstein's letter, not mentioning the fate of specific people whom the great scientist had asked about, including F. Houtermans. We know of no other instances of Soviet officials replying.

Among those who petitioned Soviet authorities about Houtermans' fate, conspicuously absent was Niels Bohr, busy at about the same time with attempting intervention on behalf of L. D. Landau. Bohr's colleague Leon Rosenfeld explained to Charlotte Houtermans that he and Bohr had discussed the issue with F. Joliot-Curie during the latter's visit to the Bohr Institute. In Bohr's opinion, the letter from the three French scientists in defense of F. Houtermans and A. Weissberg was so strong that any other intervention would only complicate the situation.

Charlotte Houtermans appeals to rights organizations for immigrant scientists and, after arriving in England from Copenhagen, to the Foreign Office and the Ministry of Internal Affairs to ensure F. Houtermans' arrival in England if released (after all, his return to Germany was out of the question!).

The Society for the Protection of Science and Learning warns Charlotte Houtermans that in order to avoid accusations of encroachment, appeals to the Soviet Embassy should be limited to requests for information. She proceeds in exactly this way, sending a telegram to People's Commissar Beria (see Document 4). Concurrently, the Society assures Charlotte Houtermans that should her husband be released, everything possible would be done to secure his arrival in England immediately after his crossing of the Soviet border – the necessary documents were already being prepared. They survive in Houtermans' file at Oxford's Bodleian Library, where the author (V.F.) had an opportunity to see his Curriculum Vitae and list of publications. At the same time, an interesting detail emerges: indications that Houtermans' 1937 work can't be presented because the author was not sent separate proofs – the reader will already understand why. The person submitting the information was obviously Patrick Blackett.

In early 1938, it was namely Blackett to whom Charlotte sent a letter from Copenhagen asking for support in her application, and perhaps her husband's, for coming to England. Even before her arrival in Copenhagen, while the steamship was en route, Niels Bohr's brother Harald had appealed to the Society for the Protection of Science and Learning in England with a request to assist the Houtermans family – emigration to England was possible because of Charlotte's husband's previous job there, whereas Danish law forbade accepting immigrants.

By January 14, the Foreign Office reports that Charlotte Houtermans is permitted to stay in England for six months, relieving the threat of winding up in Germany after the Danish visa expired. Yet in England Charlotte's situation with two children is so difficult that in letters of the time, her husband's friends and acquaintances offer clothing, household items and even furniture. After all, she has nothing.

Charlotte's task thus becomes to move with the children to the United States, where their grandmother lives. This means more searching for work and a livelihood. As of April 1939, she and her children are in America, where she tries to solicit help from her old friend from Göttingen days, Robert Oppenheimer, with whom she had once made her first trip to the United States, in obtaining research work. In the end, Charlotte Houtermans temporarily settles anew at Vassar College, where she had taught in the past.

Still knowing nothing of her husband's fate, she turns to American diplomacy. American embassies in Germany, Danzig, Vienna, Switzerland expressed their readiness to help F. Houtermans, including through financial assistance, if he should arrive in their jurisdictions. Finally, through the personal mediation of Eleanor Roosevelt she receives a message from the U.S. Embassy in Moscow that in response to her request, the Soviet authorities have reported that Professor Fritz Houtermans is not in custody and has been deported from the USSR to Germany. This message and other documents from Charlotte Houtermans' correspondence with Eleanor Roosevelt, copies of which were given to the author by the Houtermans family, are provided at the end of this chapter (documents 5-8).

At this time, the United States and Germany were not yet at war,[93] so Houtermans' arrival in the United States remained a possibility. Another fate, though, lay in store for him.

Document 1[94]

Paris, June 15, 1938

State Prosecutor Vyshinsky,
Moscow, USSR
Dear Mr. State Prosecutor:

The undersigned, friends of the Soviet Union, believe it to be their duty to bring the following facts to your attention:

The imprisonment of two well-known foreign physicists, Dr. Friedrich Houtermans, who was arrested on December 1, 1937, in Moscow, and Alexander Weissberg, who was arrested on March 1 of the same year in Kharkov, has shocked scientific circles in Europe and the United States. The names of Houtermans and Weissberg are so well known in these circles that it is to be feared that their long imprisonment may provoke a new political campaign of the sort which has recently done such damage to the prestige of the country of socialism and to the collaboration of the USSR with the great Western democracies. The situation has been made more serious by the fact that these scientific men, friends of the USSR who have always defended it against the attacks of its enemies, have not been able to

---

[93] President Franklin Roosevelt signed the U.S. Declaration of War against Germany on December 11th, 1941.

[94] Document 1 was published by A. Koestler in his preface to [5]. Translated from French.

obtain any news from Soviet authorities on the cases of Houtermans and Weissberg in spite of the time which has gone by since their arrest, and thus find themselves unable to explain the step that has been taken.

Their friends include many of the most eminent men of science, like Professor Einstein at Pasadena, Professor Blackett at Manchester, Professor Niels Bohr at Copenhagen, who are interested in their fate and will not abandon this interest. Mr. Weissberg, who is one of the founders and the editor of the Journal of Physics of the USSR, has been invited by Professor Einstein to the university at Pasadena, an invitation to which he has not been able to reply because of his arrest. Dr. Houtermans had been invited to do scientific work at an institute in London, and he was arrested in the customs office of the station in Moscow just as he was leaving.

The only official information available on the reasons for the arrest of Weissberg is a communication from Soviet authorities in March, 1937, to the Austrian Embassy in Moscow in which Weissberg was accused of espionage for Germany and activity in support of an armed revolt in the Ukraine. As to Dr. Houtermans, no official communication has been made.

All those who know Weissberg and Houtermans personally are sincerely convinced that they were devoted friends of the USSR and incapable of any actions hostile to it. They are sincerely convinced that the accusations made against Weissberg are absurd and must be based on a serious mistake which it is desirable to correct at once, for both political and personal reasons.

Official statements by responsible Soviet leaders have recently underlined the fact that errors, inevitable in critical times, have been made by subordinate offices in the course of the purge campaign which was necessary in a country so seriously threatened by external and internal enemies. These same leaders have insisted on the urgent necessity of correcting these errors and occasional abuses of authority. The undersigned and all the friends of the two accused are convinced that this is a mistake of just such a kind.

This is why they address themselves to the State Prosecutor of the USSR on the cases of Houtermans and Weissberg and urge him, in the interests of Soviet prestige in foreign scientific circles, to take the necessary steps to obtain their immediate freedom. The political significance of this question justifies us in sending a copy of this letter to Mr. Stalin, addressed to him through the Embassy of the USSR in Paris.

We urge you to give us an answer as quickly as possible, considering the urgent character of this problem. With the expression of our most sincere consideration, honorable State Prosecutor, we remain

Irène Joliot-Curie,
former Under Secretary of State for Scientific Research,
Nobel Prize winner

Jean Perrin,
former Under Secretary of State for Scientific Research,
Nobel Prize winner

Frédéric Joliot-Curie,
Professor at the Collège de France,
Nobel Prize winner

Document 2[95]

Telegram:

State Attorney General of USSR
Moscow
Same text to:
Mr. J. Stalin
Kremlin, Moscow

Please send information on the fate of well-known physicists Alexander Weissberg, arrested in Kharkov on March 1st, 1937, and Friedrich Houtermans arrested in Moscow on December 1st, 1937. Their detention threat to provoke a political campaign from the enemies of the USSR and at the same time is incomprehensible to the

---

[95]Dated June 1938. Translated from French. Sent by Frédéric Joliot-Curie, 76 Avenue Le Notre, Antony, Seine.

friends of the USSR since they are convinced that Weissberg and Houtermans are incapable of actions hostile to the Socialist Construction and that their arrest is a serious mistake of subordinated organs. Please pay attention to this case, we underline its political meaning, and urge a prompt answer. Signed by: Irène Joliot-Curie, former Under Secretary of State for Scientific Research, Nobel Prize winner; Jean Perrin, former Under Secretary of State for Scientific Research, Nobel Prize winner; Frédéric Joliot-Curie, Professor at the Collège de France, Nobel Prize winner.

Document 3[96]

May, 18, 1938

Mr. Joseph Stalin,
Moscow,
USSR

Dear Mr. Stalin:

I have recently learned of several cases in which scholars who had been invited to Russia – men who have, as human beings, the full confidence of their foreign colleagues – have been accused of serious offenses. I understand how easily suspicion may fall, in times of crisis and excitement, on innocent and valuable men. But I am also convinced that from a general human point of view as well as in the interests of the successful development of Russian construction it is of the highest importance to move only with the greatest care against men of rare energy and rare abilities.

So I urge you to direct your attention to the proceedings against Dr. Alexander Weissberg at Kharkov. Dr. Weissberg, an Austrian citizen, is a physicist and engineer who has been working at the Ukrainian Physical Technical Institute in Kharkov. I would especially like to make sure that consideration is given to the judgment of Dr. Weissberg's work for the People's Commissariat of Heavy In-

---

[96]Added by the Editor. Document 3 was published by A. Koestler in his preface to [5]. Translated from German.

dustry which was given in the beginning of 1937 by Professor Martin Ruhemann, head of the Experimental Institute on Low Temperatures.

Very respectfully yours,
Albert Einstein

Document 4

PEOPLE'S COMMISSARIAT OF INTERNAL AFFAIRS, MOSCOW

People's Comissar Beria

As the wife of Dr. Fr. Houtermans, a physicist of the Ukrainian Physico-Technical Institute, I appeal to your generosity to provide me information about my husband. I and my children, the younger of whom was born in Kharkov, were separated from him on December 1, 1937, when we were in Moscow, already having exit visas. My husband was arrested on December 1, 1937, at customs in Moscow, by arrest warrant number 104 dating from November 29. I conjecture that he was transferred to Kharkov and then to Kiev, but I have been told neither his precise address, nor what he is accused of. I am very worried about him. My husband is well-known in the scientific community worldwide. When I am asked about him, as often happens, I am unable to give a satisfactory explanation for his disappearance. My husband and I were always grateful for the hospitality shown us in the Soviet Union, and especially for the opportunities for my husband's research work. Please, give me some information about him and the state of his health. I am confident that justice will be maintained in his case, and I will be very grateful for any efforts to secure his freedom, which I, my children and his elderly mother await from day to day.

With thanks,
Charlotte Houtermans
56b Foyle Road, Blackheath, LONDON
Sent at 7 am, Feb. 12, 1939

Document 5

The White House, Washington

June 26, 1940

My dear Mrs. Houtermans:

Mrs. Roosevelt asked me to send with this letter a copy of a letter she received from Ambassador Steinhardt. She apologized that she could not obtain more specific information, but under current conditions this proved impossible for her.

Yours truly
Malvina C. Thompson
Secretary to Mrs. Roosevelt

Document 6

June 25, 1940

My dear Mrs. Roosevelt:

When I returned to Washington this morning, I found a telegram from the embassy in Moscow, confirming that the Soviet Ministry of Foreign Affairs informed the Embassy on June 19 that Professor Fritz Houtermans has been released from prison and deported to Germany – and that the Soviet Ministry of Foreign Affairs knows Professor Houtermans to have been "presently living in Germany" since then.

Yours truly
Lawrence S. Steinhardt

Document 7

The White House, Washington

October 21, 1940

My dear Mrs. Houtermans:

I'm very grateful to you for your letter.

I'm glad to know that your husband has been released and is at liberty and is feeling all right. Will he try to come to our country later on?

Yours sincerely,
Eleanor Roosevelt

Document 8

The White House, Washington

November 29, 1940

My dear Mrs. Houtermans:

Mrs. Roosevelt asked me to thank you for your letter. She is very happy that your husband has been saved, and hopes all will be well.

Yours sincerely
Malvina C. Thompson
Secretary to Mrs. Roosevelt

References

1. Judith Szapor, *Private Archives and Public Lives, Jewish Culture and History*, vol. 15, pp. 93-109 (2014).
2. A copy of Einstein's telegram is in the Eva Zeisel Papers. It is published in the Appendix of J. Szapor, "From Budapest to New York: The Odyssey of the Polanyis," *Hungarian Studies Review*, XXX, $N^{\underline{o}}$ 1 (Spring 2003), 29. -J.S.
3. Koestler's account in *Invisible Writing*, p. 501, and Placzek's letter to Eva Zeisel, Paris, April 1, 1938, Eva Zeisel Papers, give slightly different versions of the process, each emphasizing their own contribution. -J.S.
4. Felix Bloch to Eva Zeisel, Stanford, June 9, 1938, Eva Zeisel Papers. -J.S.
5. Alexander Weissberg, *The Accused*, (New York, Simon and Schuster, 1951).

Descent into the Prisons: 1939-40

The interrogations resumed upon Houtermans' transfer back to Moscow. There he was made an offer of Soviet citizenship and was promised a position as head of an institute – indeed, the NKVD was already overseeing the notorious "sharashki."[97] At this institute, Houtermans was told, he could conduct his own research. Houtermans turned down the offer. First, he was afraid of losing foreign citizenship and becoming completely powerless – he had no more illusions about such things. Second, the prisoners already had evidence that such proposals were often bluffs used to obtain commitments or information from the arrested.

One of the final reports in Houtermans' case file gives an idea of his situation in Moscow. The interrogation was held in early December 1939, when Houtermans, like many other foreigners – fellow misfortunates detained along with him at Moscow's Butyrskaya Prison – had already realized that they were being prepared for deportation from the Soviet Union. The first portent of this came when all of them were dressed in decent clothes (Houtermans was virtually shoeless) and began to be decently fed. Besides this, arriving in Moscow sometime in early October 1939, they learned of the start of the Second World War and likely of the non-aggression pact between the USSR and Germany. Here, then, is Houtermans' interrogation report.

Interrogation report for detainee Gautermans Fritz Ottovich,[98] from December 3-4, 1939, native of Danzig, member of the Communist Party of Germany since 1925.[99] Before his arrest, worked as a research supervisor at UPTI. Resided in Kharkov, Tchaikovsky Street, 16, Apt. 2. Interrogation be-

---

[97] *Sharashki* is a jargon name for research institutes and design bureaus of a prison type subordinated to the NKVD/KGB, which employed imprisoned scientists, engineers and technicians.
[98] The Russified Goutermans becomes Gautermans.
[99] Other sources indicate that Houtermans joined the Communist Party in 1926 or 1927. -V.F.

gun at 21:40. Completed at 14:45.

Question: When did you come to the Soviet Union?

Answer: In late February 1935.

Q: Where did you find work?

A: At the Physico-Technical Institute.

Q: How long did you work there and in what position?

A: I worked there until early September 1937 as a research supervisor.

Q: Why did you leave this position in October 1937?

A: Because I was dismissed.

Q: For what reason?

A: The order from the director [100] didn't specify the actual reason for my dismissal, but the institute director told me a week beforehand that he was forced to dismiss me from my position because of my foreign citizenship and that for this reason my contract wouldn't be renewed.

Q: And when you were arrested?

A: December 1, 1937.

Q: What did you plead yourself guilty of?

A: I plead guilty of giving false testimony in which I incriminated both myself and a number of others whom I knew to be absolutely honest people.

In addition, I confess that in private conversations, in a circle of my acquaintances who visited my apartment, I criticized, from anti-Soviet positions, certain actions by Soviet institutions and the government. For instance, a law banning abortion, etc. In Soviet circles, such criticism is called counter-revolutionary, so I plead guilty to this. Then I spoke in an anti-Soviet manner while in my cell.

Q: While under investigation, you gave extensive testimony about your being an agent of the Gestapo. Are you saying this is testimony you now recant?

A: Yes, I recant all the testimony I gave before, since I was forced to give it under difficult moral and physical conditions.

---

[100] At that particular time the director was A. Leipunsky. -V.F.

Q: What do you mean by difficult moral and physical conditions?

A: Before I began to give my testimony in Kharkov, I was continuously interrogated, with no chance of to sleep, for about 10 days. Along with this, I was placed in this state in a cell where other arrested people told me just what I needed to write in my testimony, and gave me the names of individuals known to me, people whom investigators apparently had told them about.[101]

In addition, during the investigation I was presented with some kind of evidence against my wife, on the basis of which I was directly threatened that if I didn't testify, my wife would also be arrested and our children sent to an orphanage with registration under some other name so I wouldn't be able to find them later.

Affected by all this, I decided to give fictional testimony about myself, moreover because in the investigation I was assured that no Soviet court would ever seriously punish me based on this testimony and that as a foreigner I would only be expelled from the Soviet Union.

Q: Why do you consider your Kharkov testimony to have been false?

A: During the investigation I gave two versions of my testimony. The first version was that I was recruited by Lieutenant Schimpf, who put me in touch with resident Gestapo agent Tisza, who at one time worked in Kharkov and went abroad in 1937. Next, I testified that for espionage work, Tisza supposedly put me in contact with Fomin, my assistant, and with Rupp, an electrical engineer at the Metrology and Standards Institute in Kharkov, and with Benjamin Margo, a pediatrician who also worked at some children's center on the outskirts of Kharkov.

Next I testified that from what Tisza said, I had real-

---

[101] A. Weissberg, a man with a fate just as dramatic as that of Houtermans, wrote that one of his cellmates was a specially placed provocateur who sought to induce him to provide whatever testimony was needed for the investigation. -V.F.

ized that espionage work for Germany was being carried out by Rozenkevich, Walter, Shubnikov, Reiter or Ritter, Oskar Gail. That was basically the first version of my testimony. It was false because none of the people I named is known to me as having any involvement, of whatever degree, in German intelligence work.

Q: Did you know the people you named in your testimony?

A: I knew German Reichswehr Officer Schimpf in 1931-1932 while he was a physics student at the institute in Berlin where I worked as an assistant. I wasn't closely acquainted with him; I just remember his name as a student, and have no knowledge of Schimpf as a spy.

In my testimony, I indicated that in England, on orders from the Gestapo, a certain "Hans" tried to make contact with me. I declare in this investigation that in fact no such person exists at all. I invented him in order to supply a motive for my coming to the USSR on an espionage mission.

Tisza worked as a researcher at UPTI for a year and a half or two years, and then left to take up residence in Hungary. I have no knowledge of him being a spy, and chose his name so that the primary initiator of the spy ring would be someone there was no way to ask about this.

Q: Why did you take such a course of provocation?

A: In the cell, we, the arrested, constantly discussed forms for giving testimony about espionage. We came to the conclusion that it would be best to identify as spies people who were already dead, and it was considered very valuable when someone among the arrested could offer the name of whatever deceased Latvian or someone else of another nationality; the other detainees would immediately start including this name in their testimonies.

Q: Do you think it works out that everyone arrested gave false testimony?

A: I should clarify that obviously this wasn't a mass phenomenon, but in the cell where I was, it was a fact.

We'll end our interrogation report citation with the second version of the confession that Houtermans mentions.

Houtermans: I was read Obreimov's testimony, where he said I had recruited him for spying in 1929. For my part, I had given testimony about starting espionage work in 1933. This presented the issue of needing to backdate my spy experience, as after all I couldn't have recruited Obreimov for espionage work in 1929 if I myself weren't spying before that. I had to think up some new recruiter, since Schimpf, whom I'd known in 1931-1932, didn't fit this scenario. After considering this question, I decided to write a second version of my testimony where I would name Professor Westphal as my recruiter. I wrote that Westphal had recruited me for espionage work in 1929 on the grounds that he had learned of my membership in the German Communist Party and threatened me with loss of employment, since I worked for him as an assistant, and in this way had lured me into spying.

The Bridge over the River Bug

Up until just a few years ago, it had seemed that the brutal act of German emigres' transfer from the Soviet Union to Fascist Germany had occurred as a result of the pact of 1939. It now appears that negotiations began much earlier.[102] In the autumn of 1936, the German Ambassador to the USSR, F. von Schulenburg, made a request to the USSR People's Commissariat for the extradition to Germany of German subjects arrested on suspicion of spying for his country. The first ten from this group were sent to Germany in early 1937. The German side sent lists of people to "fetch." The Soviet side relayed a "counter-offer" – lists of people approved for deportation from the USSR.

Figure 24.   Vyacheslav Molotov, Foreign Affairs Minister of the USSR, greets Heinrich Himmler, SS Reichsführer, 1939.

---

[102]See I. Shcherbakov's article "The NKVD and the Gestapo. A Marriage of Convenience" in the newspaper *Moscow News*, June 2, 1991. -V.F.

These lists turned out to contain names of people whom neither the Gestapo nor other similar German institutions had known to be staying in the Soviet Union – the whereabouts of many who had emigrated from Germany after 1933 had remained unknown.

The NKVD lists included arrested political emigrants, technicians working in research institutes and factories, and simply Germans who had lived for many years in the Soviet Union. The above-cited *Moscow News* article contains an excerpt from a letter sent to the Soviet People's Commissar for Foreign Affairs through the German Embassy: "The actual friendly relationship between the Third Reich and the Soviet Union is incompatible with the large number of German citizens to be found in Soviet prisons."

A corresponding agreement was struck, after some stalling from the Soviet side, and a large group of "undesirable foreigners" was conveyed to Brest-Litovsk and, on the bridge over the River Bug, on the eve of 1940, handed over by NKVD officers to members of the Gestapo (A. Weissberg was part of this contingent).

What motivated the Nazis in initiating such an action? For one, plans were already being made for war against the USSR, and people who had lived in the Soviet Union a few years, who knew the situation, spoke Russian and had been aggrieved and embittered by imprisonment in Soviet prisons and camps, could be useful. What motivated the NKVD? People who had connected themselves with the leftist movement, who had come voluntarily to a country that seemed to them to fulfill their ideals and to struggle against their enemies, were now being given up to the Gestapo. Among these people were many communists and Jews – one can imagine what awaited them in Germany! Apparently, it was a gesture of "good will" – a twistedly justified act intended to demonstrate faithfulness to the pacts with the new ally. The deportees may also have included representatives of our intelligence services, dispatched into Germany by this means. According to testimony from Houtermans and others, in the last stage of their stay in Butyrskaya they had to sign an agreement not to disclose the circumstances and conditions of their stay in Soviet prisons, along with a pledge to cooperate with the NKVD.

The bulk of the deportees may have been exchanged as the price for a few of our actual spies.

There are several pieces of evidence about the fate of immigrants who crossed the bridge over the River Bug to the German side. The historical record also tells of those who decided not to make the crossing – some flung themselves off the bridge into the river. One young worker's tragic fate is known. In Germany, when his labor brigade had a fight with stormtroopers, he was implicated in murdering one of the Nazis. Because he managed to escape (after some wanderings, he wound up in the Soviet Union), his arrested comrades testified that namely he had struck the fatal blow. After this, he was sentenced to death. And now he was being sent to Germany!

Not all but many were sent to concentration camps after a trial – after all, everything had to be legal! A. Weissberg, as already mentioned, wound up in the Krakow ghetto, where he fled without waiting for his demise. It's unlikely that F. Houtermans, already exhausted by this time, could have done the same. As he himself wrote, he probably would have just died of exhaustion in a German prison, even if no harsher sentence were given him.

Here is an extract from one of the final pages of F. Houtermans' case file.

Extract from report № 29

Special Committee of the People's Commissariat of
Internal Affairs (NKVD), April 25, 1940

  Heard:

Case number 15844/Investigative Division, Chief State Security Directorate (GUGB), on charges against Gautermans Fritz Ottovich, born 1903, native of the city of Danzig, German, German citizen, formerly a German Communist Party member since 1926.

Before arrest, employed as a researcher at the Ukrainian Physico-Technical Institute.

Charged under Articles 58-6, 58-9, 58-10 of the Criminal Code of the RSFSR.

<u>Resolved:</u>

Expel Gautermans Fritz Ottovich from the USSR as an undesirable alien.

In late April 1940, the undesirable foreigner Fritz Houtermans was taken to Brest-Litovsk and, on the bridge over the Bug, handed over to Gestapo officers.

On the Other Shore

By the time of Houtermans' crossing into occupied Poland, the Gestapo already had a dossier on him.[103] The documents it contains give a sense of the workings of the German secret police system.

The negotiations between the Germans and Soviets on the return of German nationals from the Soviet Union to Germany find reflection in a long list – marked "Classified!" and dated June 2, 1937 – compiled by the Gestapo office in Dresden. The list's title, *Flüchtige Kommunisten,* can be translated as "escaped" or "fugitive Communists." With the list are instructions to send it to different cities and various officials in Germany, including the head of the country's border service. The number of people in this alphabetical list can be surmised from the fact that Houtermans figures as number 3727 (and his name starts on the seventh letter of the German alphabet!). The list includes the time and place of his birth, as well as a case number assigned to him by the Gestapo. His location at that time is given as "unknown."

In August 1937, when Weissberg and other UPTI staff were arrested, Houtermans, as the reader knows, had decided to leave the USSR. His only option was to appeal to Kharkov's German consulate for a passport extension and documents for his entire family.

From this moment on, the wheels of the Gestapo machine begin to spin. Information about Friedrich (Fritz) Houtermans is sent to Germany, and there, on September 21, 1937, a document appears about a "Russland Rückkehrer" (Russia returnee). The card index now contains records about him: residing in Kharkov, street, building number, last place of residence in Germany at Uhlandstrasse 189, Berlin. His racial origins are given: "Mischling II Grade" – a second-degree cross-breed – with a quarter Jewish blood. The term for this in Germany was "Ein-Viertel" – "quarter-part." The racists of the

---

[103]The author is grateful for the assistance of Mr. Thomas Stange (German Institute of High Energy Physics in Zeuthen near Berlin) and the State Archive in Potsdam for sending certain documents relating to Houtermans. The referenced materials are contained in case file numbers ZB-7271 (A.3 and A.4), ZB-7268 (A.8), ZR-925 (A.4), ZR-926 (A.2). -V.F.

Third Reich seemingly pardoned no more than a sixteenth part of Jewish blood.

Houtermans is described as an activist in the Communist Party of Germany. No longer is he a person whose status is "unbekannt" – unknown.

But here is the document that seemingly picks up the baton from the "Decisions of the Special Committee of the NKVD on the Expulsion of Gautermans from the USSR" (April 25, 1940), provided above. In fact, it anticipates it, with a date of April 19, 1940, appearing after the title, *Ausweisung von verhafteren Reichsdeutschen aus der USSR*, ("Expulsion from the USSR of German Citizens Arrested There").

Houtermans' case file, renumbered at this point, now contains details about his role as a Communist Party functionary, and about his final place of employment in Berlin at the Graduate School of Engineering, from which he had been dismissed in accordance with the law, with no previous record of his bearings thereafter. An official at the German Embassy in Moscow relayed to Berlin by telephone (on the same day – April 19, 1940) that in the coming days another batch of German citizens would be transported from Moscow to Germany. The full list has not yet been received, the official adds, but there is exact information about nine of the deportees. Their names are relayed to Berlin. Houtermans figures among them as Number 3.

The full list of deportees arrived in Berlin on May 6, 1940. It names 33 people, 33 fates. Their number is apparently not accidental – other sources indicate that "undesirable foreigners" were dispatched by the NKVD in namely such batches. Maybe this was exactly how many people fit in a boxcar? Whatever the case, in this list Houtermans moves to eighth position. And as with two or three others, a brief note is made: "Houtermans, appearing as Number 8, should be especially noted. He is a Mischling II Grade and a former functionary of the Communist Party of Germany, and was an assistant professor at the Technische Hochschule in Charlottenburg." And a few lines down, further instructions are provided to the Berlin police that upon Houtermans' arrival in Berlin, he is to be arrested, interrogated and turned over to the Imperial security service. The trap is set.

While Houtermans and his companions are en route to Germany, documents on them are also forwarded there. One is a list of people who testified during preliminary interrogation (apparently at a transit camp in Poland) that before leaving the USSR, they had expressed their willingness to perform work for the NKVD. In the copy of the first two pages of this list that was conveyed to the author (-V.F.), only Houtermans' name is decipherable – the other names are concealed, with only their numbers visible, covering names from A to K – 16 people. It appears that more than one-half of the deportees from the Soviet Union expressed – in oral or written form – their willingness to cooperate with the NKVD after returning to Germany. Houtermans himself, in one of his autobiographical documents,[104] confirms that while still in the USSR, during his final meeting with

Figure 25.   Lublin Castle overlooking the Jewish Quarter, 1940. The castle served as a prison during the Nazi occupation of Lublin from 1939 to 1944. In 1944, just days before their retreat, the Nazis massacred Lublin Castle prison's remaining 300 inmates. After 1944 the castle continued to serve as a prison for Soviet secret police for some time.

---

[104]See Houtermans' "Chronological Record," page 366.

NKVD agents, he agreed to cooperate with the organization. In a footnote, the Gestapo indicate that the listed people have been automatically placed under police surveillance and must report all their movements and check in at police stations twice a year.

There is a final series of documents on the transport of the deportees. On May 24, 1940, the Lublin transit prison reported that on May 14 it incarcerated 33 people conveyed there from the Polish border town of Biała-Podlaska. Apparently Lublin was a filtration point.[105] On May 24, only 32 of the deportees were sent on to Berlin. The train departed from Lublin, the document meticulously states, at precisely 14:35. The next day, May 25, at 7:30 in the morning, it arrived at the Friedrichstrasse station.

Houtermans is put in a Gestapo prison, and on June 3 is transferred from there (now along with only three others) to the jail at Berlin police headquarters.

---

[105]The article in the Polish Wikipedia devoted to Alexander Weissberg-Cybulski (see http://pl.wikipedia.org/wiki/Aleksander_Weissberg-Cybulski) says: "The Germans imprisoned all the deportees first in Biała-Podlaska, then moved them to Pawiak in Warsaw, where they performed racial selection. Five Jews, including Weissberg were transferred to the prison at the Castle in Lublin, while others were transported to the Reich."

Back in Berlin

Houtermans recalled that when their "Russland-Rückkehrer" group arrived in Berlin, he was taken to a prison at Alexanderplatz in the city center. In one respect Houtermans expressed a preference for Soviet prisons he experienced, which, despite the terribly overcrowded cells, were far cleaner!

At the Alexanderplatz prison, each cell held several people. Here fortune smiled on Houtermans: one of his cellmates was soon to be released. He agreed to carry out his companions' requests – to phone or write home for them, to pass along greetings. Houtermans' request appeared quite innocent. The phone number of a Berlin acquaintance of his, the physicist Robert Rompe, had to be found. Houtermans asked the man to convey, by phone, a single phrase to Rompe: "Fisl is in Berlin." Fritz Houtermans' Berlin friends called him "Fisl." (This nickname's origins are lost in the mists of time.)

Rompe immediately told Professor Max von Laue about this.[106] Max von Laue, 1912 Nobel Laureate in Physics, valued F. Houtermans' talent and respected his wife: in the summer of 1933 namely he had seen her off at the railway station in Berlin when she had left with her little daughter Giovanna to join Houtermans in England. There she had carried out his request to deliver a letter to one of his colleagues who had moved beyond the borders of the Third Reich. And in 1938, Laue had hurried to Copenhagen, where, at Bohr's, he met with Charlotte Houtermans and her two children, just back from the Soviet Union. It was there that Laue learned the sad news about Houtermans.

A brave man, Professor Laue immediately took the necessary and, of course, very difficult steps to save his young colleague from prison. To this end, the world-famous Nobel laureate's name was weighty

---

[106]The author met Professor R. Rompe in 1987 in Berlin. He held major administrative positions in the GDR, was chairman of the Physical Society, and, when we met, was more than 80 years old and considered one of the patriarchs of German physics. The patriarch was very accessible, but – alas! – the idea for this book had yet to be born back then. Professor Rompe probably could have said a lot about this important episode in F. Houtermans' life. -V.F.

enough for even the Nazi bosses. Laue's intervention fairly soon brought positive results.

Laue sent postcards, still extant, to Houtermans' family in the United States, where Charlotte had moved from England and where Houtermans' mother Elsa lived and worked. (Such mailings were still possible, as the U.S. entered the war with Germany only in November 1941.) Here is what he wrote in the first of them, dated June 7, 1940, to his acquaintance, Edna Carter, who taught in the state of New York at Vassar College, where Charlotte Houtermans had taken a job: "To my surprise, a former Technische Hochschule assistant, Dr. Fritz Houtermans, has 'popped up' here again. I think this will interest people who live in New York with whom you can share this." This phrase is hidden in a rather banal text about Laue's daughter and her success at work, and how in Berlin, after a cold May, lovely weather had finally arrived. It's clear enough what dictates Laue's caution: at this point Houtermans is still in prison, but he's made his presence known ("popped up").

On June 20 Laue writes to Houtermans' mother, Dr. Elsa Houtermans, telling her, "Your son, Dr. Fritz Houtermans, is back in Berlin. True, I haven't yet conversed with him, and I don't know when this conversation will occur. But the fact itself is beyond doubt!" A third postcard to the U.S. is finally addressed to Charlotte Houtermans herself. It was mailed from Berlin on July 13. Here, the conspiracy continues. Laue writes, "The day before yesterday, in a phone conversation, your husband delayed his visit to me until the beginning of next week. But Dr. Rosbaud [107] has already talked with him in Tegel.[108] His voice hasn't changed, and sounds quite confident. He has the money he needs. If I understand correctly, he got it from his stepsisters. Rosbaud said he wants for nothing except reading mat-

---

[107]Paul Rosbaud was a scientist who worked at the Springer publishing house and who knew all the physicists. A book by the American writer Arthur Kramish describes Rosbaud's anti-Fascist activity, as will be touched on below in connection with F. Houtermans' own fate. -V.F.

[108]Tegel is a suburb of Berlin. At one time the prominent German scientists Wilhelm and Alexander von Humboldt had an estate there. As of 1940 the suburb was the site of the notorious Plotzensee prison. Thus for those who lived in Berlin, this phrase's meaning was quite clear. -V.F.

Figure 26.   Berlin after Hitler's rise to power. Mid-1930s.

ter, especially scientific literature. During his two-and-a-half years
of sickness, he couldn't read at all." As Houtermans later recalled,
Laue was the first to visit him in prison in Berlin and bring him
food and money ("he has the money he needs") and could hear for
himself how Houtermans' voice sounded. Houtermans was supposed
to be released, but the release was delayed ("delayed his visit"). And
we know what sickness he suffered from (Soviet conspirators in the
1930s referred to imprisonment as a "sitting disease").

F. Houtermans was finally released from prison on July 16. The
Gestapo documents mention that on October 12 he settled on Uhlandstrasse again, in the same building number 189 he had left in
1933. The next signs of his presence in Berlin, though, already had
a physics connection. In 1940, Volume 36 (September 6) of the very
prominent German scientific weekly journal *Naturwissenschaften* featured (on page 578) a short, 12-line note, "On the Half-life of Radio-

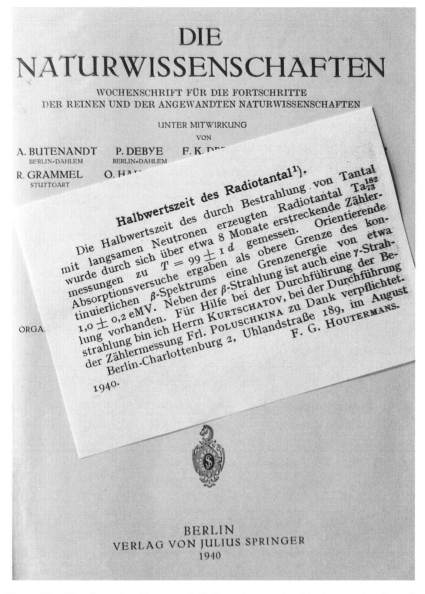

Figure 27.   The first scientific note of F. Houtermans after his deportation from the USSR is published in the September 6 issue of *Naturwissenschaften*.

tantalum." This note has three interesting aspects. The first is a footnote: "The publication of these measurements, completed in October 1937, was delayed due to external circumstances." Another is the following sentence: "I am grateful to Dr. Kurchatov for help with these measurements, and to Fraulein Polushkina for numerical calculations." As this was the time of the brief Soviet-German alliance, Houtermans wasn't afraid of hurting Dr. Kurchatov and Fraulein Polushkina by mentioning their names. And finally, the third notable fact – the most important for Houtermans himself – beneath the report on the half-life of radiotantalum appears the author's address: "Berlin-Charlottenburg, 2, Uhlandshtrasse 189, August 1940." His friends could read this as saying, "I'm alive, I'm back in Germany. Write."

Once again, Houtermans had to find a means to make a living. He had hopes of finding a job, but it was certain that without being a pure Aryan, and as a former communist under suspicion besides, he couldn't work for the public service under German law – couldn't return, for instance, to the Technische Hochschule or find an opening at some university. For a start, he went to *Physikalische Berichte*, a periodical analogous to contemporary abstracting journals. The journal gladly hired him – an outstanding specialist, and also fluent in Russian! At that time, subscriptions to physics and technical journals from the Soviet Union could be maintained from within Germany, including *Journal of Experimental and Theoretical Physics*, which published the results of the most important studies, including in nuclear physics. Issues of *Physikalische Berichte* for 1940 and 1941 are full of abstracts of papers by Houtermans' recent Soviet colleagues. He doesn't limit his attention to papers on nuclear physics, but also writes abstracts of articles on technical and condensed matter physics. Among the whole broad spectrum of papers his abstracts covered, we'll note a quite important one – both for physics and for Houtermans' later fate – Yakov Borisovich Zeldovich's and Yulii Borisovich Khariton's article [109] positing a chain

---

[109] Yakov Borisovich Zeldovich (1914-1987), an outstanding Soviet physicist who played an important role in the development of Soviet nuclear and thermonuclear weapons, and made important contributions to the theory of shock waves, nuclear physics, particle physics, astrophysics, physical cosmology, and general relativity. Yulii Borisovich Khariton (1904-1996), a Soviet physicist, who directed the Soviet nuclear program for many

reaction associated with the neutron-induced fission of uranium (in *Physikalische Berichte* issue 23, 1940).[110]

Undoubtedly, physics-starved Houtermans' in-depth review of the field got him thinking about continuing his nuclear physics research after its interruption by prison – during his absence, Otto Hahn and Fritz Strassman,[111] namely in Germany, had discovered neutron-induced nuclear fission of uranium, and every nuclear physicist understood this discovery's consequences. For F. Houtermans it was also important that his friends and colleagues were working on this problem. The scientist's life took a new turn.

Later, prominent German scientist and inventor Manfred von Ardenne,[112] in his autobiography, covering the most important events of his life, writes [1], "January 1, 1941. F. Houtermans an employee at the laboratory." The note marks the fruition of Laue's efforts to secure Houtermans a permanent position, this time at Baron von Ardenne's renowned private lab. (Houtermans himself considered his work for M. von Ardenne to have begun on November 1, 1940.) For a long time, the main interests of the head of the laboratory had

---

years. He was Director-General of the Nuclear Research Center in Sarov.

[110]It's noteworthy that even during the war with the Soviet Union, German scientists' papers often cited Soviet scientists' papers, including work on nuclear physics. Looking through binders, say, of *Zeitschrift für Physik* for 1942 or 1944, even the most cursory examination turns up more than a dozen citations referencing papers written by Soviet scientists. It's entirely possible that German scientists became acquainted with the contents of at least some of these papers through abstracts by F. Houtermans. -V.F.

[111]In 1938 Otto Hahn, Lise Meitner, and Fritz Strassmann, working together, became the first to recognize that the uranium atom, when bombarded by neutrons, actually splits. Lise Meitner was not among the official authors: after the Anschluss she had to flee Germany because of her Jewish origin. She wrote a separate paper with her nephew, Otto Frisch, in which they formulated a theory of how the nucleus of an atom could be split: uranium nuclei after fission had to produce barium and krypton, accompanied by emission of several neutrons and a large amount of energy.

[112]Manfred von Ardenne (1907-1997), a German applied physicist and inventor. Approximately 600 patents in such fields as electron microscopy, medical technology, nuclear technology, plasma physics, and radio and television technology belong to him. From 1928 to 1945, von Ardenne directed his private research laboratory *Forschungslaboratorium für Elektronenphysik*. For ten years after World War II, he worked in the Soviet Union on the Soviet atomic bomb project and was even awarded the Stalin Prize. Upon his return to what was then East Germany, he started another private laboratory, *Forschungsinstitut Manfred von Ardenne*.

involved development and improvement of the electron microscope. F. Houtermans was well-versed in this topic. At that time, the laboratory's research was focused on creating Germany's most powerful accelerator – the cyclotron. Moreover, Ardenne was devoting ever more intense study to nuclear physics and its possible applications, trying to establish a connection with the German uranium project and receive government funds for his laboratory's research. Here again Houtermans proved himself an extremely useful employee.

F. Houtermans' articles began to be published in various German physical and technical journals starting in mid-1941 (see [2–4]). But in this book we'll focus on a paper he had begun even before started work for Ardenne, and finished in August 1941. It remained unpublished – and for very serious reasons (see the next chapter).

Another paper by Houtermans, which he had worked on from inside Soviet prison cells, also remained unpublished, but due to a quite different set of circumstances. In 1943, he reconstructed its contents from memory (see [5]) and even discussed it with colleagues.

The reader can easily see that any given period in Houtermans' life turned out to yield productive results. It's not surprising that even in prison he sought to occupy himself with scientific problems! In his own statement on his confinement in Soviet prisons, he reports the results he obtained in the field of number theory at that time. Houtermans was not a mathematician – in this case, knowing only Euclid's proof of the existence of an infinitely large set of prime numbers, he tried to prove this proposition for certain special cases. During the hardest year of his life, he sought a proof, despite having no means to write, and regardless of punishment for attempts to use "improvised" means. As a result, he formulated and proved a series of theorems in number theory and found a proof of Fermat's famous theorem for exponent $n = 3$. Trying to attract attention, Houtermans wrote about his findings to the head of the Ukrainian People's Commissariat of Internal Affairs (NKVD), but received no answer, and even declared a hunger strike.

Naturally, when freed from prison, he turned to mathematicians to assess his results. Professor B. van der Waerden,[113] whom he was advised to consult, confirmed the validity of all his conclusions and proofs, but disappointed him with the news that these results, important for number theory, had already been obtained by others. (Indubitably, had these solutions been original, the history of science and this book would have allotted much more space for them.) However, as a persuasive example of how scientific creativity can facilitate survival in inhuman conditions, these studies fulfilled another purpose – they saved Houtermans for science.

In a letter written to his mother (who held a Ph.D. in science) immediately after his release, Houtermans says:

> Completely alone, independently, with no paper, with no conditions to work in, I carried out a thorough investigation, but so far I haven't told anyone about it, because I'm not sure what's known about the subject of my research. Probably everything, because I had to grapple with what for me was a totally new field – the theory of numbers. And in all those years, step by step, phrase by phrase, I built my little building, much as Pascal,[114] while a shepherd, composed Euclidean geometry. But he had the sun, the air, and whatever he needed to write with... I don't think anyone before me ever studied mathematics in such conditions in a Bolshevik prison!
>
> After I showed some of my results to the mathematicians whom Laue had told me about when I met with him, I found out how many interesting things I had discovered: Euler's phi function, Euler's (or someone else's) constant from the theory of logarithms... Fermat's little theorem, Dirichlet's theorem, and, finally, an elementary proof of Fermat's great

---

[113]Bartel Leendert van der Waerden (1903-1996), a Dutch mathematician and historian of mathematics.

[114]Blaise Pascal (1623-1662) was a French mathematician, physicist, inventor, writer and Christian philosopher. He was a child prodigy who was educated by his father, a tax collector in Rouen. Before Pascal turned 13 he had proven the 32-nd proposition of Euclid and discovered an error in René Descartes' geometry.

theorem [115] for exponent 3. I didn't know Euler's proof, but of course mine came later. I'm writing all this down now as a document for you, for myself, for my children and descendants: I've already written 20 pages, and even now I'm barely half done. I have to reconstruct my thoughts, and only then, when everything is ready, I'll read the literature to find out that others – probably – already know everything, but nothing will ever deprive me of the subjective happiness of creativity, which has always given me strength. It was only through this that I survived.

Houtermans writes that the mathematicians with whom he discussed his results had convinced him that if as a novice in this area, under such conditions, he had achieved so much, he would do even more if his work continued. "And I'd gladly continue, but I don't know whether one can serve such different gods as experimental physics and number theory at the same time. To do everything, a person has to live a thousand years."

References

1. Manfred von Ardenne, *Ein glückliches Leben für Technik und Forschung. Autobiographie*, (Verlag der Nation, 1972, in German), pp. 135-136; see this Collection, pp. 54-55.
2. F. Houtermans, "Über die Raumladungswirkung an einem Strahl geladener Teilchen von rechteckigem Querschnitt der Blende," *Archiv f. Elektrotechnik*, Bd. 35(11), 686-691, 1941.
3. F. Houtermans, "Über den Energieverbrauch bei der Isotopentrennung," *Ann. Physik*, Bd. 40(7), 493-508, 1941.
4. F. Houtermans, "Zur Frage der Auslösung von Kern-Kettenreaktionen. Mitteilung aus dem Laboratorium Manfred von Ardenne," *Unveröffentlichter Bericht*, S. 115-145, 1941.
5. F. Houtermans, "Über einen elementaren Beweis für die Existenz unendlich vieler Primzahlen der Form $(2px + 1)$ und eine Verallgemeinerung des Euklidischen Beweises für die Existenz unendlich vieler Primzahlen," *Unveröffentlichtes Manuskript*, 1943, 9 Seiten.

---

[115]Also known as Fermat's last theorem.

The Plutonium Report

For half a century now, issues related to research in the field of nuclear physics, which paved the way for the harnessing of atomic energy, have been a central concern for physicists, politicians, historians, and simply the "reading public." In the case of the American project (in which immigrant scientists, particularly from Germany, played an active role), the question is: what was the initial stimulus and how did it happen? For the Soviet project, the question is probably a bit different: why did it succeed? With an obvious subtext: how did it happen, in a country shaken and exhausted by a terrible war, by the purges of the prewar years and the enormous losses in all spheres of society? In the case of Germany, the question is: why didn't they do it? The subtext here is that fission was discovered by Germans, and Germany had the best school of physics in the world. Even after 1933, despite the exodus of many major scientists, the country still had great physicists, technical resources and developed industry. Another aspect of this issue can be seen in the story of Fritz Houtermans' paper "On the question of the initiation of a nuclear chain reaction," subtitled "A report from the laboratory of Manfred von Ardenne, East Berlin, Lichterfeld."

This typewritten report was never published, despite the topic's significance. The date at the end of the report, "August 1941," merits attention. More than six months had passed since Houtermans started working at the laboratory. The problem of producing a nuclear chain reaction was already on the table and was beginning to be solved in the United States, England and – before the war – in France and the USSR. Up to that time, the warring sides had not yet decided to suspend nuclear physics publications, so Houtermans must have known about them. His list of references, containing 16 items, confirms this. It features classic works by scientists from France (F. Joliot-Curie, H. Halban, L. Kowarski, F. Perrin), America – including the most extensive survey of nuclear research, by L. Turner in *Review of Modem Physics* [1] – and England (D. Chadwick). Of course, Houtermans references the famous paper by N. Bohr and D. Wheeler on the mechanism of fission of heavy nuclei. He also mentions a rela-

Zur Frage der Auslösung von Kern-Kettenreaktionen

von Fritz G. Houtermans

Mitteilung aus dem Laboratorium Manfred von Ardenne

Berlin-Lichterfelde-Ost

Inhalt:

I.	Allgemeine Gesichtspunkte.	S. 1
II.	Die Konkurrenzprozesse.	S. 2
III.	Kettenreaktionen durch Kernspaltung mit schnellen Neutronen.	S. 5
IV.	Kernspaltung durch thermische Neutronen.	S. 10
V.	Möglichkeiten zur Auslösung von Kern-Kettenreaktionen mit thermischen Neutronen.	S. 16
	1. Isotopentrennung.	S. 16
	2. Wahl einer schwereren Bremssubstanz als Wasserstoff, insbesondere schweren Wasserstoffs.	S. 16
	3. Relative Erhöhung der Wahrscheinlichkeit für 1/v-Prozesse durch Anwendung tiefer Temperaturen.	S. 19
	4. Selbstregulierende Wirkung und Bedeutung des Doppler-Effekts bei tiefer Temperatur.	S. 23
VI.	Kettenreaktionen bei endlichem Versuchsvolumen.	S. 26
VII.	Die Bedeutung einer Kettenreaktion bei tiefen Temperaturen als Neutronenquelle und Apparatur zur Isotopenumwandlung.	S. 28

Figure 28.   The first page of Houtermans' *Plutonium Report*. The full text is published in German in [2].

tively insignificant Soviet work on resonance neutron capture – a phenomenon that impedes the chain reaction.

But here's an intriguing detail – the list of references doesn't cite the Zeldovich and Khariton papers, already mentioned here, which give the most extensive analysis of the kinetics of nuclear reactions and details extraordinarily important findings. After all, Houtermans himself wrote an abstract of it!

There exists, however, a separate sheet, typed on the same typewriter used for Houtermans' main report, which in fact does contain a reference to the Leningrad physicists' papers.[116] The text of the report also implies that Houtermans had these papers in mind. It thus appears that there's no reason to expect any surprises in his survey.

However, the report's second page contains the following intriguing paragraphs:

> Only the discovery of the neutron as a particle that has no electromagnetic interaction with the electron shell of the atom revealed the fundamental possibility of a nuclear chain reaction, given that essentially the neutron can lose its energy only through collisions with nuclei. As early as 1932, the author, in his inaugural lecture at the Technische Hochschule in Berlin, pointed out the fundamental possibility of, and formulated the necessary condition for, producing a nuclear chain reaction. This condition is as follows. A nuclear chain reaction must occur in processes in which a nucleus impacted by an incident neutron produces a new neutron (with probability one); the emitted neutron must have energy which is in turn capable of triggering the production of yet another neutron from a different nucleus.[117]
>
> Only after the discovery of the splitting of heavy elements by neutrons, as we know, was such a reaction mechanism actually found. Characteristic for this mechanism is not only the fact of the release of the reaction energy on the order of 180 MeV, but also that during this reaction, besides the appearance of two large fragments into which the heavy atom

---

[116]This sheet was kindly provided to the author by I. B. Khriplovich, author of the first Russian-language paper on F. Houtermans [3]. -V.F.

[117]This refers to an unbranched reaction. A branched chain reaction implies the release of more than one neutron (on average) after absorption of the incident neutron by a nuclei, the so-called multiplication coefficient. -V.F.

splits, there appears a certain quantity of free neutrons capable in turn of causing the fission of heavy nuclei.

It's doubtless a pity that Houtermans didn't publish his ideas back in 1932. Because of this, he lost priority, yielding this to his friend from Berlin in the late 20's and early 30's, and from London in 1933 through 1934 – Leo Szilard. The story of Szilard's statement of a similar idea has appeared in many publications [4]. Moreover, prudent Szilard in 1934 even patented the idea (the patent was classified), despite not knowing, at the time, any specific "explosive" substance that would behave as Houtermans and Szilard wanted. However, Szilard, to his credit, from the start had in mind a branched chain reaction with two released neutrons. Later, he posited that this substance could be beryllium, which really does release neutrons in nuclear reactions of various types.

Yet the most important part of Houtermans' report comes in the closing paragraphs, which refer to another such "explosive" – the 94th element in Mendeleev's periodic table – although the author doesn't emphasize this point in the text. How important is this particular conclusion?

In March-May 1941, a group of physicists in the United States (G. Seaborg, E. McMillan, et al.) announced the discovery of the 94th element, called plutonium (Pu). The element proved to be alpha-radioactive, with a half-life of about 24,000 years. It was shown that plutonium splits under the influence of slow neutrons, much as does a light isotope of uranium, U-235. The report on these findings was released as a preprint ($N^{\underline{o}}$A-33), dated May 1941. With the ban on publications about nuclear physics in the open press already in effect, Houtermans could not have known about this report.[118]

The best testament to the significance of Houtermans' work may be found in contemporary assessments, which run very high:

"Houtermans' lucid argument can be seen as a first turning point

---

[118] Another German physicist, Carl von Weizsäcker, wrote about the significance of the 94th element, in a report which also went unpublished. Houtermans knew about this work, but Weizsäcker essentially mentioned the 94th element's role only hypothetically. In addition, some think that Weizsöker had in mind element 93, neptunium, not yet knowing that this is a short-lived element. -V.F.

in the story of the German uranium research effort..." (D. Irving, in his book about the German uranium project, *The Virus House* [5].)

"This excellent paper...concentrates on...the use of [the slow neutron moderated reactor] as a generator of new radioactive nuclides. Two points of particular interest which it makes are that...one could economize in the effort for fuel enrichment, if needed, by working at reduced temperature...and that one of the products would be element 94 (plutonium), which would probably have similar fissile properties to uranium-235, and be much easier to separate." (Charles Frank, in the introduction to the book *Operation Epsilon* [6].)

"From 1941 until shortly before the war's end...he was one of the mainstays on [our] team, with his imaginative, ingenious ideas... [He] was concerned with estimating the energy consumed in isotope separation... Houtermans summarized his main results in a classified report...which was then communicated to all prominent German nuclear physicists. In this manuscript, Houtermans predicted the splitting and the prospects of plutonium. He examined the advantages of plutonium and pointed toward the method that is used today for so-called breeder reactors and as an economical method for power generation. It is surprising that this work receives only perfunctory mention in post-war official reports, although Houtermans' study was read with great interest by both Soviet and American scientists." (Manfred von Ardenne, in his memoirs [7].)

An obvious conclusion can be drawn: Houtermans' report contains quite contemporary ideas, later put into practice both in nuclear weaponry (the plutonium bomb) and in reactor physics (breeders), although, of course, for him these were only hypotheses which might serve as the starting point for work on a broader scale. Naturally, in the context of a private laboratory supported only by a civil government agency like the Reich Ministry of Posts, this was unfeasible.

The German project, unlike those of the Americans and Soviets (after the war), was never established on a large-scale industrial basis; moreover, in February 1942 it was officially acknowledged that it would be impossible to create an atomic bomb before the war's end. As for the continued research, it focused on the creation of a research reactor (termed a "uranium machine") for staging a chain reaction. The project involved the Imperial Council for Scientific Research, the Ministry of Weapons, and a number of other government agencies with aspirations to operate autonomously. (The Imperial Security Service, including the Gestapo, clearly was not involved in the project, which was never selected as a top-priority critical initiative.) A Uranium Society ("UranVerein"), founded in 1939, included a fairly narrow range of leading physicists, such as Heisenberg, Hahn, Geiger, Bothe, Weizsäcker, and others. Houtermans, confined in Soviet and then in German prisons at the time, never became a member.

Dry dates and a list of events in the "nuclear race" may tell more than a lengthy narrative. On June 9, 1939, E. Flügge, then a young German physicist, published what at the time was the only German-language paper to examine the issue of the critical mass of nuclear "explosives" [8]. Before this, a similar calculation had been made by the French physicist F. Perrin. The same summer, Leo Szilard, an immigrant physicist from Hungary who had once found employment alongside Houtermans at Britain's Electrical and Musical Instruments, advanced the idea of a heterogeneous nuclear reactor (at first – and in Germany even much later – experiments had been conducted only in a homogeneous mixture of uranium power or its oxide, and water, both normal and heavy).

Almost concurrently with the beginning of World War II, N. Bohr and D. Wheeler published what was then the most detailed theoretical analysis of the problem of fission. In the USSR, as already noted, these topics were being studied by Zeldovich and Khariton (critical mass) and Ya. I. Frenkel (the theory of nuclear fission). In Germany, W. Heisenberg became an active leader in this research. And then it was September 1939...

Before Germany's invasion of the Soviet Union, the German physicists had more or less successfully solved their "fission" problems, with Heisenberg reporting on the properties of U-235 as a material for nuclear detonation. True, it even now remains unknown whether he had calculations for, or at least a plausible idea of how to calculate, the critical mass of such explosives,[119] but at that point no

---

[119]From the Farm-Hall transcripts and other sources, see Addendum on p. 241, it is

one had anything close to accurate results. In February, Heisenberg again presented a report, at a closed meeting, this time about the possible implementation of a chain reaction with slow neutrons for energy generation. In May 1940, the Wehrmacht made its own contribution while occupying Norway, capturing the world's only plant for producing heavy water. The first tons of pure uranium material had also been received by German industry.

Later, in October 1940, the idea of a reactor began to be developed simultaneously in both Berlin and Leipzig (Heisenberg himself directly supervised this work). But by January 1941 there came an event with a "negative sign" for the German project: in the laboratory of prominent physicist W. Bothe, based on measurements made there, an unfavorable conclusion was reached about graphite as a possible moderator in the reactor [120] (not so with the Americans, for whom graphite became a primary material, based on their correct results). For the moment, this didn't slow the work of the Germans, who made do with heavy water (the plant was only later bombed in Allied air raids).

The first encouraging (but incorrect) data about critical mass were obtained in England in 1939 – by R. Peierls and O. Frisch, whom we've already encountered. The incorrect answer only prodded the British to work harder. Meanwhile, Einstein's letter on the need to start work on an atomic bomb had just reached U.S. President Franklin D. Roosevelt's desk... Yet as early as 1940, the Americans' start was yielding impressive results (the research was not yet classified). L. Turner concluded that a new element suitable for use as an explosive could take shape in the reactor, and Frisch and Peierls maintained that only a kilogram of it would be needed, if pure uranium-235 were used. After words came deeds – in mid-1940, the American scientists P. Abelson and E. McMillan obtained the first transuranium element, neptunium (albeit in trace amounts)

known that Heisenberg made a mistake in his wartime evaluation of the critical mass. Neither his colleagues nor Heisenberg himself bothered to verify the critical mass calculation in earnest until the news of the Hiroshima bombing came.

[120] Due to a gross mistake. The graphite used by the Bothe team in their experiments was not pure enough.

and hypothesized that namely neptunium is yielded by plutonium decay.

Yet another encouraging result was obtained in December 1940 – in England, F. Simon proposed a method for separating uranium isotopes in order to yield a lighter isotope – U-235 – via gas diffusion. Germany, however, had its own inventor of this method: Gustav Hertz![121]

Events involving Houtermans developed as follows.

In the first month of 1941, Houtermans, in a personal, confidential interview with Weizsäcker, informed him of his work and said he was not disclosing anything related to building nuclear weapons. Weizsäcker, in turn, spoke of his own conjectures, and after discussion, both physicists concluded it was best not to tell the authorities about these prospects. This conversation receives mention in T. Powers' book *Heisenberg's War* [9]. Afterwards, Houtermans met in Berlin with Weizsäcker and Werner Heisenberg, essentially the head of the scientific side of the German uranium project. According to Powers, this meeting's participants decided to conceal the results from the authorities.

In August 1941, F. Houtermans finished his report and presented the text to Ardenne. Copies were sent to several of the physicists participating in the uranium project: W. Bothe, K. Diebner, O. Hahn, F. Strassmann, H. Geiger, and of course C. von Weizsäcker and W. Heisenberg, along with some others. The report was later discovered in the papers of the Reich Ministry of Posts – Ardenne used namely its head, his old friend Ohnesorge, to obtain funding to run his laboratory. Research on isotope separation was conducted there as well. Also in 1941, Houtermans published an article comparing the methods of separation known at that time – thermally induced gas diffusion, electrolysis, and ultracentrifuge – using the example of light isotopes.

In the fall of 1941, Houtermans visited the Technische Hochschule and spoke with its employee Otto Haksel, who was also doing ura-

---

[121]Prior to the "Alsos Mission" no one knew that G. Hertz as a "non-Aryan," would not be admitted to the German uranium project. His knowledge proved useful after the war, when he wound up in the USSR! -V.F.

nium research. It was probably from him that Houtermans learned more about the German research project, which was considered confidential. Haksel believed that technically implementing a nuclear chain reaction for weaponry would be an extremely difficult task, since nature itself produced no such reaction without human intervention.

In the U.S., the following events occurred. The main fission research results were probably obtained by March: plutonium became available in weight amounts, its properties as a fissile material were defined (by G. Seaborg and E. Segré), which opened a plutonium alternative for the Americans, and, finally, the fission cross-section of uranium was clarified, enabling a more accurate determination of its critical mass – more than eight pounds. That summer, the Americans not only established the necessary physical parameters of the fissile materials, but also conducted successful experiments for splitting uranium isotopes. After Pearl Harbor (December 7, 1941), the U.S. government had no further doubts as to whether to build or not build an atomic bomb.

Then came February 26, 1942 – an important date in the history of the German uranium project.

In Berlin, Werner Heisenberg spoke before a gathering of scientists and leading representatives of government and military institutions. Here is an important excerpt from his secret report, published in August 1995 in the American journal *Physics Today* [10].

"As soon as such a machine is in operation, the question of how to obtain explosive material, according to an idea of [Carl Friedrich] von Weizsäcker, takes a new turn. In the transmutation of the uranium in the machine, a new substance comes into existence, element 94, which very probably – just like U-235 – is an explosive of equally unimaginable force. This substance is much easier to obtain from uranium than U-235, however, since it can be separated from uranium by chemical means." [122]

---

[122] Now knowing the events on both sides of the "scientific front," we can say that by this point, the German project had started lagging that of the United States: in March 1942 R. Oppenheimer and G. Breit finally identified the critical mass of nuclear explosives. -V.F.

Notably, Heisenberg mentions only Weizsäcker, not Houtermans – perhaps to avoid revealing his contact with an "uninitiated" man still being monitored by the Gestapo.

Houtermans found himself in a unique situation. Building on his early ideas of 1932, which had been more like "technical dreams," he had made a fundamentally significant discovery, yet showed no interest in its realization. On the contrary, the situation motivated him to take extremely risky steps, as will be outlined in the following chapters.

As for his fellow physicists from the Uranium Society, they experienced their "moment of truth" on August 6, 1945, upon learning of the explosion of the atomic bomb at Hiroshima, while interned by the Allies at Farm Hall – the headquarters of British Intelligence, near Cambridge. In the secret recordings of their conversations [11], among more than a dozen physicists mentioned in discussions of the German uranium project, Houtermans' name never came up. Yet another of his discoveries had dropped out of scientific circulation for the time being.

References

1. L. A. Turner, "Nuclear Fission," *Rev. Mod. Phys.*, Vol. 12, p. 1-29.
2. Dieter Hoffmann, *Viktor J. Frenkel, Professor Friedrich Houtermans: Arbeit, Leben, Schicksal. Biographie eines Physikers des zwanzigsten Jahrhunderts Herausgegeben und ergänzt von Dieter Hoffmann, unter Mitwirkung von Mary Beer*, Report No. 414 of the Max-Planck-Institut für Wissenschaftsgeschichte, Berlin, 2011, in German.
3. I. B. Khriplovich, "Zvezdy i Ternii Friedricha Houtermansa", *Priroda*, 1991, Issue 7, pp. 86-91, in Russian; English translation: Iosif B. Khriplovich, "The Eventful Life of Fritz Houtermans", *Physics Today*, 1992, Volume 45, Issue 7, pp. 29-37.
4. See, for example, the book by Leo Szilard: *His Version of the Facts*, Eds. S. R. Weart and G. W. Szilard, (The MIT Press, Cambridge, Mass., and London, England, 1978).
5. David Irving, *The Virus House*, (London, Kimber, 1967); Russian-language edition, Moscow, Atomizdat, 1969.
6. Charles Frank, *Operation Epsilon. The Farm-Hall Transcripts*, (Bristol and Philadelphia, Institute of Physics Publishing, University of California Publishing, 1993);
Jeremy Bernstein, *Hitler's Uranium Club: The Secret Recordings at Farm Hall*, (Copernicus, 2000).

7. M. von Ardenne, *Ein Glückliches Leben für Technik und Forschung*, (Zürich und München, Kinder Verlag, 1972). After the war, M. von Ardenne participated in projects leading to the creation of nuclear weapons in the Soviet Union.

8. S. Flügge, *Kann der Energienhalt der Atomkerne technisch nutzbar gemacht werben?*, *Die Naturwissenschaften*, 27. Jg. 1939. pp. 402-410.

9. T. Powers, *Heisenberg's War*, (Alfred Knopf, New York, 1993).

10. W. Heisenberg, *Lecture on Bomb Physics*, *Physics Today*, 1995, v. 48, No. 8, p. 27-30.

11. See *Operation Epsilon*, Ref. [6]. The events referenced here are covered in greater detail in V. Ya. Frenkel's article (co-authored by B. B. Diakov) "Operation Epsilon, or the End of the German Uranium Project," published after his death in the journal *Zvezda*, $N^{\underline{o}}$5, 1997.

"They should Accelerate..."

A few words about the German uranium project may enable a better understanding of the events to be described. After the puzzle of why German physicists made no serious efforts to build nuclear weapons, with many leading figures simply leaving the stage, there remains a more tangible inquiry, with an opportunity, in this case, to base answers on solid evidence, never again to be lost. This is the question of what the project's German participants saw as the major scientific (not only technical) problems in developing nuclear weapons.

Firstly, no one will dispute the view that creating an atomic bomb means being able calculate the critical mass of its "explosive." In Germany, as of the beginning of the project, only one paper relevant to the subject is known to have existed – the aforementioned article by Flügge, who became a Uranium Society member. Neither he, nor anyone else, including Heisenberg, either made such calculations or elaborated on what was known at least through available printed sources. No matter what anyone might say, the Germans never did this – as the August 6, 1945, moment of truth at Farm Hall proves irrefutably, as do further recordings of eavesdropped conversations.

Accordingly, the second problem in atomic bomb design, the isotope separation with the aim of accumulation of the necessary amount of U-235, effectively faded away: after all, the necessary amount of U-235 remained unknown. At the same time, the project's ideologists had a quite realistic idea of the scale of the scientific and technical work that would be needed. It was no accident that at Farm Hall, Heisenberg and others among his colleagues expressed the view that during the war, no one would have dared submit a government proposal for the multi-million dollar implementation of any of the methods in the other side's research.

The achievement of a "German-crafted" plutonium alternative, about which little more is known than the previous chapter relates, was unrealistic not only because the main developer – Houtermans himself – was, as it turned out, far from inclined to support this. From a purely scientific standpoint, many more things would still

have needed discovery, including the physical properties of plutonium that make it essential, as we now know, to use an implosion
method (internal explosion) in a plutonium-driven bomb. There was
no formulation of this problem, nor could there have been, although
German physicists probably could have managed to solve it.

There remained a third problem, which basically everyone was in
fact working on during the war – that of building a "uranium machine" for obtaining a controlled chain reaction. Houtermans saw
this machine as a source of plutonium, while other scientists, led
by Heisenberg, viewed it more as a source of energy. In this case,
the course that was chosen was correct but unfeasible: a reactor using natural uranium, with heavy water as a moderator. It would
seem that the failure to address another problem – the creation of
a uranium-graphite reactor – stemmed simply from an experimental error causing graphite to be ruled out as a moderator material.
Accordingly, E. Fermi's 1942 triumph could not have been repeated
by the Germans, even in principle. But this leads us away from the
matter of Houtermans – he wasn't researching that problem...

Robert Jungk, in his *Brighter than a Thousand Suns*, quotes the
following statement by Houtermans, apparently from one of their
many conversations [123] during the book's preparation: "When faced
with a totalitarian regime, every man should have the courage to
commit high treason."

Various witnesses attest to Houtermans realizing his principle.
Among them, the most important source of information was the
German physicist Friedrich Reiche. As it happened, after Reiche's
return to Berlin from Breslau, where he had taught at the university,
he failed to leave Germany in time, unlike many of his "non-Aryan"
colleagues. But in the spring of 1941, he had a chance to emigrate to
the United States (Germany closed its borders to Jewish emigrants
in May 1941). Laue knew of Reiche's planned departure. He made
Houtermans aware of this chance to send word to his family, who by
then had moved from England to the United States. The very day

---

[123]In the German original [1]: "Einem totalitären Regime gegenüber muss jeder
anständige Mensch den Mut besitzen, Hochverrat zu begehen."

before his departure, Reiche met with Houtermans – not a personal acquaintance of his before, but vouched for by Laue's recommendation. Houtermans' message had nothing to do with family affairs. As Reiche recalled [2] in an interview 20 years later (March 30, 1962), Houtermans requested that he contact their colleagues in the U.S.:

> Please remember if you come over, to tell the interested people the following thing. We are trying here hard, including Heisenberg, to hinder the idea of making the bomb. But the pressure from above... Please say all this; that Heisenberg will not be able to withstand longer the pressure from the government to go very earnestly and seriously into the making of the bomb. And say to them, say they should accelerate, if they have already begun the thing.

About two weeks later, Reiche and his family safely reached America, where he was welcomed at the home of Professor R. Ladenburg (a student of Roentgen), whom Reiche had known for a long time, having himself worked for Roentgen at one time in Munich. Within a few days' time, Reiche shared Houtermans' message with a gathering of about a dozen physicists. Among those Reiche recalled as present were E. Wigner, W. Pauli, H. Bethe and J. von Neumann. "I saw," he says in the same interview, "that they listened attentively and took it. They didn't say anything but were grateful."

At that time (April 1941) E. Wigner was the only one among the guests who was already involved in the atomic bomb project,[124] but that was enough – Wigner worked closely with E. Fermi.

Some time later, Wigner received another message from Houtermans, this time addressed to him directly. In his memoirs [3], published in 1992, Wigner writes:

> One day while we were working at the Met Lab,[125] a telegram reached us from a fine theoretical physicist named Fritz

---

[124]Some of them worked for the Manhattan Project later on. -V.F.

[125]The Metallurgical Laboratory, the Chicago-based American nuclear research center where in late 1942 the world's first nuclear reactor was launched, with the development the theory of heterogenous nuclear reactors credited to E. Wigner himself – V.F.

Houtermans. Houtermans understood fission; he also knew Heisenberg quite well. Houtermans wrote from Switzerland: "Hurry up. We are on the track."

Apparently Houtermans had entrusted this information to one of his close friends who had an opportunity to travel to neutral Switzerland. The warning reached its intended destination...

Of course, this act was extraordinary. In the context of Nazi Germany, with its ubiquitous surveillance and hypertrophic cautiousness, if not cowardice, it took true courage for Houtermans to propose such a mission, and no less for Reiche to accept. Reiche could have been detained, and no one knows what might have come of that. Not to mention that he could taken Houtermans to be simply a provocateur (although in this case the recommendation from ultra-honest Laue probably did its work). The same also holds true with regard to sending the telegrams.[126]

Until long after the war, these important episodes were not known either to a wide circle of physicists or to historians of science. Professor Friedrich Hernek was among the first to call attention to them [4]. Moreover, the fact of Houtermans' communication with the Americans was important not only for him but also for its impact in speeding up the Manhattan Project. This issue is discussed in the already-cited book by Powers.

Editor's Addendum

It is undeniable and well-documented that Fritz Houtermans indeed showed no desire – nor had he any means – to help Hitler's regime to acquire the nuclear bomb. As for Heisenberg's role in this story, it is ambiguous, to say the least.

From the early postwar years till 2002 most historians of science followed a theory according to which the team led by Heisenberg

---

[126]Recall the popular Soviet television series *Seventeen Moments of Spring*'s episode depicting all that came of an attempt to transmit important information through absent-minded Professor Pleischner (a role brilliantly played by Yevgeniy Yevstigneyev). And this was not a movie, but life itself! -V.F.

deliberately sabotaged the German nuclear project, accounting for its failure. This myth can be traced back to a letter Heisenberg sent to Robert Jungk, see [1]. Thomas Powers, who wrote [5] the monumental treatise *Heisenberg's War*, was an ardent proponent of this theory. Victor Frenkel refers to Powers' monograph in his book.

What changed in 2002?

It was known that in 1941 Heisenberg visited Bohr in Copenhagen. They had a private conversation. No details of this conversation were available to historians of science, which gave rise to unlimited speculations. In 2002 a letter written by Bohr to Heisenberg around 1957, sealed in the Bohr personal archive, was made available to the public. To my mind, this letter leaves no basis for the myth of sabotage. This conclusion seems to be shared by historians in more recent publications. In particular, Robert Jungk himself no longer stands behind the interpretation of his 1956 book. Moreover, he accused [6] von Weizsäcker, whose interviews were a source for his book, of misleading him, and Heisenberg of confirming von Weizsäcker's claims:

> I accuse a few [eyewitnesses], who even today are respected by the public, of conscious distortion of his tory by means of deliberate misrepresentations and – I do not even hesitate to use this devastating word – the occasional lie. [...] It was Carl Friedrich von Weizsäcker who described to me very forcefully that the German scientists did not want to build the atomic bomb. At that time he used the expression "passivists" to describe this circle of people.

Because of its importance for the history of science, I quote here Bohr's letter [7] in full:

> Dear Heisenberg,
>
> I have seen a book, "Stærkere end tusind sole" ["Brighter than a thousand suns"] by Robert Jungk [1], recently published in Danish, and I think that I owe it to you to tell you that I am greatly amazed to see how much your memory has deceived you in your letter to the author of the book, excerpts of which are printed in the Danish edition.

Personally, I remember every word of our conversations, which took place on a background of extreme sorrow and tension for us here in Denmark. In particular, it made a strong impression both on Margrethe and me, and on everyone at the Institute that the two of you spoke to, that you and Weizsäcker expressed your definite conviction that Germany would win and that it was therefore quite foolish for us to maintain the hope of a different outcome of the war and to be reticent as regards all German offers of cooperation. I also remember quite clearly our conversation in my room at the Institute, where in vague terms you spoke in a manner that could only give me the firm impression that, under your leadership, everything was being done in Germany to develop atomic weapons and that you said that there was no need to talk about details since you were completely familiar with them and had spent the past two years working more or less exclusively on such preparations. I listened to this without speaking since [a] great matter for mankind was at issue in which, despite our personal friendship, we had to be regarded as representatives of two sides engaged in mortal combat. That my silence and gravity, as you write in the letter, could be taken as an expression of shock at your reports that it was possible to make an atomic bomb is a quite peculiar misunderstanding, which must be due to the great tension in your own mind. From the day three years earlier when I realized that slow neutrons could only cause fission in Uranium 235 and not 238, it was of course obvious to me that a bomb with certain effect could be produced by separating the uraniums. In June 1939 I had even given a public lecture in Birmingham about uranium fission, where I talked about the effects of such a bomb but of course added that the technical preparations would be so large that one did not know how soon they could be overcome. If anything in my behavior could be interpreted as shock, it did not derive from such reports but rather from the news, as I had to understand it, that Germany was participating vigorously in a race to be the first with atomic weapons.

Besides, at the time I knew nothing about how far one had already come in England and America, which I learned only the following year when I was able to go to England after being informed that the German occupation force in Denmark had made preparations for my arrest.

All this is of course just a rendition of what I remember clearly from our conversations, which subsequently were naturally the subject of thorough discussions at the Institute and with other trusted friends in Denmark. It is quite another matter that, at that time and ever since, I have always had the definite impression that you and Weizsäcker had arranged the symposium at the German Institute, in which I did not take part myself as a matter of principle, and the visit to us in order to assure yourselves that we suffered no harm and to try in every way to help us in our dangerous situation.

This letter is essentially just between the two of us, but because of the stir the book has already caused in Danish newspapers, I have thought it appropriate to relate the contents of the letter in confidence to the head of the Danish Foreign Office and to Ambassador Duckwitz.

From this letter it seems clear that Heisenberg's team worked in earnest to make the bomb. They failed not because they sabotaged the project, but because they were not qualified to solve the problems that arose in the course of their work. I mentioned already a fatal mistake in Bothe's experiment (see footnote 120 on page 233). As for the critical mass calculation, this issue is discussed in great detail in Jeremy Bernstein's paper "Heisenberg and the Critical Mass" [8]. I will try to summarize the main points of this paper as follows.

The 1939 wartime report [written by Heisenberg] is called "Die Möglichkeit der technische Energiegewinnung aus der Uranspaltung" – "The possibility of the technical use of the energy gained from uranium fission," see [9]. In this report Heisenberg derives a rather crude formula for the critical mass. No numerical estimates were presented. Using the Heisenberg formula one can obtain the critical radius and the corresponding mass, 31 cm and approximately one ton, respectively.[127] These numbers agree with the first estimate Heisenberg presented to his colleagues at Farm Hall (see below). In 1940 Karl Wirtz heard Heisenberg commenting on this calculation.

Figure 29.   Farm Hall, circa 1945. Ten German physicists – Erich Bagge, Kurt Diebner, Walther Gerlach, Otto Hahn, Paul Harteck, Werner Heisenberg, Horst Korsching, Max von Laue, Carl Friedrich von Weizsäcker, and Karl Wirtz – were interned here from July 3, 1945, to January 3, 1946.

The Farm Hall was bugged so that conversations of all detainees were recorded and transcribed. On August 6, 1945, the detained German physicists learned that a new weapon had been dropped on Hiroshima. They did not believe that it was nuclear.

When they finally were persuaded that it was, they began trying to explain it. That evening, Otto Hahn and Heisenberg had a conversation. Heisenberg gave Hahn an estimate based on the

---

[127]I.e. approximately 50 times larger than the actual value of the critical mass.

data concerning the Hiroshima explosion published in newspapers. Heisenberg reasoned as follows. He knew that the Hiroshima explosion was about equivalent to 15,000 tons of TNT, and he knew that this amount corresponded to the fission of about 1 kg of uranium. Then he estimated that this would require about eighty generations of fissions assuming that two neutrons are emitted per fission. He then assumed that during this process the neutrons flow out to the boundary in a random walk of eighty steps with a step length equal to the mean free path for fission. This gave him a critical radius of 54 cm and a critical mass of several tons. (The correct estimate would give 15-20 kg.)

On August 14, 1945, Heisenberg gave a lecture on this subject at Farm Hall to the other nine detainees. From his August 14 lecture one can infer that he had finally understood the basics of the problem. This time Heisenberg derived a reasonable critical mass of 15 kg.

Then Bernstein continues:

There is one especially surreal aspect of this discussion that took place after the second bomb was dropped on Nagasaki. The mass of material for this bomb was given in news reports and it seemed too small. The Germans indulged in all sorts of wild speculations as to why this was so. It never occurred to them that the Nagasaki bomb was made of plutonium, despite the fact that von Weizsäcker, who had introduced the idea of transuranics into the German program, was in the audience.

To have admitted that plutonium was used was to admit that the Allies had a vast reactor development and that everything the German scientists had worked on for so long and so hard had been insignificant. Heisenberg's lecture, which represented the high water mark of the German understanding of nuclear weapons, shows that in the end they understood very little.

Prior to Hiroshima the Germans were absolutely convinced on the basis of their own experience that a nuclear bomb could not be built in the immediate future. Their belief was based on the idea of their superiority: they were absolutely convinced that they were ahead of everyone else in their study of nuclear chain reaction. Because they had not been able to build a nuclear reactor, they were sure that no one else had done so. These points are made very explicitly in the Farm Hall transcripts.

References

1. Robert Jungk, *Heller als tausend Sonnen. Das Schicksal der Atomforscher*, (Stuttgart, 1956), in German.
2. *Oral History Transcript Program*, American Institute of Physics (AIP), http://www.aip.org/history-programs
3. *The Recollections of Eugene P. Wigner as told to Andrew Szanton*, (Plenum Press: N.Y. and London, 1992), p. 241.
4. F. Hernek, "Eine alarmierende Botschaft," *Spektrum*, Januar 1976, pp. 32-34, in German.
5. Thomas Powers, *Heisenberg's War: The Secret History of the German Bomb*, (Knopf, 1993).
6. Mark Walker, "Physics and Propaganda: Werner Heisenberg's Foreign Lectures under National Socialism," *Historical Studies in the Physical and Biological Sciences*, Vol. 22, No. 2 (1992), pp. 339-389.
7. Niels Bohr Archive, Draft of letter from Bohr to Heisenberg, never sent. In the handwriting of Niels Bohr's assistant, Aage Petersen.
8. J. Bernstein, "Heisenberg and the Critical Mass, *American Journal of Physics*, 70 , 911 (2002).
9. W. Heisenberg *Gesammelte Werke/Collected Works*, Eds. W. Blum, H. P. Dürr, and H. Rechenberg (Springer, Berlin, 1989), Ser. A, Pt. II. p. 378.

Back in Kharkov

On October 24, 1941, German troops captured Kharkov. This had tremendous consequences for F. Houtermans. The authorities certainly remembered that he had spent several years there, studying not just anything at all, but namely nuclear physics. The bureaucratic machine may have done its job again. Houtermans himself may have wanted to get out of Berlin, as a way to extricate himself from involvement in implementing his own ideas. In any case, Houtermans reappeared in Kharkov, but now as a representative of the German government. What then transpired makes it possible to conclude that he also went to Kharkov with his own agenda.

It also ought to be said that scientists are not uncommonly sent into an occupied country which has great scientific and technical potential. In occupying France, the Germans were well aware, for instance, of the benefits they might obtain for their uranium project. A "mission" was dispatched to Paris to see to the "capitalization" of France's leading nuclear laboratories. Kharkov was similarly known to the Germans as a city of science, and the "mission" sent there may have had the same purpose, as indicated by former "Kharkovite" F. Houtermans' involvement from the outset.

In Kharkov, the following events occurred. In late October 1941, a tiny crew of UPTI employees who for one reason or another had not evacuated went out at lunchtime into the courtyard adjacent to the institute building. By that time, a new institute director had already been appointed: a certain Ebert, a chemist, a native of Riga and a graduate of that city's Polytechnical Institute.[128] Suddenly

---

[128]The Editor was unable to firmly establish the first name of Oberingenieur Ebert. According to S. L. Kudelko, see [1], it could have been Julius Ebert, the elder son of German experimental physicist, engineer and textbook writer Hermann Ebert (tentatively). The very existence of Oberingenieur Ebert and his role at UPTI under the German occupation is confirmed by German archive documents. In the book by Stefan Alker, Christina Köstner, and Markus Stumpf [2] one can find the following passage (p. 313): "Important physical-technical devices and the UPTI library were transported to Munich to a Luftwaffe research center under the command of Chief Engineer (Oberingenieur) Ebert," with the reference to the Documents BA-MA, RW 31/528, Zahlreiche Fernschreiben und Aktenvermerke der Wirtschaftsinspektion Süd zwischen dem 25.6 und 26.8.1943. See

those present saw a group of SS uniform-clad motorcyclists ride into the courtyard, and in one of the men they recognized their former colleague, Professor Houtermans.

At UPTI he was thought to have long since disappeared in prison or a labor camp, and seeing him alive and healthy was amazing in itself. But in occupied Kharkov and, on top of it all, in an SS officer's uniform – that was incredible! This episode largely determined the prevailing Soviet attitude toward Houtermans. One can cite, for instance, the memoirs of USSR Academy of Sciences corresponding member S. E. Frish, who first met Houtermans in Germany before the war. In a book dedicated to the memory of the fallen Shubnikov, he wrote [3]:

> During the war, when Kharkov was under German occupa-
> tion, the following happened: Houtermans, the same man
> who had so vividly described his persecution by the Nazis,
> showed up at the institute in an SS uniform... He came with
> orders to assume responsibility for running the institute. The
> institute was almost empty. An overwhelming number of the
> employees had been evacuated... Throughout the entire Ger-
> man occupation, Houtermans remained the institute's direc-
> tor. This was, in all probability, the one case that was truly
> criminal. What's more, in 1937 Houtermans hadn't yet been
> exposed; back then, he was only sent back to Germany, along
> with other Germans.

Unfortunately, Frish never verified this information, compiling these memoirs based on the testimony of others who also had no adequate knowledge of the facts. First, Houtermans, as we know, didn't stay "unexposed," but spent 2.5 years in Soviet prisons. He wasn't just "sent back" but was expelled after being sentenced as an "undesirable foreigner," and he was sent into the hands of the Gestapo despite his pleas to be allowed to go to Sweden or any other country. Second, he was in occupied Ukraine for a little more than a month, and not "throughout the occupation." It is true that he

---

also Addendum on p. 258.

became the institute's acting director, but immediately after his departure he was replaced, with Ebert becoming director again. A few words, too, about Houtermans' SS uniform.

Documents from German archives indicate that Houtermans was sent on the "mission" under the Luftwaffe, and it's not impossible that he was wearing a military uniform. (Houtermans himself, in 1947, claimed that in Kharkov and later in Kiev he wore only civilian clothes.) But of course what's more important is not the uniform [129] but the content of what Houtermans was doing in Ukraine.

Certainly, in October 1941, the institute employees had few grounds to believe that Houtermans had come for a friendly visit. Houtermans' task was to assess the state of UPTI's nuclear research program: who among the employees from those laboratories had stayed in Kharkov, and which equipment hadn't been removed and might be used in Germany.

What are the facts? The UPTI equipment remaining in Kharkov was not taken to Germany. This held true for the large van der Graaff accelerator – the pride of the Kharkov nuclear physicists – as well as for its smaller counterpart. Significantly, at this same time, there were plans in Germany to build this very same kind of accelerator, and moreover, on a smaller scale than at UPTI – 1 million volts compared to 2.5 million for UPTI's larger accelerator. Moreover, none of the UPTI staff underwent deportation to Germany.

In February 1992, in Kharkov, the author met with Ukrainian Academy of Sciences corresponding member A. P. Klyucharev. He said that Houtermans, in his short time at UPTI in October-November 1941, generously furnished the remnant of the Kharkov physicists with certificates stating that they were working on Luftwaffe orders. This served to safeguard the certificates' bearers from being shipped off to Germany. Alexei Pavlovich had seen Houtermans at UPTI many times before the war, but not during the occupation. He said, though, that Houtermans had indirectly played a critical role in his life. This happened as follows.

---

[129]It is known that many Soviet experts, including scientists engaged in the nuclear project, were sent to occupied Germany and wore Ministry of Internal Affairs uniforms

Figure 30.   In occupied Kharkov, 1942.

Because food in Kharkov was hard to come by, the townspeople exchanged their belongings for food in the surrounding villages. The longer the occupation lasted, the farther they had to travel from Kharkov for this purpose. Klyucharev and UPTI physicist M. D. Borisov [130] agreed to embark on a joint foraging outing that would take them more than 25 kilometers outside the city. Leaving the 25 kilometer zone required a pass from the town council. They agreed to meet on the square in front of the State Industry Building, not far from the council headquarters. As their meeting place, they chose the gigantic flower bed in the middle of the square. Klyucharev left home early on the morning of November 14 and immediately found the streets full of German soldiers, with almost no townspeople in sight. He reached the prearranged spot, which Borisov approached as well. The following conversation took place between them.

---

with fairly high-rank insignias -V.F.

[130] Mikhail Borisov (1903-1960) began working at UPTI in 1934. In 1956, he became head of the laboratory. One of his papers was a collaboration with I. V. Kurchatov -V.F.

Figure 31. In occupied Kharkov, 1942.

Borisov: "I was hoping you wouldn't come." "Why?" "Didn't you hear what happened?" "No." "The mansion where the top-ranking German officers were staying was blown up.[131] Some people were killed. They're rounding up people in the city. We can't go anywhere, we've got to get home."

They tried to head homeward, but the huge square was already cordoned off. All documents were checked, and most of the townspeople were sent to the International Hotel building. Borisov and Klyucharev also reached the cordon. Mikhail Dmitrievich Borisov presented his certificate, signed by Houtermans: "The bearer is working on orders from Luftwaffe-Kommando." The soldier nodded him past. "And he's with me," Borisov pointed to Klyucharev. This got them through the cordon on November 14, a day when more than 2,000 people in Kharkov were arrested. Toward evening, detainees were lined up on the square, and every tenth person was executed.

---

[131]The explosion of the mansion on Sumska Street in Kharkov, triggered by radio signal from Voronezh, is described in Yu. Medvedev's report "On That Day" in the anthology *The Way into the Unknown* [4]. The explosion killed the chief of Kharkov's German garrison, Georg von Braun (brother of rocket scientist Wernher von Braun) -V.F.

Scaffolds with the victims of fascist terror were erected all the way down Sumska and Sverdlov Streets. "So Houtermans, without knowing it, saved my life!" said Alexei Pavlovich, completing his story.

Over time, other evidence, in this case documentary, has surfaced about Houtermans' "mission" activities. These are presented most fully in A. Kramish's book *The Griffin* [5]. According to Kramish, who had access to documents from the American "Alsos" mission in Germany, Houtermans, although sent to Kharkov as a Luftwaffe representative, in fact got the assignment from the Department of the Navy. The head of the department of naval artillery was General-Admiral Carl Witzel.[132] Houtermans had been introduced to him as a specialist in nuclear physics. After learning more about Houtermans' work, Witzel sent him to the occupied territories. In Kharkov, Houtermans surveyed the UPTI laboratories and spoke with the employees. He outlined the results of his activities in a report, which has been preserved.[133] Given the importance of these documents for F. Houtermans' reputation, we will examine them in detail. Houtermans' official report is entitled "An evaluation of the qualifications, political opinions and current situation of physicists, engineers and technical personnel in Soviet Russia (Sowjetrussland)." The report contains a general overview of Soviet science (the "Qualifications" section), with a high assessment of specialists in physics and mathematics (N. N. Luzin and A. F. Ioffe are among those given special mention), a description of the internal situation in the country (the "Effects of Politics" section), with this conclusion: "The young and capable intellectuals are absolutely convinced of the correctness of the Soviet system (Sowjetsystem), and blame the terror and material deprivation not on the system but on Stalin and his henchmen."

---

[132]In the Kramish book, among the people who enabled Houtermans' participation in the "mission," mention is made of Rompe and Rosbaud, already encountered in these pages. Given that the latter, at least, is well-known as a member of the Resistance, it's not impossible that Houtermans was led to them along these lines. C. Witzel's department was also working on magnetic mines. Using his acquaintance with Witzel, P. Rosbaud also relayed other information to British intelligence (through Scandinavia) -V.F.

[133]A. Kramish graciously provided the author with a copy of this report in English translation -V.F.

In the next section, "Science and technology professionals remaining in the occupied territory, and their attitude towards us," Houtermans gives a rough estimate of the number of scientists and technicians left in Ukraine: 10 percent of the pre-war number of researchers, and 80 to 90 percent of the technical workers with higher and secondary qualifications. At the same time, university employees, in his opinion, had mostly abandoned their research. He reports that evacuation to the East had often been forced, and that the science and technology employees from certain institutes in Kiev and Kharkov had resisted the destruction of their plants and equipment during the evacuation. Houtermans obviously assesses their loyalties from a standpoint that he himself shares. In a supplement to the report (and only there), three groups of researchers are listed, respectively relating to three academic institutions in Kiev and Kharkov: scientists, technicians and teachers, but with only eight specific names provided. Houtermans immediately emphasizes that he is unable to judge the extent of their willingness to cooperate with the Germans.

Let's try asking ourselves: what ought the report to have said, if the author wanted to save his former colleagues and laboratory equipment? If he had characterized them as anti-fascists, wouldn't that have meant signing their death warrants? Hence the elliptical formulation that they were not enemies of the Soviet system but were strongly opposed to Stalin and therefore had no wish to be evacuated to the East. For Houtermans it was clear that if they were perceived as valuable, they might be removed to Germany. He therefore stays muted in gauging their qualifications, stating that there are no important specialists among those left behind. The implicit conclusion: leave them alone.

With a cover letter and no commentary, the report was sent to ministerial director Rudolf Mentzel at the Imperial Research Council (which, as already noted, oversaw all research projects in Germany). This happened in the wake of the February 26, 1942, council meeting, so fateful for the uranium project. Mentzel's decision on the lot of Soviet scientists in the occupied territory is worth citing:

Imperial Research Council,
March 31, 1942
Secret!

Dear General-Admiral!

I have received and carefully studied your report and highly important proposals on the issue of possible involvement of Russian scientists and engineers in research development, as outlined in your letter of March 13. The current position of the Research Council is that all research activity must focus entirely on resolving state issues associated with the war, and that therefore this work must be secret. Under these circumstances, the feasibility of using Russian personnel is highly doubtful. In addition, the German security service would be unable to provide the required security guarantees for potentially eligible persons. Finally, at present, there are also difficulties associated with determining the whereabouts of these persons, because only in very rare cases can one hope to find them at their former workplaces.

The letter goes on to express considerations about using such people only to train qualified personnel in educational institutions in the occupied territories – the Baltic States and Western Ukraine. As for equipment at the research institutes examined by Houtermans, the letter gives this no mention. We can thus say that Houtermans acted in the interests of his colleagues, whom he esteemed, not conflating them with his torturers in Soviet prisons.

Undoubtedly, the Kharkov van der Graaff generator would have bolstered the German project.[134] What did Houtermans' former colleagues see after returning from evacuation? Here is a short excerpt from V. S. Kogan's book [6] *His Name was K. D.* (about K. D. Sinelnikov, an Academician of the Ukrainian Academy of Sciences and the postwar director of UPTI):

The main building had been blown up .... The staircase and

---

[134]In a conversation with the author of this book, Academician B. G. Lazarev said that indeed, not all of UPTI's valuable equipment was evacuated to the East -V.F.

the central part of the building had collapsed, but the side wings were intact... In the High-Voltage Building there was also an explosive device with an aerial bomb..., but it hadn't detonated... Dirt, desolation, ruins were everywhere. Yet the electrostatic generator stood in its place by the discharge tube. And the globe, as it should, was resting on the support columns.

Having been in Kharkov only in the first months of the occupation, Houtermans was not involved in the destruction– it was carried out by the Germans before they abandoned Kharkov, which Soviet troops liberated on August 23, 1943. Neither the staff nor the institute's equipment were taken to Germany, and these two factors speak in Houtermans' favor, although this has long been debated by both Soviet and Western scholars. In this regard, we consider it necessary to expand our narrative with a few episodes and documents from a later period. The participation of German scientists in the "development" of the occupied territories, according to the plans of the Reich leadership, included two "components": direct management of scientific institutions, and adaptation of their activity to the needs of the Reich – whether "in the field" or by removing equipment and science personnel to Germany. Namely this was the task put to Houtermans and the participants in his "mission." There are at least two widely known similar examples involving F. Houtermans' colleagues and acquaintances, prominent German physicists.

The first was an attempt to adapt the equipment and staff of the College de France and the Radium Institute to the needs of the German uranium project. The participants in this physics "mission," Walther Bothe and Wolfgang Gentner, acted in much the same manner as Houtermans, and neither employees nor equipment were removed. There is evidence that they, especially, W. Gentner, who stayed in France for over a year, did so not under duress, but quite intentionally, out of a desire to help his French colleagues.

The second case pertains to a trip to Copenhagen by German scientists participating in the uranium project. Events there were no less dramatic than in Kharkov, so is no matter of indifference to know how Houtermans' colleagues behaved under the circumstances.

In January 1944, in the wake of Niels Bohr's and his family's dramatic flight from Denmark to Sweden (on the night of September 30) along with thousands of Danish Jews who were threatened with extermination,[135] the Bohr Institute was occupied by the Germans. Prior to this, the institute had retained the semblance of independence, with no direct German intervention as yet, and the staff had been left untouched.

But then came the arrest of Jorgen Boggild, who had stayed on as the institute's director after Bohr's departure. Of course, the institute staff understood that their German colleagues weren't at all to blame, and they sought help from W. Heisenberg. Heisenberg knew of the events of January 1944 and at the last moment joined the commission traveling to Copenhagen to see to the institute's "utilization" for the needs of the Reich. The situation was made worse by the fact that after Bohr's flight from the institute, the German occupation authorities accused the institute staff of working for the Allies. There was word of a plan to make Weizsäcker the institute's director. The commission met with the leadership of the German administration in Denmark, with the same questions raised as Houtermans had been required to answer. After touring the institute along with representatives of the occupation government, Heisenberg, as the committee's most authoritative member, recommended not only leaving the high-voltage equipment and institute's cyclotron undisturbed, but also reinstating the Danish leadership. Boggild was even released. Heisenberg may have done everything that was in his power. After the war, his behavior has been positively assessed. Houtermans was less fortunate in this regard, and it took years to rehabilitate his reputation.

Another side of German scientists' activities in the occupied countries activities probably also merits interest. We'll touch on it only briefly, having no evidence of Houtermans' recruitment for this work.

This is the "cultural mission" – lectures presented for various audiences consisting mainly of science professionals, pursuing the

---

[135]In the coming days, the Jews were to have been deported to concentration camps. -V.F.

"grand purpose" of propaganda for the ideas of the Nazi Reich. Groups of lecturers were supposed to receive spontaneous and partly sincere invitations, providing opportunities for demonstrations of Germany's "cultural identity." Taking part in this unseemly activity when it was essentially foisted on him, Heisenberg traveled to Denmark, Holland, Hungary and Switzerland. Like some of his other physics colleagues, he tried to limit the scope of his lectures, choosing theoretical physics topics (as was quite natural for him). Some of his lectures were boycotted, some welcomed. Their post-war assessment has varied.[136]

Editor's Addendum

After Victor Frenkel's death new documents pertinent to the events that happened at UPTI under the German occupation were discovered. Some of these findings are discussed in my Introduction, pp. 55-57. Kharkov was under Nazi occupation from October 24, 1941, to February 16, 1943, and, for the second time, from March 15, 1943, to August 23, 1943.

Leonid Pyatigorsky's letter published by Yuri Raniuk [8]:

"I will present some verified facts concerning events during this ill-fated time. Under the German occupation UPTI was converted into a "Scientific Research Institute" which was christened "Eberti" by the employees who stayed in Kharkov. This name was related to the fact that its director was the son of Professor Ebert, a German scientist in physical chemistry. Our Nina Mikhailovna Shestopalova told me that one day all employees of *Eberti* were ordered to come to the Institute and line up on the stairs leading from the first to the second floor of the High-Voltage Building in order to meet a guest. To

---

[136]Extensive information on the subject may be found in M. Walker's "Physics and Propaganda" [7].

their great surprise, the guest who entered the building and started ascending the stairs was ... Houtermans! He shook hands with each employee and entered the office that used to belong to the UPTI Director Shpetny. Then he asked where was Shpetny. Of course, Shpetny had left Kharkov with retreating Red Army. Houtermans was in a brand-new Nazi uniform, with a military cap on. He said that he had come to Kharkov to lend a hand to the UPTI employees."

Excerpts from the deposition[137] of I. P. Korolev and G. A. Milyutin,[138] October 13, 1943, published in Collection [1]:

In March there appeared Oberingenieur Ebert. He had received his education in physical chemistry. He was 27 years old, fluent in Russian. Ebert's task was to organize scientific work of the Institute. The first laboratory he launched was the Electromagnetic Oscillation Lab. Then came Brailovsky's lab, seemingly intended to research on radioactivity... A General Mathematics Group was organized to perform calculations for Ebert. It was headed by Professor Sushkevich... and was a rather strong group. They occupied a special office and reported directly to Ebert... One of the Germans, Jansen, warned me that Ebert was a member of the National-Socialist German party, but covertly rather than overtly.

Ebert was rather soft on us. He was not a stupid person. Before his departure for Germany he said: "Farewell, be happy, and when the Reds come, tell them that there are good people among the Germans."

Damage to the Institute inflicted by retreating Germans was rather minimal. This is because it was directed by such people as Ebert. Otherwise nothing would have been left of the Institute. We had the largest Van de Graaf in Europe. They put a mine there, but it was never detonated, despite the fact that they had such an order. The most precious UPTI possession that they grabbed and moved to Munich was our library, 50 thousand volumes. It was an excellent

---

[137]Kharkov Oblast State Archive, Π2-31-17-37-43.

[138]Georgi Anatolievich Milyutin (1914-1990), Professor of Kharkov University (since 1950), Dean of the Faculty of Physics and Technology (since 1962).

library. Fortunately, a similar one, situated nearby, remained intact.

References

1. *City and War: Kharkov in the years of the Great Patriotic War*, Eds. S. M. Kudelko et al., (Aleteya, St. Petersburg, 2012, in Russian), p. 321.
2. Stefan Alker et al., *Bibliotheken in der NS-Zeit*, (Vienna University Press, 2008), in German.
3. L. V. Shubnikov, *Selected Works. Memoirs*, (Kiev, Naukova Dumka, 1990), pp. 39-44, in Russian.
4. Yu. Medvedev, "On That Day," *The Way into the Unknown*, (Moscow, Soviet Writer, 1986), pp. 39-44, in Russian.
5. A. Kramish, *The Griffin*, (Boston, Houghton Mifflin Co, 1986).
6. V.S. Kogan, *His Name was K. D.*, (Kharkov, Prapor, 1990), in Russian.
7. M. Walker, "Physics and Propaganda: Werner Heisenberg's Foreign Lectures under National Socialism," *Historical Studies in the Physical and Biological Sciences*, Vol. 22, Part 2, pp. 338-389, (1992).
8. Yuri Raniuk, "Two Books on Friedrich Houtermans," in *Victor Frenkel: Last Works, Recollections of Colleagues and Friends*, Eds. V. G. Grigoriantz et al., (Ioffe Physico-Technical Institute, St. Petersburg, 2002, in Russian), p. 254.

The Kharkov Trace

(What Happened at the Session of the Academy of Sciences)

In June 1945, the USSR Academy of Sciences held extensive celebrations of the 220th anniversary of its founding. 220 years are not a jubilee occasion, but for the jubilee's organizers, as well as for their guests, who traveled to the Soviet Union from all over the world, the event was clearly celebrating victory over fascism, proclaiming a return to pre-war traditions of international scientific cooperation. The transfigured country, whose heroic struggle against fascism had given it an unprecedented level of authority worldwide, was opening a new era of friendship and cooperation with the international scientific community.

Many physicists gathered for the festivities, which began in Moscow and continued in Leningrad. Some of the foreign guests had visited the Soviet Union before. Especially impressive was the delegation from France – spouses Frédéric and Irène Joliot-Curie, F. Perrin, P. Auger. From England came one of the founders of quantum mechanics, Max Born (who had previously been in the Soviet Union while attending the Sixth Congress of Russian Physicists in 1928, but as a representative of Germany).

In the preceding 10 years, contact with foreign scientists had been limited by technical difficulties – primarily postal – but exchange of scientific literature had continued uninterrupted. True, by the war's end, other kinds of difficulties arose. After all, it was no accident that none of the nuclear physicists invited from England and the U.S. attended.[139] In the Soviet Union, it was no secret that a number of the country's major institutes were intensely pursuing work on military applications of nuclear fission – and leading Soviet nuclear engineers' absence from the meetings held during the jubilee session

---

[139]The United States was represented by Irving Langmuir, the 1932 Nobel Prize laureate in Chemistry, and a number of less famous scientists. An extremely interesting report on Langmuir's visit to Moscow can be found in [1].

was likewise no accident.

Figure 32.   Stalin ordered the dispatch of army planes to pick up foreign guests in the countries of their residence and deliver them to Moscow, see [1]. Courtesy of ARAN.

Figure 33.   The opening session of Celebrations of the 220th anniversary of the USSR Academy of Sciences, Bolshoi Theater, June 16, 1945. Courtesy of ARAN [2].

The session included forums and official receptions for the participants, including a Kremlin reception and a chance to attend the Victory Parade. Soviet physicists welcomed their foreign guests in their homes, in a relaxed atmosphere, exchanging the latest news. What's the latest in physics? Where is this or that colleague? How is he? What's he working on? Where had people been scattered by the war that now was over?

A conversation between Max Born and Piotr Leonidovich Kapitsa turned to the fates of German physicists, among whom they recalled Houtermans – both knew him fairly well. Two years later, on November 10, 1947, Born wrote about this conversation in a letter to Ilse Ursell, secretary of the Society for the Protection of Science and Learning,[140] which, as we know, Charlotte Houtermans had recourse to during hard times:

> When I was in Moscow in 1945, Professor Kapitsa called him [Houtermans -V.F.] a traitor and said the Russians would hang him for it if they found him. He said that Houtermans had come with the German army to Kharkov, where he had previously been Professor, and had denounced his former colleagues to the Gestapo. Although I didn't believe the whole story, I thought it best to warn Houtermans about what the Russians had told me, in case he would be caught going into the Russian zone.

Toward the end of the letter, Born writes:

> Some months ago, a young Austrian physicist, Dr. B. Touschek, who is now working under Professor Dee at the University of Glasgow, came to Edinburgh [141] and said that he was a friend of Houtermans, so I told him some of what I had heard oft Houtermans. Touschek communicated with Houtermans and told him what I had reported, and he has had a reply from a letter in which he defended himself... Concerning my own opinion, I think Houtermans' explanation sounds quite credible.

Given the letter's date of November 1947, it seems that a trail of suspicion had followed F. Houtermans for a long time already, and not only in the USSR. Thus Touschek's visit to Born was no matter of chance. Born subsequently contacted the advocacy organization to report the information he had received, and expressed an opinion, as we've seen, supporting Houtermans. Apparently this was preceded by Touschek's communication with Houtermans and Born. In the interim, Houtermans wrote Touschek a letter presenting his

---

[140]Currently the Council for At-Risk Academics, CARA.
[141]M. Born taught at the University of Edinburgh from 1936 till 1952. – V.F.

arguments.[142]

Recalling his nearly three years of detention in Soviet prisons, Houtermans writes:

> I have good reason to be angry at a government that played such a cruel trick on me ... all the more so as I found that the fruits of my three years of work, the text of an article I had written, was published... with no mention of my name, as is customary there when one of the authors "disappears" (yet I don't blame the physicists; *Glavlit* [the censorship office] erases the names of the "disappeared" from titles). For my part, I lodged an unofficial protest against deleting Shubnikov's name from one of our papers. It's clear where that led. Later I was often approached about publishing memoirs of my experiences in Russia – the last time by Herr Brüche,[143] who told me he was on very good terms with the Propaganda Ministry, but I told him that could write only good things about Russian science (with which he is now again on the best of terms also), and I always refused... I accepted the proposal (to go to the occupied territories -V.F.): 1) because in my situation, my refusal would have inevitably meant a concentration camp, and 2) because I saw it as my only opportunity to provide support and protection to the institute and its personnel... I can easily imagine that, with everything I know about Russia, the NKVD organs and some people who were probably charged with collaboration because they stayed behind (in the occupied territory – V.F.) made every effort to use me as a scapegoat, and I'm not angry with them, just as I'm not angry with the Russian physicists who decided that when Born, a foreigner, came from abroad, they <u>must</u> (the

---

[142]The above-cited materials on Houtermans, which are stored in the Manuscript Division of the Bodleian Library at Oxford University, are referenced in I. B. Khriplovich's article "The Eventful Life of Fritz Houtermans," see [3]. Through the kind assistance of Professor R. Stuewer (Minneapolis, USA), the author received copies of these materials [4], including M. Born's letter, from the library archives. -V.F.

[143]Apparently, Ernst Brüche (1900-1985) who was a German physicist, pioneer in electron optics. -James Manteith

emphasis here is Houtermans' -V.F.) tell him this nonsense.

Houtermans' letter ends with this statement:

Today, as before, I have the highest esteem for Russian science and its representatives, and I feel connected with them, despite all the bitter experiences I had there, and I hope that the day will come when this relationship again will be free of all political obstacles.

It was after acquaintance with these arguments that M. Born found it necessary to voice his opinion. There are exceptional grounds, too, for why namely Bruno Touschek came to serve as a kind of mediator, and why his opinion was esteemed by interested people and by F. Houtermans himself. Bruno Touschek (born 1921) was also a Viennese. Due to his half-Jewish origins, he barely passed matriculation exams, which he had to change schools to take. For the same reason, in 1940 (the *Anschluss* of Austria already having occurred) he was expelled from the University of Vienna. Yet Touschek had attracted notice: A. Sommerfeld, the famous German physicist, in the second edition of his famous work *Atomic Structure and Spectral Lines* [6], thanked Touschek, who was still a student, for critically analyzing and finding errors in the text. Throughout the war, Touschek was based in Hamburg, where in 1945 he was arrested (in the Gestapo prison, he produced a description, writing between the lines of a book, of his idea of radiation deceleration of electrons in the betatron – an effort more than a little reminiscent of Houtermans' in Soviet prisons!). Reduced to utter exhaustion, while being taken along the streets of Hamburg en route to a concentration camp, he was simply shot. Yet the guard was in a rush, and Touschek remained alive, although he was handed over to the police again and sent to prison, where the Allies freed him.

After this he reached Göttingen and continued his scientific work. There he met F. Houtermans. In 1947, B. Touschek was invited to Glasgow as a specialist in accelerators. The above makes clear that Touschek's reputation – as a physicist and anti-fascist – had serious potential to help Houtermans' reputation among his colleagues.[144]

Another document, dating from 1945, with the Denazification Committee already actively at work, was provided to the author by the Bodleian Library. In this document, Nazi regime survivor Baroness Marie Rausch von Traubenberg relates how Houtermans supported her and her husband, and what role Houtermans played in saving her from a concentration camp. Baroness Rausch von Traubenberg was the widow of Prague University professor Heinrich Rausch von Traubenberg, who died of a heart attack during Marie's arrest in Hirschberg (Silesia)[145] in 1944. She also provides information about others helped by Houtermans in various degrees, and expresses the opinion that he ran a still greater risk, given his surveillance by the Gestapo.

The shadow of suspicion that has hung over Houtermans might have dissipated sooner had his letter to P. Blackett, written in 1945, reached its intended recipient. This was impeded by an event we will focus on later.

References

1. A. Rosenfeld, *Men of Physics: Irving Langmuir*, (Pergamon Press, 1966).
2. http://arran.ru/?q=en/exposition15_1
3. Iosif Khriplovich, *Physics Today*, 1992, Volume 45, Issue 7, pp. 29-37.
4. Special Collections, Weston Library, Bodleian Libraries, University of Oxford: MS. SPSL 330/8. fol. 573 and MS. SPSL 330/8, fols. 570-2; the full Houtermans' file from CARA can be found at MSS. SPSL 330/8, fols. 409-607.
5. E. Amaldi, *The Bruno Touschek Legacy (Vienna 1921 - Innsbruck 1978)*, CERN Yellow Report 81-19, (Geneva, 1981), available at http://ccdb5fs.kek.jp/cgi-bin/img/allpdf?198203034
6. Arnold Sommerfeld, *Atombau und Spektrallinien*, Vol. 2, 2nd Edition, (Friedrich Vieweg und Sohn, Braunschweig, 1939).

---

[144]This information is based on an article by E. Amaldi [5]. -V.F.

[145]Currently Jelenia Góra, Poland.

Who are Beck and Godin?
(The author's search)

I already had taken an interest in Houtermans and his life when, in mid-January 1991, I found myself at the Niels Bohr Archive in Copenhagen. I had also heard that apparently Houtermans had written a book with a biographical basis. In consequence, one of my first steps at the Bohr Institute was to visit its wonderful library. There I found a collection dedicated to Houtermans. But it was a memorial anthology – the result of efforts by his students, colleagues and coworkers – published in 1980 and already mentioned above. This collection includes a very good, warm piece by G. A. Gamow about his colleague.

My next step was to review the huge file of N. Bohr's correspondence. I started by making a list of Bohr's potential correspondents who interested me; they were mainly Soviet physicists, but also included Houtermans. Comparing my list with the complete list of Bohr's correspondents reminded me of studying tables of state loan awards. In my list, all the names came out "winners," including Houtermans. The first of his letters to Bohr was sent from Berlin on August 25, 1940, that is, a little more than a month after his release from the Berlin jail. Denmark had been occupied by the Germans since April 9. Like other letters from Houtermans I later saw, I found this letter interesting not only in its own right, but also as my first glimpse of the handwriting of a man I had thought about a lot – for some reason this proved a significant milestone in my work. In the letter, Houtermans thanks Bohr for tremendously helping his family, and says that he has found a way to correspond with him. He goes on to talk about his research on the theory of numbers while in Soviet prisons, and speaks of this mental exertion as a source of physical strength. The letter also contains a "Russian" motif: in a postscript, Houtermans tells Bohr that to his delight, he has learned that his Russian colleagues and friends – L. D. Landau, P. L. Kapitsa and the German Communist Fritz Lange, who had emigrated to the Soviet Union and worked in Kharkov at UPTI – have survived and are free.

Another letter to Bohr from Houtermans, sent much later, from Göttingen on February 3, 1949, contained a few odd phrases. It began in the usual way – Houtermans thanks Bohr for his greetings, conveyed to him through German physicists Hans Kopfermann [146] and J. Hans Jensen (later a Nobel laureate), who had visited Copenhagen. Houtermans then writes, "Herr Kopfermann told me about your interest in a non-physics manuscript written by two authors, one of whom is a historian and the other a physicist. These authors, writing for the time being under the pseudonyms Bernstein and Lagodin, would like to give an objective portrayal and explanation of the political situation in the Soviet Union at a certain stage in its history, while doing so otherwise than by describing escapades. On the contrary, they have attempted a historical analysis that may help in forming a certain idea of the current situation in that country."

Houtermans adds that it would be very important for him to know whether this manuscript would interest Bohr and whether it gave him an objective picture of life in the USSR, and thus whether the authors succeeded in doing so. And Houtermans finishes the letter by earnestly asking Bohr to inform him whether he has read the manuscript and what impression it's made on him.

About two weeks later, Bohr lets Houtermans know that Jensen and Kopfermann have told him about current living conditions in post-war Germany, about what life was like there during the war, and especially about Houtermans' fate. But no one at our institute, Bohr continues, has seen the manuscript Houtermans mentioned, which would of course interest Bohr greatly. Bohr adds that he would be very grateful if Houtermans could send it.

Rather strange letters, which reminded me somewhat of Max von Laue's "conspiratorial" correspondence with Houtermans' family in spring 1940!

I found neither Lagodin nor Bernstein in the library's catalog. In the evening of the same day, as I was looking through book-lined

---

[146] See page 58, footnote 37.

shelves of the room provided me for work, there happened what Pushkin, in one of his letters, called a "strange convergence," a coincidence. My attention was drawn to a small book in a gray dust-jacket, *Russian Purge and the Extraction of Confession* [1]. Its authors, F. Beck and W. Godin, were unknown to me. The book had been published in England in 1951 in English translation from a German original. On the title page I found an inscription: "To Professor Niels Bohr in gratitude and admiration from the authors. July 10, 1951." The signature of the inscription's author was missing, but I recognized the writing immediately: it was in Houtermans' hand.

With growing interest, I started leafing through the book, whose authors tell of the events of 1937 in the Soviet Union, of the arrested in those years, of the prisons where they were held, of the accusations brought against them, and of the interrogations where NKVD agents obtained confessions from the arrested.

The dust jacket went into a fair amount of detail about the book, and the publisher's note succinctly echoed the same thoughts:

> For their own safety and that of many close friends and former colleagues living in the USSR and other countries beyond the Iron Curtain, the authors must conceal their identity under pseudonyms. The authenticity of their experience has, however, been checked as well as their scientific authority, not only from their papers published in the USSR and elsewhere but also from a number of celebrated scientists, including several Nobel prize winners. Of their bona fides there can be no possible doubt.

At the very least, it sounded intriguing!

The next day I had a meeting scheduled with Professor Stefan Rozental, Niels Bohr's longtime personal assistant,[147] and a charming man, as I realized during my very first conversation with him. Despite his more than venerable age (he was then already 88 years old), he had an excellent memory and was exceptionally easy to talk

---

[147] Stefan Rozental (1903-1994) was a nuclear physicist and Niels Bohr's "right hand" for fifteen years, after Hendrik Anthony Kramers and Léon Rosenfeld.

with (like all the Danes I've ever encountered). Professor Rozental engagingly described events from his life and the people whom fate had connected him with. His perfect fluency in Russian made our interaction all the better. I remember how I phoned him at home on one of the first days after my arrival in Copenhagen and began explaining who I was, my interests and so on. After listening to me and interjecting a few words in perfect English, he added in perfect Russian, "Really, you can speak Russian with me. I was born in the Russian Empire, and attended gymnasium in Warsaw. So call me Stefan Adolfovich and, if you'd like, we can talk in Russian – it'd be my pleasure."

When Stephen Adolfovich, with his constant friendly smile, came into my room, I immediately told him about my strange discovery and some of my own conjectures about the Beck and Godin book.

"I know the book well," said Professor Rozental. "It was written by Houtermans and his Russian friend. Bohr helped him greatly with its publication. Houtermans was afraid that the Russian secret service might pursue him. Gamow was the same – for a long time after the war, he didn't risk travel to Denmark, because he saw it as too close to the Soviet Union."

The space afforded here, of course, can hardly accommodate a full survey of the Beck and Godin book's contents (we'll call them by those names for now). Here is the final paragraph of the author's preface to the book:

> This book was written by two men whom chance threw together in a Soviet prison, and is the result of months of discussion in a cell. The two authors differ in nationality, career, and outlook; and perhaps their differences made a certain objectivity easier for them. One is a historian and the other a scientist. The sharing of a professional prejudice in favor of objectivity may have been valuable in encouraging them to tabulate and check their observations carefully and to be cautious in drawing conclusions.

The book as a whole is preceded by an epigraph [148] that sounds

---

[148]This epigraph represents two lines from a popular song written by Vassily Lebedev-

all the more ironic in light of the contents: "For I know no other land where man can breathe so freely."

Now it's time to tell about the book itself, moreover in that it merits attention, as does Alexander Weissberg's *The Accused* [2], already familiar to us.

Both books can undoubtedly be regarded as forerunners to A. I. Solzhenitsyn's *Gulag Archipelago* [3], which recounts the fate of prisoners in Soviet prisons at that time.

In the book, the authors fully realize the plan their preface outlines. Primarily addressing the Western reader, they describe the Soviet Union's political situation and the Communist Party line, commencing with a brief period which they call the "lull before the storm" (1933-1937). The book's greatest value, I think, lies in its thorough and systematic analysis of the categories of persons imprisoned in 1937-38. (A. Weissberg's book contains a similar analysis.)

The book lists 22 such groups, and the account of almost every one of them includes an example of the fate of one its characteristic representatives. There is also equally detailed explication and classification of "theories" explaining the role of at least minimal logic (generally twisted) in what happened in those years. The authors heard most of these theories from the victims themselves. As a rule, the latter thought the trouble that had befallen them resulted from some awful, random error, basically a "glitch" in a good, fair system, and not as a consequence of the Party line.

The book compares detainment in Soviet prisons with the regime in Nazi prisons. At the same time, the authors draw a clear distinction between the Soviet prison butchers who led the interrogations and the guards and wardens, who are portrayed without hatred and sometimes with sympathy, as contrasted with Gestapo prison guards, who were cold, always heartless, and sometimes vicious.

Finally, beyond all these categories and theories, the fates of three prisoners are traced in detail. The narrative in this case is handled not by both authors but by one of them – in the first person. As

---

Kumach (lyrics) and Isaac Dunaevsky (music) in 1936, just before the beginning of Great Terror.

other sources have established, the first fate described is that of one of the authors – the one whom the preface refers to as an historian. To tell his tale, let's return to Houtermans' dismal prison odyssey, to his time of incarceration in Kiev in 1938. It was namely there that the theory of numbers helped Houtermans survive. And in 1943 in Germany, when he set forth his proofs on paper, at the end of the manuscript, he thanked Professor van der Waerden for his review of the manuscript, and further expressed his gratitude to a certain Professor K. Shteppa.

Who was Shteppa? It would have been natural to seek his name among mathematicians, but such a search would have turned up nothing: Shteppa was that very historian mentioned in the book's preface.

Konstantin Fedoseevich Shteppa (1896-1958), a professor at the University of Kiev, was arrested around the same time as Houtermans. Much later, Shteppa recalled his first sight of Houtermans in a small cell at the Kiev NKVD prison at 33 Korolenko Street. When Shteppa was led into the cell, he saw an emaciated man lying on the top bunk with his eyes closed. He looked so dreadful that Shteppa had a frightening thought – was his cellmate dead? Happily, Houtermans was alive. He and Shteppa became friends, and the historian, who was supported by money and food parcels from his family, shared all this with his comrade in misfortune – also supplying him with cigarettes, apart from everything else. Much later, after F. Houtermans' death, K. F. Shteppa's memories of their meeting were recorded by his daughter. The Houtermans family has preserved these several pages. When Houtermans and Shteppa first met in prison, they used their real names, unlike the scene of acquaintance in the book. In 1939, during a brief period of relative liberalization associated with the purge of People's Commissar Yezhov, Shteppa was released and even allowed to teach at the university again. Shteppa did not evacuate from Kiev, which German troops occupied on September 20, 1941. Like many, he unfortunately gave no credit to reports about the fascists and their conduct in the occupied territories. His daughter has harrowing memories of the fascist invaders' barbarity in the early days of the occupation [4].

But Shteppa's fate was decided almost immediately after the Germans came – he was made rector of the University of Kiev, probably in light of his arrest and imprisonment in 1937-39.

Well aware of what he could expect after Kiev's liberation by Soviet troops, K. F. Shteppa clearly left the city before this. The hardships he and his family experienced in Germany came to an end only with a lucky chance meeting with Houtermans in Göttingen in 1945. (Shteppa's daughter A. Gorman preserved his memories of this.) Apparently it was then that they decided to write a book about their experiences...

In concluding this story, I should add that the authors' conspiratorial efforts to conceal their authorship were extremely naive. Figuring out who wrote *Russian Purge* is incredibly easy, given all that the authors tell about themselves. One describes himself as a Kiev-based historian who was persecuted by the Ukrainian press for his "incorrect" interpretation of the character of Joan of Arc, and for inappropriate references to the myth of King Midas. He was released in 1939. Did that description fit many historians in Kiev, or even in the Soviet Union? The case of the other author, described as a natural scientist, is hardly more complicated. The book contains scattered phrases identifying him as a physicist and as knowledgeable about the development of science in Ukraine, and also as a foreigner who was held in prisons in Moscow and Ukraine and deported to Germany before the war. The figure of Houtermans is barely veiled at all!

The mystery, then, is why Houtermans and Shteppa chose pseudonyms, and why namely these ones? I haven't succeeded in solving this completely. The Lagodin from Houtermans' letter to Bohr has obviously turned into Godin. Where did Beck come from, and why did Bernstein vanish? Shteppa's daughter, A. Gorman, recalled that in a prison conversation with her father, Houtermans once referred to himself as Beck. Maybe these things aren't too important. I was able to trace the later life of Houtermans' co-author based on his daughter's memoirs, which appeared in *Novoye Russkoye Slovo*, a Russian-language newspaper published for many years in the United States. Additionally, in the United States, where Shteppa and his family eventually immigrated from post-war Germany, I browsed the catalog of the Library of Congress and found he had written several books on Soviet science.

This tale of pseudonyms has something else I find meaningful. It reflects, if not fear, at least caution on the authors' part after what they'd heard from Born after his return from travel to the USSR and his conversation there with P. L. Kapitsa.

To close this chapter, we present some excerpts from the above-mentioned book, likely unfamiliar to most readers.

> Outside [149] the Soviet Union it is taken for granted that there is a direct connection between a man's imprisonment and some offense he has committed, or has at any rate been accused of. People accept this idea so completely that they find it hard to understand that in the Soviet Union no such necessary connection exists. Arrests in Russia – particularly at the time of the purge – were based on an entirely different system. For an analogy one cannot do better than to refer to the statistical determinism of modern physics. According to this, the fate of an individual atom in a given set of circumstances cannot be foreseen. All you can say about it is that in such-and-such circumstances there is a degree of probability, which can be stated mathematically, that so-and-so will happen. The same was more or less true of individuals in Russia. The causes that led to imprisonment were the now familiar "objective characteristics"; it was sufficient to belong to one of certain categories. A comparison is provided by what happens in time of war, when enemy aliens are automatically interned, or by what happened in Nazi Germany, when being a member of one of the persecuted groups involved penalties that had nothing whatever to do with personal guilt. But there was an important difference. In the case of an enemy alien in wartime, or of a Jew in Nazi Germany, the unpleasant consequences were practically inevitable. They were not inevitable in the case of a member of one of the compromis-

---

[149]The excerpts quoted are from [1], pages 95-98, 129, and 134 of the American Edition.

ing categories in the Soviet Union. His chances of escaping
were by no means negligible. Generally speaking, the higher
the rank of the person concerned, the less likely he was to
escape; and in the case of someone who had the misfortune
to belong simultaneously to more than one category – e.g., a
Soviet party official who had been a member of a Soviet mission abroad – the chances of his escaping arrest diminished
in accordance with the laws of mathematical probability.

Whether any particular individual was arrested or not depended on a host of secondary factors, such as the state of
overcrowding in the prisons, the state of the NKVD files, the
personality of the official concerned, the number of denunci-
ations that had come in, any damaging confessions, and so
forth. Incidentally, the last two factors' mentioned did not
seem to play a particularly important role. In the great majority of cases there was no point whatsoever in asking the
reason for an individual arrest.

Some people managed to escape arrest by knowing the
ropes. A well-known scholar told me that his friends, including a number of experienced Communists, advised him
at the time of the purge to pretend to be a drunkard, and
occasionally to give his lectures when he was slightly under
the influence. This enabled him to escape the first purge
of specialists at the beginning of the thirties. Another favorite method was to change one's job and place of residence
frequently. It always took a considerable time, at least six
months or a year, before the local NKVD started paying attention to a new worker in a Soviet undertaking. It took time
to accumulate sufficient secret reports, commonly known as
"material," about him, and there was an inevitable delay
until he had filled in enough questionnaires to be put in a
particular category and until his NKVD personal file and secret documents had been forwarded from his previous place
of work – particularly as all such documents were dispatched
by special NKVD express messenger and not through the ordinary post; this meant that they took a very long time to

reach their destinations and sometimes did not arrive at all.

Another way of avoiding arrest, which was used by many party and Soviet officials, was to have oneself arrested for some minor criminal offense, such as careless accounting or squandering State funds. A well-known teacher, for example, who, after being checked up, was afraid of losing his job and being arrested for deviations from the party line, escaped arrest by getting drunk and creating a disturbance in a public park. The result was that six months later he was able to find a new job in a different neighborhood.

Finally, it is probable that the NKVD left a few people free in each of the arrest-worthy categories to demonstrate that membership in one of them did not automatically lead to arrest and to render plausible the personal guilt of each accused. Thus among those not arrested were several senior officers of the Red Army, such as Zhukov and Shaposhnikov, and a few prominent leaders of the Communist parties of European countries, such as Pieck and Ercoli.[150] Among scientists and scholars membership in the Academy of Sciences of the Soviet Union, but not in those of the Ukraine or other Republics, seemed to bestow a certain, though by no means universal, immunity, so that most of the older academicians were spared. We know of cases in which scientists in the provinces who had had tremendous political difficulties at the check-up meetings and were definitely threatened with arrest transferred themselves to one of the academic institutions in Moscow and either escaped arrest altogether or were released after a relatively short time.

Here is another excerpt from [1] describing a subcategory of potential prisoners. This subcategory is referred to by the authors as "those who correspond with the outside world."

All correspondence with foreign countries was regarded as incriminating not only by the NKVD but by the Soviet public,

---

[150]Now known under his real name of Togliatti. –Beck and Godin

which expressed its opinion at "criticism and selfcriticism" meetings. Many people, particularly those who had relatives abroad, often conducted such correspondence for years, though always very discreetly. In the years from 1929 to 1935 such correspondence was prevalent, for goods of Soviet manufacture, such as provisions, clothes, and other necessities, could be bought at world prices in any quantity in exchange for foreign currency at the special *Torgsin* shops.[151] During the famine many families kept themselves alive on the occasional few dollars or pounds they received from relatives abroad, and this naturally encouraged them to keep the correspondence alive. After 1936, however, most of them had to suffer for it, for they were arrested as spies.

Scientists also conducted extensive correspondence with their colleagues in foreign countries, and many Russian scientists, particularly those engaged in the natural sciences, published their findings in foreign journals, especially in Germany, and later in Britain and America as well.

Between 1925 and 1929 many scientists and engineers went abroad on behalf of Soviet institutions to work in corresponding institutions in Germany, England, Holland, and the United States, to renew scientific relations abroad or to start new ones. It was these who were in the gravest danger [of arrest]. But scholars who had worked abroad before the First World War, engineers, members of Soviet purchasing and selling missions also fell into this category.

---

[151]See footnote 46 on pp. 135-136.

Editor's Addendum

I believe that before Frenkel's book [5] very few people in the world were aware of the existence of the Beck and Godin book [1] and fewer still knew that this book had been written by Fritz Houtermans and Konstantin Shteppa.[152] It was published in 1951, almost simultaneously with Weissberg's book [2]. One might think that this was a mere coincidence, while in fact this was a natural consequence of the similarity of the past experiences of the authors. A decade later these first testimonies of the Stalin dictatorship were eclipsed by Varlam Shalamov's *Kolyma Tales* [7] and Alexander Solzhenitsyn's *The Gulag Archipelago* [3]. The value of the first testimonies due to Houtermans, Shteppa and Weissberg will never fade, however, moreover in that they tried to study the phenomenon of totalitarianism inherent to the Soviet regime as scientists rather than as writers. The authors themselves emphasize this aspect of their treatise. For instance, the following phrase (see [1], p. 94): "We shall now enumerate and describe the various categories of prisoners...," quite typical of a scientific paper, can be found more than once on the pages of [1]. It reminds me of a note by two entomologists whom I knew in the past, who classified a rare species of bees and described their beehive.

I would like to note one more detail. Frankel mentions in passing that the Beck-Godin book is prefaced by an epigraph (see p. 270). In fact, there are two epigraphs in the book. The second one is a quotation from a 1935 speech by Stalin:

Life is getting better, happier!

This is complemented by commentary from the authors (p. 47 of [1]): "By this time the system had reduced itself to absurdity."

---

[152]Edoardo Amaldi was among those few who knew the names of the authors from the very beginning, from Fritz Houtermans himself. However, Amaldi's book [6] was published only in 2013, sixteen years after Frenkel's publication. Thus, Frenkel's accidental find of a copy of [1] in the Niels Bohr library, with Houtermans' inscription "To Professor Niels Bohr from the authors, with gratitude and admiration, July 10, 1951," (and opportunity to corroborate his discovery at once with Professor Rozental) is a striking example of good fortune.

As far as I have been able to determine, in postwar Russia Victor Frenkel was the first to mention the name of Konstantin Shteppa (sometimes spelled as Shtepa), who was completely forgotten in the USSR and in the West despite his reputation as a historian in pre-war Ukraine and, later, in the United States [8]. The chapter which the reader have just finished reading aroused interest in this man and his fate. During the 20 years that have elapsed since Frenkel's publication, many historians, both in Ukraine and Russia, have published papers and books devoted to Konstantin Shteppa (in some Ukrainian publications he is referred to as Kost Shteppa), see e.g. [9]. Among others, let me single out the book of recollections *A Story of Professor Konstantin Shteppa's Family* [10]. Among the authors are Konstantin Shteppa himself, his son Erasm and his daughter Aglaya. Recently Konstantin Shteppa's daughter Aglaya Gorman published a touching and informative memoir *A Choice Between Two Evils* [4]. Yuri Raniuk translated from English the Beck and Godin book *Russian Purge and the Extraction of Confession* and published it in Ukrainian under the title *Purge in Russia* [11]. For the first time ever, the names of F. Houtermans and K. Shteppa appeared on the title page of this book. Raniuk's foreword which opens the Ukrainian edition summarizes the results of years of his thorough investigations in Kharkov archives.

After Konstantin Shteppa's death his personal archive was split in two parts: one of them is currently in the Rare Book and Manuscript Library of Columbia University [12] (New York), while the second part was generously donated to the State Archive of the Russian Federation by Aglaya Gorman in 1998.

Needless to say, now we know much more than 20 years ago when Victor Frenkel worked on this chapter. Frenkel had to undertake a special – practically a detective – investigation to uncover the true names of the authors of *Russian Purge and the Extraction of Confession* hidden under the pseudonyms of Beck and Godin. A part of this chapter describes how he solved the puzzle.

Figure 34. The cover of the Ukrainian edition of *Purge in Russia* (2000). Photos on the cover, from left to right: Konstantin Shteppa and Friedrich Houtermans. Courtesy of Yuri Raniuk.

Professor Shteppa (1896-1958) was born into a priest's family in a small Ukrainian town of Lokhvitsa, Poltava province. He got his education at the Department of History of St. Petersburg University. During the Civil War after the Bolshevik coup d'etat he fought against the Bolsheviks, later concealing this fact. In 1922 he began teaching at the Nezhinsky Institute near Kiev; he earned his doctorate in 1927 at Odessa University after successfully defending the thesis "On Demonology, or the History of Medieval Inquisition." In 1930 Shteppa became the head of the Department of Ancient History and the Middle Ages of Kiev University. In 1931 he was appointed as a chairman of the Commission on the History of Byzantium.

And then ... then in 1938 he was arrested by the NKVD and spent 19 months in the Kiev NKVD prison without being formally charged. A succinct summary of Shteppa's arrest and imprisonment, which exhibits the highest degree of absurdity not only of the NKVD, but of the Soviet mentality at large, is given by Robert Conquest in the revised edition of his famous treatise *The Great Terror* [13], from which I quote three paragraphs:

A professor of ancient history, Konstantin Shteppa, first lost favor as a result of describing Joan of Arc as high-strung. Joan had been treated in a hostile fashion or ignored until the mid-1930s, but with the coming of the Popular Front in France she had been referred to as a heroine of a national resistance movement, so that the professor's remarks deviated from the Party line. After considerable trouble about this, he was again censured for a reference to the legend of Midas in an unfortunate context. Then, speaking of ancient and Christian demonology, he happened to remark that country people are always backward. Unfortunately, Trotsky, like many others, had expressed the same thought. Finally, in dealing with the Donatist movement in North Africa, at the time of the Roman Empire, he had shown that it was in part a national as well as a peasant rebellion, thus becoming a bourgeois nationalist. At this time, in 1937, his friends and colleagues were being arrested on a large scale.

"I was naturally sorry for my friends, but I was not only sorry for them. I was also afraid of them. After all, they could say things about conversations we had had, in which we had not always expressed the orthodox view. There had been nothing criminal in these conversations; they had contained no attacks on the Soviet power. But the trivial criticisms and grumbles and expressions of resentment and disappointment which occurred in every conversation forced every Soviet citizen to feel guilty."

Then came the suicide of Lyubchenko and his wife N. Krupenik. Unfortunately, the wife had been a university lecturer, and the whole staff of Kiev University naturally became high-grade suspects. A vast network of bourgeois nationalists in the universities and cultural agencies came to light. Nevertheless, the professor was not arrested until March 1938. After a severe interrogation for fifty days, by a series of thirteen "magistrates," he was charged with complicity in an attempt to assassinate Kossior.[153] The fall of Kossior led to the withdrawal of this charge in his and many other cases, and for it was substituted espionage for Japan. This was based on the following facts: the professor had for some time been head of the "Byzantological" Committee of the Ukrainian Academy of Sciences, The term then came to be regarded as reactionary and was replaced by "Near East." This connection with the "East" was regarded as adequate for at least some suspicion of sympathy with, and espionage for, a country a good deal farther east. It was shown that the professor had lectured on Alexander the Great and Hannibal to senior Red Army officers. This had given him contact with the Army and therefore the opportunity to carry out espionage. It was then proved that he had actually met foreigners in the person of Professor Hrozny, the great specialist in Hittite history, who had "recruited" him through another Byzantologist

---

[153]Stanislav Kossior (1889-1939) was the First Secretary of the Ukrainian Communist party from 1928 to 1938. He was arrested by the NKVD, tortured and executed by a firing squad in 1939.

who had lectured in the Soviet Far East, thus getting very near Japan. Finally, an indirect contact was found with a professor in Odessa who had actually met the Japanese Consul there. The reports passed through this espionage link to Tokyo consisted of remarks about the "political morale" of the Army, and here a genuine fact was established in that the accused had once told a colleague that some senior officers had confused Napoleon III with Napoleon I, and Alexander the Great with Caesar.

It was in this Kiev NKVD prison that Shteppa's fateful encounter with Fritz Houtermans occurred in 1938. According to Aglaya Gorman [4], here's how her father described it.

I entered the cell which contained a single piece of furniture a wooden bunk-bed. Immediately I was shocked. On the top bed laid a corpse. The man's face was grey and the skin was so thin that one could see every bone under it. I was terrified. "Is it possible that they've become so cruel? That the degree of their mockery has reached the point of putting the dead and the living together?" That was my first thought after I saw his face.

After a while he opened his eyes. He stared at me with a look of expectation, hopeful I would bring him all kinds of news, which he needed so desperately.

"Are you new? I can tell by the way you walk, you move and you look," he said in his broken Russian. He lifted himself up and offered his thin hand for a handshake. "My name is Fritz Houtermans, a German... a physicist... a former member of the communist party... former emigrant from Nazi Germany... former professor at the Institute of Physics in Kharkov... former human being – and who are you?"

Those were my first weeks in prison, so I hadn't forgotten how to smile. I shook his hand and introduced myself properly: "Professor Konstantin Fedoseevich Shteppa, Professor of History at Kiev University."

"Pleased to meet you," Fritz Houtermans replied. "I think

we will have a lot in common. Do you smoke?"

"No, sorry, I don't."

"That's a pity. If you did, I would hope to occasionally smoke your stubs.[154] You know, I don't get any money from the outside. My family is abroad. I tried a hunger strike several times, but they don't care, so I gave up, and you can see the only results." He pointed out his emaciated limbs. "I also used to exchange rations for cigarettes," he added with sorrow in his voice.

I answered, "My wife is allowed to send money every month. I don't know for how long, but as long as I have money, we'll share."

"You are a lunatic," he said frankly. "Nobody does that here. Everyone cares only for one thing, to survive. And you can't survive on what they give you... Forget about that; just tell me the news... When did they arrest you? What are the news from the West?"

Then Aglaya Gorman continues:

They stayed in the same cell for several months. They became great friends. They told one another everything about themselves, about their families, their experiences, their knowledge. They just had to talk. They recalled the books they had read and the letters they received. They talked about good and bad, beautiful and ugly, about wonders and terrors. They had the same fears, the same agonies, the same despair and hopelessness. They both were at the mercy of the NKVD. Each of them was completely sure that the other would never come out alive.

---

[154]Yuri Raniuk writes [14]: "All Kharkov colleagues noted Houtermans' passion for smoking. His wife Charlotte was not very happy about this and once in a while would convey her dissatisfaction to her husband, especially after Jan's birth. The Houtermans' apartment № 2 on 16 Tchaikovsky Street was located on the ground floor, and Fritz has attached to it a sort of open-air terrace, to which he would retreat for smoking. This is the only material memory of Houtermans the tenant he left in Kharkov. His neighbors on the third floor remember that they enjoyed the smell of Houtermans' tobacco smoke rising to them from the first-floor balcony."

My father kept his word and shared his small allowance with Fritz Houtermans. This embarrassed him, but there was no other solution, so he accepted.

When one was called out for interrogation, the other one prayed. They prayed together. One Catholic, the other Orthodox, but the cell made them compromise. They swore that if one of them came out alive, he would take care of the other's family. Both had a wife and two children left behind. And there was very little hope for either man.

Fate brought them together and fate separated them. When they said goodbye, they meant goodbye forever. But the will of God is not ours to know. They both came out of prison at different times and under different circumstances. They met again in a free world and stayed friends. They wrote a book which they had conceived in their thoughts while still over there, in a cell of the NKVD building at Korolenko 33 in Kiev.

In 1941, Konstantin Shteppa decided not to evacuate with the retreating Red Army, but rather to stay in Kiev and wait for the arrival of the German army. During the German occupation, he first headed Department of Public Education of the Kiev Administration, and then was appointed rector of Kiev University. After his dismissal from this latter post, Shteppa became editor of the Ukrainian newspaper *New Ukrainian Word* and the Russian newspaper *Latest News.* According to B. Yakubskii, a literary critic, under Shteppa all articles in these newspapers were limited to two topics characteristic for periodicals in the occupied territories of the USSR, namely, anti-communist and anti-Semitic.[155] Shteppa himself recalls [10] that this became a problem for him much later, after his emigration to the United States. Most of the Russian liberal immigrants in New York were Jewish and could not forgive him this sad page of his life.

---

[155]Some Western scholars of Ukrainian history believe that in his views Shteppa was a supporter of a "Great Imperial Russia." Whether or not that was the case is still being debated. The only firmly established fact is that under his editorship the "Ukrainization" campaign in the newspapers he headed faded away.

Shteppa left Ukraine with the retreating German Army in 1943. Aglaya Gorman describes his miraculous second encounter with Fritz Houtermans as follows [10].

> After the war ended in 1945, we had to flee again, since under the Yalta Agreement Plauen remained in the Soviet zone of occupation. It was a long and painful escape to the North. I do not remember now why my father wanted to go to Hamburg. In Göttingen he met his friend Professor Houtermans, who persuaded him to stay in Göttingen. Göttingen was in the British zone of occupation, and perhaps this fact helped us survive.
>
> Being afraid of repatriation and inevitable Gulag, after two days in Göttingen, my father took his backpack and left Göttingen bound for the West. He had many misadventures before he reached Westphalia. There he was advised to seek assistance from Cardinal von Galen. Cardinal listened to his story and offered him a job as a librarian in his monastery.
>
> Father lived in Münster until 1947. By that time his situation had become easier in that he no longer faced forced repatriation to the USSR. Fritz Houtermans still was in Göttingen, and the two of them, with the help of a German typist, wrote the book *Russian Purge and the Extraction of Confession*. The book was published in England in German, and then translated in English by Eric Mosbacher and Eric Porter and published in the United States. Later it was translated into many foreign languages, including Arabic and Chinese.

Frankly, I was unable to find any traces of the German edition of this book. Some historians say it never existed. I will not describe further adventures and misadventures of Konstantin Shteppa in the West, referring the reader to [4, 10].

It is worth adding that life in Germany, and in particular in Göttingen, was not easy even for world-famous physicists in the first postwar years. In the summer of 1945, Max Planck (who was 87 years old at that time) was taken to Göttingen by the US military who were sent to help him. In Göttingen he settled with his niece. Widely known is a letter from Marga Planck, Max Planck's wife, to Lise Meitner, dated June 15, 1947. In this letter Marga writes: "But I can assure you of one thing: without the help of our friends abroad, my husband would very certainly not have survived the winter."

Figure 35. This snapshot was made on March 31, 1947. The poster on the left reads: "We want coal, we want bread."

References

1. F. Beck and W. Godin, *Russian Purge and the Extraction of Confession*, (Hurst & Blackett, London, 1951); American edition: The Viking Press, New York, 1951.
2. Alexander Weissberg-Cybulski, *Hexensabbat*, (Frankfurt, Frankfurter Hefte, 1951, in German), English translation: Alexander Weissberg, *The Accused*, (New York, Simon and Schuster, 1951).
3. Alexander Solzhenitsyn, *The Gulag Archipelago 1918-1956*. The first "samizdat publications" in Russian circulated in 1967-1968; English translation: Harper & Row, 1974 and 1975.
4. Aglaya Gorman, *A Choice Between Two Evils*, (Xlibris, 2006); see also the

letter from Aglaya Gorman to Charlotte Houtermans, "In memory of Professor Dr. F. Houtermans," Giovanna Fjelstad's family archive.

5. Victor Frenkel, *Professor Friedrich Houtermans: Works, Life, Fate,* (A. F. Ioffe Institute, St. Petersburg, 1997), in Russian.

6. E. Amaldi, *The Adventurous Life of Friedrich Georg Houtermans, Physicist* (Springer, Berlin, 2013), Eds. Saverio Braccini, Antonio Ereditato, and Paola Scampoli.

7. Varlam Shalamov, *Kolyma Tales.* The first "samizdat publications" in Russian circulated in 1960-1962; English translation: Penguin, 20th Century Classics, 1995.

8. K. Shteppa's most important publications are
"Imprisoned by Communism," *Novy Zhurnal,* vol. 57, New York, 1959, in Russian; "Ezhovshchina," *Novy Zhurnal,* vol. 58, New York, 1959 (reprinted in [10]), in Russian; *A Syllabus on Soviet Communism: a Compilation From the Commentaries on Soviet Development Prepared for Radio Liberty, 1951-1959,* (New York, American Committee for Liberation, 1960); *Russian Historians and the Soviet State,* (Rutgers University Press, New Brunswick, NJ, 1962).

9. I. V. Verba, *Kost Shteppa,* Parts 1 and 2, *Ukrainian Historical Journal,* 1999, $N^{\underline{o}}$ 3, pp. 97-111 and $N^{\underline{o}}$ 4, pp. 98-114, in Ukrainian; *Kost Shteppa as Orientalist,* in Ukrainian, in the Collection *The World of the Orient,* dedicated to 2000 years of Christianity, Kiev, 2001; I. V. Verba and M. O. Samofalov, *Historian Kost Shteppa: The Man, the Scholar and the Teacher,* (Kiev, 2010); Yuri Raniuk, "Ukrainian Historian Shteppa and German Physicist Houtermans," Based on the K. F. Shteppa dossier, Security Service of Ukraine, $N^{\underline{o}}$ 49863, in *Collection of the Shevchenko Scientific Society,* 2000.

10. *A Story of Professor Konstantin Shteppa's Family,* Ed. A.V. Popov, (Moscow, Rusaki, 2003), in Russian.

11. K. Shteppa and F. Houtermans, *Purge in Russia,* translated from English by Yuri Raniuk, (Kharkov, Folio, 2000).

12. Bakhmeteff Archive,
http://www.columbia.edu/cu/lweb/archival/collections/ldpd_4078079/

13. Robert Conquest, *The Great Terror: A Reassessment,* (Oxford University Press, Oxford, 2007).

14. Yuri Raniuk, Private communication, April 24, 2015.

War's End

In the spring of 1942, F. Houtermans moved from Ardenne's lab to the Imperial Physical-Technical Institute. His reasons for leaving the lab remain somewhat ambiguous.[156] What did he research at his new place of occupation?

One thing is known to have kept him occupied, although indeed it formed his constant occupation: Houtermans smoked incessantly. But in 1944 in Germany, tobacco was hard to come by. At this point Houtermans embarked on one of his characteristic adventures, claiming to be studying tobacco smoke's light-absorption properties – obviously with military implications. Under this project's auspices, he actually obtained a shipment of tobacco, which was nonetheless quickly exhausted. He placed an order for a new shipment, but this time, the institute took notice. Houtermans, threatened with serious consequences, was saved by his Uranium Society friends – Weizsäcker and Walther Gerlach, who by that time had become the uranium project's administrative supervisor. They secured his transfer to Göttingen, where Houtermans later met the Allies.

In the Allies' front ranks, and sometimes ahead of them, went the "Alsos Mission" teams, whose scientific division was led by an old friend of Houtermans', the Dutch-American physicist Samuel Goudsmit.[157] He already knew about the group of Göttingen-

---

[156]See p. 56 and footnote 28.

[157]The Alsos Mission, a part of the Manhattan Project, was created following the Allied invasion of Italy in September 1943, to investigate the German nuclear effort. Samuel Abraham Goudsmit (1902-1978) was a theoretical physicist of Dutch-Jewish descent, famous for proposing the concept of electron spin (jointly with George Eugene Uhlenbeck) in 1925. In 1943 his parents were deported to a concentration camp by the German occupation authorities in the Netherlands and were murdered there. In 1943 Goudsmit was appointed scientific head of the Alsos Mission by Brigadier General Leslie Groves, head of the Manhattan Project. Goudsmit and other members of the Alsos team found the German group of nuclear physicists around Werner Heisenberg and Otto Hahn at Hechingen (then in the French zone) in advance of the French physicist Yves Rocard. In the book *Alsos*, published in 1947 [1], Goudsmit concludes that the Germans did not get close to creating a nuclear weapon for two reasons: first, science cannot function efficiently under a totalitarian regime, and, second, the German scientists simply did not understand how to make an atomic bomb.

based physicists associated with the German atomic project: Wilhelm Groth and Hans Kopfermann, who were working on separating uranium isotopes with centrifuges,[158] and Friedrich Houtermans. Goudsmit first met with Kopfermann. During this meeting, which took place at the latter's home, Houtermans happened to drop by. The "Alsos Mission" papers contain a report of this meeting. This report is examined in T. Powers' *Heisenberg's War* [2].

Figure 36.   Alsos members (left to right): Goudsmit, Wardenburg, Welsh and Cecil.

Both German physicists portrayed the position of German scientists during World War II as an attempt to "put the war in the service of science," a formulation they attributed to W. Heisenberg. According to Goudsmit, Houtermans himself was not a participant in the project, but he knew about and was very interested in it. He provided the mission with all the information he had, but "some of it was definitely incorrect, showing his ignorance." Goudsmit goes

---

[158]From our future perspective, this has by now emerged as the primary method for obtaining light uranium isotopes. Yet at the time, almost no one in Germany, the Soviet Union or even the United States viewed the study of this method as warranting priority. -V.F.

on to write that Houtermans spoke of the German physicists' effort to "work slowly," as a means of delaying the success of the wartime uranium project as long as possible. He also said that he'd asked Weizsäcker to tell this to Niels Bohr during the German physicists' trip to German-occupied Denmark. As we know, the trip took place, but only Heisenberg spoke with Bohr.[159]

The consequences of the meeting between Goudsmit and Houtermans indicate Goudsmit's loss of confidence in his old German friend. Prior to their meeting, Houtermans wrote a letter to his closer friend, Patrick Blackett, which he hoped Goudsmit could deliver when in England. In a postscript, apparently added in Goudsmit's presence (the extant copy of the letter contains text in handwriting recognizable as Houtermans' -V.F.), Houtermans asks Blackett to tell Max Born and James Franck about his hardships and to try to seek help with reestablishing scientific research in Göttingen.[160] The letter contains the following lines:

> This is the moment I am looking forward to for years and years... I think to you and to those who know us personally, it is not even necessary to mention how we thought about all that had been done during the war in the name of Germany beginning from Coventry [161] to the behavior of German *Sprengkommandos* in Russian institutes, so that you will not believe that all German physicists have gone mad too.

Houtermans expresses special respect for Laue and Hahn, and refers to what he sees as Heisenberg's compromise. According to Houtermans, namely Heisenberg averted the gutting of Bohr's institute in Copenhagen.

Unfortunately for Houtermans, Goudsmit did not deliver this letter to P. Blackett, and it stayed in the "Alsos Mission" archives. The

---

[159] See Editor's Addendum on p. 241.

[160] According to Powers (p. 415), Houtermans asks simply for greetings to be passed on to Born and Franck, whereas Blackett is asked to try to seek help from the Allied military authorities (as this reads, it appears as if help is sought from Born and Franck). -James Manteith.

[161] This refers to the devastating bombardment of the English city of Coventry by the Luftwaffe. -V.F.

information it contained was later confirmed, as detailed above.

References

1. Samuel Goudsmit, *Alsos. The Failure of German Science*, (Time-Life International, 1947); Modern editions: Samuel Goudsmit, *Alsos*, (American Institute of Physics, 1985 and 1996).
2. T. Powers, *Heisenberg's War: The Secret History Of The German Bomb*, (Da Capo Press, 2000).

The Age of the Earth[162]

In 1952, Houtermans left little Göttingen forever and moved to Bern, the capital of Switzerland.[163] His friends were surprised – how could this temperamental Viennese-Kharkovite-Berliner get along with the serene Swiss, with their deliberate pace of life? He got along well with them, and was loved and respected by them. He worked successfully, founded a new institute, was "overgrown" with disciples, became the head of a school – all the things that every German university graduate might have aspired to.[164] But what a lot of adventures he had before attaining this! Heading the department of experimental physics at the University of Bern gave him an opportunity to make full use of his multi-faceted talents in the natural sciences.

The new institute saw the implementation of modern equipment, including mass spectrometers and apparatus for measuring low-level radioactivity. Thus the institute embarked on a course of applying nuclear physics to earth sciences. At the same time, F. Houtermans' international authority and broad connections helped inspire many,

---

[162]See also Appendix V on p. 379.

[163]Bern has a special place in the history of physics – namely there, in 1902-1907, A. Einstein worked at the patent office while developing his theory of relativity. -V.F.

[164]It would be fitting to quote P. Enz, Pauli's assistant [1]: "The dominant and colorful personality in physics in Bern at that time was Friedrich Georg Houtermans, an old friend of Pauli's. Houtermans became a professor in Bern in 1952. He inherited an institute which he described to Casimir as follows: 'If you want to see an authentic early-twentieth-century laboratory, come and visit me. But you have to come soon, for I am going to change all that.' Here is Casimir's description: 'A little tower with a winding staircase was part of the physics laboratory. The heavy central column bore on its top the zero point of the Swiss geodesic survey. It was also supposed to provide a vibrationless support but, according to Houtermans, the stability left something to be desired.' Hence his remark: 'When I stand in my institute and push I can wiggle the whole of Switzerland.' "

In Bern Houtermans founded the internationally renowned *Berner Schule* for applications of radioactivity to the geosciences and cosmochemistry. Judging from the number of his publications and students he had in Bern, this was his most productive period [2]. One of Houtermans's former students, Hans Oeschger (1927-1998), described Houtermans's lectures in general physics as difficult to follow and error-prone but filled with brilliant comparisons to illuminate the underlying physical mechanisms [3].

many co-workers and guests to join him. His perfect knowledge of several languages played a far from negligible role in this growth.

Figure 37.   Fritz Houtermans with his first motorbike in Bern.   1954 (Courtesy of J. Geiss.)

Yet his life was punctuated by encounters with the past. Even *Russian Purge* didn't free him from memories. During the war, he and his family were separated by the front line and the ocean, with no hope of seeing each other anytime soon or even obtaining reliable information about each other. But when Houtermans' personal life fell apart, not only external circumstances were to blame. The previously mentioned letter from Max Born mentions that during the war, Houtermans took advantage of a German divorce law that existed at the time. According to this law, spouses' mutual consent did not need to be shown, with proof of the absence of one of the spouses for several years considered sufficient to obtain a divorce. Under this law, Houtermans did not commit bigamy when he married his colleague Ilse Bartz, with whom he had co-authored scientific publications during the war years. Houtermans' friends spoke highly of this fine woman, but as at least Born's letter implies, not everyone approved of Houtermans himself.

Figure 38.   E. J. Workman and Fritz Houtermans, New Mexico, USA, January 1958. Credit: American Institute of Physics Emilio Segré Visual Archives, Physics Today Collection.

Then, after the war, when the inevitable meeting with Charlotte took place, the past was reluctant to turn loose of them: Houtermans divorced I. Bartz (though by this time they already had three children) and remarried Charlotte. Their friends recalled this as accompanied by some sad yet comic episodes. The official who recorded the official remarriage asked the newlyweds how many children they had from their previous marriages.

Charlotte said two, and Fritz, five. "So, a total of seven," the official calculated. "Five," said Houtermans, correcting him. "Do you think I don't know how to count?" the official insisted. "Two plus five equals seven, doesn't it?" "All the same, five," Houtermans asserted. "Does this guy want to become a professor or something?" the official probably thought as he placed his stamp.

The renewed marriage didn't last – there was another divorce, but Friedrich and Charlotte Houtermans remained on good terms. Surprisingly for our time, Charlotte Houtermans, Ilse Bartz and a third wife, Lore Müller (from Houtermans' Bern period), all left very warm memoirs about him.[165] His children also retained appreciative memories of him.[166]

As for son Jan, he barely knew his father until meeting him after the war. He became a physicist and worked at Berkeley...

Scientific ties gradually formed anew – Houtermans began to travel throughout Europe again and was a welcome participant in many conferences and other gatherings. In addition, Switzerland become a major center for science, hosting numerous physics conferences, especially on the peaceful uses of atomic energy, and Houtermans of course took part in these. Sometimes, especially in the 1960s, Houtermans' former acquaintances from the Soviet Union also appeared, but they avoided him (we now know the reason for this), and he didn't want to put them in an awkward position.

Science always having been important in his life, his research gravitated more and more toward a different Past. The outlines of this Past emerge in his work on nuclear geophysics and geochronology, in his creation of new original methods for determining the age of rocks and minerals, meteorites and archaeological artifacts.

---

[165]Houtermans himself made light of his private life. When a student missed a lecture to attend his own wedding, Houtermans reprimanded him in front of the entire class with the words: "But Mr. Lang, if I had skipped a lecture every time I was married, where would we be now!?" [2].

[166]I had the opportunity, during my visit to the United States in 1992, to meet with Charlotte Houtermans' family. She was already advanced in age, and my main conversations about Friedrich Houtermans were with his daughter, Giovanna. She came to the U.S. when she was six and a half years and met her father again only at age 18! Our meeting took place in Northfield, Minnesota, where Giovanna Fjelstad-Houtermans, a Harvard graduate, worked as a professor. -V.F.

In this field, F. Houtermans left not only a great scientific legacy,

Figure 39. Lise Meitner (left) and Fritz Houtermans (right, in the front row) at a meeting of Nobel laureates at Lindau, Germany. Credit: American Institute of Physics Emilio Segré Visual Archives, Physics Today Collection.

but also his own school and the institute he organized at the University of Bern. Houtermans was led to work on geochronology by the interest in nuclear physics that had marked his whole life. By that time, several methods existed for using physical phenomena to determine the age of rocks. One such method, using radioactive lead, is based on measuring lead's isotopic composition in lead minerals through the stable lead isotopes they contain: "primary" Pb-204 and "radiogenic" Pb-206 and Pb-207. The first isotope has been in the earth's crust from the beginning. The second is the final product of a radioactive decay chain resulting from the uranium isotope U-238, which has a half-life of about 4.5 billion years, while the third is also a final product, but resulting from the decay of another isotope, U-235, with a half-life of 0.7 billion years. (There is a third chain, thorium, which yields a final stable lead isotope, Pb-208, but the initial element has a much longer half-life – more than 14 billion years for thorium-232.) By measuring the ratio of lead and uranium isotopes in a rock sample, taking into account the quantity of primary Pb-204 it contains, and knowing the half-lives, it is possible to gauge rocks' absolute age and, on this basis, to date the formation of the Earth's crust or of meteorites.

Figure 40.   Fritz Houtermans lecturing at Varenna, Italy. 1960 (Courtesy of J. Geiss).

Usually, these elements appear in very small quantities; therefore, uncertainties in determination of these quantities led to significant errors in dating. One needs precision measurement methods, which were developed by Houtermans [4]. Prior to his papers of 1953-54, based on the results of research that were considered classical, the age of the Earth's lithosphere was estimated at about 2.9 billion years. Thus, the Earth's age as a planet was deemed to be not much greater than this. Interestingly, in his article "Determination of the age of the Earth from the isotopic composition of meteoric lead" [5] Houtermans cites the estimate of 3.3 billion years quoted not only in then-fundamental papers by G. Gamow, C. Weizsäcker and P. Jordan, but also in a Papal address.[167]

Houtermans' paper reports his own estimate based on study of numerous samples – 4.5 billion years, a result later repeatedly cited in the scientific literature. Moreover, he argues for a variable ratio of uranium and primary lead content in the formation of the lithosphere, and pushes back the time of the formation of rocks to 5.5 billion years. Houtermans' paper undoubtedly gave additional momentum to contemporaneous efforts to clarify the geologic scale of Earth's history.

Houtermans and his students also contributed groundbreaking ideas to the precision technique for measuring weak activities in various fundamental isotopes in other methods – potassium-argon [6] and osmium-rhenium [7] – as well as to the study of thermoluminescence of rock samples [8] and to improving the method of nuclear photoemulsions [9]. In 1954, he identified the following directions for nuclear geophysics research in the future [10, 11]: cosmic radiation traces in the Earth's past, alpha radioactivity of rocks and minerals, and isotopic composition of lead.

During this period of F. Houtermans' creative activity, luminescence again, many years after his dissertation and papers associated with it, appears in the titles of his scientific works. Fundamental to this series of works is the following idea – if a sample being studied

---

[167] Address by Pope Pius XII to the Pontifical Academy of Sciences on November 22, 1951. Tipografia Poliglotta Vaticana. Rome, 1951. -V.F.

(terrestrial rocks, a meteorite fragment, an ancient work of art) has, over the course of its existence, been exposed to any kind of radiation, then when it is heated, a glow appears as the formerly obtained energy transitions into the ground state. The papers' titles eloquently describe their content: "Measurement of weak thermoluminescence in geology and mineralogy" [8], "On the dating of ceramics using thermoluminescence" [12], "Thermoluminescence glow curves as a research tool on the thermal and radiation history in geological settings" [13], "Radiation effects in space and thermal effects of atmospheric entry by thermoluminescence on meteorites" [14], "Thermoluminescence of Meteorites" [15].

Showing his interest in thermoluminescence technique, Houtermans created an installation to measure thermoluminescence in meteorites and demonstrated the possibility of using the measurements to determine meteorites' age. The subsequent extensive research in this area essentially followed his idea. The glow curve contains all the information for determining age, since the high-temperature peak serves as a cumulative dosimeter and the low-temperature peak as an indicator of the dose strength as long as the sample temperature remains constant. If, on the other hand, the age of the samples is identical, it can be determined whether they had the same thermal history, that is, the extent of the differences in the conditions under which they existed.

With his typical penchant for originality also reflected in his statements on scientific topics, Houtermans explained why these studies were undertaken in the Swiss institute he headed: "Switzerland is the country of precise time!" [16]. In scientific retrospectives of the last period in Houtermans' life, it's legitimately stated that Switzerland became the leader in this field of knowledge.

In Switzerland, Houtermans had a new family, a new "scientific" family, ten years of a basically quiet life – a reward for the hardships of the past. In this field of knowledge, new for F. Houtermans, he became a major authority.[168]

---

[168]In "Fritz Houtermans in bad times and in good" [17], American geologist Bruce Doe provides interesting details that are informative for an understanding of Houtermans and

In *Earth Science and Meteoritics* [18], an anthology released in honor of F. Houtermans' sixtieth birthday, the book's compilers note the speed of the development of this field of science. They also note that the volume to be released should satisfy the need for a review of its current status and serve as a guide to the existing publications on the subject. "The stories of Houtermans," they write in the preface, "have become legend, and this volume might seem to be incomplete without them. However, the compilers intend to issue a compendium of such tales on the occasion of his seventieth birthday."

But on March 1, 1966, Houtermans succumbed to lung cancer...

References

1. Charles Enz, *No Time to be Brief: A Scientific Biography of Wolfgang Pauli*, (Oxford University Press, 2010).
2. Ann M. Hentschel, "Peripatetic Highlights in Bern," in *The Physical Tourist. A Science Guide for the Traveler*, Eds. John S. Rigden and Roger H. Stuewer, (Birkhäuser, Basel, 2009).
3. *Leonium und andere Anekdoten um den Physikprofessor Dr. F. G. Houtermans, 1903-1966*, Ed. Haro von Buttlar, (Institut für Experimentalphysik III, Ruhr-Universität Bochum, 1982).
4. J. Geiss, C. Gfeller, F. Houtermans, and H. Oeschger, "Special low-level counters," in Proceedings of the United Nations International Conference on the Peaceful Uses of Atomic Energy, **21**, 147-149, (1958).
5. F. Houtermans, "Determination of the age of the Earth from the isotopic composition of meteoritic lead," *Il Nuovo Cimento*, **10**, 1623-1633, 1953. For further developments see F. Houtermans, "Die Blei-Methoden der geologischen Altersbestimmung," *Geolog. Rundschau*, Bd. 49(1), 168-196, (1960).
6. O. Haxel, F. Houtermans, and J. Heintze, "Die Halbwertszeit des K^{40}," *Zeitschrift für Physik*, **128**, 657-667, (1950).
7. W. Herr, F. Houtermans, E. Merz, J. Geiss, and B. Hirt, "Isotopenanalysen des Osmiums aus Eisenmeteoriten und irdischen Proben," *Helvetica Physica Acta*, **32**, 282-284, (1959).
8. F. Houtermans, E. Jäger, M. Schön, and H. Stauffer, "Messung der Thermolumineszenz als Mittel zur Untersuchung der thermischen und der Strahlungsgeschichte von natrlichen Mineralien und Geisteinen," *Annalen der Physik*, **20**, 283-292 (1957).
9. F. Houtermans, "Die Kernemulsionsplatte als Hilfsmittel der Mineralogie und Geologie," *Naturwiss.*, Bd. 38(6), 132-137 1951.
10. F. Houtermans, "Problems of nuclear geophysics...," *Suppl. al Nuovo Cimento*, $N^{\underline{o}}$ 2, 1954, **11**, 390-405.

his scientific achievements in this period. -V.F.

11. F. Houtermans, " L'eta della Terra e dell'Universo," *Suppl. al Nuovo Cimento, N⁰* 1, 1954, **12**, 17-25.

12. N. Grögler, F. Houtermans, and H. Stauffer, "Über die Datierung von Keramik und Ziegel durch Thermolumineszenz," *Helvetica Physica Acta*, **33**, 595-596 (1960).

13. F. Houtermans, "Thermoluminescence glow curves as a research tool on the thermal and radiation history in geologic settings. Lecture 8," in *Summer Course on Nuclear Geology*, Varenna 1960, (Comitato Nazionale per l'Energia Nucleare), Pisa 1961, S. 233-253.

14. F. Houtermans, "Radiation effects in space and thermal effects of atmospheric entry by thermoluminescence measurements on meteorites," Technical Report AF EOAR, grant 61-51 (1962).

15. F. Houtermans and A. Liener, "Thermoluminescence of Meteorites," *Journal of Geophysics Research*, **71**, 3387-3396 (1966).

16. F. Houtermans, "Les elements radioactifs en tant qu'horloge geologique," *La Suisse Horlogere*, 71e Annee, 1956, *N⁰* 1, 3-6.

17. Bruce Doe, "Fritz Houtermans in bad times and in good," *Physics Today*, June 1994, p. 106.

18. *Earth Science and Meteoritics. Dedicated to F. G. Houtermans on his Sixtieth Birthday*, Eds. J. Geiss and E. D. Goldberg, (North-Holland Publishing Company, Amsterdam, 1963), 312 pp.

Friends on Houtermans

Let's review the course of this physicist's life, now from the perspective of our own time.

Brilliant gifts, attendance of a superb vocational school, an excellent general education, a progressive outlook, active involvement with social issues, an intense commencement of creative work, immediately accompanied by the authoring of original papers. And his path in life is initially providential: work at the Technische Hochschule in Berlin – with the promise of a thesis defense in the future – as an assistant professor and eventually quite likely with a full professorship. F. Houtermans is full of ideas and ready to bring them to life.

Then 1933 arrives, and because of his convictions, Germany is closed to him. He emigrates to England, and then to the Soviet Union – following his convictions, but in fact playing a dangerous game with fate, with 1937 just around the corner. It's unlikely that Houtermans thought much beforehand about the possibility of being spurned by the state he set out to live under, in spite of the advice of more cautious friends such as W. Pauli, who like Houtermans had visited the Soviet Union. Namely there his nuclear physics research gains prowess. His actual capabilities in this area, like those of other emigrant German physicists during the war, can be imagined based on his "Plutonium Report" alone! Instead, he faces prison and a long two-and-a-half years of solitary struggle with the ruling system in the country where his convictions and professional interests had made him so eager to go...

Germany's downfall, and the disruption of his research, slows but doesn't stop him: another sharp turn in his life, and another change of host country, finds him this time in Switzerland. And only then, in 1952, does the path of an academic scientist open for him, as it might have 20 years earlier, under different circumstances! Yet I hope the reader has seen that Friedrich Georg Houtermans managed to do many things, until the very end of his life.

This man's story would be incomplete if our book didn't reflect his wit, which made such a memorable impression on his colleagues, friends and even casual acquaintances. Houtermans became the source of specimens of physics humor that have made their way into the folklore of science. Some of their authors have become anonymous in consequence of repeated retelling and variations. One such specimen supplied the title for a collection of jokes and anecdotes associated with Houtermans, *Leonium* [1].

HOW TO FIND A LION (LEONIUM). If you're on a walk and notice a rustling in the bushes, hurry up and make an announcement that a lion has been found in town – what else rustles in the bushes? So if a physicist hears some strange rustling, he immediately writes an article about it. If the lion acquires a Latin name, everyone will believe in it.

And here are a few more examples.

EVEN NUMBERS. Many scientists have an even number of publications. In one article, they assert something, and in the next, they retract it. I do this, too. My number of publications is growing, and they've all been cited.

THE PRINCIPLE OF MECHANICS. France created a new type of jet aircraft. But the first prototypes crashed because the wings broke off in mid-air. The designer decided to consult a professor of mechanics. After some thought, he proposed perforating the wings near the fuselage. And lo and behold! There were no more crashes. "Where did you get that idea?" the professor asked. "It was quite simple: have you ever seen toilet paper tear at the perforations?"

A PRINCIPLE OF THEORETICAL PHYSICS. One night a drunk is staggering around a lamppost, always in a circle. A policeman comes up and asks what he's doing there. "I'm looking for my apartment key," the man replies.The policeman also starts searching. "Are you sure you lost the key here?" "No, it wasn't here, but at least here it's light."

WHY THE GERMANS DIDN'T USE HOUTERMANS' PLUTONIUM IDEA. When I wrote a report about it, I had no interest in seeing it used. So I made sure it was stamped "Strictly Confidential" and had it sent to the deepest vault of the Reich Ministry of

Magisches Auge

Eines Tages kam Houtermans ins Labor und verkündete, dass er sich ein neues Radio gekauft habe. Da sei etwas ganz Neuartiges daran, nämlich ein magisches Auge. „Wozu mag das gut sein?" sinnierte er. „Angeblich soll man damit den Sender scharf einstellen können. Aber jeder Mensch schafft das doch viel besser mit dem Gehör."
Er rätselte stundenlang, wozu das magische Auge denn wirklich notwendig sei. Am nächsten Tag kam er triumphierend ins Institut und sagte:
„Jetzt weiss ich, warum das Radio ein magisches Auge hat: Damit auch die Taubstummen den richtigen Sender finden."

We

Gerade Zahl

„Viele Wissenschaftler", dozierte Houtermans, „schreiben eine gerade Zahl von Veröffentlichungen. Jeweils in der ersten Arbeit behaupten sie etwas und nehmen es in der zweiten zurück. Ich mache das auch gelegentlich so. Dann wächst das Publikationsverzeichnis, und man wird überall zitiert."

vB

Deutsche Sprache

Wir hatten eine Arbeit zur Veröffentlichung bei der Zeitschrift für Physik eingereicht. Der Herausgeber, Prof. Dr. R.W. Pohl, residierte im gleichen Hause im oberen Stock des Göttinger Physikalischen Instituts. Da Pohl ein sehr korrekter Mann war, gab es zwischen ihm und Houtermans gelegentlich Spannungen.

Figure 41.   A page from the original German edition of *Leonium*.

Posts. It lay there for the whole war. And it'd be lying there still, if the vault had survived when the bombs hit the building.

PAULI'S EXCLUSION PRINCIPLE. Pauli was best man at Fritz Houtermans' wedding. When Houtermans married for the fourth time, he said he wouldn't ask Pauli this time around, because in physics, the Pauli exclusion principle was in effect. Pauli sent a telegram: "Congratulations, as usual."

TEST RESULTS. Every time Pauli visited Houtermans' institute in Bern, the radiation counters would begin to tick furiously when he and Houtermans would enter the lab together. After many possible reasons for this effect were discussed and rejected, Houtermans finally said that someone must be carrying around a source of radiation. All eyes turned to Pauli. "Pauli," Houtermans said, "I'll bet this is your doing. All right then, trousers off!" Pauli took off his pants and set them on the radiation counter. "Your turn, Fisl, trousers off!" said Pauli. Houtermans took off his trousers and the counter became to tick violently. Houtermans' handkerchief turned out to be strongly "beaming." Delighted, Houtermans sealed it in a plastic bag and labeled it "Radioactive. Property of Prof. Houtermans."

ALTITUDE SICKNESS. On a visit to the institute's Jungfraujoch research station in the Alps, Houtermans met a group of doctors who were conducting trials of an altitude sickness drug. However, in talking with the scientists, it came out that there were two "homeopathic" remedies: carbon dioxide and alcohol. Houtermans immediately invented a "drug": "Obviously combining the two would work twice as well. So let's drink champagne!" It worked wonderfully.

Of course, as with any respected professor, there are numerous anecdotes about Houtermans' absentmindedness.

A FANCY SUIT. One day some of the institute staff encountered Houtermans, dressed in striped trousers and a black jacket, standing in the street, lost in thought. *"Kinder,"* he said to them, "I'm so rarely dressed like this. If only I knew where I was going!"

TWINS. One of Houtermans' employees became the father of twins. This event was was raucously celebrated at the lab, with assistance from the boss. That night at home, the happy father heard his phone ring. Worried that something might have happened at the hospital, he picked up the phone and heard Houtermans' voice: "Listen, some character at our lab had twins, and I'm bent out of shape. Could you fill in for me at tomorrow's lecture?"

Let's finish the story of this extraordinary man, a brilliant scientist with an incredible fate, by portraying him in a mosaic of the voices of those who knew him best.

Charlotte Houtermans: Fritz seemed to attract people. He was always full of ideas. He told stories, witty jokes, he was interested in a great number of different things, running the gamut from physics to music, to economy, to politics.

George Gamow: I always remember him sitting with a slide rule at a desk covered with a paper tablecloth and laden with a dozen coffee cups.

Walter Elsasser: He was the wittiest man I ever met.

Victor Weisskopf: Houtermans was an entertaining person, cheerful, humorous, with a huge number of ideas for designing experiments.

Henrik Casimir: He was a colorful man – so colorful that one could sometimes forget that he was also a fine physicist.

Otto Frisch: A physicist of Dutch-German descent who never achieved the degree of success that his mind's originality deserved.

Edoardo Amaldi: Those who knew him will never forget his enthusiasm for science, his devotion to it, his open and friendly attitude toward everyone.

Alexander Ilyich Akhiezer: Houtermans was a clever physicist and a good guy.

Olga Trapeznikova-Shubnikova: He was such a nice man! His only fault was having an unmusical voice...

Marie Rausch von Traubenberg: I can testify with absolute certainty that Houtermans was always a man who severely condemned Nazism – not only in words but also in deeds.

J. Geiss (Physics Institute, University of Bern, Switzerland) and E. Zeller (Department of Geology, University of Kansas, USA): Perhaps his most precious gift to all of us was the ability to make us go past the limits of artificial boundaries of the physical sciences.

Here, too, is further evidence of the scientific world's respect for the merits of Friedrich Houtermans. In 1973, at its regular session in Sydney, the International Astronomical Union adopted 50 new names for a newly created detailed map of the lunar surface. One of these names was Houtermans, whom the March 1974 issue of *Sky and Telescope* magazine called a "German-Swiss physicist of astronomical importance, who as early as 1929 discussed nuclear fusion reactions as the source of stellar energy." The Houtermans crater, 30 km in diameter (87.0 degrees longitude and −9.3 degrees latitude), immortalized his name.

References

1. *Leonium und andere Anekdoten um den Physikprofessor Dr. F. G. Houtermans, 1903-1966*, Ed. Haro von Buttlar, (Institut für Experimentalphysik III, Ruhr-Universität Bochum, 1982).

Chronology

Friedrich Georg "Fritz" Houtermans
January 22, 1903 – March 1, 1966

1906: Fritz Houtermans parents divorced, his mother Elsa Houtermans and Fritz move to Vienna

1911-21: *Gymnasium* in Vienna (the last year in Wickersdorf)

1921-27: Göttingen University, studies under the supervision of James Franck

1927: PhD thesis defence at Göttingen University

1928: Houtermans collaborates with George Gamow on α decay theory

1929-33: Houtermans is Gustav Hertz's assistant at *Technische Hochschule* in Berlin

1929: Houtermans collaborates with Robert d'Escourt Atkinson on nuclear fusion in stars

1930, August: Houtermans' first visit to the USSR, marriage to Charlotte Riefenstahl

1933 (early summer)**-1934** (November or December): England, work at Shoenberg's *Electrical and Musical Instruments*

1934: June 23: Knoll-Houtermans-Schulze patent claim (Electron microscope invention)

1935, early February: Houtermans' arrival at Kharkov

1935, November 28: First arrest of Moisei Koretz in Kharkov

1936, May 26: Arrest of Éva Striker in Moscow

1937, March 1: Arrest of Alexander Weissberg

1937, March 4: Arrest of Konrad Weisselberg (executed on December 16, 1937)

1937, July 5: Arrest of Lev Rozenkevich (executed on November 9, 1937)

1937, August 6: Arrest of Lev Shubnikov (executed on November

10, 1937)

1937, August 6: Arrest of Matvei Bronshtein in Kiev (executed on February 18, 1938)

1937, September 21: Arrest of Vadim Gorsky (executed on November 8, 1937)

1937, October 7: Arrest of Valentin Fomin (executed on December 2, 1937)

1937, December 1: Fritz Houtermans arrested in Moscow

1937, December 16: Charlotte Houtermans leaves the USSR (with Giovanna and Jan)

1938, January 4: Fritz Houtermans transported to Kharkov

1938, January 11-22: Eleven day continuous interrogation of Fritz Houtermans (Conveyor)

1938, January 22: Fritz Houtermans told of alleged Charlotte's arrest and transfer of children to orphanage

1938, April 28: Arrest of Lev Landau, Yuri Rumer and Moisei Koretz in Moscow

1938, June 22: Arrest of Ivan Obreimov

1938, July 14: Arrest of Alexander Leipunsky (released on August 9, 1938)

1940, January 1: NKVD hands over Alexander Weissberg to Gestapo on the bridge of Brest-Litovsk

1940, May 2: NKVD hands over Fritz Houtermans to Gestapo on the bridge of Brest-Litovsk

1940, June 3-July 16: Gestapo prison in Berlin

1941, January 1: Houtermans starts working for Manfred von Ardenne

1941, Autumn: Houtermans' "field inspection" visit to Kiev and Kharkov with König and Bewilogua

1942, May 15: "Guest" of C. Weiss at the Imperial Physical Technical Institute

1945, January 31: Leaving the Imperial Physical Technical Institute and moving to Göttingen

1945, September 3: Houtermans' petition for an appointment with Göttingen University

1946, August: Assistant at the *II. Physikalische Institut*

1949, October: Houtermans obtains a supernumerary lectureship

1951: Job offers from Bern and Berlin

1952-1966: Full Professor at Bern University and Head of Experimental Physics Institute

312

Appendices

Compiled by the Editor

Charlotte Houtermans: Last Diary

Brione,[1] Summer 1966

Again I am looking down onto the lake. I found a bench on the road above the village, half hidden under a tree so that I can write in the pleasant half-shade. Today the water is slate gray and brownish and the mountains have sharp silhouettes. It is peaceful and beautiful and I am at rest.

Many things I seem to have left behind me beyond the mountains. It may be good in this slightly detached mood, in which I find myself, remote from any interference, to take stock and to draw the final line under my life with Fisl, if I can. Somehow it is doubtful, that this should be possible. Too much was involved, too many invisible Threads still tie me to him in ways which I really do not quite grasp. Our life might have been easier if I had understood him. May be I never even knew him, never really found out a single thing about him. I believed in him, I loved him, I invested much love and thought to help him achieve what I thought at the time he wanted to accomplish and what I firmly believed was a very worthwhile goal.

It shocked me realizing how lonely Fisl must have been towards the end. Jan's visit last October was apparently one of the few, very good things he enjoyed. There was also an encounter on New Year Eve with Bamsi in which he was very outgoing and loving and happy to see her.

At the Wilbrandts[2] I talked one evening with Karl Heinz Mayer,[3]

---

[1] Brione is a municipality in the district of Locarno in the canton of Ticino in Switzerland.

[2] Walther Wilbrandt (1907-1979), a German-Swiss physiologist and pharmacologist who worked from 1944 until 1977 as a professor and director of an institute at the University of Bern. Renata Wilbrandt (1912-1972), his wife.

[3] Probably Charlotte Houtermans is mistaken here. The University of Bern has kept record of all its professors since 1528. The closest name is Klaus Peter Meyer (1911-1986). In 1961, Klaus Peter Meyer was appointed to direct the newly founded Institut für Angewandte Physik (Institute of Applied Physics) in Bern. See *Phys. Bl.* 42, No 7,

who is the Director of the Institut für "Angewandte Physik." According to Renate Wilbrandt (who brought Fisl to the hospital last August) K.H. Mayer really loved Fisl. It was he who also made all the funeral arrangements. He spoke to me for more than an hour and gave such a warm picture of Fisl as the director of the institute, that I felt exactly as I did in Göttingen years ago when I only anticipated, wishfully, his future achievements. There seems to be no doubt about the importance of the Institute as it now stands. Contrary to all expectations Fisl managed to keep all research projects moving. But ever since his fall in 1961 and his long illness afterwards, he must have aged rapidly, not only physically. Growing old happens to all and lucky are those who can accept it and can make their peace with new conditions. Fisl apparently could not. It might have been his character, that made him over-exaggerate the importance of youth, but I rather think it was the sudden onslaught of age after his illness which did not allow for a gradual adjustment. In spite of this he was in a limited way very much aware of what was happening in the laboratory. Everybody mentioned particularly, how lucid and clarifying were all his remarks during the colloquia until the very last time. All were quite sure that as the guiding genius, it would be difficult to replace him ever.

I went home after this meeting at the Wilbrandts with a good feeling. This had been the testimonial of an achievement, which would last.

I had also wished to see the Institute itself. During my first week in Bern Paul took me to a colloquium, where Wolfgang Paul (Bonn),[4] who is now at CERN, spoke about his machine. Afterwards I met Geiss,[5] Mayer and Oeschger,[6] who all invited me to come again. But

---

p. 245 (1986).

[4]Wolfgang Paul (1913-1993), a German physicist, who co-developed the non-magnetic quadrupole mass filter which laid the foundation for what is now called an ion trap. He received the 1989 Nobel Prize in physics for this work with Hans Georg Dehmelt.

[5]Johannes Geiss was appointed as Head of the Institute of Physics, Bern University, after Houtermans' death.

[6]Hans Oeschger (1927-1998) was the founder of the Division of Climate and Environmental Physics at the Physics Institute of the University of Bern in 1963 and director until his retirement in 1992. Oeschger was the first to date the age of Pacific deep water.

since it was the end of the semester and the exam period it seemed difficult to find a convenient time. At last, on Thursday July 21, I met Geiss at the Institute. He showed me the first mass spectrograph, which I still remembered from 1953, and all the new ones, Oeschgers C^{14} counters, etc.

Most of the time, though, we sat talking in Fisl's office. Geiss still had not moved into it, and though most of the books had been removed, there was still a little of the old atmosphere left behind.

Geiss filled out many of the blank spots, still there even after Mayer's talk. He told me for instance about the difficulties Fisl had had about the financial records of his various scientific accounts. To dispel ugly rumors, Geiss and the others insisted on an investigation and succeeded – as they had hoped – in vindicating Fisl completely, which not only cleared him but also raised his status and that of the institute considerably. So in the end the administration of the university were even proud of Fisl's achievements and of their importance for the Institute.

I also got the impression that Geiss must have been very fond of Fisl and had managed the last years with a great deal of tact. This became especially difficult after he had been promoted to Vice-Director and *Ordinarius*. Geiss gave me a copy of the volume published by Fisl's friends for his 60th birthday and also promised to send me a photostat collection of Fisl's papers. (They never came, though.) I had inquired particularly about these papers and was glad to learn that they were going to be collected. One of the last papers Fisl apparently wrote was a contribution for Gentner's[7] 60th birthday, which was this July and to which Geiss went. All this is in good hands.

***

I do not know any facts, only stories told me at odd moments, out of context and ill remembered. Whatever they might tell, it will

---

The Oeschger counter was the leading instrument in geochemical studies for many years.
[7]Wolfgang Gentner (1906-1980), a German experimental nuclear physicist. In 1956, Gentner was appointed as Director of the Synchrocyclotron Department at CERN. In 1958, he became director of the new Max Planck Institute for Nuclear Physics at Heidelberg.

rather be what I felt when I listened to them, and I suppose I only remember those which not only fascinated me but contributed to my image of Fisl. He was from the beginning when I met him in Göttingen during the winter of 1926-27, a singular figure quite apart from all the others, not attractive at first, but becoming increasingly more engaging and also more intriguing. What must have puzzled me most was that there seemed to be no ordinary explanation for his personality, no common denominator to shed light on his actions or sayings, his likes or dislikes. He was brusque and tender, aloof and social, attentive and remote. Because I believed he loved me, I set out to understand him, may be not rationally, but by trusting and loving him and believing everything he said in his good moments.

***

The name of course is Dutch. It was Fisl's grandfather, who came to Germany. His family lived in the Catholic part of Holland, southwest of Eindhoven. They were probably merchants, one brother was a stonemason and sculptor and gave a statue of St. Sebastian to a church. The grandfather's name was Joseph Cornelius Houtermans, born in 1848 in Voerendal. (He died in 1921 in Thorn, West Prussia.) Joseph H. himself became an architect. He must have had acquired considerable knowledge and experience in his profession, because he was later on commissioned to build the Navy Harbor in Bremerhafen. He was still a young man at the time and the family legend – as related to me by Elsa H., Fisl's mother – has it that he made a million marks. With an enormous amount of money in any case he decided to travel, stopped first at the Riviera, became intrigued by the Casino in Monte Carlo, tried to break the bank like so many before him and lost.

Rather penniless now, he followed the traditions of the time and joined an army, specifically that of the Pope, who was involved in the Italian Civil War. Later he as well as his son Otto H. went to Rome to present their newly wedded wives to the Pope. Fisl did not follow this tradition, but much later sought an audience with another Pope, Pius XII, together with Harold Urey.[8] Their interests were neither religious nor based on the old family tales but strictly scientific. Another Pope, Pius XII, I think in a Marian year, had pronounced "Ex Cathedra" that the church recognized all the scientific findings concerning the age of the Earth as absolutely true. It was vey much like Fisl to use this as a reason for seeking an audience.[9] Gamow before that quoted the papal statement in one of his publications.

Joseph H. returned to Germany, again became very successful and probably at this time was engaged with the Naval Harbor. He also married a German girl from the neighborhood of Bielefeld: Ida Strathmann, born in 1856 in Lenzighausen near Herford. The name Strathmann was very familiar to me when I was a schoolgirl. My father knew the Strathmanns; of course I do not know how close their relationship with Ida was. I always passed the Strathmann House on my way to school and wondered about it. It was always called "Das Figürchen Haus," because of its late gothic facade decorated with innumerable small sculptures.

The next thing I remember to have heard was that he must have been a fairly shrewd businessman. He got wind of government plans to build a fortress in Thorn, Posen, and not only was he chosen to build it, but he also sold to the government vast areas of land, that he had previously acquired. These land speculations must have been very extensive, because his son years later still owned some real estate in Posen, which he sold bit by bit whenever he needed money. At his father's death Fisl could have inherited the last remnants but refused since at that time in 1936 he already lived in Kharkov. The grandfather Joseph H. retired from business sometime around the end of the century. He lived in Zoppot, near Danzig, with his wife

---

[8]Harold Urey (1893 – 1981) was an American physical chemist whose pioneering work on isotopes earned him the Nobel Prize in Chemistry in 1934 for the discovery of deuterium.
[9]Fritz Houtermans was the first to estimate the age of the Earth combining experimental data on radioisotopes with cosmochemistry and geosciences. His paper "Determination of the Age of the Earth from the Isotopic Composition of Meteoritic Lead," *Nuovo Cimento*, 10, 1623-1633, 1953 was ground-breaking. The Holmes-Houtermans model estimated the age as app. 4.5 billion. As for the age of the Universe, the current measurements yield app. 13.8 billion years.

and only son Oscar Otto H., but spent a great part of the winter in his Villa in Capri.

Many many years later a little aftermath happened, a kind of footnote to family history. It was the year 1939 or probably 1940 when Bamsi, Jan and I lived in Poughkeepsie, NY. Bamsi went to the Arlington school and for a little while had to be tutored in mathematics. I would walk with her and Jan to the tutor's house and always passed the home of Dr. Leiser, whose wife was a cousin of the Loewenherzs and Roses, my friends from Beverungen and Lauenfoerde. I knew the Leisers only slightly, but the destiny of my Jewish friends was of constant concern to us and we would occasionally exchange news. Dr. Leiser had finally succeeded in bringing his old parents safely to the United States, and we stopped at the house just a few days after their arrival.

The old gentleman was very deaf and had the somewhat wooden bearing of a statue. He made me vaguely think of Hindenburg. Dr. Leiser introduced us in a loud voice, particularly mentioning Jan's name, who looked up to the octogenarian with a scared little face. "This is Jan Houtermans." He repeated it twice more, whereupon a sudden smile softened the stern face: "Houtermans?... Houtermans? Oh, I know that name well; I sold to a man of that name many, many bricks when they built the fortress of Thorn."

So here was a man who had known Jan's and Giovanna's great-grandfather!

***

Brione, Thursday, July 28

Of Fisl's father I know very little, but I liked him. He was a heavy man with a round neck and a red moonlike face, and wore rimless glasses. He does not sound too attractive and to imagine him as an over-slender youth was difficult for me. Fisl had not inherited any of his features, but in his twenties Fisl was also very thin and his dark face with the blue eyes was so narrow that he seemed mainly profile. While Fisl was dark, his father was reddish, very short cropped. Otto H.'s youth must have been very conventional. He studied law, belonged to one of the fraternities, who were fighting *mensuren*[10] and even much later went to all their reunions in Munich. While still a *Referendar*[11] he met Elsa Wanek,[12] when he stopped in Vienna with his parents on their way to Capri. They married and lived in Zoppot near Danzig. I do not believe he practiced law, but lived comfortably on very generous allowances from his father. The style of life in Zoppot has partly dictated by the frequent presence of the German crown prince. One gave elegant parties, played tennis, ate often food out of season, brought in at great expense. Elsa H., who was used to the intellectual atmosphere of Vienna, never adjusted to the new lifestyle.

Otto H. was conservative, you may say bourgeois. He had rented a beautiful house, which I visited once, had several expensive hobbies like *Photographie*, fishing and hunting, a collection of lovely etched wine glasses from Bohemia with individual hunting scenes, scores of oriental rugs. I was quite overwhelmed by it all, especially by the decorations of horns and antlers in the entrance hall. But for me most important was his sense of humor, which Fisl inherited from him. We got along very well with each other, he teased me about my cooking abilities, praised my turkish coffee, presented me with a cookbook called "Only for Men" in which utensils were not named but only referred to by numbers matching the illustrations on the front leaf. He probably also hoped that I would be able to improve the unconventional ways of his son.

Elsa H. was obviously ill fitted for the life in Zoppot; after only a few years, when Fisl was three, she divorced his father and returned to Vienna with her son, asking no alimonies, since she was quite well situated financially.

---

[10]The traditional kind of fencing practiced by some student corporations (Studentenverbindungen) in Germany.

[11]In Germany the graduate in law who seeks a legal career must embark upon a period of practical training as a Referendar.

[12]Elsa Wanek (1878-1942) was born and brought up in Vienna. She was half-Jewish, since her mother belonged to the Karplus family, well-known in Austria because it owned a liberal newspaper, "Das Wiener Tagesblatt." This would make Fritz Houtermans *jüdischer Mischling zweiten Grades* according to the Nazi classification. According to the Jewish tradition he would have been considered Jewish.

Figure 1.   Fritz Houtermans with his parents, Elsa Houtermans (née Wanek) and Oscar Otto Houtermans, and his grandfather Joseph Houtermans, Toruń (now in Poland), 1905. Courtesy of the Physics Institute of the University of Bern.

I had returned from America in the summer of 1929 and had found a job with Springer in Berlin, when I first met Otto H. At that time Fisl was first assistant at the Technische Hochschule in Berlin under Westphal and in charge of the advanced laboratory. The director of the Physics Department was Gustav Hertz. We both lived in Halensee, near to each other and near to Bimbus (Charlotte Schlesinger) and Fisl's cousin Anna Gmeyner-Wiesner. I knew very little of Fisl's family, which was large, with numerous cousins, half-brothers and sisters, uncles, aunts, etc.

Certain facts emerged, though. He had met his father for the first time since he was a baby at the age of 15. His father paid for the university years with rather elaborate checks and was proud of his career. In the summer when I left for the USA to teach at Vassar College, his father gave him a beautiful present for his completed PhD exam, financing for him and Elsa a trip to Spain, including Tenerife if I remember correctly. They must have enjoyed it tremendously.

Not knowing any Spanish, they spoke Latin with what they imagined to be a Spanish pronunciation. They got along quite well, especially with some Spanish priests, who planned to travel to New
York where they were to post a letter to me in Poughkeepsie, which
confused me for a while.

Back in Vienna they found so many accumulated letters from me
that Fisl's mother for the first time admitted that the obvious liaison
between Fisl and me must really be a serious one. During 1929-30
Fisl's father asked us once to come to Danzig for a visit, probably to
have a look at me. I too was anxious to have a look at his father's
family and went quite happily.

At that time Otto H. and his family lived in a large beautiful
house in Zoppot, as I have already mentioned. Shortly after his
divorce Otto H. had married again the daughter of (I believe) a
Gymnasium professor, a very nice, kind and understanding person,
not very beautiful. She had the good sense to fall in with his various
hobbies and eccentricities. They went for a short while to Windhuk,
German South west Afrika, where their first son Peter Africanus
was born. When they came back to Germany, they settled down in
Zoppot and he became director of a bank.

The house in Zoppot had a large entrance hall decorated with
trophies, huge stuffed birds, to me all rather gruesome looking but
obviously the proud takings of hunting trips all over Europe. Besides
Peter there were two more children – Rosemarie, called Rolly, and
Hans (Hänsi), whom Fisl liked particularly. Nothing in the house
seemed to agree with my impression or anticipation of Fisl's family.
The rooms were doubly carpeted, the wine glasses specially blown in
Bohemia and etched with hunting scenes, the precious Meissen porce-
lain – it all did not blend with my dreams of Fisl. Fisl indeed was
very much the outsider in Zoppot. He was not interested in money
or being a banker, in wine collections or etched glasses, in being a
Corpsstudent[13] or hunting trophies. His posture alone aggravated his

---

[13] Corps (or Korps), are the oldest still existing kind of Studentenverbindung, Germany's
traditional university corporations. Their roots date back to the 15th century.

father and his taste in jackets appalled him. The upstairs bedroom disclosed yet another hobby of his father, which Fisl actually liked and showed to me very proudly. It was a beautiful built-in cabinet with innumerable drawers for all photographic equipments and films. Orderliness in his later mineral collections Fisl must have inherited from his father, and probably also his sense of humor, though I thought Fisl's was more sophisticated and not so earthy.

He had one whole day in Danzig, an old Hansa city, where Fisl showed me all the historic places of the old town. But then, with tongue in cheek, he began to point out various sites and documented them with dates of their historical connections, all referring to "Danziger Lachs" (salmon), which I took to be true quite religiously, astonished about his detailed historical knowledge. I must have been even more besotted and in love than I thought, because only in the evening did I find out, that it was, all of it, sheer invention. In am sorry now that I cannot remember anything at all of the story itself.

After this visit to Zoppot I never met the family again except for Otto's short stop-overs in Berlin. Usually he came from a meeting of his "Alte Herren," his "Corps" in Munich, or from a hunting trip, or from a shopping trip buying elegant fishing tackle. We were married by that time and often felt very disgruntled by these visits. He had cut Fisl's allowance by 50% as soon as we married for the lovely reason that two could live cheaper than one. I had to give up my job on account of German tax laws, and we felt suddenly very poor. When he was in Berlin, he lived at Kempinski's and always asked us there for dinner. Kempinski was a fashionable and expensive place at the Kurfürstendamm. Fisl and I went there sometimes, but only ordered *kleine Zwischengerichte,* cheese and coffee, pretending that we had eaten a whole menu. With his father of course we ate a proper menu, enjoying it and inwardly protesting because the bill usually ran into two figures, a sum which would have been enough to feed us for a week.

Two things I remember which are rather funny. Once when his monthly check had not arrived on the 10th or so, I became desperate and sent Otto a telegram. He had been in Berlin the month before

and had left two precious fishing rods in my keeping. There was also
a pigskin bag with priceless flies and other fishing gear. The fishing
rods were resting flat on the armoire. I had strict orders never, never
to lift them. My telegram simply said: "Rods already at 20 degrees,
will lift them to 90 degrees, if money not received immediately."

The money came promptly. He had thought the telegram to be a
great joke.

During his students days, being as usual out of funds, Fisl had
telegraphed him: "Lichtzeiger (Lightbeam) of the ammeter [14] broken, please send immediately 75 Mark. Fritz." To this also he had
responded by return mail, laughing, and sent the money.

Once at Kempinski's, when I was alone with him for a moment,
he complained to me about the shabbiness of Fisl's overcoat, asking
me why I did not buy him a decent one. I pointed out that we simply
did not have the money.

"How much do you need?"

I told him and he took his wallet and gave me the money. Fisl of
course was delighted, also astonished, but had no intention of buying
a coat. There was a theoretical conference at Pauli's in Zurich, and
it just paid for our tickets.

Later on when his father visited again, Fisl always had to borrow
a good coat from a friend, and since he did not always borrow the
same coat, it was finally revealed, to our sorrow, because this time
his father did not think it was a joke.

* * *

Danzig was at that time still a free city (Freie Hansastadt), separated from Germany by a strip of Polish territory, called the Polish
corridor, which one could cross by train. While crossing the corridor
the train was sealed. When Hitler came to power and life began to
become extremely precarious and dangerous Fisl went once more to
visit his father. I was terribly alarmed and had no quiet moment
until he was finally back in Berlin. My fears were justified, as I
learned. Before getting on the train in Danzig Fisl had bought as he

---

[14] An ammeter is a measuring instrument used to measure the electric current in a circuit.

always did all the newspapers he could find from the extreme right to the left. He carried them in his attache case. When the Nazi control came, they questioned him at length about those left and communist papers. The fact that he had also all the other papers did not help him, but what saved him and convinced them of his political innocence was that they found the beautiful bound cellar-book with all the vintage entries and lists according to years, when bought, when laid down, etc. This could not be a communist, just a crazy capitalist, and they let him go. I do not know whether this was the last time that Fisl saw his father, but it might have been. In 1936 when we were already in Kharkov we learned that he had been hunting. Aiming at a deer he had a heart seizure and died immediately.

My remembrances and impressions of Fisl's childhood and the years in the Gymnasium in Vienna, and the final year in Wickersdorf are vague and disconnected like episodes in a dream. Even in the earliest years of our friendship and love there was a reluctance on his part to speak of his youth and to tell me, so eager to listen, how he had lived before I met him.

Once when I urged him to speak of the past, he said there can never be an understanding, so why try. "For instance this table," he said, "will remind me of one in our room in Vienna, where Anny and Tully and I played. Since you will never see it, you will never comprehend to what kind of table, emotions, remembrances I refer, why I should call an object good or beautiful or ugly, because you will never have the same frame of reference as I."

It was a total rebuff. I am sure he had no idea how much he hurt me. I hoped he would now speak of the present, our life together, our dreams of the future, of growing understanding and love. He did not. I felt like a lonely child standing outside in the rain and nobody offering shelter and warmth. After that, suddenly, his mood changed, the present became real to him and he kissed me. There was joy and happiness in this kiss for me, but maybe rather the happiness of a butterfly rejoicing during a summer day, without past or future.

I was too involved already in this tangle of love and excitement and unable to cut loose. The only thing I had was the future and I hoped to build it on our common experiences. Thus I began to ignore his past. Rather shrewdly I had begun to understand that his past hardly included physics, which had just then burst into unexpected channels and promised scientific developments more fantastic than fairy tales and more exhilarating. Fisl was involved and in the middle of it all. This life was new to him too and quite remote from any childhood associations.

***

When Fisl's mother after her short marriage returned to Vienna, she found her younger sister married to Rudolf Gmeyner, a lawyer. He was the man she probably cared for most all her life. Whenever he was mentioned, there seemed to be an aura about his name, and I imagined him to be the wisest, the most understanding, the most likable and most intelligent of men. He was surrounded by a household of women, Lili, his wife, three daughters, Anna, Tully and Kitty, some hangers on and devoted distant cousins, all loving slaves who tried to anticipate his slightest wish. I met him only once when he came to Berlin to visit Anny who was just then getting a divorce from Berthold Wiesner, a biologist in Edinburgh. She had left him and his huge institute with rats, mice and monkeys, to live in Berlin with her little daughter Eva. "Onkel Rudolf " surprised me. He was a very slender, small man, speaking in a broad Viennese, and he certainly had none of the characteristics I had expected to find. He warned me severely against a marriage with Fisl. But if I went ahead with it in spite of all his warnings, he would wash his hands of it. He had warned me and was at least honest. Most difficulties raised by Fisl's family were based on my family background: north German, rather poor, though well educated. In short, they did not know us.

Fisl's mother took an apartment in Vienna next to her sisters. Together they occupied a whole block. She engaged maids, a governess or nurse, a cook and began to organize her life in such a way that she could go to the Gymnasium and pass the Abiturium [15] to

---

[15] Das Abitur (in the obsolescent Abiturium; from Latin *abiturire* want to depart) is the highest level of the German high school diploma opening access to university education. The Abitur diploma earlier was referred to as the Test of Maturity.

enable her to study at the University. She finished with a doctorate in chemistry (or biology), one of the first women to do so in Austria. She was brilliant, almost masculine in the way she pursuit her goals. Her memory was phenomenal and never left her. She also was endowed with tremendous energy. She walked for hours and hours, climbed mountains, read everything, making notes and annotations, kept a diary, ruled and educated not only Fisl but also the three little cousins. Her earlier photos portray her as a beautiful woman. She was very tall, rather gawky with a masculine stride and no grace. On the other hand she was imposing in the long dresses which had slight trains for the evening gowns. Most all of them came from Paris. Lissy Frandzik called her affectedly Cosima, but in America she reminded us mostly of Eleanor Roosevelt, whom she resembled in more ways than just physical likeness.

During Fisl's childhood the summer months were usually spent in Baden near Vienna where they rented a villa with a large garden. For the children it was a paradise; Fisl mentioned it often though never in great details. Once Fritz and Anni climbed into a cherry tree, ate cherries and spit out the stones. Apparently Tante Lili surprised them and sternly forbade them to spit the stones on the ground. Obediently they now swallowed them with the result of getting pretty sick.

Fisl loved his mother abjectly and admired her tremendously. But when together, they always had conflicts, different opinions, probably based on their need for independence, for freedom, their wish to be leaders. They both wanted that all their lives.

As far as Fisl was concerned it colored his whole life. In a house where so many women reigned he had only slight powers over his younger cousins and had to fight for recognition. Anny, who was a few years older, had a strong personality and was very gifted. She invented stories and plays and led the little group. In turn she and Fisl tyrannized little Tully especially during a play, in which Tully always got to be the polar bear sitting under the table while the others had the more active, better parts.

In school Fisl was apparently very good, especially in mathematics.

He had many friends; they still remember him now. They knew him as a younger schoolmate or as a good pal from the camp days in Ischl. Later on in the Gymnasium he must have had some difficulties – I do not know what kind – and was even brought to see Dr. Freud whose daughter Anna was his mother's friend or at least acquaintance. This did not last very long. As soon as he had found out that Freud was interested in his dreams Anny and he invented beautiful fairy tales before each session, and when this was discovered, the sessions ended.

One amusing story about Anna Freud. She used to take long walks in the Prater with her huge dog and afterwards drove home in a "Fiacre" (horse drawn carriage). Once the dog roamed alone in the park, came to the gate and jumped into an empty carriage expecting to be driven home. This the taximan did and delivered the dog to Freud's address.

When Fisl's school difficulties could not be resolved, the family decided, that he should spent the last year before the Abiturium in Wickersdorf, where Wyneken [16] had founded a "Land Erziehungsheim" – something similar to the American private boarding or prep schools.

Much has been said about the value of Wickersdorf. The negative criticism it received was mainly based on Wyneken's private life, the strong emphasis on the Greek eros, a tendency to condone homosexual relationships. Apart from this, which was very private and came to public attention only in later years, the whole setup was very modern and the children profited enormously. Instead of separating the children into age groups, living in separate houses, they formed family units, where a teacher and his wife lived in a house with a group of children, boys and girls, of all ages. Fisl loved the head of his house. Years later we visited him in Stuttgart where he lived in a charming house with his wife. From its windows one could look down into the city, enjoying a fantastic view. It was in this "family"

---

[16]Gustav Wyneken (1875-1964) was a German educational reformer, free thinker and charismatic leader. His ideas and practice on education and youth became highly influential but were also controversial.

that Fisl met Heini Kurella and Irmin von Holten,[17] only 12 years old at that time, and who loved Fisl all these years like an older brother. Irmin later married Robert Atkinson, who worked with Fisl in Franck's Laboratory and followed Fisl to Berlin. They too left Germany and lived alternately in England and America. Between them in age was Heini Kurella the most gentle and lovable human being. I met him when I first came to Berlin. Heini shared an apartment in Berlin with his sister Tanja, a dance and gymnastic teacher, who married James Stern, an English writer, and lives with him in England. We sometimes would spend a weekend with Heini when Tanja was out of town. I never met anybody who was so pleasant to live with, so amusing and friendly and also so invisible, if one needed to be alone. Heini became editor of the *Rote Fahne,* the communist newspaper; finally he went to Russia and was killed there during the early purges [18] according to an account in Jan Valtin's book "Out of the Night." [19]

The impression I received about the people they mentioned, the tales they talked about them, was that of a very friendly, intellectual crowd, of an artistic atmosphere. All their young fantasies and philosophical queries were taken seriously, they read poetry, they studied philosophy, languages, economics, and whatever ... and loved it all. It also encouraged – which seems to be obvious - any kind of individualism. This might not be strange or even undesirable from an American point of view, but it was certainly unusual for a German school. Nothing slightly "smelling" of militarism was tolerated or encouraged. Conventions were kept at a minimum , and the inner necessity of each blossoming individual was the guiding line of his individual education.

When Fisl appeared in Göttingen after having earned the Bac-

---

[17] Irmin von Holten (1907-1990), the future wife of Fritz Houtermans' co-author, Robert d'Escourt Akinson.

[18] NKVD records show that Heinrich Kurella was arrested by NKVD on October 19, 1937, sentenced to death on charges of participation in a counter-revolutionary organization, and was shot by a firing squad on October 28, 1937.

[19] Jan Valtin was the alias of Richard Julius Hermann Krebs (1905-1951), a German writer during the interwar period. He settled in the United States in 1938. His bestselling book "Out of the Night" was released in 1940.

calaureate in Wickersdorf he consequently behaved and also looked quite differently from everybody else who had gone through a regular school. With his blue eyes and dark hair, which was not cropped but cut in a Viennese fashion, his lanky behavior and slight stoop, he was as different from the ordinary run of young German academics as if he had come from the moon. I always thought he looked Italian, which impression grew even stronger after I had met Beppo Occhial-ibi [20] in Cambridge. Though Beppo's eyes were more beautiful, as types, he could have been Fisl's brother, allowing for some stretch of the imagination.

During the first years of our mutual stay in Göttingen we never met, though one seemed to be aware of each other. The city was very small. It had only 30,000 inhabitants, 10,000 of whom were students. The university buildings and laboratories were spread out over the whole town; students rented private rooms, ate in restaurants or in the Mensa; as far as I remember, we owned the world.

I came to Göttingen in 1922, a difficult time in Germany because the inflation was growing at such a rate, that finally the money one had was loosing its value from one day to another. The student body was threatened with starvation but ingeniously enough found a way of getting food without paying for it. They formed a committee whose members wrote letters to the major German food industries asking for their help in form of free food supplies. The German government was also approached and agreed to have all donations shipped without charge. What arrived did not exactly constitute the basis for a balanced diet – flour, sugar, beans, peas, margarine, etc. We cooked the meals in the kitchen of the Mensa and whoever cooked or served or washed dishes, got a free meal. The actual price for everybody else was an absolute minimum. One year we fed 3,000 students at least. Most of us had just this one meal, watery rice soups, beans and such, but nobody seemed to mind. We also received gifts from America, huge bales with clothing which must have been

---

[20]Giuseppe Paolo Stanislao "Beppo" Occhialini, an Italian physicist, who contributed to the discovery of pion decay in 1947, with César Lattes and Cecil Frank Powell (Nobel Prize for Physics). At the time of this discovery, they were all working at the H. H. Wills Laboratory of the University of Bristol.

robbed en route, because they contained nothing very useful, like ballet shoes, evening dresses ... With one meal a day and hardly any cash, we still studied, were excited about our various studies, about love and life in general and took all these miseries more or less for granted and managed to forget or overlook them.

It was the time of premieres of Händel operas, and, more important, of the Bohr "Festspiele" (concert, performance) when he showed in the large auditorium the models of the H and He atoms on large cardboards and created wild enthusiasm and countless fantasies and new theories. These were also the years when Quantum Mechanics was born, when the spin of the electron was discovered. One sat around the small marble tables at the cafe "Cron und Lanz" and somebody would explain matrices or the Schrödinger equation writing directly on the table. The waiters, who were our financiers and moneylenders, addressing each one as "Herr Doktor," would calmly wipe it off later on. These waiters had their own huge stake in the future of the students and got paid in most cases when the final exams were passed, the jobs secured, and the first salaries received.

The great center where physics was discussed was the Pro-seminar of Max Born and James Franck,[21] and also the Colloquium in the Physics Institute. All students who were already engaged in their PhD theses, all 5th and 6th semesters, professors from everywhere – USA , England, Russia, France, etc. attended these meetings.

***

In the first part of his book "Brighter Than a Thousand Suns" Robert Jungk [22] refers to this time. His account I believe is based on an interview Fisl gave him. It is hard to discribe the excitement of these years. Time stood still or maybe jumped forward in a big leap into the unknown. One talked physics and listened and discussed the

---

[21] James Franck (1882 - 1964), a German physicist and Nobel laureate (1925). In 1933, after the Nazis came to power, Franck, being a Jew, resigned his post in Germany. He assisted Frederick Lindermann in helping dismissed Jewish scientists in finding work overseas, before he left Germany in November 1933 to continue his research in the United States. There he became involved in the Manhattan Project.

[22] Robert Jungk (also known as Robert Baum-Jungk, 1913 - 1994), was an Austrian writer and journalist who wrote mostly on issues relating to nuclear weapons.

fabulous developments and discoveries which seemed to materialize out of wind and air.

At a meeting in Hamburg in the early part of 1927 I met practically all the Göttinger physics community: Elsasser,[23] Fisl, Dirac, Oppenheimer, Condon,[24] Pauli, Hogness,[25] Wiersma[26] and many more.

Fisl worked at that time in the Franck institute on the 2537 Hg. line. His room was next to Robert Atkinson's. Fisl introduced Robert to Irmin von Holten when they were in Berlin. Irmin and Robert married and lived alternately in England and America and finally settled in Bloomington, Indiana, where Robert died in 1982.

My own life in Göttingen definitely contained two periods, a long one of about four years and a short one of one year. My first room in the "Kirchweg" was very small but had a window overlooking the hills. The apartment belonged to a Mrs. Rabbethge, a widow, whose husband had owned sugar farms near Magdeburg. She also sublet a second, larger room to a classmate of mine, Eva Harlinghausen, who studied medicine. We were great friends, sat together in the evenings and shared all the gossip and tales which circulated in the university. She let me use her room to bring my rented piano. There was one semester when I hardly went to any lectures but practiced

---

[23]Walter Maurice Elsasser (1904-1991), a German-born American physicist considered a "father" of the presently accepted dynamo theory as an explanation of the Earth's magnetism. In 1935, while working in Paris, Elsasser calculated the binding energies of protons and neutrons in heavy radioactive nuclei.

[24]Edward Uhler Condon (1902-1974), a distinguished American nuclear physicist, a pioneer in quantum mechanics, and a participant in the development of radar and nuclear weapons during World War II as part of the Manhattan Project.

[25]Thorfin R. Hogness (1894-1976), Professor of Chemistry at the University of Chicago, who also served such as the Manhattan Project and defense research. In 1926-1927 Hogness held a research fellowship at the University of Göttingen, Germany.

[26]E.C. Wiersma (1902-1944), a Dutch experimental physicist known for his work at the Kamerlingh Onnes Low Temperature Research Laboratories at Leiden. Both independently and in collaboration with W. J. De Haas, Wiersma had published a number of papers on the influence of low temperatures on paramagnetism. Wiersma was invited by UPTI to Kharkov. In 1936 Wiersma, who had been helping Shubnikov's laboratory on behalf of W.J. De Haas and was eager to move to Kharkov to work at the Cryogenics Lab there (he had sold all he had in Leiden for this purpose) was refused admission to the USSR. This probably saved his life.

Schumann's "Carnival." Eva was very domineering, and while we roomed together, I never made other friends, because Eva was hard to please. She was two semesters ahead of me (I had first taught school for a few years after the Abiturium), and when she finished her exams and moved away to become an intern somewhere, I also left my little room and took a small two room place in the Friedlander Weg. This was my last year with Tammann.[27] I worked in the Physico-Chemical institute for my doctorate, not as a chemist but as a physicist. I took all the necessary physics courses and attended the Colloquium and the Pro-seminar in the Physics Institute. In general, I was rather unhappy with my situation at Tammann's Institute. I had very little choice. At Franck's Institute there was a long waiting line, and I was not sure that I would be admitted at all. Work for the doctorate at Tammann's was guaranteed to last not longer than 15 months, and since I could not survive financially longer than that, I applied for a working place in his lab. Being the only girl among more than 30 students was complicated, but the research projects in progress were fascinating.

Of Fisl's life in Göttingen before I met him little is known to me. Later on I learned that he was already in the Franck institute, when he suddenly disappeared into Italy for several months. During a vacation Heini Kurella and he decided to bicycle over the Semmering to Italy. They reached Milano or Turin, I do not know which, when Heini decided to go back home, while Fisl wanted to continue. He found himself rather tired and broke in Turin where he met a driver from the Fiat Works who was commissioned to run a new model without the chassis as far as Naples. Fisl probably thought of it as a nice adventure and asked to go along. The driver, liking to have some company, took him as far as Naples and invited him to stay with his family for dinner. By now the two had become good friends, Fisl liked the family, loved Naples and decided to stay on. Having no money at all, the next problem was how to find a job. The family inquired about his skills, but could not understand what on earth a physicist

---

[27]Gustav Tammann (1861-1938) was a prominent chemist-physicist of Baltic-German descent who made important contributions in the fields of glassy and solid solutions, heterogeneous equilibria and crystallization.

was. Fisl tried to explain, mostly by gestures, that is had to do with electricity, with mechanics, wheels, "revolvera"... They finally decided that he must be a plumber, a technician of sorts. It is not quite clear what happened next. At one time he had a commission to sell buttons. His one and only customer was a men whose name was Cavour. Fisl remembered the famous Count Cavour who had been a minister of King Victor Emmanuel II and was interested in the unification of Italy, met secretly with Napoleon III and continued to be important in Neapolitan politics. Signor Cavour was so flattered that somebody believed him to be a descendent of Count Cavour, that he ordered six dozen buttons right away. Unfortunately Fisl never made another sale and Cavour never paid him. Fisl led a very precarious existence in those months, sold postcards to American tourists, found a job with a loading company as a longshoremen, and almost ruined his health because the loads he had to carry onto the boats were far too heavy for him. The Italian fellows took pity on him, carried his sacks, and made him do the clerical work. By this time he was very fluent in Italian, but unfortunately never lost his Neapolitan accent. Life near the seashore, though, agreed with him. Watching ships coming in from all over the world and leaving for strange places touched the romantic adventurous streak in him and when he was just about ready to sign up on a merchant ship bound for Australia, he received a telegram from his mother. Else H. had been frantic when Fisl disappeared without leaving any address. She only knew that he must be in Italy, she tried everything and finally traced him through the Vatican. Her telegram asked him to meet her in Würzburg on the following Thursday, (unless he wanted to loose his lab place in Franck's institute. The telegram had said cryptically: "Komm Wurzdonner Mother," which Fisl interpreted rightly, using the accompanying money to make the trip home.

***

Still in Brione, writing on an enormous granite table in the garden.

It is strange that of all the happenings the early spring of 1927 remains the vaguest in my memory. No particular facts are standing out. I only recall the intense feeling of happiness, excitement, work and love. We went for long walks in the evenings from one side of the town to the other and then back and usually ended up in Fisl's lab to check on the vacuum and, if there seemed to be a leak, to caulk it immediately. Caulking in German means *dichten*, meaning also to write poetry. Fisl was finishing his experiments and preparing for the oral examination. I was still in the midst of my Gold and Silver experiment, and was not certain whether I would ever have any decent results. Tammann was a difficult chief and did not like female students. He never bothered to learn my name but called me "das Fräulein" and usually shouted it when he wanted to see me in his office. He summoned everybody the same way, daily: "Results, results..." I was always glad to escape into the atmosphere of my physicist friends. On one of our walks Fisl found four tiny stray kittens, which I kept.

Since I now had a tiny living room, I invited Walter Elsasser, Robert Oppenheimer and Fisl to tea, which was kind of festive for me. Once we all met in Robert's room when Uhlenbeck came back from Rome. Robert was all packed to leave for the United States, only some beautiful white papers were still on his desk for the next paper to be published. Uhlenbeck brought a Dante edition. He and Fisl could read Italian, Robert was just learning and I could vaguely understand. They read the fifth canto aloud, each of them in succession; in the middle of it Dirac walked in, asking for a German word.

At one of the general outings to the Hainberg, there was a short conversation between Dirac, Oppenheimer and Elsasser. They were wondering what they would do after the present papers were finished. I think Oppenheimer and Elsasser had some special problems in mind, but Dirac? What would he try to do? Everything, he said.

Once Fisl was very upset and dejected. His work did not go well, the results were unsatisfactory and he honestly believed that he was not cut out to become a physicist. He played with the idea of switching over to history, and we argued about it for hours. It must have been the lowest point; shortly afterwards he finished and passed his doctoral exam. He stayed on with Franck to continue his research with a Rockefeller grant (I believe). Most of the time though

Figure 2.   University of Göttingen Physical Institute. 1927. James Franck, Houtermans'
advisor, is fourth from the left. Next to him to the right are Robert W. Wood, Fritz
Houtermans, and Hertha Sponer, future collaborator of Edward Teller.

he was merry, irrepressible, the *enfant terrible* of the institute. Once
he asked Franck whether he could bring some Russian visitors to the
Colloquium, an unusual request because guests were always welcome.
But who turned up were two dancing bears with their owner, whom
the assistant unfortunately turned back at the door.

On another evening we all sat on the window edge of Max
Delbrück's first floor rooms and sang French folksongs: "Auprès de
ma blonde, les cloches de Nantes."[28]

One always went around on bicycles, whistled at each other's
houses, because Göttingen had neither telephones nor taxis. I never
could whistle properly to answer with a motive from the Unfinished
Symphony or the slow movement of a Beethoven Trio. I had to
develop my own "Leitmotiv" (German for leitmotif), which we still
whistle in our family.

---

[28] A popular chanson dating to the 17th century.

***

Los Gatos, Brione, August 5.

The spring of 1927 brought several final doctoral exams. Fritz's was around April. Oppenheimer's followed. This last one was of special interest to us, because Robert had been only a short time at the University, where admittance to a doctoral exam usually required a much longer residence. His oral exam was in theoretical physics with Born, experimental physics with Franck and physical chemistry with Tammann. Tammann almost spoiled Robert's record by insisting he should elaborate on the constant K, which Robert could not know. He had studied with Bridgman in Harvard and had not attended lectures by Tammann, who identified constants in a different way than Bridgman. We all waited in the hall after the exam and wanted to know from James Franck whether everything went well. Franck said, "I am glad it is over, he (Oppenheimer) just began to question me." Walter Elsasser and I passed our exams a few weeks later and celebrated it together with a group of friends. In the weeks before, Fritz coached me in theoretical physics, particularly about the Schrödinger equation.

After receiving his PhD in Göttingen, Fritz got a position as first assistant in the Physics Department of the Technische Hochschule in Berlin Carlottemburg.

Shortly after our marriage we moved into an apartment across the road from his laboratory. It was one end of the long barracks left over from World War I and converted into students' housing. These were very fruitful and interesting years. Robert d'E. Atkinson had come with Fritz to the Technische Hochschule in Berlin and was one of the great number of assistants conducting the advanced laboratories. Walter Elsasser and also Alexander Weissberg joined this group for a while.

In 1929 Atkinson and Houtermans published the paper on energy production in stars, suggesting that the fusion process producing helium was the source of the sun's radiant energy.

Fritz worked closely with Hertz, but also was able to conduct his own research project. He submitted its results to the faculty as an application for the *venia legendi*,[29] the first step of becoming a "Privat-dozent" (lecturer) and the necessary qualification for a future Professorship.

Parallel to this went the work with Max Knoll in developing the first small electron microscope. They were granted the patent for the magnetic lens.

These years also saw the speculations about the "Lichtlawine" (light avalanche) which much later became known, through the work of Townes, as the laser.[30]

***

Our private life also was very exciting. Our daughter Giovanna was born and brought us great happiness. Life in Berlin between 1929 and 1933 was unforgettable. The city vibrated with new ideas in practically all fields. The physics colloquia at the university saw people in the audience whose names alone were an inspiration: Einstein, von Laue, Nernst ...

The "Kurfürstendamm," Berlin's entertainment center, was alive with new plays, films, concerts. The numerous cafés were meeting places for the intelligentsia. All social life was of extraordinary vigor, and the levels of conversation were higher than ever experienced before or since.

We had many friends. Fritz seemed to attract people. He was always full of ideas, he told stories, witty jokes, he was interested in a great number of things, running the gamut from physics to music, to economy to politics. Wolfgang Pauli came to visit one Christmas, George Gamow and Lev Landau were frequently in Berlin, Vicki

---

[29]Habilitation (from Latin *habilis* – fit, proper, skillful) is the highest academic qualification a scholar can achieve by his or her own pursuit in Germany. The habilitation is awarded after a public lecture, to be held after the thesis has been accepted, and after which the *pro venia legendi* (Latin: petition "for permission to read", i.e. to lecture) is bestowed.

[30]A device that emits light through a process of optical amplification based on the stimulated emission of electromagnetic radiation. The 1964 Nobel Prize was awarded to Charles Townes, Nicolai Basov, and Aleksander Prokhorov "for fundamental work in the field of quantum electronics, which has led to the construction of oscillators and amplifiers based on the maser-laser principle."

Weisskopf came from Vienna. Then there was Michael Polanyi [31] with his interest in economics and politics. His niece Éva Striker, a gifted ceramic designer who later married Alexander Weissberg, Manès Sperber, the psychologist a student of Adler's.[32] Alex Weissberg, who came to Berlin in 1929, was a physicist and engineer and one of the most intelligent persons, with an astonishing command and knowledge of history, politics, Marxism, literature, and an incredible gift of quoting and reciting Rilke by the hour.

The small house and tiny garden were always bursting with guests. It was not unusual to have 35 people dropping in for tea. There were also relatives: Elsa Houtermans, Peter Houtermans, my sister Ursula Riefenstahl, a law student, Anna Wiesner,[33] a writer, Lotte Schlesinger, a young friend and talented musician. Other friends and physicists from abroad were the Blacketts, Maria Goeppert-Meyer and her husband, Professor Tamm from Moscow, Obreimov from Kharkov...

Parallel to all this high-pitched excitement, though, ran the ever-growing awareness of the increasing power and influence of the National Socialist Party. People became more and more afraid to speak openly, to be linked rightly or wrongly with one or other political parties. Our apartment was raided by Nazi students, who in those early years, though fanatics, were poorly initiated in Nazi theories. When raiding book-cases, they did not know what was – in their own belief

---

[31]Michael Polanyi (1891–1976) made important theoretical contributions to physical chemistry, economics, and philosophy. His research in physical science included chemical kinetics, X ray diffraction, and adsorption of gases. He pioneered the theory of fibre diffraction analysis in 1921, and the dislocation theory of plastic deformation of ductile metals and other materials in 1934. In 1933 he emigrated to England, becoming first a chemistry professor, and then a social sciences professor at the University of Manchester.

[32]Manès Sperber (1905–1984) was an Austrian-French novelist, essayist and psychologist. He also wrote under the pseudonyms Jan Heger and N.A. Menlos. In 1927 Sperber had moved to Berlin and joined the Communist party. He lectured at the Berliner Gesellschaft für Individualpsychologie, an institute for individual psychology in Berlin.

[33]Anna Wilhelmine Gmeyner (after her marriage Anna Wiesner, 1902-1991), an exiled German and Austrian author, playwright and scriptwriter, who is known for her novel *Manja* (1939). She also wrote under the names Anna Reiner, and Anna Morduch. She was in Berlin from 1928 until 1933 when she had to flee because of the Nazis' rise to power.

– controversial and what was not. I remember a raid on an apartment building, where many actors and writers lived. Some were imprisoned on trumped-up charges but were allowed visitors who brought food and books. The Nazi guard inspecting it all seized one of the books, Karl Marx, *Das Kapital.* Very pleased he exclaimed: "You, dumb communists, here is a good book for you to study!"

After the raid on our apartment, the Technische Hochschule forced the Nazi students to apologize, thus protecting us, for a little time at least. Any liberal attitude was interpreted as anti-Nazi or communistic. Since the police itself was under attack, they became gradually unable to help an ordinary citizen, whether Jewish or not. Thus, fear and uncertainty and anticipation of terrors to come were increasing every day.

After the raid we inspected our bookcases for incriminating materials. Fritz had bought books, pamphlets, periodicals, representing the whole gamut of the political spectrum. Some books like Marx seemed to us to be classics, some liberal writings legitimate criticisms, others may be doubtful or even dangerous. We began a private purge destroying compromising papers by tearing them apart and flushing them down the toilet, since we had no facilities to burn them. We had to stop this soon, because the Nazi student neighbor might have become suspicious. Fritz then remembered that he had some relatives on his mother's side, an elderly Jewish couple, who – we hoped – might have a coal stove, and asked them whether he could burn the rest of the material in their kitchen. He was asked to come late in the evening, so they could be sure that their non- Jewish maid was a sleep in her upstairs room. Fritz left our house with his large package, very apprehensive whether he would manage to cross the dark Savigny Place unmolested. When he arrived at his uncle's flat, he felt very nervous and became suddenly conscious of the danger for these nice people. But his uncle did not allow him to apologize: "Never mind," he said, "its nothing new, Father did it also in 1848."

As time went on the Nazis got stronger and bolder. Then came the horrible day, when Jewish houses and homes were attacked and vandalized, pianos thrown out of the windows ... people were arrested, the police were helpless. When they could not protect anybody any longer, when one day the Jewish faculty members were not allowed to enter the university, it was time to think of leaving. People began to emigrate, smuggling money and valuables, if they were suspected of having no legitimate reason for going away. It was easier for those who had relatives abroad or were invited to new jobs. Everyone who could help to find connections to foreign universities, suggested jobs. Fritz was involved in these projects, but the greatest pillar who helped so many people was Max von Laue.

Fritz was only $\frac{1}{4}$ Jewish on his mother's side and in no immediate danger. But since he did not look like the Nazi prototype, more like an Italian, and since he never would have said "Heil Hitler," his safety might not have been of long duration. When Vicki Weisskopf came through Berlin on his way to Copenhagen, I asked him to do something for Fritz abroad, because he was not taking steps on his own behalf. Vicki made the connection with the "Electrical and Musical Industries, His Master's Voice," in Hayes, Middlesex, England. The head of their research department was the father of D. Shoenberg, himself a refugee of the Russian revolution of 1905, and only too eager to help a refugee from another political upheaval.

In the spring of 1933 Hitler seized power, and we decided to leave. Fritz went first to Copenhagen and from there to Cambridge, England. I followed him in June, after packing and shipping our belongings and saying goodbyes. The last person I saw was Professor von Laue, who had messages for me to take abroad. I went by train to Rotterdam, after having been seen off at the Bahnhof Zoo by a large group of friends, we might never see again. Crossing the border into Holland was nerve-wracking.

I had to face the Nazi patrols, their inspections and questions. On the boat we were safe finally. It was peaceful in spite of the crying baby who was thoroughly upset and would not sleep.

We stayed in Cambridge for a few weeks. Fritz had again met with the Blacketts and now became friends with Occhialini and some other Italian physicists who all stayed in the same boarding house. As soon as we found a place to live, we moved to Hayes, because Fritz wanted to be near his laboratory. Settling down in this small town was rather an anticlimax after the high-pitched atmosphere of the last weeks in Berlin and the intellectual companionship with the friends in Cambridge.

***

After the constant tension in Berlin with all its fears and pressures, Hayes presented us with quietness and peace. It was unfortunately the calmness of a suburb, a very tiny village with ugly little houses, semidetached, with identical gardens in streets with pretentious names. Fritz had to contend with a well organized working day and its fixed hours. He was used, if necessary, to working all night if a research project required it. To stop exactly at 5 PM as well ads to begin in the morning at 9 AM was to him aggravating.

We were not quite as isolated as we had feared during the first weeks. Our concern for the refugees and the friends who were still in danger inside Germany kept us busy and brought all kinds of people from London to discuss ways of helping. Fritz got a rather princely salary from "His Master's Voice" and was able to spend a great part of it on these financial projects. The Quakers in London had organized the Coordinating Committee and collected names and curricula vitae of scientific personnel still inside Germany. They tried to connect them with jobs in Turkey, India, Scotland... Leo Szilard worked with them and devoted all his time and energy to this task. Fritz made contact with professors in Oxford and Cambridge, collecting signatures for letters pleading for the release of political prisoners.

Our house was constantly full of guests, many of them refugees, who stayed for days or weeks or even months. Hayes was quite far from London, but the stream of visitors kept on coming. Fritz attracted them. He was very hospitable, generous, always full of ideas of how to help, how to organize whatever was needed. I remember Otto Frisch, George Gamow, who had just been able to get out of Leningrad, Wolfgang Pauli, who visited with his wife, Leo Szilard, Manès Sperber, Lotte Schlesinger, Fritz Lange. Lange stayed very long and took over the second floor of the house. He did not bother to furnish it, he did not even buy a bed and slept in a long chair, because he believed it to be only temporary and that Hitler should

be overthrown soon. Every morning he would come down for breakfast with new elaborate plans of how to assassinate Hitler. Fritz and
Lange equipped the upstairs kitchen as a dark room. They developed
micro–photography and finally succeeded in reducing whole pages of
the *London Times* in the size of a postage stamp. The idea ways
to send news and information into Germany to people who had no
other means of learning what's was going on in the world outside.
These tiny films, often undeveloped, were pasted under the postage
stamps or into cigarette packages.

But in spite of all these useful and important activities, in spite
of the visits of so many friends, the isolation in Hayes became more
and more oppressive. We went of course to parties at the Blacketts,[34]
where we met the French scientists: Auger, Perry, the Joliot-Curies.
Somehow, though, this contributed only to Fritz's misery instead of
alleviating it. He missed the scientific inspiration, the exchange of
ideas, which is the essence of university life.

One day Sasha Leipunsky arrived from Kharkov. He had a two-
year stipend to work in Cambridge with Rutherford. He spend all
his weekends with us in Hayes and was loved by everybody. He was
sympatico, gentle, entertaining, pleasant and intelligent. He came
with no luggage whatsoever, just a toothbrush. In Cambridge he
bought a second-hand (probably fourth-hand) car. When he turned
up on the following weekend without it and we inquired about it, he
said that it had broken down and he had just left it on the road and
hitchhiked to Hayes.

He told Fritz about the scientific work in Kharkov. He was the
Director of the institute called UPTI, his interests were the same
as Fritz's. Sasha painted the scientific possibilities at the UPTI in
such rosy colors that Fritz began to anticipate a possible renaissance
there for his scientific ambitions. Hayes did not look like a permanent
solution for him. The USA was closed, and now Sasha opened a new
door.

He offered him a contract with half the salary paid in foreign cur-

---

[34]Patrick Maynard Stuart Blackett, Baron Blackett (1897-1974), an English experimental physicist known for his work on cloud chambers, cosmic rays, and paleomagnetism.

rency, guaranteed vacations abroad, a house or an apartment. It all sounded so good, especially against the background of Hayes. It became more tempting as the months went by. In order to accomodate more refugees, the salary fund from which Fritz was paid was now divided among more people, a curtailment which would have made the financial assistance he had promised to others impossible. So in spite of all the warnings of our friends, in spite of all the negative aspects of such a step, Fritz finally accepted.

When Pauli visited us and warned over and over again not to go, Fisl did not listen anymore. Our political instincts were dormant. What was alive was the hatred of the Nazi regime, the danger and terror of the Third Reich – the possible dangers and risks awaiting us in Russia were minimized by comparison. It was the time of the Kirov murder, and if nothing else, this alone should have warned us and prevented us from leaving England.

***

It was late in the fall of 1934 when we decided to leave England. The little house in Silverdale Gardens, in spite of all its ugliness and its many deficiencies, had finally become a home. It had two separate flats, and we rented first only one, then added the second. We also rented two adjacent gardens, which were separated by a wire fence. Stepping out of the French windows of the lower flat, one entered a lovely expanse of green lawn with a wide flowerbed of mainly rust-colored Chrysanthemums on the left. The back part rose slightly to form a little grassy hill behind which a narrow wilderness stretched out towards a wooden fence. The hill served like an easy chair.

Bamsi's room opened towards the garden; ours was the front room. The lower flat had only these two rooms and a kitchen and bathroom. When we added the upper flat we opened a connecting door which led to the staircase into the second storey. Thus we gained two more rooms used for guests, another bathroom and a tiny kitchen which eventually served as a photographic laboratory. This dark room was used by Fritz Lange, while he stayed with us.

Bimbus stayed with us for a long time. Her uncle or rather her stepfather Rudolf Schwarzkopf remained in Prague and was glad that we had invited her. She made some friends in London, but could not really settle down in England. The job situation was difficult, and she finally left and joined Schwarzkopf in Barcelona.

Elsa Houtermans also visited us. She had accompanied some English students of hers on a trip through the cathedral cities of France. Arriving in England she stayed with Lady Bonham-Carter, enjoying the luxuries of a great mansion, sleeping in a bed which had once harbored Queen Elizabeth I. She fitted very well into the aristocratic life of the Bonham-Carters.

These last months in England became more and more trying as days went by. The ordinary frictions, Fisl's growing dissatisfaction with his job, our inability for planning for an unknown future made these last weeks very trying. We had some apprehensions about life in the USSR, but trusted Sasha more than those who constantly warned us.

The first relief after leaving Hitler's Germany, the first relaxing days when we felt safe and free, had worn off a little. We became more and more aware of the drudgeries of our life, of the shabbiness of the little house, the isolation of Hayes. Fritz had liked his position , but could not adjust to the regulation it demanded. He often escaped to London to visit the Blacketts or Szilard, or other friends. I felt even more trapped, because I had to look after the house and anyway would not have been able to carry the baby with me.

There was always this feeling of this being a temporary arrangement. This in itself was bad. It prevented us from buying curtains for the windows, buying a table, a little carpet. We laughed it off. "Camping indoors." Lange was worse than we. In his opinion it would not take very long until Hitler would fall or be murdered. He was so convinced of this... Fritz hoped to go back to Germany after Hitler's death, or may-be to America. Consequently we never settled down, which was a great mistake.

We finally had to buy curtains because our landlord and some neighbors complained. Alas...

Odessa 1930[1]

B. Diakov, G. Nikolaev, and Olga Cherneva

A large, elegantly decorated hall, the site of the First All-Union Congress of Physicists, including international participants. Above the Presidium's table hangs red fabric lettered with a proclamation in many languages: "Physicists of the world, unite! In the name of a bright future for all mankind!"

Friedrich Houtermans presents a report which only physicists can comprehend: "The width of nuclear states and the possibility of resonant absorption of particles by atomic nuclei." He finishes his lecture, and the audience gives him a round of warm applause. Friedrich returns to his seat in the hall, near Charlotte, Alex and Éva. The physicists sitting near them shake Friedrich's hand and congratulate him on a brilliant presentation. Charlotte kisses Friedrich... Other speakers give their own lectures, and the Congress is declared complete...

Scientists in groups head into the banquet hall, exchange business cards; some disputes flare up – purely scientific. The atmosphere is lively, friendly...

Friedrich, Charlotte, Peierls, Éva and Alex Weissberg get to know their Soviet colleagues. Help with introductions comes from Yevgenia Kanegisser, a student of the Physics and Mathematics Faculty of Leningrad University and a cousin of the poet Leonid Kanegisser, the assassin, in 1918, of the Red Terror's Petrograd mastermind, Moisei Uritsky. Yevgenia Kanegisser, a woman brilliant in all respects, would wed German physicist Rudolf Peierls, later knighted as a British "Sir," which made her the Lady Peierls.

"Friends," she says, "let me introduce our famous 'jazz' physicists. George Gamow, nicknamed 'Joe,' solos on quantum instruments."

---

[1] This excerpt is taken from the book by Boris Diakov, Gennady Nikolaev, and Olga Cherneva, *Fisl, or the Man Who Overcame Himself*, in *Den i Noch*, a Literary Magazine for Family Reading, Nos. 3-4, 2005, in Russian. Translated from Russian by James Manteith.

Gamow shakes hands all around, then excuses himself, letting his friends step in.

"Dmitry Ivanenko," continues Kanegisser, "nicknamed 'Dimus,' duets with Fock and Ambartsumian on themes based on Dirac and on good people's universal attraction to each other..."

Ivanenko bows.

"Matvei Bronshtein," continues Kanegisser, "also known as 'Abbot.' I don't know why 'Abbot,' but he's a nice, clever fellow, of course, and a know-it-all with great things ahead. His main fault is his excessive modesty..."

Bronshtein shyly nudges back his glasses, which tend to slide down his nose, and shakes hands with his new friends. "Lev Landau," continues Kanegisser, "nicknamed 'Dau.' Naturally, he's a soloist – a lover of quantum symphonies, second-degree phase transitions, superfluidity in the essence of fine ladies and the theory of their excitation..." Landau takes a few polite bows, shakes hands and smiles.

"Valentin Fomin," Kanegisser continues, "the future of Soviet and, I'm sure, world physics. Besides that, he's a wonderful singer and guitarist."

Fomin, young and shy, smiles and shrugs, not daring to extend a hand to such formidable, as he sees them, scientists. "And this is Eva, Alex Weissberg's wife," Kanegisser warbles. "She's talented at everything, but most of all at painting..." Fragile, shy Eva, protesting, brushes off the compliments.

"Vadim Gorsky," says Yevgenia, "on familiar terms with X-rays; he sees through everything, and he emits rays himself, but good ones, nice ones..."

Gorsky shakes everyone's hand, bows to the ladies, stays dignified and serious. "And this is charming Lev Shubnikov," Yevgenia Kanegisser says, continuing the introductions. "He's almost reached absolute zero – he's laughing – but that's only in the low-temperature field. In real life he's as hot as the sun, and even hotter! And to prove it, his charming wife Olga Trapeznikova is the expectant mother of a new genius!" Everyone laughs and shakes hands with Olga Nikolaevna and Shubnikov.

"Yuri Krutkov!" shouts Kanegisser. "Professor at Leningrad Uni-

Figure 1. Olga Vladimirovna Cherneva is on the right. On the left: Mme Dirac and Paul Adrien Maurice Dirac. Leningrad, 1973. Courtesy of Emilio Segré Visual Archives, Frenkel collection.

versity! Interested only in quantum and solid-state physics. No threat to us..."

Elegant, restrained Yuri Aleksandrovich makes everyone's acquaintance. "Moisei Korets," Kanegisser tells the guests. "Young, but very promising..."

"Alexander Ilyich Leipunsky!" Yevgenia Kanegisser solemnly declares. "A serious man, interested only in the nuclei and protons, but watch out, someday he'll split a lithium nucleus and find a Nobel Prize inside!"

"Ivan Vasilievich Obreimov!" Yevgenia Kanegisser announces. "Not only the wonderful director of the Ukrainian Physico-Technical Institute, but also a first-class physicist!"

"Lev Rozenkevich," Yevgenia Kanegisser wearily concludes. "A very good physicist and person. You won't find a nicer person in this whole banquet hall."

Rozenkevich humbly extends his hand in greeting.

All the names spoken by Yevgenia Kanegisser, and many others, hidden from view, will be printed on the grey pages of an official NKVD folder headed by a grim black label: "UPTI CASE. 1937"...

A festive orchestra raises its strains. The Congress hosts and guests sit at generously laden tables; someone says an incomprehensible speech, drowned in the general hubbub and racket. Champagne glasses clink. From somewhere overhead, an unnerving voice calls out: "For Comrade Stalin! The leader and teacher of all peoples!..." But not everyone stands and raises their glasses in solidarity with the toast.

Off to one side, behind a curtain, a cameraman secretly films the banquet hall. He films everyone, but pays special mind to those who refrain from hailing the "leader and teacher of all peoples." His film also captures Friedrich Houtermans and his friends from the Kharkov Physics and Technology Institute...

On a large passenger boat, a contingent of Physics Congress participants, mostly guests from abroad, sails the Black Sea, eager to see the sunny Crimea and Abkhazia and most of all for relaxation after their days of effort. Among the ship's passengers are Charlotte and Friedrich; they take a separate cabin and rarely appear on deck... Popular Soviet songs of the era waft in the air...

The first stop is Yalta. Subtropics, palms, heat... In the public square, in the shade near the fountain, lie dust-caked, exhausted people, barely alive. The guests surround them, taking a closer look. The people stretch out their arms, plead for food, show their emaciated children, who also hold out tiny hands to beg.

Charlotte seizes Friedrich's arm and tugs him along after her. They dash back to the wharf, climb aboard the ship, go to their cabin. They hastily pack a large bag of everything edible they have: rolls, cheese, chocolate, bottled water. Then they go to the buffet and buy up a whole parcel of food. They run back to the people lying in the dust and give them this nourishment. Yevgenia Kanegisser energetically calls on everyone to follow Charlotte's and Friedrich's example. The scientists hurriedly make for the ship and return with food-laden bags. Yevgenia Kanegisser, Eva and Charlotte distribute foodstuffs, trying to ensure no one is left out. The unfortunates nervously stuff these priceless gifts into bags, knapsacks, pockets. Out of the bushes comes a young guard in an NKVD uniform, sleepy-faced, dour and irate; he looks around suspiciously at everyone, adjusts his belt with its holstered revolver, recounts the people by the fountain like a shepherd counting sheep in a herd, and signals the foreigners to move along.

The guests are baffled, incensed. Why are these people so hungry and miserable? What are they, beggars? Alex Weissberg explains:

"Comrades, gentlemen! The Soviet Union is now completing a struggle with kulaks, a bitter fight, a fight to the death! These people are kulaks, enemies of the new order! They're against the collectivization of agriculture, so they're being deported for resettlement in the north..."

"These old men and women, these mothers with children are enemies?!" says Peierls, astounded.

"Is that really what 'enemies' look like?" says Sommerfeld incredulously.

Gamow calls Houtermans and Charlotte to one side and points to Alex.

"The way I see it, this talented young gentleman is too entranced by the idea of universal brotherhood. Wiser men of science, say, Academician Ivan Petrovich Pavlov, the Nobel laureate – who lives in the USSR, by the way – has a bit of a different perspective than Mr. Weissberg's." He takes a sheet of paper from his pocket and shows everyone. "Here, ladies and gentlemen, are fragments of public speeches by Pavlov. These are words that people are passing around, copying, sharing. Listen! We live under the rule of a cruel principle: the state and power are everything. The common person's personality is nothing. Life, liberty, dignity, convictions, beliefs, habits, the opportunity to study, means of livelihood, food, housing, clothing – everything is in the hands of the state. And from the common person, only unquestioning obedience... On this foundation, gentlemen, not only can no civilized state be built, but no state at all could ever stand for long... Because a state should consist not of machines, not of bees and ants, but of representatives of the highest species in the animal kingdom..." Gamow neatly folds the paper, hides it in his pocket and, pointing at the prostrate people, asks Alex, "Who do you think they are, people or ants? Why are they kept like that? For what?!"

Alex is discouraged, but doesn't give up: "What's there to explain? There's a class struggle; without struggle, life itself can't possibly exist!"

"Personally, I can't accept a society where the 'happiness' of the majority means destroying people – absolutely defenseless people!

"You people don't understand. You ought to read the works of Bukharin," retorts Alex. "I met with him in Moscow, I spoke with him – he's an outstanding person!"

"Yes, I've read his articles. He speaks out against Stalin, so unfortunately his days are numbered..."

Alex disagrees, but considers it unseemly to keep arguing in front of the physicists.

"We'll just have to see," he says, ended the discussion with a dismissive commonplace.

The guests, shaken by what they've seen and heard, leave the "fountain" and hurry back to the ship, away from the awful reality...

The second stop is Sukhumi. A beautiful white city, palm trees, friendly Abkhazians. Stalls with fresh fruit, taverns with wine. Loudspeakers on poles pouring out folk melodies, girls in fancy dresses, young men sitting in the shade, sipping fresh wine. Idyllic...

Friedrich and Charlotte, holding hands, run to the sea. A breaking wave, washing inland, wets them up to their knees. They laugh, happy. Friedrich, fully clad, leaps into the waves, swims parallel to the coast; Charlotte runs along the sand, waving her shoes...

Dressed to the nines, serious, Friedrich and Charlotte, accompanied by Alex Weissberg, Eva, Yevgenia Kanegisser, Peierls, Lev Landau and other physicists, formalize their marriage at the Sukhumi office of the civil registry. A jolly, portly Abkhazian – or maybe a Georgian – examines Friedrich's and Charlotte's passports and, clucking with surprise, says:

"To the best of my knowledge of wines, you must be Germans!"

"Yes, yes, we're Germans. You, comrade, know your wines well."

"Wai-wai-wai, friends, I don't know the most important thing: can I solemnize the marriage of these two lovely Germans?" the Abkhazian says cheerfully, clearly looking to have fun with the guests. "In such an important matter, our people say, all these stamps, seals and registries are like ropes for mountain goats. They're free and jump around in the mountains where they want to. Germans, French, Russians, who cares! If such beautiful young people are looking for happiness and find it in our sunny Abkhazia, that happiness has to be given to them! That's what I think! What are formalities, anyway, all those cans and can'ts? I say give it to them! Sign here!"

Amidst his emotional, ornate explanations, he manages to make notations in his "granary" logs, fills out (in the Abkhaz language!) a Certificate of Marriage, places stamps. Bottles of champagne and wine glasses materialize, and the Abkhazian says solemnly:

"In the name of Soviet Sunny Abkhazia, I now pronounce you husband and wife! I wish you happiness and, of course, children," he narrows his eyes, looks first at Charlotte and then at Friedrich, and finishes, – "at least six! We mountain people think six is a lucky number of children!" Turning to Friedrich, he says, "Dear Friedrich! We have equal rights under the Constitution, but men are traditionally stronger. So please, while we're opening the champagne, try taking your beloved in your arms and lifting her as high as you can. And we'll pour the champagne..."

Alex provides simultaneous interpretation of the good Abkhazian's speech, and when the champagne bottle opens and the glasses are foaming with champagne, Friedrich seizes Charlotte in his arms and lifts her to his arms' full length. Charlotte hugs Friedrich's neck and kisses him firmly. They are truly happy. Champagne glasses clink, the Abkhazian embraces the newlyweds, bestows them with the Certificate and, at the last minute, wets one tip of the Certificate in the wine glasses with the newlyweds' champagne. The friends congratulate Charlotte and Friedrich. Yevgenia Kanegisser tries to read the writing on the certificate, but the Abkhazian tongue overwhelms her. Then emotional Lev Landau snatches the Certificate away from her and reads confidently, improvising as he goes:

"This Certificate of thus and such is issued so that he, the husband, might work worthily in the field of love and creativity, make six great discoveries in physics and get a Nobel Prize, and she, the

Figure 2. Luzanovka, 1930s. An Odessa beach which was used by many conference participants for heated scientific debates.

wife, might bear him three little ones and – so help them God! – for their happiness from minus infinity to plus infinity! Hooray!"

Editor's Addendum

Wolfgang Pauli's recollections of the same conference present an interesting "view from another side" and tell yet another version of the wedding of Charlotte Riefenstahl and Friedrich Houtermans. They are summarized in a book by Charles P. Enz, Pauli's assistant [1] (Enz also cites from Peierls [2]):

Pauli and his assistant Peierls arrived in Odessa on August 18, and Pauli and Tamm gave talks on the 20th. Peierls found the conference "lively and interesting," and he met Yakov Frenkel and Tamm, "one of the most charming personalities

Figure 3.   George Gamow, Abram Ioffe, Rudolph Peierls, and others conversing outside of the Odessa All-Union Physics Conference. Courtesy of Emilio Segré Visual Archives, Frenkel collection.

in physics. He had an agile mind, and an equally agile body, and the first impression he gave was of never standing still." However: "A good deal of our time was spent at Luzanovka, the beach in Odessa," where Peierls took a picture of Pauli with Frenkel and Tamm in bathing suits. This congress, in fact "was a grandiose one: 800 participants, 200 talks, plenary sessions in the City Council building. The opening session was broadcast on radio, and the participants got to ride the trams free. And of course, there were Odessa's splendid Black Sea beaches."

Peierls continues: "After the conference, all participants were taken by boat across the Black Sea," and he "was sharing a cabin with Pauli" From the boat Pauli, Sommerfeld and an unidentified Russian sent a postcard to Ehrenfest: "Greetings from the 'Gruzia' to the friend of Russian physics [in Cyrillic]. The Pauli effects so far have been quite harmless. Many greetings from God's whip. Sommerfeld.' The boat called at Yalta on the Crimean peninsula and then sailed on to Batumi in Georgia, from where Pauli travelled through Turkey to Istanbul and on to Vienna, returning to Zurich only on September 26. To be more precise, from Batumi Pauli went to Tbilisi, the capital of Georgia, situated in the foothills of the Caucasus. He was accompanied by the experimental physicist Fritz Houtermans from Berlin and his girlfriend from their student days in Göttingen, Charlotte Riefenstahl, herself a physicist. Fritz and Charlotte decided to get married in Tbilisi and asked Pauli to be the best man. Thus started a lifelong friendship between Pauli and Houtermans to which we will have occasion to come back repeatedly.

References

1. Charles P. Enz, *No Time to be Brief: A Scientific Biography of Wolfgang Pauli*, (Oxford University Press, 2010) p. 220.
2. Rudolf Peierls, *Bird of Passage: Recollections of a Physicist*, (Princeton University Press, 1985).

Friedrich Georg Houtermans: Chronological Report of my Life in Russian Prisons

On December 1, 1937, I was arrested in the Custom House in Moscow, where I was preparing my property to get looked thorough for my departure from Russia. I was immediately brought to the Lubianka prison where I was shown the order of arrest, dated from Kharkov from November 27th, on account of Paragraph 28 (political reasons). After a quarter of an hour I was brought to the big Butyrka prison into a cell for 24 men. Gradually this cell was filled until it held 140 men, sleeping on and under wooden boards, about 2-3 men per m^2.

While still in Moscow, eleven days after my arrest I was called by an officer of the NKVD to give a full confession of my alleged counterrevolutionary activities on behalf of the German fascist government, but no concrete charge was brought against me; only the names of a number of my Russian and foreign colleagues from the Kharkov Physical Technical Institute were mentioned as being members of a counterrevolutionary organization, as Shubnikov, Landau, Ruhemann, Weissberg, Fomin, etc. I was told that if I gave a full confession I would immediately be sent abroad. Of course I did not make a false confession and denied any activity against the USSR.

On January 4th, 1938, I was brought up in a prisoner car by railway to Kharkov and put into the prison Kholodnaya Gora in Kharkov, in a cell which was still more overcrowded than that in Moscow, but without any sleeping accommodation so that we all had to lie on the floor. I remained there till January 10th when I was brought to the central Kharkov prison of the NKVD, into a cell perfectly clean and not too overcrowded. Here many fellow prisoners tried to persuade me to make a false confession of things of my own invention as they had done themselves, which I would have to do anyhow sooner or later in order to save a lot of trouble. The same day I was asked to make a confession again by an interrogator, named

Drescher, who threatened to beat me and to get anything out of me.

On the evening of January 11th began an uninterrupted questioning of 11 days, with only a short break of five hours the first day and about two hours the second day. No concrete charge was brought against me, as in nearly all cases of people I have seen in Russian prisons, and I was told to give all "facts" myself. The only two questions that were asked were: "Who induced you to join the counterrevolutionary organization" and "whom did you induce yourself?"

Three officials questioned me in turn, for about eight hours each, the first two days I was allowed to sit on a chair, later only on the edge of a chair and from the 4th day on I was forced to stand nearly all day, I was always kept awake, and when I fell from lack of sleep I was brought to by means of fainted cold water that was poured on my face. The chief official who led the questioning was named Pogrebnoi.

The night of January 22nd, shortly after midnight, Pogrebnoi showed me an order of arrest for my wife and another order to bring my children into a home of "besprizornykh"[1] under a false name so that I would not be able to find them ever again. I was of the opinion that they were all still in Moscow. I have learned since that they had left shortly after my arrest so all I was told was bluffing, but in my state of weakness after nearly ten days without sleep I fell for it.

In this state I tell unconscious nearly every 20-30 minutes but I was awaked every time and my feet were so swollen that my shoes had to be cut off. I was beaten little, only occasionally, and not with instruments as many other prisoners I have seen, and I was told by them that the treatment I had to undergo myself was very mild indeed compared with what they had to endure. At the end I declared, I was ready to sign any statement they wanted on condition that my family was to be sent abroad immediately and I would be shown a letter from abroad by my wife telling me her whereabouts, after three months. In case I would not get such a letter I would revoke any statement I had made. I signed a short statement as they

---

[1]Orphanage, from *besprizornik*, a homeless child, waif.

asked me, admitting that I was sent to the USSR by the German Gestapo for espionage. Then I was able to eat luxuriously and got tea and was sent to sleep to my cell where I slept for about thirty six hours. Then I was asked upstairs again and there I wrote a long confession of about 20 pages in German and I was very careful to give only names of people whom I knew to be abroad, or whose evidence against me – of course forced by 3rd degree methods – was shown to me. I had to write about espionage, sabotage and counterrevolutionary agitation and I was absolutely free to invent anything I liked, no corroboration by facts or by evidence being needed. I made nuclear physics the theme of my espionage, though at that time no technical applications of nuclear physics were known, since fission was not yet discovered, but I wrote a lot of phrases that nuclear energy is existent and that it needed only the right way to start a chain reaction as described in popular novels on this matter. Another instrument I wrote I had spied on was an instrument for measuring absolute velocities of airplanes by the number of magnetic lines of force which went through a coil, a device contradicting the law of conservation of energy, and being obviously a perpetual mobile. I intentionally made my confession as stupid as possible in order to be able to testify that it is nonsense in case of a trial, and I put in a short statement in English in ciphered form that I was under third degree torture and that all I wrote was pure invention.

During the last year of my stay in Kharkov many acquaintances I knew perfectly well as being innocent had been arrested already and it was said that they all had given evidence of being guilty. I did not know then about the methods how these statements were forced from people but I had told my wife in case a signature should ever be forced from me, I would leave out the full stop after my signature, and in case my signature were given by my free will I would always put a full stop after my name. I had the opportunity to do so and I left out the full stop in the written confession. My written confession was translated into Russian and I was left alone and was not troubled anymore till August 1938, living till March in a clean prison cell not too overcrowded in the central Kharkov prison.

On March 17th I was called again and a letter from my wife dated from Copenhagen was given to me. The same day I was transferred to the Kholodnaya Gora prison in Kharkov, to a small cell, rather dirty and very overcrowded, where I remained till August 2nd. Food was very scarce and we suffered from hunger. The daily rations consisted of 600 grams of black bread containing more water than ordinary bread (equivalent to about 500-550 grams of ordinary bread), about 15-20 grams of sugar, a mug of soup containing little nourishing value and 1-2 spoons of porridge of some kind a day, from fair estimates made by physicians I met and by myself about 500-1000 kcal per day. Food was always given regularly and I don't know of any cases that prisoners were not given their rations. Treatment by prison officials was hard but not sadistic, but there existed cells where conditions were much worse for people who had not given the confession of evidence wanted. I remained there till August 2nd when I was sent to Kiev in a "Stolypin car,"[2] a special sort of railway car for prisoners. I remained in Kiev till October 31st, 1938, when I was asked to give more evidence especially against a friend of mine, Professor Leipunsky, a member of the party and an absolutely sincere man. From prisoners in my cell I learned that he was arrested in another cell in Kiev and a man in my cell tried to persuade me to give evidence against him and told me what I should say. No especially hard pressure was used against me then and therefore I did not give any evidence against him or against Professor Obreimov, another member of our institute that I was asked to accuse. Prison conditions in Kiev were much better than in Kharkov, the rooms being very clean and food a little bit better. It was hard though because it was not allowed to sleep during the day time.

On October 1st, 1938, I was sent back to Kharkov and put into a clean cell in the central prison. Prisons were not so overcrowded any more at that time, but still there were 1-2 prisoners per m^2 of room. I was not questioned again till January 1939 when I was asked to sign an application for Soviet citizenship. For that case they promised me

---

[2] A Stolypin car consisted of two compartments: one for passengers and another for livestock or agricultural tools. After the Bolshevik coup d'etat, Cheka and NKVD used these carriages for transport of large numbers of political prisoners and exiles: the passenger part was used for prison guards, whereas the cattle part was used for prisoners.

the chair of a big institute for my research, to be built by the NKVD itself, but I did not consider that offer to be sincere, having met foreigners in prison cells who had agreed to such an offer without having been released, and therefore I said I could talk about this matter only after release and after communicating with my family. This was the only time I got some of the things that were sent to me by my wife and by Mrs. Cohn-Vossen, a friend of mine in Moscow.[3]

I got a blanket and a few pieces of underwear. I did not get any letters nor any money that was sent to me from abroad, as I have learned since. This was rather bad because all the time there was the possibility to buy some additional food supply and smoking material for about 20 rubles a fortnight, and this helped a great deal but since I had less than 100 rubles on me when I was arrested I nearly never could make use of this possibility and therefore I had lost about 18 kg in weight and became more and more feeble.[4]

I could not consider a revocation of my confession of the year before and when I was asked to give more evidence against persons like Obreimov whom I knew to be in the USSR I declined but I confirmed my former confession, not wanting to have all the trouble over again. On the new evidence they were not pressing very hard.

In February 1939 I was sent again to Kiev where I was put again in the central prison but in an underground cell without any daylight (artificial light was in all cells during the night) which was very humid. I was asked again by a new official to give evidence against Obreimov and Leipunsky and I was threatened to be beaten in case I refused and shown written evidence of both men against me in their own handwriting. I was very weak by then, I could hardly walk about and so I decided to confirm their statements on counterrevolutionary activity about myself and that I knew about theirs. I put in some

---

[3]Margot Maria Elfriede Cohn-Vossen, née Ranft, a widow of the famous mathematician Stephan Cohn-Vossen (1902-1936) best known for his collaboration with David Hilbert on the 1932 book *Anschauliche Geometrie*. Stephan Cohn-Vossen was barred from lecturing in Germany in 1933 under Nazi racial legislation. In 1934 he emigrated to the USSR where he soon died of pneumonia.

[4]I have to acknowledge though that I got a lot of help from prisoners in my cells and occasionally also from kind prison officials who risked a lot being kind to an "enemy of the State." –F.H.

slight discrepancies concerning dates etc. with their evidence, and my evidence was accepted. Again I was told I would be sent abroad.

In May 1939 I was asked by the People's Commissar of the Interior of Ukraine himself to give evidence against Professor Fritz Lange, a good physicist and friend of mine who was working in the Ukrainian Physical-Technical Institute, and also against Professor Landau, Professor Ioffe and Professor Kapitsa, all of them prominent physicists of the USSR. He told me he knew well that all of these people were active spies and members of a counterrevolutionary organization and he only wanted me to confirm this. I said I knew nothing about it but did not try to revoke my own statements given earlier. This confirms the fact I had often heard about in prison cells, especially by men who once had been officials of the NKVD themselves, that it is quite usual to collect evidence about counterrevolutionary activity of prominent people in case their arrest should be effectuated later on. Neither Lange, nor Ioffe or Kapitsa have ever been arrested as far as I learned since.

No paper or books were allowed in prison cells and therefore it was nearly impossible to do any work. Yet from the very beginning of my prison time, I decided to work under all conditions and, since it was the only field I could do, I started already at the end of 1937 to think about problems of the theory of numbers. All I knew was Euclid's proof about the existence of an infinite number of primes and I started thinking on the problem whether there exists an infinite number of the type $6x + 1$ and $4x + 1$ also, while for the $6x - 1$ and $4x - 1$ I could find Euclid's proof to hold with a slight alteration off hand.

I had no writing materials, so I tried to write some numbers with matches on a piece of soap or on places of the wall where it could not be seen, but I had to erase it all every day before leaving the cell for the toilet.

I thought about that problem for more than a year and finally in Kiev in the first days of March I found that any form $x^2 + xy + y^2$ with x, y being relative primes cannot contain any other factor than primes of $6x + 1$ type or 3, and the sum of the squares of relative primes contains only primes $4x + 1$ or 2.

After solving this problem I discovered Fermat's theorem (I only learned its name after I left the prison, as with all theorems I found) and quite a number of theorems in the elementary theory of numbers.

When I found on August 6th an elementary proof for Fermat's famous problem for $n = 3$, which as I have learned since is essentially the same as Euler's, by "descent infinite," I got very excited about it, because I did not know Euler's elementary proof to exist, and I applied to the People's Commissar of the Ukraine to get paper and pencil. (I said I wanted to work out an idea of mine on a method in radioactivity which might be of economic importance). When my petition was not granted, I went on hunger strike (only declining food, not water). I was alone in a cell then and succeeded in getting paper and pencil after 8 days of hunger strike, by which time I was very much weakened since I had been in a bad state when I started. I wrote a number of theorems: I had found the so-called indices of theory of numbers, a theorem of Lucas and a new proof of a theorem of Sylvester which is in course of publication at the *Jahresbericht*[5] upon the advice of Professor van der Waerden[6] whom l told about my prison studies in the theory of numbers. I could even keep my writing materials when Professor Melamed[7] (a philosophy Professor from Odessa) was put into my cell, so that I could make steady progress in the theory of numbers.

In August all the evidence I had given $1\frac{1}{2}$ years earlier was rewritten and I was summoned up together with Professor Obreimov for a so-called "double questioning" in which he – of course it was all pure invention – stated before my eyes that I had induced him while still in Berlin to do espionage work for the Nazis, though at the time of his visit to Berlin the Nazis were not in power and a quite small party. I affirmed all his statements because I did not want and, in the state of health I was in, could not afford to suffer all the tortures

---

[5] Jahresbericht der Deutschen Mathematiker-Vereinigung, Annual Report of the German Mathematical Society.

[6] Bartel Leendert van der Waerden (1903-1996), a Dutch mathematician and historian of mathematics.

[7] Boris Moiseevich Melamed (1896-1978), arrested in 1938 and sentenced to five years in Gulag.

by which I was threatened.

Suddenly on September 30th, 1939, I was called out and brought to the station in a closed car and sent to Moscow. I did not know about the war till January 1940. The isolation of prisoners is extreme in Russia, the only source of information being what is told by newly arrested prisoners, and I had not seen such people for a considerable time.

In the train I saw that the official, who had questioned me before, travelled with me in the same train and in Moscow I was brought immediately to the central prison of the NKVD on the Lubianka. While I was still in the shower bath that everybody arriving there has to go through, I was already called for questioning. I was brought into a luxuriously furnished room in which a man in the uniform of a general of the NKVD sat and beside him in civilian clothes a very intelligent looking man who presided and who asked me politely to sit down. Then he asked me what I felt guilty of. I asked: "Do you want to hear what confession I signed or do you want facts?" "Of course, facts," he replied. "This is the first time I am asked this question within these walls," I said. "But since you want to know, the only thing I feel guilty of is that I stole a pair of underwear in the Kharkov prison a year ago, removing the prison stamp on them by calcium chloride in the toilet. That's all." "And what about your confession?" he asked. "That's all pure invention!"

Then he asked who had forced me to give a confession and by what means I was forced. I gave all the names as far as I knew them and all details. "We are going to get it all cleared up," he said shortly and I was brought back to my cell, a good cell, where I was alone.

I liked it better that way, since I could work. Everything was extremely clean and I got books, very good ones, too, special food in quite sufficient quantity and a package of cigarettes every day.

Though my Kiev manuscript had been taken away from me when I entered the Lubianka, I got writing materials again without any effort and I went on to occupy myself with what I have learned since to be "Pell's problem" and other things in theory of numbers. In this cell I remained without being called a single time until the beginning of December of 1939, being all the time alone. After all I had gone through it was a treat.

In the first part of December I was called up again by another official who asked me absolutely correctly about everything and I answered all questions truthfully. When I asked to write or to cable to my family (I supposed them to be in England, from where I had last heard from them in August of 1938) he said I would soon be sent out. I then asked especially not to be sent to Germany and he made a note of it.

About a week later I got new clothes and was sent to Butyrka prison, into one of the big cells where I had been 2 years previously, but now it was not overcrowded there. All people in the room were Germans, not all of them foreigners, some had taken the Soviet citizenship. Among them I was glad to meet another Professor, Professor Fritz Noether,[8] former Professor at the Breslau University for applied mathematics and later a refugee living in Tomsk. He had been arrested as a German – though being a Jew – and was forced to invent an espionage story, also. But in contrast to my case a sentence of 25 years of imprisonment had been passed on him. Shortly after my arrival he was removed from the cell and I have never heard about him since.[9] In this cell we all got special food in sufficient quantity and cigarettes and we had the impression that we were kept there because most of us were in a very bad state of health and they did not want to send us abroad like that. Most of the people were German workers, skilled workers, or engineers, specialists and many of them former communists. Among them was Hugo Eberlein,[10] friend of Lenin and Liebknecht and former member

---

[8]Fritz Alexander Ernst Noether (1884-1941) was a famous German mathematician, Emmy Noether's brother. Not allowed to work in Germany under the Nazi racial laws, he emigrated to the Soviet Union, where he was appointed to a professorship at the University of Tomsk. In November 1937 he was arrested by the NKVD at his home in Tomsk. On October 23, 1938, Professor Noether had been found guilty of allegedly spying for Germany and committing acts of sabotage. He was sentenced to 25 years of Gulag. On September 11, 1941, Fritz Noether was executed in Orel.

[9]See footnote 9 on page 17.

[10]Hugo Eberlein (1887-1941), a German Communist politician. When the Nazis came to power in Germany in 1933, Eberlein fled to the Soviet Union. In July of 1937 Eberlein was arrested by the NKVD. In 1938, he was tortured for weeks at a time in the Lefortovo Prison, and then in 1939, sentenced to 15 years of Gulag. In 1941 Eberlein was returned

of the Executive Control Committee of the Comintern, president of
the communist fraction of the Prussian Landtag for many years. He
had been beaten severely, like nearly all of them. Some were called
out and presumably sent abroad, some arrived directly from camps
in Siberia and the far North.

Figure 1.   Orel NKVD Prison. On September 11, 1941, 157 victims of the Great Purge,
were shot here by a special NKVD squad, without trial and sentencing. Fritz Noether
was among them.

In March I was called out alone and asked to sign a paper, agree-
ing that I would not tell about what I had seen in Russian prisons
and that I would agree to do secret work for the USSR abroad. This
I signed because I had learned from many people that most of them
were asked to sign such a paper, otherwise one would be kept indef-
initely.

I again asked as a condition not to be sent to Germany and this
was promised me by the official who made me sign the paper.

On April 17th, 1940, some of us were gathered into another cell in
the same building and on April 30th we all were called out, a sentence

---

to Moscow, tried again and executed on October 16, 1941.

was read to each of us, that we were condemned to be exiled from the USSR by a special court of the NKVD, and we were transported in a prison car to Brest-Litovsk where we all were taken over by the officials from of the Gestapo.

We were not set free, but taken to a German prison in Biała Podlaska, a small town near the frontier line and after some days we were all transferred to the citadel of Lublin.

Isolation was not as strong as in Russian prisons, the regime was more military and food and accommodation conditions much worse than the last time in Moscow. Every day we heard the songs and the noise of drunken Gestapo officers below our windows, while we learned that every day about a hundred Poles and Jews were executed in the prison court.

We had passed the frontier on May 2nd, 1940, and were transported to Berlin on May 25th. Some of us were brought to "Nazi-Rückwandererheim" where they were set free after a few days, but some of us, among them also I, were brought to the police prison on Alexanderplatz. By the way, the only prison in my experience where there were lice. Here I met people from concentration camps who told me about German camps and a well experienced communist who advised me how to behave in front of the Gestapo.

A week later I was brought to a small prison at the Gestapo headquarters in the Prinz-Albrecht-Strasse where I was asked about my Russian experiences, why I had left Germany and gone to Russia, and about some communist friends of mine in Germany before 1933. I told them I had known those people but I did not know about any illegal activity of theirs, confirming my information nevertheless on such people I knew to be abroad. I was asked to give an account of my Russian experiences, which I did, also mentioning by precaution the paper I had been made to sign but not the fact that I had asked not to be sent to Germany.

On July 16th finally I was set free. A few days later I met Professor von Laue [11] from whom I learned the whereabouts of my family.

---

[11] Max von Laue (1879-1960), a German physicist who won the Nobel Prize in Physics in 1914 for his discovery of the diffraction of X-rays by crystals. A strong objector

As soon as he had heard that I was in Germany in a Gestapo prison he went there himself, brought me some money and did all he could to accelerate my liberation.

May 19th, 1945

---

to National Socialism, he was instrumental in re-establishing and organizing German science after World War II.

Alexander Weissberg's Letter

*Alexander Weissberg sent this letter to Marcel and Anna
Weisselberg and their close friend Gertrude Wagner (undated, circa 1946). From Mica Nava's personal archive.*[1]

Dear,

As you can imagine, after the experience of the last ten years I
too am happy to meet someone from the old days. I ought really to
write up a detailed account of everything that has happened to me
but if I were to do that you would never get this letter, or not for
three months at least. In any case, it's not possible to write freely
from Warsaw and in two days I'm leaving [for Sweden?] so I'm very
busy. As my life over recent years has been somewhat complicated,
not to say surreal and unlikely, I find it difficult to give a faithful
historic account on less than ten pages. I will have to limit myself to
an abbreviated version.

On January 1, 1940, I was handed over to the Gestapo on Brest-
Litovsk bridge. Four months of prison in Warsaw and Lublin, then
released. I weighed 30kg less than now, possessed no shoes or clothes
and was infinitely tired. I went to Krakow and rested for six months.
Then I started a company with Rosalowski and Emmi Meder (whom I
accidentally met on the street) to avoid being deported from Krakow
and to be protected from the Germans. I realized that I would need
funds to survive the German terror so focused on making money. My
business talent, which for years had been inhibited by my political
principles, was now able to flourish.

I benefitted from the organizational experience I had gained in
Russia. I founded factories, organized undercover companies, broke
all the German laws and bribed and double-crossed them. As a
result the Jewish workers, who the Germans had incarcerated in the
ghetto in order to starve them, had more work and bread than their
Polish comrades who lived in freedom. When you wanted to buy

---

[1]Translated from German by Ina Wagner, Mica Nava and M. Shifman.

good merchandise in Krakow you had to go to the ghetto. That's where it was produced.

This continued until the beginning of 1942. At that point the Germans changed their strategy and started the liquidation. On March 18, 1942, they dragged fifty of the best-known members of the Jewish community out of their beds in the middle of the night and shot them. I was on their list but luckily they didn't find me. I went underground and began to remake contact with political groups, first of all the socialists. At the same time I started feverishly to make money. Every few days I changed my address and moved to a new hiding place. The Gestapo was looking for me yet despite that, during the next few months, until August 1942, I earned about 200.000 dollars [approximately 3,000,000 USD in 2015]. Over the following three years all this money was spent on supporting comrades and friends, buying out those who had been arrested, organizing passports, apartments and weapons.

In August 1942 the Germans went all out. They began the mass gassings. I tried to save my most valuable comrades. I had good contacts in the Polish organizations. I was able to get Aryan papers for most of them. I sent people across the Carpathians to Hungary and tried to smuggle groups into Switzerland with the help of Ella Reiner in Vienna. We fell into a trap. People were arrested at the border, among them Ella and Kurt [Lingens]. The Vienna Gestapo issued a warrant for my arrest as the main organizer. At the same time, a group in Warsaw who had collaborated with me got caught. Then my wife, Janka Skarowa, was arrested with her mother in Warsaw on an entirely different matter.

Janka was a delightful person, blessed with a combination of physical grace, high intelligence, character and style. She was very assimilated, estranged from her [Jewish] people and completely absorbed into Polish society. Yet during the days of hardship and danger she had gone into the ghetto and worked day and night as secretary for the Jewish community in order to alleviate the fate of the poorest and most oppressed. On August 22, 1942, under pressure from me, she left the ghetto and went into hiding in Warsaw. On September 9 she was arrested. I moved heaven and hell to get her [and her mother] free. It did not help. Through Polish comrades I offered the Gestapo half of my fortune to release them. The Gestapo took the money and arrested the messenger. On October 26 Janka and her mother were shot. I was devastated. I could think of nothing else for years. She was torn from me at the heyday of our great love. And great love is so rare. I think she was the only true love of my life.

The next period was dark. Comrades perished daily in the unequal struggle. A permanent tournament with danger. A mistaken word, an unthinking gesture could cost lives and freedom. The work in the revolutionary organizations was still preparation rather than open confrontation. That came a year later. The first partisans surfaced in the area of Lublin. Stalingrad and El-Alamein came later. They [the Gestapo] were still looking for me obsessively. It is almost comical that they should have mobilized such a large-scale operation in order to find just one man. I moved hiding places 32 times but finally they did find me. On March 4, 1943, I was arrested at the home of Countess Z., the mother of my current wife.[2]

The situation was so hopeless that none of my comrades even considered doing something to free me. Every Jew who left the ghetto with false papers was sentenced to death by law. All were shot without mercy, even though all they had done was to try to avoid being gassed.

And now to me. They [the Gestapo] had all the evidence they needed: smuggling people abroad, arming the ghetto in preparation for the uprising, etc. I didn't have the slightest hope. I was obsessed by the thought that I might die before Hitler and so would not see the end, the defeat of the fascists. In their pursuit of me they had arrested eleven comrades and executed all of them. They only spared the two Germans, Ella Reiner and Kurt Lingens. Ella was sent to concentration camp, first Auschwitz, then Dachau. Kurt was demoted to the ranks and as a punishment sent to the front. What chance did I have?

Although it may seem fantastic and highly improbable, this is what happened. The Germans picked me up twice. The first time

---

[2]Zofia Cybulska.

they arrested me with a Pole from the resistance without knowing who I was. I had a Swiss passport. I was insolent and they let me go. The second time they arrived with my photo, knew who I was, executed the comrades they had arrested with me and kept me in order to conclude the investigation. Then they lined us all up against a wall. They shot eighty of us and sent the rest to concentration camps. Because of an error in their records about me, which I had managed to set up, I was put in the group that was sent to a concentration camp. I arrived at the camp on the Tuesday. On the Wednesday I contrived to establish contact with the comrades in Warsaw. On the Saturday I escaped to Warsaw. I cannot tell you how. It would be going too far.

After this heavy treatment it took me a month to regain my strength. Then came a period of hope. Things gradually improved in Europe. The defeat of the Germans on the Eastern Front, the landing in Africa, the surrender of Italy. London radio was our only consolation. Every day we received secret reports [of events as they happened]. Illegal resistance spread slowly through the whole country. There was no decent family that did not participate. In Warsaw more than twenty illegal newspapers made their appearance and the partisan movement grew. The "divisions" restarted their activities. A tragic and heroic episode during this time was the uprising of the Warsaw Ghetto. After the fall of the ghetto I slowly lost contact with the Jews. My network was made up almost exclusively of people from the Polish resistance. When the Germans arrested me they confiscated most of the assets I had invested in diamonds. But I still had enough to be able to help people who needed help. And it was this humanitarian activity that kept me connected to those surviving Jews in hiding with [false] Aryan documentation. Later the [Polish] government in London was able to parachute in money for the illegal Jews. My current wife, who is Polish, helped with the distribution of these remittances.

The terror increased but we were no longer helpless. Everyday on the streets of Warsaw our young people were shooting down Gestapo big shots as though they were wild dogs. The Germans retaliated by capturing innocent people on the streets and lining them up against

Figure 1.   Warsaw Ghetto Uprising (April 19-May 16, 1943).

Figure 2.   After the defeat of the Ghetto defenders.

a wall as hostages. They didn't find the revolutionaries. The repression became more and more ferocious. It became more and more difficult for Polish people between 15 and 60 to be on the streets during the day. They would be hunted down and captured, and whether they were sent to a concentration camp or to Germany to do forced labor or lined up against a wall to be shot was completely arbitrary.

I organized forged German documents and because of my knowledge of German was safer on the streets than my Polish comrades. The Soviet troops were approaching. All of us sensed that a reversal was imminent. On July 31, 1944, we received the unexpected order to revolt. On August 1 the Warsaw uprising started. I was part of it from the very first day until the capitulation. Even after the defeat I stayed on for some time, hiding in a cellar in Warsaw. It was a remarkable time in my life. These were the first days of freedom. In spite of falling walls and burning houses, in spite of bombs, smoke mortars (*Nebelwerfer*), incendiary shells and heavy artillery, I felt completely safe and calm. A person who has lived in continuous fear of the Gestapo is not perturbed by heavy weaponry.

My best friend Marcel Robinsky fell in battle. His life had once been miraculously saved. The Gestapo had arrested him on October 28, 1943, in connection with my case. After 14 days they took him out of prison and shot him in the back of the head. He was left lying on the ground. The SS thought he was dead. But the bullet had travelled through his head and exited through his mouth without killing him. That night he was found by a passing Jewish group and taken to hospital. He hovered between life and death for three weeks. Then he regained consciousness and contacted us. We managed to get him out and moved him first to a convent and then later to an estate near Warsaw. It took him two years to recover completely. He came to see me in Warsaw a few days before the uprising. He immediately enlisted in the insurgent army and was killed on August 19. This was the second heavy loss for me. He was a beautiful lively human being, and very close to me despite our age difference (he was 15 years younger than me).

Figure 3.   Warsaw Uprising (August 1-October 2, 1944).

Figure 4.   After capitulation.

My family – parents and siblings, etc. – were all liquidated by the Gestapo. The defeat of the uprising was a real tragedy for me. I cried when the communiqué about the capitulation was issued. The thought of being incarcerated again was excruciating. For over 60 days, we had managed, almost unarmed, to withstand the concentrated attacks of a regular army equipped with the most advanced weapons. And now we had to remove the barricades ourselves and let the steel-helmeted SS onto our streets. And this at a moment when the Soviet troops were already on the other side of the Vistula. It was hard to take.

In addition, there was the danger to me personally. Unlike the Poles, I couldn't go into a German prison camp as an officer. I would have been identified as a Jew and been shot. Polish nuns hid me in the cellar of a convent.[3] Then I made contact with some Austrian soldiers. They helped me and my family across the barbed-wire lines. We settled in a suburb of Warsaw. It was good there because the front was close by, which meant that the Gestapo was far. We were secluded and isolated, and we waited there for the German front to collapse. Then on January 17, 1945, the advancing troops of the Red Army liberated us.

What happened next is less important. After the surrender of Germany and the end of the war I tried to keep a low profile, given my past in the East and my political views. So I did not attempt to carve out a political career. At that point it was easy to have a great career in the Polish state apparatus. I joined none of the newly founded Polish political parties. I kept my name from my underground days, which was allowed by the government in a newly passed law, and finally received a Polish passport for foreigners issued in that name. After demobilization I founded a foreign trade company of which I am director. On behalf of the Ministry of Foreign Trade we mediate trade between the Danube countries and Scandinavia, and in the future may include England.

---

[3]Polish Wikipedia states that after the defeat of the Warsaw uprising on October 2, 1944, later in the fall Weissberg found himself at the Pruszków concentration camp. Pruszków is a suburb of Warsaw used by the SS to intern the Jews expelled from the capital after the uprising, before sending them to Auschwitz. This would explain the next sentence.

My intention is to work in Poland for another year and then, when the occupation of Austria has ended, to return to Vienna. As to my political views, I am now considered a heretic by all sides. I have remained an internationalist in the old sense, but have revised some things. I now place more importance on democracy, personal civil rights and liberties and legal guarantees, etc. I will most probably return to the Social Democratic Party [4] when I go back to Austria. However, I'm not under the illusion that parliamentary democracy can, achieve socialism on its own, without a revolution. But I have to acknowledge that what has happened in some European countries, France for instance, as a result of the war, the surrender of 1940, the resistance movement and collapse of the German power apparatus, equals a revolution and that therefore in France socialism is possible

The situation is fundamentally different in England. The Brits have not yet had their revolution but it will come.. As for the question of freedom, this is an issue not only for the West but also for the East. After my experiences of the last ten years my view is that freedom is a fundamental postulate for all progressive classes in modern society. It is needed in the East as much as in the West and maybe even more. And we can assume that the majority of mankind will not be willing to renounce the old idea of freedom in order to accelerate the path to socialism. I am not prepared to make this sacrifice either.

Gerti,[5] you now have a rough picture of my life over recent years. The reality was much more exciting and adventurous.

Konrad [Weisselberg] was arrested 5 days after me in 1937.[6] Gustl

---

[4] In a few years political views of Alexander Weissberg drastically changed. In 1949 he was a key witness of Kravchenko in a sensational trial "Victor Kravchenko vs. *Les Lettres Françaises*," the communist weekly published in Paris (till 1960s), see http://spartacus-educational.com/RUSkravechenko.htm. *Les Lettres Françaises* acted as an ardent supporter of the hard-core communism until its demise. In the 1950s Michael Polanyi enlisted Weissberg as a participant in the work of the Congress for Cultural Freedom, an anti-communist advocacy group founded in 1950.

[5] Gertrude Wagner, my parents' closest friend and a sociologist who worked in UK before the war and went back to Vienna afterwards. –Mica Nava

[6] The Kharkov NKVD arrested Alexander Weissberg on March 1, 1937, and Konrad Weisselberg on March 4.

Deutsch,[7] as I learned recently, was arrested a year later.

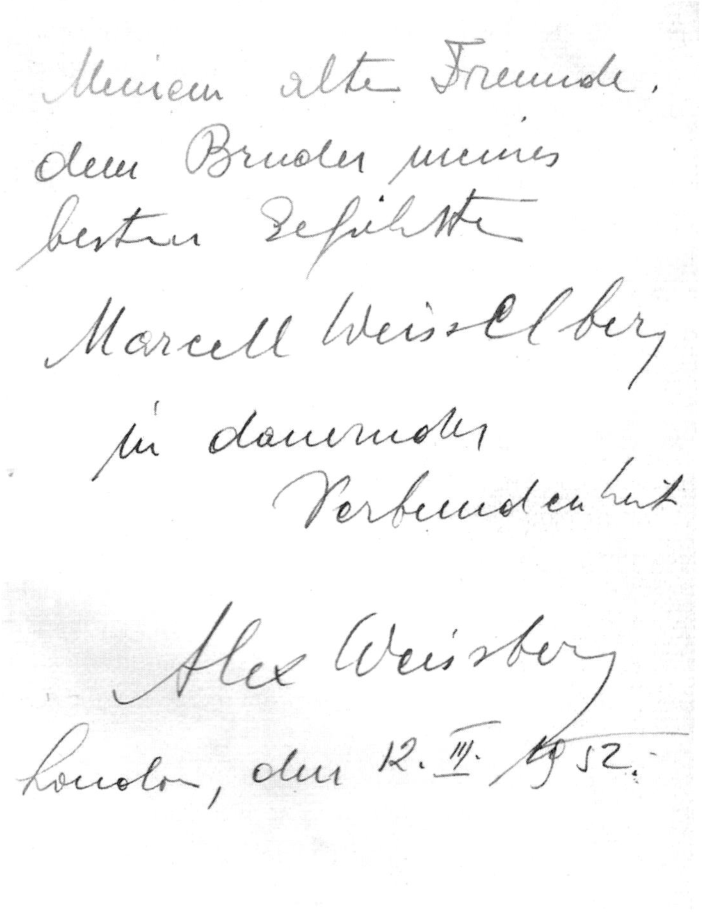

Figure 5.   Dedication to Marcel Weisselberg by Alex Weissberg on the frontispiece of the German version of *The Accused*. Courtesy of Mica Nava.

---

[7]From https://en.wikipedia.org/wiki/Ernst_Fischer_(writer): "When Fischer and his wife arrived at Hotel Lux Moscow in 1938, the Stalinist purges were still taking place and the expats living at the hotel were living in a climate of fear and terror. The autumn after their arrival, Fischer came home from work one evening, looking terrified. Gustl Deutsch, an Austrian who had been arrested and imprisoned, had managed to smuggle him a note to alert him to the danger facing Fischer. Under torture, Deutsch had named Fischer as being involved in a plot against Stalin's life."

After the War[1]

Edoardo Amaldi

When Fritz decided, in 1944, to marry Ilse Bartz, he did not inform his first wife Charlotte of his desire of divorcing her, but took advantage of a law which exempted from such a "formality" any person living separated from his wife or husband for more than five years. The law, promulgated by Hitler's Government, had been used to terminate many marriages of "pure Aryans" to Jewish people.

As an announcement to Charlotte of his second marriage, Fritz sent her a reprint of one of the papers he had published in collaboration with Ilse.

Charlotte was already aware of the existence of these papers, which had been pointed out to her by Otto Oldenburg, an old friend from Göttingen and now professor of physics at Harvard University. But only a few months after the arrival of the "reprint," Charlotte learned of Fritz's divorce from her and of his marriage with Ilse.

In 1951 Charlotte went to Europe in order to visit her mother in Bielefeld. Coming back, with Casimir,[2] from a conference in Copenhagen, Fritz went to see her. After a first rather stormy encounter, Fritz told Charlotte of difficulties he had with Ilse, expressed to her his affection and insisted that she should remain in Europe and immediately go live with him. But such an unexpected radical change was not possible for Charlotte. She had commitments at Sara Lawrence College, and Giovanna had to finish school in the United States.

---

[1] This excerpt is taken from the book Edoardo Amaldi, *The Adventurous Life of Friedrich Georg Houtermans, Physicist* (Springer, Berlin, 2012), pp. 105 and 109.

[2] H. B. G. Casimir, born in the Hague in 1909, for many years was Extraordinary Professor at the University of Leiden and Director of the Philips Physics Laboratory at Eindhoven; later the President of the Royal Academy of Sciences of Amsterdam. He worked in close contact with Niels Bohr in Copenhagen, and W. Pauli in Zurich, especially during his formative period. As a theoretical physicist he worked on the applications of the group theory to quantum mechanics (the so-called Casimir operator), on the thermodynamics of superconductors and on the Van der Waals forces (the so-called Casimir effect). In his memoir [1] Casimir mentions Houtermans' adventures and jokes at various points (pp. 133 and 220 to 223). He died in Heeze on May 4, 2000. -E.A.

Charlotte came back to Europe with Giovanna and Jan a first time during summer 1950. At their landing in Amsterdam, they were received by Fritz who had organized a vacation in Überlingen am Bodensee. All the children were there with Fritz and Charlotte: Giovanna, Jan, Pieter, Elsa and Coja.

In spring 1953 Charlotte and her two children were awarded fellowships from three different organizations, which facilitated their second trip to Europe. After their landing, she drove with a friend through France and met Fritz again in Bagneres de Bigorre, in the French Pyrénés where, from 6th to 12th July 1953, took place "Le Congrès International sur le Rayonnement Cosmique." That week was just in the middle of the Second Expedition to Sardinia for the study of cosmic rays at high altitude by means of balloon flights,[3] in which also the Bern physicists Houtermans and Teucher[4] were involved.

Among the many participants in the Bagnéres de Bigorre Conference I should recall P. S. M. Blackett, B. Rossi, G. Bernardini, Cecil Powell, L. Leprince-Ringuet, G. Occhialini, C. Dilworth, etc., many of whom were old friends or more recent friends of Houtermans. I also was there and thus had the opportunity of taking up some of the conversations I had started with Fritz not long before when he passed through Rome on his trip to Sardinia.

During the conference we read in the international press that recently Beria[5] had been condemned and executed. I will always recall Fritz's excitement when we talked about this event.

After the conference, Fritz, Charlotte with Giovanna and Jan

---

[3]Three international expeditions, promoted by C.F. Powell of the University of Bristol and based on the support of the Milan, Padua and Rome Universities, were made in the Mediterranean area in the years 1952, 1953 and 1954. The Physical Laboratories of the following Universities took part in the second one (June-July 1953): Bern, Bristol, Brussels, (Université Libre), Catania, Copenhagen, Dublin, Genoa, Göttingen (Max Planck Institute), London (Imperial College), Lund, Milan, Oslo, Padua, Paris (Ecole Politechnique), Rome, Sydney, Turin, Trondheim, Upsala. -E.A.

[4]Martin Teucher (1921-1978), worked on his PhD in the field of nuclear physics with F. Houtermans. Later worked at DESY, Germany, in experiments with bubble chambers.

[5]Lavrentiy Pavlovich Beria (1899-1953) was Stalin's right hand, Marshal of the Soviet Union, chief of the Soviet security and secret police (NKVD) since 1938. In December 1944, Beria's NKVD was assigned to supervise the Soviet atomic bomb project.

Figure 1.   Fritz Houtermans with his daughter Giovanna. Germany, 1950. Their first encounter after 1937 Moscow. (From I. Khriplovich's article). With kind permission of *Physics Today*, Courtesy of Ursula Riefenstahl.

went to Marseille, where Fritz and Charlotte left the children with a friend. They themselves visited James Franck in Bad Kreuznach, Germany, that was there for a few weeks cure for heart troubles. Asked for advice by Fritz about his planning of marrying again Charlotte, Franck expressed a clear negative view, which, however, was not followed by Fritz in spite of his almost filial devotion.

From Kreuznach they went to Hamburg to participate in a meeting of people that had been communists or very close to them, in the 1930s, had moved to the USSR with the idea of helping in the construction of the socialist society and that, once over there, had experienced very awkward adventures and had the great luck to be still alive [2].

Towards the end of August 1953, Charlotte arrived in Bern. At their marriage on August 28, the witnesses were Giovanna, Jan and W. Pauli.

The "third family" of Fritz that settled in Bern included two children, Pieter and Elsa, but not Coja, who was only five years old and still needed the devotion of her mother. Giovanna was in Tübingen as a Fullbright student and Jan at the University of Rochester (USA).

Houtermans and Charlotte went to the annual conference of the Italian Physical Society that in 1953 was held in Cagliari from 23rd to 27th of September. Ilse Bartz was also there.

In October of the same year a meeting was organized at the Department of Physics of the University of Bern, by Houtermans and Teucher for the distribution of the packages of nuclear emulsion exposed to cosmic rays at high altitudes among the participants of the Second Expedition to Sardinia. I was also there, and one evening after work, Fritz and Charlotte invited all participants to their house, where all enjoyed their hospitality and the friendly atmosphere created by the cordial and witty conversation and jokes of Fritz.

During the winter 1953–1954 Fritz started to drink abundantly and the relationship with Charlotte deteriorated rapidly.

On March 1, 1954, she left Bern and went to Paris, where she remained for a few weeks and had the opportunity to meet once more old friends like Manés Sperber and Alex Weissberg-Cybulski. From Paris she went to Bristol where, from April to September, she worked as a microscopist at Cecil Powell's Laboratory on the investigation of events produced by cosmic rays in nuclear emulsions.

At the end of August Charlotte went back to the United States and took up again her teaching work at Sarah Lawrence College. The divorce from Fritz was accorded her in 1954. It was a shock for both of Charlotte's children, in particular for Jan, who by now was 18 years old and had started to study physics at the University of Rochester.

Figure 2.   Charlotte Houtermans, left, and Laura Polanyi Striker in Eva Striker-Zeisel's Rockland County, New York, studio (circa 1955). See pp. 159, 162, 165. Courtesy of Jean Richards.

***

In 1955 Fritz married Lore Müller, the sister of the wife of his stepbrother Hänsi that he had met a few years before in Göttingen. For their marriage Wolfgang Pauli sent Fritz the following telegram: "The usual congratulations."

Lore already had a few years old daughter, Sabine (b. 1951) who was later adopted by Fritz. In 1956 Fritz and Lore had a son, Hendrik, who unfortunately died a few years after the death of his father, at the age of seventeen, in a car accident.

Houtermans Charlotte			
		1979/01/08	121,1/0
		1979/01/08	72,1/0
		1979/01/23	72,1/0
		1979/02/19	121,1/0
		1979/02/19	72,2/0
		1979/02/26	72,2/0
		1979/03/20	72,2/0
		1979/04/09	121,1/0
		1979/04/09	72,2/0
		1979/10/16	72,2/0
		1979/11/09	72,2/0
		1979/11/09	121,1/0
		1979/12/15	72,2/0
		1980/01/14	72,2/0
		1980/01/14	121,1/0
		1980/02/14	72,2/0
		1980/02/14	121,1/0
		1980/03/18	72,2/0
		1980/04/09	121,1/0
		1980/04/18	72,2/0
		1980/04/18	72,2/0
		1980/06/10	72,2/0
		1980/06/10	121,1/0
		1980/06/23	72,2/0

Figure 3.   Edoardo Amaldi kept a meticulous log of his correspondence. This is one of the log pages showing the record of Edoardo Amaldi's correspondence with Charlotte Houtermans which was especially intense in 1979 and 1980. A note on the left (in Amaldi's handwriting) reads: "In 72,2/0 there are no letters, only copy of manuscript Ed on Houtermans. The letters are in 72,1/0." The Editor failed to find out what was the contents of correspondence marked as 121,1/0. Courtesy of Ugo Amaldi and Saverio Braccini.

In 1957 Houtermans took a sabbatical year and went to the United States, where he spent months at the California Institute of Technology (Pasadena, California) and the Scripps Institution of Oceanography (San Diego, La Jolla, California). In both places he was in close contact with the well known figures in the Earth Sciences: Harrison Scott Brown (1917-1986), Samuel Epstein (1919-2001) and Gerald J. Wasserburg (b. 1927) in Pasadena, and Roger Randall Dougan Revelle (1909-1991), Director, and Hans Eduard Suess (1909-1993) in La Jolla.

Nuclear geology had become perhaps the most important part of the scientific program set up by Houtermans in Bern. Another subject was the investigation of particle physics by means of nuclear emulsions, and Lore started to take part as a microscopist, in the work of the group composed of eight or ten people that were active in this field under the direction of Teucher.

Lore remembers these years with great pleasure not only for the trip to the United States, but also for a number of other trips in Europe, in particular to Italy, where they visited many towns that combined artistic and natural interest either with new friendships, like Pisa and Rome, or Fritz's youth recollections, like Naples.

The year 1961 marked a break in Houtermans' life. He was supposed to go to a country in Far East and therefore had to have a certain number of preventive injections. He had a rather strong reaction with high fever, and when at a very early hour of the day he tried to get up for greeting Lore's daughter that was going on an excursion to see the sunrise, he fell and hit his head against the banister of the stairs. The concussion he had was not too serious, and, after six months the neurologist declared him normal. The accident, however, had triggered some damage that the doctors never really identified. The hard experience of his life, his demanding work and lifestyle, in particular his rather heavy drinking habit during the last few years, caught up with him.[6] Thus, from about 1962 on he was never again able to work with the enthusiasm and the success which had characterized the first eight or ten years of his life in Bern.

At the beginning of autumn of 1965 Fritz Houtermans was diagnosed with a lung cancer: a dark stain was clearly visible in the radiographies. After about three months of irradiation the stain dis-

---

[6]Also, Fritz Houtermans was a heavy smoker.

appeared and Fritz started to regain part of the weight he had lost. He felt much better and enjoyed again sitting in his house, at his working table. He wrote a paper on the history of the WAr-method of geochronology for the book dedicated to Wolfgang Gentner's 60th birthday [3]. Lore still remembers when Fritz went out of their house to mail his manuscript.

Shortly after, on 1st March 1966 he had a stroke: a pulmonary artery broke, his heart stopped and he suddenly died.

References

1. H. B. G. Casimir, *Haphazard Reality: Half a Century of Science*, (Harper and Row Publ., New York, 1983).
2. *Encounter: Literature, Arts, Current Affairs* Vol. V, No. 6 December, 1955. *Encounter* was a literary magazine published in the United Kingdom from 1953 till 1991.
3. F. Houtermans, *History of the WAr-Method of Geochronology*, in *Potassium Argon Dating*, (Eds. O. A. Schaeffer and J. Zähringer) Springer, Berlin, 1966.

PART II

Golfand

Yuri Golfand

THE LIFE AND FATE OF YURI GOLFAND

BORIS ESKIN

eskin7@yandex.ru

The Mount of Rest

The funeral procession moved slowly along the wide cemetery avenues. A capricious February wind billowed the women's black capes and plucked at the men's clumsily pinned yarmulkes. They were burying a "Russian" professor, and most of those present were also "Russian" – that is, Jews from Russia: colleagues, friends, acquaintances, neighbors.

In Hebrew, the burial ground is called *Har HaMenuchot.* This can translate as "Mount of Burial," or as "Mount Solace," "Mount Tranquility." And all three renderings are correct: for three thousand years, souls of Jews have found tranquility and solace here – since the time of the First Temple. Now the professor, too, had come to rest on the ancient hill, overlooking nearly all of Jerusalem.

Everything happened so quickly, unexpectedly. Yet death is always unexpected, even when inevitable and awaited.

Yuri Abramovich had come home to Jerusalem from Haifa, taking a short vacation from the Technion to relax with his family – his wife Natasha, his young daughters, his sister Kira.

He'd felt an immense weariness, although in a fine, combative mood. A few days before, he'd gotten word of his latest article's acceptance for publication in the international scientific journal *Modern Physics Letters.*

...A black-clad rabbi mumbles the Kaddish in a studied and habitually hurried manner, as if rushing to move on to the next prayer memorial. Wrapped in a snow-white shroud, the body of the deceased is slowly lowered into the ground.

...The people by the grave stood in silence, not yet grasping that Yura had left them, that his soft, velvety baritone would never sound again, that his clear, calm and infinitely benevolent gaze would never again turn toward them.

Yet maybe now, from the high hill, he'd find it even easier to see a world invisible to most alive on earth...

On "Yom Rishon," Sunday, the week's first workday, Yuri Abramovich had planned to return to the Haifa Technion. Natasha had persuaded him not to go. Call the administration, ask for another couple of days off. Her husband appeared so awfully pale, completely unrested, unusually tired.

Natasha had to leave in the morning for work in Kiryat Arba – not far from Jerusalem, halfway to Beersheba – visiting a family who had recently suffered a terrorist act. Natasha worked for an aid organization for victims of terror.

Yura had wanted to go with her. Natalia convinced her husband to stay home and not worry. She promised to call him as soon as she returned to Jerusalem, right from the bus station.

It was February 14, 1994. The very day of the stroke.

He was taken to the hospital. With unblinking, childishly naive eyes, he looked around at the bustling medics in light green robes. He couldn't figure out what all the fuss was for.

The doctor asked Natasha her husband's age. Seventy-two, she said. Uncomprehending, he asked again. He'd thought the patient, draped in tubes and sensor wires, could hardly be more than forty. Handsome, cheerful, face unmarred by wrinkles. Robust body, muscular arms. He'd suffered from uncompensated cardiac arrhythmia throughout his life, but couldn't stand trips to the doctor, preferring hiking and kayaking trips instead. He amiably called all doctors "bunglers."

In a sense, he proved right. No Israeli Asclepius could save him. For three days his body desperately fought death. He remained conscious until the last second. And until the last second, Natasha and Kira hoped their Yura would pull through yet again.

He didn't pull through...

Far from everyone attending the funeral realized who they were seeing off on his final journey. "Big things can be seen from a distance" – alas, this well-worn truth is still more precise than the laws of Newton.

On the thirtieth day of mourning for the deceased, over his grave appeared a Hebrew and Russian inscription, carved as simply as thousands of others around it:

Yuri Abramovich Golfand
Jan. 10, 1922 - Feb. 17, 1994

First digression

Yuri Abramovich Golfand was among the discoverers of supersymmetry, perhaps the most beautiful construction in modern theoretical and mathematical physics.

Mikhail Marinov, his friend and colleague at the Haifa Technion, wrote:

"The fundamental discovery of supersymmetry gave new impetus to theoretical physics and will forever remain a part of the history of science. Yura came first to this work, and his name will never be forgotten."

The prominent Israeli physicist Professor Yuval Ne'eman stated that "experimentally verifying the theory of supersymmetry as created by Yura is one of the main tasks of modern quantum physics."

"A Mozart of physics," Andrei Dmitriyevich Sakharov called Golfand.

They worked at the same institute, FIAN – the Lebedev Physical Institute of the USSR Academy of Sciences – in the theory department. The great Sakharov, not overly free with lofty epithets, writes in his book *Memoirs*:

"Golfand and Likhtman (a graduate student of Yuri Abramovich) were the first to consider supersymmetry as a principle for constructing a theory of elementary particles. It was a great idea. In the following years, the ideas of supersymmetry were developed in hundreds of remarkable works. It became clear that supersymmetry was the most natural and practical way to construct a unified field theory."

In 1989, Academician [1] Leonid Veniaminovich Keldysh, a Lenin Prize winner and a specialist in the field of solid state physics and semiconductors, became FIAN's director. In connection with the award of the I. E. Tamm prize to Yuri Golfand, just before his colleague's departure for Israel, the director delivered the following address in his honor:

"On behalf of the scientific community of the USSR Academy of Sciences' P. N. Lebedev Institute of Physics, I would like to personally express to you my deep gratitude for your outstanding contribution, recognized throughout the world, to the development of modern theoretical physics, which you have made through many years of fruitful scientific activity within our institution's walls."

The message of condolence that Professor Yuval Ne'eman sent the Golfand family contained these words:

"When Yuri joined Israel's scientific community, it was an important event, and greatly bolstered science in our country... We will remember him, although he is no longer with us. We're left with grief at this irreparable loss, and with his scientific and spiritual legacy."

"What do you think?"
(Kharkov childhood and adolescence)

1922. The Civil War's rage has just recently passed. The despotic era of "war communism" has unexpectedly given way to the lax NEP (New Economic Policy),[2] with its syndicates and cooperatives, innu-

---

[1] The academic hierarchy in Russia follows the German rather than the Anglo-American pattern. An approximate Russian equivalent of PhD in the US is the so-called *candidate* degree. The highest academic degree, doctoral, is analogous to the German *Habilitation*. The doctoral dissertation is usually presented at a mature stage of the academic career; only a fraction of the *candidate* degree holders make it to the doctoral level. The most outstanding scholars can be elected as members (or corresponding members) of the Academy of Sciences. In this case they acquire the title *Academician*.

[2] NEP was an economic policy of the Soviet Government from 1922 till 1928. The NEP was slightly more capitalism-oriented than the so-called War Communism of 1917-1922 which practically ruined the country. The goal behind the NEP was stimulating the ruined economy. The complete nationalization of industry during the period of War Communism was partially revoked and a system of mixed economy was introduced, which allowed private individuals to own small enterprises, while the state continued to

merable banks and vigorous trade. Seemingly the half-dead Lenin
has realized the country can only be saved by returning to natural
market relations. The dying "leader of the world proletariat" is essentially no longer running Red Russia. Two portraits – Lenin and
Trotsky – hang everywhere. The authority of Trotsky, the Minister
of War and commander of the October Revolution, looms unusually
large. Needless to say, this also holds true among the Jewish populace. In his near-mythic "Tale of Reddish Motel," written in those
years, the poet Iosif Utkin[3] bears witness:

And the days were jabbering
Like the hawker Med
And the Jews were arguing:
"Yes or no?" they said.
There was faith and there was doubt,
Joy and tragedy.
"No" –
Of course – they said to Lenin,
"Yes" – they said to Trotsky.

Kharkov was the official capital of the Ukrainian Socialist Re-
public. And so it would remain right up to 1934 and basically un-
til the start of World War II. All party and state institutions, the
All-Ukrainian Central Executive Committee, headed by Bolshevik
Grigory Petrovsky, a variety of ministries – all were concentrated in
Kharkov.

Kharkov's famous factories come back to life – among them the
locomotive works and the electromechanical factory – which in its
time had shifted south from Riga – the iron-smelting works and
the plant for manufacturing agricultural equipment, bicycle workshops and more. Cultural life is at a boil. In 1922 Kharkov became
the birthplace of the "Berezil" theater, led by a bold experimenter,
the "Ukrainian Meyerhold" Les Kurbas,[4] subsequently shot during

---

control major banks, foreign trade, and large industries. Six years after its introduction
Stalin dismantled it, and virtually all "NEPmen," or petty entrepreneurs, were sent to
the Gulag.

[3]Iosif Pavlovich Utkin (1903 - 1944) was a Russian poet of the World War II generation.

[4]Vsevolod Emilevich Meyerhold (1874 - 1940) was a Russian and Soviet theater direc-

the Great Terror. In the twenties and thirties, two more glorious troupes arose there: the Opera and Ballet Theater and the Pushkin Russian Drama Theater. There were famous Ukrainian writers and poets working in Kharkov: Ostap Vishnya, Alexander Korneychuk, Vladimir Sosyur, Pavlo Tychyna. There were the famous artists Nikolai Samokish and Vassily Kasiyan, and the composers Yuliy Meitus and Andrei Shtogarenko. Here the outstanding singers Ivan Kozlovsky and Ivan Patorzhinsky won their first acclaim.

In Kharkov on January 10, 1922, young married couple Abram Golfand and Nina Petrova welcomed their first child, Yuri. As Yuri Golfand's younger sister Kira says:

"Our father Abram Dmitriyevich was a fascinating personality. He was very remote from Jewish life – assimilated, to use the current term. He graduated from the Kharkov Institute of Technology and became a successful engineer. An extremely capable, creative person, he received a series of promotions. He became chief engineer of the Ukrainian Meat Trust. He basically created the meat industry in the Ukraine. Meat packing plants in Poltava, in Darnitsa (Kiev) and in Dnepropetrovsk were built according to his designs. The work was hellish. He seemed to work around the clock. Constant business trips, treks to Moscow to squeeze something out of the authorities, sign papers. The whole apartment was crammed full of blueprints, documents, directories. There was a drafting table in the living room... I think the rush job was non-stop..."

With the relocation of the capital, Abram Dmitriyevich was transferred to Kiev. He essentially lived in two households. And this situation lasted three years. The darkness of 1937, the year of the Great Terror, loomed on the horizon.

"I still don't understand," Kira says, "how our father stayed clear of that bloody meatgrinder. Almost all the chief engineers of the Ukraine's meat packing plants, which he oversaw, all the directors and party secretaries were arrested, deported to camps or executed

---

tor, actor and theatrical producer. His provocative experiments and symbolism in an unconventional theater setting made him one of the seminal forces in modern international theater. In 1939 Meyerhold was arrested, and in 1940 sentenced to death by firing squad. He was executed the next day.

on instantaneous *troika* verdicts.[5] It must have been obvious to our father that they would come for him soon. He filed one application after another, asking for release from his post due to health issues, for family reasons, and so on. But his applications went unsigned..."

Then came a stroke of luck: a new boss, uninformed, let the last application slip through. Abram Dmitriyevich soon wound up on the operating table with purulent appendicitis. He then took a couple of months to recuperate. In short, he disappeared, miraculously eluding the bloodthirsty hunters of "enemies of the people." He returned to Kharkov.

"Our mother's name was Nina Gregoriyevna Petrova. Her father was Russian, and her mother... A lot of things mixed together! Our grandmother used to say: 'My mother had French, Polish and Russian blood, my father was a Pole, and I'm Orthodox. My father was one of the Polish aristocrats sent into exile under the tsar after the uprising in the Kingdom of Poland. And since he married a woman from the petty bourgeoisie, he was tossed out of the nobility... '

Our mother studied to be a doctor. She graduated from medical school, but worked in physiology. This was in Kharkov at the Ukrainian Institute of Experimental Medicine. It was later closed. After the war, she was at the Military Medical Academy. She did very interesting scientific work whose actual significance is only now emerging.

Basically, our parents were talented people..."

And not only talented – they were intelligent and sensitive child-rearers. The family took young people seriously, appreciated their personalities. And Yura, his sister remembers, was a "special boy, with special abilities."

Their father, fond of chess, initiated his four-year-old son in the game. The two spent all their free time sitting around the chessboard. Sometimes their matches stretched over days. And Yura often called his father at work to tell him he thought he'd found a very strong

---

[5]Troika or NKVD troika were institutional commissions of three persons who issued sentences to people after a simplified superficial investigation and without a full trial. These commissions were used as an instrument of extrajudicial punishment for quick execution or imprisonment of the "enemies of the people."

countermove. But without braggery, with incredible tact for a child his age: "What do you think, if I move to e5?.."

More and more, son began winning against father. Seeing Yura rapidly gaining strength, Abram Dmitriyevich started bringing him books on chess theory, collections of chess problems, selected matches of Lasker, Capablanca, Alekhine.

And one day father told son he had nothing more to give him as a chess player. "From now on you're on your own ..."

But when Yura started school, an area emerged where he was a long way from overtaking his father: mathematics. As an inherently disciplined, restrained person, the boy didn't let on in class that he grew bored with listening to the basics of arithmetic, algebra and geometry. At home, he and his father worked problems that the teachers never dreamed of.

His conversations with his mother were more philosophical.

"What do you think, if matter's eternal..."

Nina, hearing out the question, smiles softly and retorts in parody of her son's habit: "What do you think?"

Smart people seem to come in two categories: some love to express their own opinions, while others glean opinions from conversation as a means to form their own perspectives, sometimes radically different from those they've encountered.

"When Yura was still a boy," his sister Kira says, "Our mother was doing serious work in science. Really, she was always working on something new and unexplored. And my brother took an avid interest in my mother's work. She said a lot of interesting things about it. Yurochka listened to her tales of biological experiments with no less interest than he did my father's news of math and chess..."

Reaching his teens, Yura wasn't particularly muscular. And one day he made a firm decision to catch up. He brought five-kilo dumbbells home from the store. His father, seeing them, gasped:

"Do you think it's a good idea to start off with those weights?"

"What do you think?"

Abram Dmitriyevich happened to think otherwise. He put the dumbbells in a briefcase and headed for the sporting goods store.

"Excuse me, did my boy just buy these from you?"

"Yes. It came as a surprise that he needed such big ones..."

In short, the dumbbells were exchanged for a two-kilo set. Then six months later he needed the five-kilo weights, and later on, ten...

In 1939, Yuri, having successfully graduated from school, applies to study at the Department of Physics and Mathematics of Kharkov State University.

"More than a fourth of all the physics in the country"

Kharkov is a city of education and science: the Technological Institute (now Polytechnic), the oldest Russian agricultural institute, the Institute of National Economy, the Institute of Civil Engineering, the Medical Institute, the Institute of Mathematics and Mechanics, the Pedagogical Institute. The Ukrainian Institute of Physics and Technology (UPTI)[6] was founded in 1928 in Kharkov on the initiative of Academician Abram Ioffe.[7] In 1932, the Institute was the site of the first splitting of an atomic nucleus (!) in the Soviet Union. The country's first radar installation was built here. As early as 1940, a group of UPTI employees under Friedrich Lange[8] filed a proposal for development of the atomic bomb based on nuclear fission! Incredible but true.

Academician Sergey Vavilov maintained "more than a fourth of all physics in the USSR" was done at UPTI. It's also worth knowing that the most famous tank of World War II, the T-34, was developed at the Kharkov Design Bureau, headed by Mikhail Ilyich Koshkin.

The city takes special pride in its university, the south of Russia's oldest, founded by Tsar Alexander in 1805.

The university's first rector was the outstanding Ukrainian poet Hulak-Artemovsky. In the mid-19th century, the chemistry department was headed by future academician Nikolay Beketov. Notable

---

[6] Currently Kharkov Institute of Physics and Technology.

[7] Abram Fedorovich Ioffe (1880 - 1960), a prominent Russian and Soviet physicist.

[8] Friedrich "Fritz" Lange (1899 - 1987), a German physicist and active member of the German Communist Party. He emigrated to the USSR in 1935 and returned to (East) Germany in 1959.

alumni include historian Nikolai Kostomarov, playwright Michael Staritskiy, composer Mykola Lysenko and artist Genrikh Semiradsky. The university developed a stellar School of Mathematics: Alexander Lyapunov, Mikhail Ostrogradsky, Vladimir Steklov (incidentally, Yuri Golfand completed his postgraduate studies at the Steklov Mathematical Institute in Moscow).

The names of three Nobel laureates – alumni and faculty – are associated with this illustrious institute: Ilya Ilyich Mechnikov, the prominent Belarusian-American economist Simon Abramovich Kuznets and, finally, the head of the Department of General Physics, Lev Davidovich Landau.

When Yuri Golfand enrolled at the university in 1939, Landau had already left: in 1937 Pyotr Kapitsa had invited him to head the department of theoretical physics at the new Institute for Physical Problems in Moscow.[9] Landau had also spent a year in prison[10] (more on that below). Nevertheless, Landau's spirit remained palpable in the university's auditoriums and lab classes.

Turbulent years

And so, in 1939, Yuri became a student of Kharkov University. The war was a little less than two years away. In this time, he managed to finish the courses that took regular students three years. This saved him from immediate mobilization to military service. Freshmen and sophomores were drafted regardless of academic success and other factors – the harvest took them all... In 1941, when the war began, third-year student Yuri Golfand was in his twentieth year.

Almost everyone with at least three years of study – those who had already received basic technical training – were sent to Sverdlovsk for an accelerated study at the Zhukovsky Air Force Engineering Academy, relocated from Moscow to the Urals. Thus Yura avoided active army service a second time. He didn't suffer the sad fate of most the younger undergraduates, who went to the front to die in

---

[9]Currently P.L. Kapitsa Institute for Physical Problems. The Institute was founded in 1934 by P.L. Kapitsa.
[10]From April 1938 till April 1939.

the first weeks of the war.

Kharkov was captured by Nazi troops in October 1941. Hundreds of thousands of Red Army troops were killed or captured in the fierce battles for the city. In 1943, Soviet troops liberated the city, but hung on there only briefly before being forced to retreat again with enormous losses. The "Kharkov meat grinder" is one of the darkest and bloodiest pages of the history of World War II.

Meanwhile, the Golfand family – father Abram Dmitriyevich, mother Nina and sister Kira – were in evacuation in Semipalatinsk, East Kazakhstan, with its harsh, extreme continental climate. The first Soviet atomic bomb was detonated in 1949 near Semipalatinsk at the USSR's largest nuclear test site.

In Sverdlovsk, Yura progressed quickly in his military aeronautical engineering studies, with no desire to work as an engineer or military professional in the future. The army barracks were a prison for him. Golfand fell seriously ill twice in the course of a year and was released to stay for a while with his parents – fortunately, the Ural Mountains aren't overly far from Semipalatinsk by Russian standards.

Visiting on family leave, Yuri was more than a little surprised at his father's and mother's feverish activity. As a doctor, Nina Grigoryevna had military duties, working day and night at a hospital. And their father had proved heavily in demand. The Leningrad Technological Institute of the Refrigeration Industry had been evacuated to Semipalatinsk. Abram Dmitriyevich taught twenty-five courses – the prominent Ukrainian specialist's engineering, scientific, pedagogical and organizational talent was a tremendous asset.

"When Yura visited us in Semipalatinsk," Kira recalls, "he brought my mother an absolutely amazing book. He saw it in a shop, opened it, and it turned out to be about physiology. He immediately bought it and wrote a touching gift inscription. For mother, it was a tremendous gift!...

He was interested in our father's work, because our father, seemingly a civil engineer, working on design theory, was also writing something completely unrelated to his work. He probably showed someone, but no one understood... After our father's death, Yura gave these notes to a geometer acquaintance for reading... Cybernetics were in the air then, and the geometer told Yura afterward that our father's notebooks contained material on spontaneous cybernetics, that he'd arrived at cybernetic laws intuitively, not knowing the work of Wiener...

That was how our father was..."

Abram Dmitriyevich kept teaching at the Institute of the Refrigeration Industry throughout the three years of the family's evacuation.

With this same institute, the family moved to Leningrad in 1944. After finishing his academic courses, Yura served at a military airfield.

In the spring of 1945, immediately after the war's end, Yuri passed the exams for four years at once and entered Leningrad University as a fifth-year student. In a year, he had a university degree. Subsequently, he cheerfully said that he had only really been a student as a freshman in Kharkov and as a fifth-year student in Petersburg.

Kira (four years younger than her brother) recalls:

"The graduation ceremony at the university on Vasilievsky Island... White nights, happy faces... A young girl, I'm dying with pride: old professors raise their glasses to Yura, saying words about his future that are fit to fly to heaven... Yura blushes, hangs his head... And drinks with anyone who comes by to kiss up to him..." Kira laughs. "It was his first and probably last time in life to get drunk as hell... I dragged him home through the city..."

He hopes to attend graduate school but has no luck. The early postwar years saw the start of a campaign of extreme anti-Semitism, culminating in the "case of the Kremlin doctors," the execution of the Jewish Anti-Fascist Committee and the dying Stalin's decision to deport all Jews to Siberia.[11] Yura, never having encountered open

---

[11] The Doctors' case (or Doctors' plot) is considered to be the most dramatic anti-Jewish episode in the Soviet Union under Joseph Stalin's regime. At the end of 1952 a group of professors, the very most accomplished medical specialists, were arrested. All of these, with the exception of one or two, were Jews. They were accused of acting under the orders of an American "Jewish spy organization, the Joint," and, under the pretense of healing, actually trying to kill the leaders of the Party and government. A few weeks after the death of Stalin, the new Soviet leadership stated a lack of evidence and the case was dropped. Soon after, the case was declared to have been fabricated.

anti-Semitism before, suddenly feels for the first time with his own skin what it means to be a Jew in the Soviet Union.

As Kira says, "Their student body was small after the war, and there were only two Jews: Yura, and Zhenya Plonsky. But they weren't admitted to graduate school. Zhenya went to work at some factory. And Yura was assigned to the Moscow Computing Center. He found the work uninteresting and disagreeable..."

But Golfand didn't give up. He started graduate school by correspondence through the Leningrad branch of the Steklov Mathematics Institute. Within a year, he passed all the exams, finished graduate school and defended his master's thesis.

Both the thesis and his next few publications concerned purely mathematical problems of group theory. Soon Yuri came to feel that for him, pure mathematics was only a tool – fascinating, but only a tool, which he would use in theoretical physics. Physics held a strong attraction for him. Yura knew he had to move to Moscow. "Because Moscow," as he wrote his childhood friend Alexander Frumkin in March 1948, "is the focal point of all the main opportunities. But it's much better to drive into Moscow in your own car than to cling to a closed trolleybus door, waiting for a beautiful conductress to deign to admit you."

Frumkin was nearly the only person in whom Yura could confide his secrets. In Kharkov, they lived in the same building, and their fathers were friends. Alexander rented a nook in Moscow, studied, had started working. Subsequently, for many years Associate Professor Alexander Lvovich Frumkin headed the department of the theoretical foundations of electrical engineering at the Moscow Institute of Electricity.

Two weeks later, in early April, in the following letter, Yuri says:

"I've finally found an idea (physical in nature) which may guide my work for years to come. I must admit, this is incredibly exhilarating for me. After all, remember how I whined all the time about being bored working on groups and abstract mathematics in general. Now the picture has changed completely. Although my idea still has very vague outlines, I instinctively know I've chosen the right direction. Turning it into a theory will take a lot of work. And that's just

what I need! Success, and I'm not exaggerating, will mean creating a totally new perspective in physics! For now, I'll say, like Pushkin: 'Far-off still, the free novel reposed half-hidden in my magic crystal...'
"

This "magic crystal" may have been the idea formulated in several years' time as the *theory of supersymmetry.*

He asked Alexander to check the ads in the newspaper *Evening Moscow* for openings for an assistant professor at some university or a senior researcher at a research institute, and also for help with temporary housing. And, of course, to clear up the matter of a residency permit.[12]

Soon (around 1950) Yura managed to make his way to Moscow, where he met Sara, a young woman from Kharkov whom he hadn't known before. She was also a mathematician by profession, studying earthquakes and the physics of the earth's crust. And perhaps the most unexpected "earthquake" for family and friends was Yura's hastily arranged marriage. Yura's and Sara's firstborn, Yasha, soon appeared.

Golfand worked at the Research Institute of the Electrical Industry. His articles were published in the Mathematical Miscellany of the Academy of Sciences, but Yuri was more interested in theoretical physics. And he kept dreaming of the Physical Institute of the Academy of Sciences.

He went there for an appointment with Academician Markov, one of the "demigods" of Russian science, from the institute's first generation. He introduced himself as a mathematician longing to work in theoretical physics. The "demigod" gave Yuri a tricky problem which his assistants had struggled fruitlessly to solve. It was an absolutely physical problem, but its solution required Golfand's formidable math skills and unconventional turn of mind.

A few days later, Yuri brought the Academician a solution. Markov warmly shook his hand and mumbled something about

---

[12]In Russian, *propiska*, a mandatory residence permit which, in effect, eliminated the freedom of movement inside the country. It was virtually impossible for a non-Muscovite to settle in Moscow since the residence permit was granted only rarely and only on special occasions.

"times like these," "staffing problems" – basically, sadly hinted at the insurmountable barrier of the "fifth point."[13] Thirty years later, namely Moisei Alexandrovich Markov would hire the disgraced "refusenik"[14] physicist Yuri Abramovich Golfand for his department at a time when no one else dared.

Of course, all this darkened Golfand's mood. But Yuri had no intention of giving up. What followed was peculiar. Yuri's mother Nina, a strong-willed, determined, uncompromising woman, arrived from Leningrad. Many maintain that Yuri's character resembled hers.

Says Kira:

"Our Russian mother, with her vehement hatred of anti-Semitism, agonized over what was happening. And this wasn't just about Yura, who was rushing about like a hunted wolf. She said she didn't understand at all what was happening in the country. And she visited Ilya Ehrenburg,[15] whom she'd known since back when they both were young. Our mother was friends with Ilya Grigoryevich's wife Ludmilla. During the war, Ehrenburg was incredibly renowned. He was called the 'conscience of the nation.' Basically, my mother went to Gorky Street to ask the famous Jewish writer, poet and publicist just one question: 'Is the country really sliding back to the days of Black Hundred pogroms?' "

Nina Grigoryevna later described the meeting at the office, which housed Ehrenburg's legendary collection of smoking pipes. The writer was in a kind of tense state. "A pathetic, disturbing conversation..." Ehrenburg immediately realized the reason for the visit. He asked about her son. Nina told him what was happening with

---

[13]Ethnicity — which in the Soviet parlance was referred to as "nationality" — was entry No. 5 in the Soviet passport. Entry No. 5 became a euphemism for "Jewish."

[14]A group of people treated as political enemies in the USSR in the 1970s and 80s. The only "crime" committed by these people was that they had applied for and been denied exit visas to Israel. And yet, they were treated essentially as criminals: fired from jobs and blacklisted, with no access to work (with the exception of low-paid manual labor), constantly intimidated by the KGB, on the verge of arrest. In fact, the most active of them, those who tried to organize and fight back for their rights, were imprisoned.

[15]Ilya Grigoryevich Ehrenburg (1891 - 1967), a prominent Soviet writer, journalist, translator, and cultural figure.

Yura...

And a few days later, Ehrenburg's secretary arrived with a letter from Ilya Grigoryevich to Academician Markov. Yura was to deliver this envelope to the "demigod." The secretary said nothing about the message's content, but it wasn't hard to guess. As soon as the messenger left, Golfand tore the envelope to bits without opening it.

Learning of the letter, Nina Grigoryevna told her son: "Good for you that you tore it up! I should've stayed away from that blockhead... "

This episode may have "fired up" Yuri still more than before. He sought a meeting with Tamm, who headed the department of theoretical physics at FIAN. Tamm was far from elderly, barely over fifty-five, but in the academic world he had long been a legend, a classic.

This was the head of the physical-technical department at Moscow State University, the colleague of Mandelstam, Cherenkov and Frank... The author of brilliant works on quantum mechanics, solid state physics, the theory of radiation, nuclear physics, elementary particle physics. And the brother of an executed "enemy of the people," and the winner of the Stalin Prize, received from Stalin's own hands. Just two years earlier, Igor Yevgenyevich had won a Nobel Prize.

The meeting with Tamm was a turning point in Yuri Golfand's fate. Without a doubt, the master took a liking to Yuri, with his independent views and unexpected ideas. And until the end of his days, Igor Yevgenyevich would be Yuri's wise teacher, counselor and protector.

Golfand was hired at the Physical Institute as a mathematician. From 1951 to the day of his departure to Israel, Golfand's employment record book had only one entry: "Lebedev Physical Institute of the USSR Academy of Sciences." Until his dismissal from the institute, when he spent six long years as a "refusenik."

FIAN

FIAN was officially created in 1934 by Sergei Ivanovich Vavilov, an outstanding Soviet scientist, the future president of the USSR

Academy of Sciences, and the founder of the Soviet school of physical optics.

At Vavilov's suggestion, the institute was named after the remarkable Russian physicist Pyotr Lebedev, a pioneer of studies of light, to which Sergei Vavilov had also devoted a considerable part of his life. Academician Lebedev was the first to measure the pressure of light, experimentally confirming Maxwell's conclusions about the phenomenon's presence in nature.

At one time, FIAN's staff included Leonid Isaakovich Mandelstam, who had received the Lenin Prize back in 1931; Academician Grigory Samuilovich Landsberg, the author of an acclaimed three-volume physics textbook which a generation of Soviet scientists was raised on; the brilliant radiophysicist Mikhail Alexandrovich Leontovich; Nikolai Papaleksy, the founder of Soviet radio astronomy; the future theorist of nuclear reactors Blokhintsev; Moisei Alexandrovich Markov, already mentioned above, a specialist in the quantum mechanics and elementary particle physics; Tamm himself, Pyotr Alexandrovich Rebinder, Lev Abramovich Tumerman, and others.

The names of such Academicians as Skobeltsyn, Keldysh, Rozhdestvensky, Brekhovskikh, Alikhanyan, Fradkin, Shapiro and Krokhin are also associated with the Lebedev Physical Institute. By number of academicians, FIAN ranks as the leader among all Russian scientific institutions.

Out of the nine Soviet (and later Russian) physicists who have been awarded the Nobel Prize, six were Physical Institute employees.

The first from FIAN to receive the Nobel Prize were Cherenkov, Tamm and Frank, in 1958, "for the discovery and interpretation of the Cherenkov effect." In 1964, the prize was awarded to Nikolai Basov and Alexander Prokhorov (together with Townes) for creating the world's first lasers. Few could imagine then how lasers would revolutionize our lives in a few years' time. FIAN's sixth Nobel laureate, in 2003, was Academician Vitaly Lazarevich Ginzburg, for his work on superfluidity and superconductivity.

There was also a seventh Nobel laureate at FIAN: Andrei Dmitriyevich Sakharov, recipient of the Nobel Peace Prize, the father of the Soviet hydrogen bomb and an outstanding defender of human rights. A huge cross-section of Yuri Abramovich Golfand's life would be connected namely with Sakharov.

A theoretical physicist

In his very brief autobiography, written on the eve of his departure to Israel, Yuri Abramovich stated that since 1951 he had "worked at the P. N. Lebedev Physical Institute as a senior fellow," then added: "By profession I'm a theoretical physicist."

I don't think this phrase is accidental. After all, he was hired as a mathematician in the department of theoretical physics – headed, as mentioned above, by Igor Yevgenevich Tamm.

But within days of starting work at the department, Yuri encountered an opponent, to put it mildly: Vitaly Lazarevich Ginzburg. In 1950, on the eve of Golfand's arrival at the institute, Vitaly Ginzburg produced the brilliant work that would find a place in the history of physics as the "Ginzburg-Landau theory of superconductivity." A couple years later, he followed with another great work (jointly with L. Pitaevsky) on superfluidity – a phenomenon discovered twenty years earlier by Pyotr Kapitsa. Essentially, the Swedish Academy of Sciences acknowledged these two works with the Nobel Prize a half century later.

Golfand's relationship with Ginzburg was poor from the start. Vitaly Lazarevich grumbled, "Why'd the department hire a mathematician? What does he know about physics?"

And indeed, Yuri's first scientific publications were abstractly mathematical in nature. But soon physics-dominated works began to appear. One example was his study of the interaction of π mesons with nucleons, done jointly with Tamm (1954). Yuri then published an article on the properties of the electron-positron field. Another, from 1955, examined quasifields. In 1957, Golfand published his work "Fermi Fields and Spinors in Infinite Dimensional Space," which fits on three pages of the 113-th issue of *Reports of the USSR Academy of Sciences*.

The more Igor Yevgenevich Tamm admired his protégé's sharp mind, more Ginzburg disliked him – disliked his inner freedom and lack of hang-ups.

Many years later, Golfand's colleague Mikhail Marinov, a professor of physics at the Technion, tried to explain this phenomenon:

"How did he come by this internal freedom, which everyone found so stunning? First, Yuri had a brilliant personality in his youth. He was an excellent student, and his PhD thesis was completed in record time. When he started to work – at first in the field of applied physics – his projects went quickly and successfully. In addition, he belonged to a generation of scientists who were more independent-minded than previous generations.

Second, Yuri belonged to a group of scientists formed to address 'defense tasks,' particularly in nuclear physics, and working under the guidance (and protection) of leaders like I. V. Kurchatov, A. I. Alikhanov and I. Ye. Tamm, who were recognized by the authorities in power. Unique social conditions were created for them, which were hardly comparable to those of their counterparts in the west. By the end of 1950s, 'defense tasks' had receded to a secondary role, yet privileges largely preserved. They could just sit and work, writing articles. And no one ever told them what to do. No deadlines applied. If an error occurred, not to worry, it could be corrected before the article was sent to press. The only thing most physicists (especially Jewish ones) were deprived of was the opportunity to travel abroad and maintain personal contacts with colleagues from abroad. But not everyone found this important.

This meant that Yura's inherently romantic free thinking essentially subsisted without the drag of dull daily duties. He could afford to come to work at his own convenience and work on what he thought possible, never reporting to anyone. All this, of course, didn't preclude internal discipline and extraordinary accuracy in whatever concerned his work."

Marinov's first point seems clear enough. But the second may require some elucidation. Indeed, the Soviet Union had a privileged caste of scientists engaged in secret military projects: the atomic bomb, missiles, chemical and biological weapons, and so on.

Before 1948, FIAN staff had no direct involvement in these projects. Igor Kurchatov, Yakov Zeldovich, Yulii Khariton, Abram

Alikhanov and the other pillars of the Soviet atomic project had no direct relation to the Physical Institute. But then in late June 1948...

From Andrei Sakharov's *Memoirs*:

...With a mysterious look, Igor Yevgenyevich Tamm asked me and another of his students, Semyon Belenky, to remain after the seminar. This was one of the so-called Friday seminars, in-house gatherings held in Igor Yevgenyevich's small office (by now the FIAN physicists would no longer fit there). As soon as we were alone, he shut the door tightly and made an announcement that stunned us.

A special FIAN research group was being created by decree of the Council of Ministers and Party Central Committee. He had been appointed head of the group, and we were both its members. The group was tasked with theoretically and computationally ascertaining whether it was possible to build a hydrogen bomb and, specifically, with checking and refining the calculations that Zeldovich's group was producing at the Institute of Chemical Physics...

Continuing, Andrei Dmitriyevich tries to understand why he was chosen:

As to why I'd become a candidate for this position, I later heard a story that supposedly the director of FIAN, Academician S. I. Vavilov, had said, "Sakharov's housing situation is terrible. Let's include him in the group; then we can help him." It probably also played a role that I was working on concrete nuclear physics and plasma theory and had a proposal about muon catalysis...

Really, though, I think the main grounds for my appointment were Igor Yevgenyevich giving me a strong recommendation.

Vavilov kept his promise. In May, I was given two rooms on Twenty-fifth of October Street. Although the building itself is in the heart of Moscow, it wasn't a very "fashionable" place to live – wood-heated, and with rooms accessed by a shared corridor. At the last moment, a deputy director of finances "diverted" one of the two rooms for his mother... Our room was 14 square meters,[16] we had no dining table (there was nowhere to put it), so we ate off stools or the windowsill. There were about 10 families living on the long corridor, with one small kitchen, a toilet off the staircase landing where two such "communal" apartments were to share it, and no tub or shower, of course. But we were incredibly happy...

So much for "fashionable" housing! So it's clearly an exaggeration when Marinov refers to special conditions for Soviet nuclear scientists as "hardly comparable to those of their counterparts in the West"!

Essentially, though, a new group at FIAN started work on thermonuclear weapons.

"Our group had two other members," Sakharov writes. "One was doctor of physical and mathematical sciences (now an Academician) Vitaly Lazarevich Ginzburg, who was one of Igor Yevgenyevich's most talented and beloved students; the other was Yuri Alexandrovich Romanov, a young researcher who had joined the Theory Department recently. Ginzburg apparently was included on some kind of part-time basis; later, at the time of the group's move to the 'Object,'[17] this transfer didn't apply to him."

Those years found essentially the entire Theory Department carrying out work for the hydrogen bomb project, where Andrei Dmitriyevich Sakharov would soon play a primary role. Many department employees never even suspected where their theoretical projects were leading.

This was the case with Yuri Golfand. He worked on the computing tasks that were assigned to him from above, but had no knowledge of how his solutions would be practically applied. Nonetheless, this

---

[16] About 140 square feet.

[17] A top secret classified site of the Soviet nuclear bomb research center, officially referred to as *Arzamas 16* although no such city existed in the map. The historical name of this city was Sarov, a small town in the Gorky (now Nizhny Novgorod) District, about 300 miles to the east of Moscow (currently, the Russian Federal Nuclear Center in Sarov). There the first Soviet nuclear-fission, or atomic, bomb was developed. Later the first thermonuclear-fusion, or hydrogen, bomb was developed there too.

indirect participation in secret projects would later prove fateful as a basis for long-term refusal to grant him permission to travel abroad, including to Israel.

The May vacation dissertation

As a candidate of mathematical sciences, physicist Yuri Golfand was so engrossed in more and more new developments that when colleagues told him, "Yura, it's time to defend your doctoral thesis," he carelessly brushed them aside: "This is no time for a dissertation – I'm up to my neck in more serious work!"

Then Igor Yevgenyevich Tamm fell ill. The job of managing the department effectively shifted to Ginzburg. In 1966, Vitaly Lazarevich became an Academician, and a couple of years after Tamm's death, he was officially appointed head of the Theory Department at FIAN. However, the unquestioned authority for the staff, and the conscience of the department, was still Andrei Sakharov. The fact that Sakharov didn't take Tamm's place is easily explained. By the mid-sixties, Sakharov's human rights activism had become a bogey for the Soviet party leadership. He participated in a collective letter against the revival of the cult of Stalin. In 1968 he wrote the famous article "Reflections on Progress, Peaceful Coexistence and Intellectual Freedom." In this, essentially his first major non-scientific and purely political work, Sakharov advanced a convergence theory – unthinkable for communist ideology – positing the mutual rapprochement of the socialist and capitalist systems as the basis for progress and peace on the planet. The article's total circulation in the West reached 20 million. After its publication, Sakharov was banned from pursuing further classified projects in the closed city of Arzamas, where he had spent 18 years of his life.

In early 1968, Tamm called Golfand aside for a private conversation. The master was very honest:

"Yura, I'm asking you to act urgently to defend your doctoral thesis, because I know that when I'm gone, things will be bad for you..."

Yuri heeded the master's fatherly advice. On the eve of the May holidays in 1968, he suddenly appeared at his sister Kira's house in

Peterhof.[18] It was her birthday, April 28. He always holed up in this quiet, congenial abode when he urgently needed to focus his mind on particularly difficult problems.

This time, after kisses and congratulations, Yura set copies of his works on the table and said with unusual solemnity:

"Kísanka, I'm going to do a dissertation. Will you help?"

"You bet, of course I'll help!" said the birthday girl.

She brought a large pair of scissors and a bottle of silicone stationery glue.

"Work!"

Then she left for the May break on a long-planned canoe camping trip with her institute friends.

Spring lingered that year. Kira returned four days later.

Yuri, pointing to the manuscript lying in the middle of the table, said calmly:

"You see, I finished in time. There it is – the dissertation."

The phrase "in time" was not accidental: there was almost no time left before the Higher Attestation Commission of the Ministry of Education and Science closed for summer vacation. Before then, he had to at least register his application. And also write thank-you letters to his opponents – no getting around that!

Kira set her typewriter on the table, offering her services.

"No, no, I'll take care of it."

Then he rushed off to the station. Back at the institute, he immediately headed for the typing pool. He laughed afterward, "The typist worked twice as long as I did!"

His dissertation made it in before the honorable Commission went on vacation. He also managed to hold his defense while Igor Tamm was still alive. Academician Tamm passed away a year and a half after Yuri earned his doctorate.

What a dissertation defense was in those days, what kind of hassle and hubbub were involved, is known to everyone who went through one. Still, in Golfand's case everything happened surpris-

---

[18]Peterhof is a small town not far from St. Petersburg, located on the southern shore of the Gulf of Finland.

ingly quickly.

Problems arose, though, where Yuri had least expected them. The work had to go out for at least two reviews. Opponents also needed copies. And at this point the country turned out to have very few scientists who actually understood what the work was about. One of the reviewers was then-young Lev Okun from the Institute of Experimental and Theoretical Physics.

Yuri asked Sakharov to serve as his opponent. Alas, Andrei Dmitriyevich was unable to attend the defense: at this time, his first wife Klavdia Alekseyevna was dying from a serious illness. (She had borne Sakharov two daughters and a son.) He relayed his opinion to the Commission in writing, not so much expressing the conclusions of an opponent as providing a rave review of a colleague's work.

The doctoral dissertation which Golfand defended in the early fall of 1968 said not a word about supersymmetry, which would soon fill all his thoughts, subduing his mind and heart.

A few months later, the freshly minted doctor of physical and mathematical sciences finally received his first graduate student. As Kira says:

"He and Sarah, his first wife, had just moved into an apartment on Vernadsky Prospekt. Their children, Natasha and Yasha, were still little. I happened to be in Moscow on business, and one evening as we were walking, Yura said happily, 'Guess what, I have a graduate student.' (He'd never had a graduate student before – just many trainees, including Chinese students.) 'His name is Zhenya. Evgeny Likhtman, a really sharp guy. You know, there's this thing I've been thinking about. Evgeny will help me a lot, because I just have two hands. I need 'physical' assistance. We need to sit down and write squiggles together...' "

The "squiggles" were the mathematical apparatus explaining the hypothesis that would be called supersymmetry. In the early 1970s, Golfand and his assistant Evgeny Likhtman made a first official statement on their idea. This was followed by two joint publications: "Extensions of the Algebra of Poincaré Group Generators and Violation of P-Invariance" (*Journal of Experimental Theoretical Physics, 1971*) and "On Extension of the Generator Algebra of the Poincaré Group by Bispinor Generators" (*Problems of Theoretical Physics, 1972*). This statement took no more than three journal pages.

"The kind of guy he was..."

At the conference "Thirty Years of Supersymmetry," held in the U.S. in 2000, Evgeny Pinkhasovich Likhtman concluded his speech with these words: "For me, Yuri Abramovich Golfand remains not only a teacher of craft, but also a man who gave me a taste for the risky work of walking the road less traveled."

Dozens and dozens of people who knew Yuri Abramovich have recorded their memories of him.

Eduard Batkin, physicist (Haifa Technion):

"He always went against the flow, was never 'mainstream'... He had no need for self-affirmation, for recognition, and that could annoy others. Yura was a scientist, not a person who earned money as a scientist.

He never held himself at a distance. He had his own style of communicating: 'That, old chap, is baloney' – that was the maximum he could allow himself. That was his style: simple and open. Here in the West, people's style of behavior is more flamboyant. Many people – the kind who write huge works with loads of formulas or turn out lots of articles, and who work in big teams – were annoyed by how he was. But what he did, he did alone. He didn't congregate with groups, didn't write many articles. He knew his ideas would be implemented, and didn't think about their propaganda.

The main reason he died so suddenly was his character; that was how he lived. It was possible to be angry with him for being that way, but it came from God... My chances of meeting anyone else like that in my life are next to nothing."

Boris Bolotovsky, Doctor of Physical and Mathematical Sciences (FIAN veteran):

"I realized fairly soon that his qualities of friendliness and attentiveness to people were unfeigned. When I came to him with a question, no matter what – whether about a book translation or work – he immediately dropped his own work, which may have been more important than my own, and started discussing my problems. He asked me about details, clarified nuances and, if our conversation didn't lead to a solution, kept turning over the question in his mind and, at our next meeting, went back to discussing the question on his own, not worrying about the time this took."

Alla Vapdysheva, music teacher (Moscow):

"Life depends on people like him. It was breathtaking when he talked about his science, even though I didn't understand his theory. I always sensed his tremendous magnetism. And this is paradoxical, because you couldn't call him easy to talk to; he wasn't very socially responsive, didn't let everyone get close to him. It was only possible to talk with him about the essential, only what was great and important. Although not a convivial person, he instantly understood others.

He detested worldliness, he couldn't stand empty words. You might say that he and I represented totally opposite fields, but we understood each other perfectly... We could keep silent for a long time, and we felt good. You could just sit with him for a cup of tea – and you'd leave as a different person..."

Leonid Mittelman (Tel-Aviv University):

"Happiness, unhappiness, all problems – they're only internal sensations. Sergei Kovalev, for example: he was free in his prison cell... And a person can be unfree while having everything. This isn't a genetic concept, it's a matter of environment – it comes from spending time, for instance, with people like Yura. You could tell at first sight that nothing could ever overwhelm him. In the Soviet Union that was amazing..."

Irina Marakhova, biologist (St. Petersburg):

"His intelligence was always there, it was natural – from his family and upbringing. But also from a certain isolated lifestyle typical for scientists of that level...

He didn't waste time on nonsense. He knew how to avoid squandering himself on what didn't exist on his own wavelength and would only have worn him out. Even being around mindless conversations is exhausting – it's better, he thought, to go for a walk..."

Irina Brailovskaya, mathematician:

"To judge by how he acted, Yura was always young. When his daughter Masha was born, he was 50, and I remember how he took her on walks. They lived near the Lenin Hills.[19] Yura would go downhill with a stroller, and then would make his ascent holding the stroller stretched out almost at arm's length.

Yura taught my daughter to swim: the advice he gave her was just to not be afraid and to move as if she were on land. And off she swam!

Yura had no faith in and never took any medicine. He thought you should heal yourself by focusing on yourself."

Alexander Yomin, physicist (Haifa Technion):

"I used to work at an institute where even the minor scientists behaved like royalty... Yuri knew his own worth well enough not to bother with outward demonstrations of his significance. I saw a man so simple, so homespun... You could always approach him with questions... We shared an office for a year. Usually the other person in the room somehow gets in the way, but this time... As soon as Yuri Abramovich appeared, I dropped whatever I was doing and talked with him. Since he started working at the Technion later than I did, his work space wasn't as comfortable as mine, but he didn't mind... He was demanding about work conditions, though – about noise, for instance.

He had an interesting way of starting a 'scientific' conversation: 'May I ask you a question, teacher?' – and then it would turn out that I knew nothing. At the same time, Yu. A. wasn't at all domineering. On the contrary: for my part, I'd try to look up to him from below, but he'd nip that attitude in the bud and we'd go on talking as equals..."

Lyudmila Boytsova-Kovaleva, biologist (Moscow):

"The thing about Yura that always delighted and even surprised me (because it's so rare to encounter) was his unconditional response whenever anyone asked for help. Whatever someone asked for, he got up and did. When you were all still here, I told many people

---

[19]A neighborhood in Moscow. Currently Vorobiev Hills.

what an amazing and rare quality that was in Yura. Usually people adapt others' requests to suit themselves, but Yura always adapted to whoever was asking. It's a rare gene, and it probably died with Yura."

Victor Brailovsky, Professor of Mathematics, Tel Aviv University:

"I've known very few absolutely free people. The most prominent among them was Sakharov. And Yura. He always lived the way he wanted..."

Kira Golfand:

"Always even-tempered, calm, full of smiles, he grew withdrawn, even angry, when he was working on something. Then, exhausted, frazzled, he'd exclaim, "That's it. I did it!" And he often went to Peterhof to rest under our mother's wing. We walked a lot in the park and often spoke of my research – I worked at the Institute of Cytology – and then he became interested in biology issues. He knew all about whatever was happening at our institute. Yura's ideas found their way into my work. He had a way of asking, 'Well, how'd it go?' I'd tell him, 'Imagine that, it worked!' And he was happy as a child: 'Nice!'... And then would come his famous phrase, 'So then, what's next?...'"

Natalia Koretz:

"I had many chances to see him working. Sometimes even while lying down and resting he would 'write' with his finger in the air and sing. Then he'd sit down at the table and work for several hours without a break. His drafts, like the rest of the workspace around him, were a model of neatness. And it seemed miraculous when a hundred pages of densely scribbled pages turned into two or three pages of printed text, which always contained some new idea."

Figure 1. Family picture, Perm, 1931. Moisei Koretz and his first wife Alexandra Simonova are on the right (in the second and first rows, respectively). To the left of Moisei Koretz is his mother Slava-Simcha Koretz (née Eisurovich) with his and Alexandra's baby daughter Esther-Irina (in the first row) and his sister Lipa (in the second row). Courtesy of Michael Koretz.

Second digression
The "Koretz-Landau-Rumer" Case

Document No. 1

NKVD, Kharkov Regional Department,
UGB Department 3, July 5, 1937, No. 813321.
Top Secret NKVD [20] **Div. 3,**
Voronezh Region, City of Voronezh.

According to our data, Koretz Moisei Abramovich, born 1908, an engineer-physicist, is living and working in Voronezh. We are building a case against Koretz as a member of a counter-revolutionary Trotskyist sabotage organization. In 1935, we arrested Koretz, but the latter's guilt was not completely proved, such that Koretz was not convicted and his case was suspended.

At this time we have commenced the liquidation of the entire counterrevolutionary subversive group at UPTI, and the investigative materials we have obtained identify Koretz as an active participant in the aforementioned counterrevolutionary group and the closest friend of this group's leader – a Trotskyist, Professor Landau.

We have targeted Koretz for arrest.

We urgently request that Koretz be traced and put under active undercover surveillance, and that we kept informed of all materials this yields.

Kharkov Region NKVD Deputy Director Grishin
Third Division Deputy Director Tornuyev

Document No. 2

From Landau's testimony:

"By the beginning of 1937, we had concluded that the [Communist] Party had degenerated, that the Soviet government was not

---

[20] The Soviet acronym for the name of the secret police at that time. The Soviet secret police has changed acronyms like a chameleon. It started out as the Cheka, and then became the GPU, the OGPU, the NKVD, the NKGB, the MGB, and finally the KGB. Even today, however, people often simply refer to the secret police as "the Cheka" and the secret agents as "the Chekists." Currently FSB, Federal Security Service.

acting in the interests of workers but in the interests of a narrow ruling group, that it was in the country's interests to overthrow the existing government and establish a state in the USSR that would preserve collective farms and state ownership of enterprises but would be structured along the lines of bourgeois-democratic states."

Document No. 3

From the undercover report for March 7, 1938,
the day before the arrest of Landau and his two friends,
Yu. B. Rumer,[21] and M. A. Koretz:

"Professor RUMER, at a March 5 social evening at the House of Scholars with his friend, Professor Doctor LANDAU, told me: 'Have you read what's going in the leadership circles? Traitor sitting on traitor – and in fact they were nearly all running the country. Good grief, what a fine government – nothing but secret service agents, traitors and murderers. The ones up for trial are no better than the ones left behind.'

LANDAU, present for this remark, added: 'Degraded, inferior moral qualities are typical for our Bolsheviks – what else do you expect?'

...At his apartment, Koretz introduced the source to two individuals calling themselves LANDAU and RUMER. The source was introduced as a participant whom KORETS had recruited to the organization once more. The source's conversations with Koretz made it obvious that LANDAU and RUMER are completely committed to the ongoing preparations for issuing anti-Soviet leaflets."

Document No. 4

May Day leaflet, 1938

"Comrades!

The great cause of the October Revolution has been foully betrayed. The country is flooded with streams of blood and filth. Millions of innocent people have been thrown in prison, and no one can

---

[21]Yuri Borisovich Rumer (1901-1985) was a Soviet physicist known in the West as Georg Rumer. At the early stages of his career he worked as an assistant of Max Born at the University of Göttingen in Germany.

be sure when his own turn will come.

Don't you see, comrades, that the Stalinist clique has carried out a fascist coup? Socialism remains only on the pages of newspapers grown incapable of anything but lies. In his rabid hatred of true Socialism, Stalin has made himself the equal of Hitler and Mussolini. To preserve his own power, Stalin is destroying the country, making it easy prey for the beast of German fascism.

Comrades, organize! Don't be afraid of the NKVD executioners. They're only capable of beating defenseless prisoners, snaring unsuspecting, innocent people, plundering public property and concocting sham trials over nonexistent conspiracies.

Stalinist fascism survives solely by virtue of our disorganization.

The proletariat of our country, which overthrew the rule of the tsar and the capitalists, has the power to overthrow the fascist dictator and his clique.

Long live May 1 – the day of the struggle for socialism!"

The flier never went into circulation. The KGB learned of its existence. Who handed over the flyer to the authorities? Based on her father's words, Natasha is sure this was done by an agent provocateur, whom she confidently identifies by name. Namely he relayed the names of the authors of the daring appeal, so incredible for the time – Moisei Koretz, Yuri Rumer and Lev Landau. The friends were arrested in Moscow, where they had moved two years before.

Lev Landau, a student of Abram Fyodorovich Ioffe, since 1932 had headed the theoretical division of the Kharkov-based Ukrainian Physico-Technical Institute (UPTI). In 1934, at the age of twenty-six, with no thesis defense, he had become a doctor of physical and mathematical sciences. The following year, he had received the title of university professor.

In 1935, Kharkov was swept by the hysterical search for "enemies of the people," and the repression became unbearable. A number of institute employees were shot, including Lev Vasilyevich Shubnikov, one of the pioneers of low-temperature physics, with whom Landau had ties not only of friendship but also of shared scientific interests.

Landau fled from Kharkov to Moscow. He was fortunate to have an invitation from Pyotr Kapitsa to take a position as head of the theoretical division at the Institute of Physical Problems, which he led (and which now bears his name).

Then on April 28, 1938, just before May Day, all three of them were taken on the same evening, when Landau, Koretz and Rumer had gathered to celebrate the latter's birthday.

The future Nobel laureate, the country's youngest Academician (elected at age 38), spent a year in prison. There were interrogations where he was made to stand for seven hours straight while the investigator blinded him with a strong lamp. Lev Davidovich was saved thanks to Pyotr Kapitsa.

Landau never again entangled himself in political affairs.

The fate of the two other participants in the "Trotskyist conspiracy among physicists" proved far more lamentable.

Yuri Borisovich Rumer never returned to Moscow. At first, the "enemy of the people" worked in the suburbs of Omsk at CDB-29, a "sharashka" (in the jargon of imprisoned engineers and scientists, this was the name of secret scientific research institutions and design bureaus reporting to the NKVD/MVD). In 1946 he was transferred to Taganrog, then moved to Eniseysk under the law of "disenfranchisement." In 1953, having completed his term of exile, he was hired as a senior research fellow of the Siberian branch of the USSR Academy of Sciences, and later became director of the Institute of Physics and Electronics. He died at age 84 and was buried in Novosibirsk.

Moisei Koretz had it the worst. For him, it was already a second arrest. In 1935, he'd spent eight months in the internal jail at the Kharkov NKVD. He was threatened with the death penalty for "impeding the progress of Soviet science." But in a happy turn of events, he was released "for lack of evidence" – strangely enough, such things were also known to happen! True, he had help from Landau and his highly placed Moscow patrons. Back then, with the first arrest, they had succeeded in saving him.

Figure 2.   Moisei Koretz with two granddaughters, Anya and Masha Golfand, early 1980s. Courtesy of Michael Koretz.

Moisei Abramovich Koretz was born in Sebastopol in 1908. His family had a house there on the shore of the North Bay. He spent his childhood in Simferopol.   At age 16 Koretz went to Moscow, where he worked as a bookbinder, a pastry chef, and a loader to support himself.   In 1927, he became a student of the Karl Liebknecht

Industrial and Pedagogical Institute. There, he met his first wife, Alexandra Simonova. After two years of studies, the family – Moisei, Alexandra, and their baby daughter Esther – moved to Leningrad. In 1929, Koretz entered the Leningrad Polytechnic University, then after graduation worked for some time at the Sverdlovsk Institute for Physics and Technology. Later, at Landau's invitation he transferred to the UPTI theoretical division, concurrently serving as Lev Davidovich's assistant at the university. In 1937, he followed Landau in moving to Moscow, where he worked at the Moscow Pedagogical Institute until his next arrest.

He stayed in the Pechora-Vorkuta camps and in exile for 18 years, returning to Moscow only in 1958.

Facing cold, hunger and abuse by guards and criminals, Moisei Koretz was on the verge of death several times. Once, bandits stabbed him in the neck, miraculously missing an artery. He wound up in the infirmary, where fellow prisoner Serafima Rudova was working. A high-caliber economist, in the camp she had become a nurse. It was Serafima who saved Koretz. Moisei fell head over heels in love with his guardian angel, and the imprisoned Ru dova later became his wife.

Serafima was born in Vitebsk. Her family later moved to Latvia. Her father, highly educated, became the director of the Jewish gymnasium in Riga. His daughter, though, had revolutionary leanings. The convinced Bolshevik engaged in underground activities, then took part in the Communist International. Serafima received a death sentence while the tsar was still in power. Her Party comrades illegally smuggled her across the border. That was how she came to the USSR. She started working at the Institute of Red Professors.[22] Then in 1938, Serafima Iosifovna Rudova, like many other Communist International activists and employees, was arrested, tried under the notorious Article 58/8 – suspicion of espionage – and sent to a camp in the Gulag.

---

[22]The Institute of Red Professors was organized in 1921 as a special higher educational center of the Central Committee of the Communist Party for fostering high-level ideological leaders and professors of the social sciences. Later it became The Marxism-Leninism University, which existed until the demise of the Soviet Union in 1991.

The future wife of Yuri Abramovich Golfand, Natasha Koretz, was born in January 1946 in the godforsaken northern wilderness, in the obscurity of the forests and swamps. Understandably, the camp had no maternity hospital. Natasha's birth certificate listed her birthplace as "Village of Mezhog, Ust-Vymsky district, Komi Autonomous Republic of the Soviet Union."

Love

"Here's the story," Natasha Koretz continues. "I wasn't supposed to have been born there at the labor camp. According to my parents' calculations, my mother ought to have been released before she gave birth. My father's sentence was, so to speak, 'measureless.' You know, prisoners have a grim joke: 'They gave him a year, and year and a half later he got out early.' And what's interesting: if the release order had come when I was even 10 months and one day old, I would have just been taken to a children's orphanage. And the children there died like flies... As it turned out, my mother was able to keep me and raise me... She and I later lived together next to the zone... Of course, it was a terrible environment..."

By the time they returned to Moscow, Natasha had turned twelve.

Moisei Abramovich was released under amnesty. He was soon cleared of one set of charges, but full rehabilitation unfortunately came only posthumously, in 1990. Freed from the labor camp, the family received a separate room in a three-room apartment – an unheard-of luxury!

Natasha's parents were an amazing two-pronged magnet with two poles of attraction: her mother was a Communist to the bone, while her father was an opponent of the Stalinist regime. Serafima Iosifovna was strong, purposeful, "correct," while Moisei Abramovich was a restless intellectual. She was the embodiment of wisdom and prudence, while he had a fine poetic soul, writing poetry even in the camp barracks. Theirs was a magical fusion, and one reflective of the era. "My father was naturally gifted, no less so than Yura," Natalia Koretz-Golfand believes.

Moisei Abramovich was hired by the magazine *Nature* (*Priroda*), very popular in those years. To become an employee and then one of the editors of this natural science illustrated monthly, published by the Academy of Sciences of the USSR, was very prestigious for a physicist who for almost twenty years had been barred from his profession.

This wonderful magazine (I remember how we hunted for a subscription to it!) first appeared in 1912. It was conceived as a guide for self-education in all branches of the natural sciences and the history of science. The publication's motto was "Science first-hand." Indeed, it was a chance to read in-depth surveys and articles by eminent scientists, written so anyone could understand.

The editors of *Nature* in various years included such luminaries as zoologist Vladimir Wagner; Academician Lev Pisarzhevsky, author of the esteemed textbook *Inorganic Chemistry*; geneticist Nikolai Koltsov; geochemist and mineralogist Alexander Fersman; and microbiologist Lev Tarasevich.

The magazine stopped publishing for a while, but relaunched in 1952.

Natasha started sixth grade at an "English school." Really, Koretz grins, in their neighborhood on Leninsky Prospekt, around FIAN, there were several elite schools, mainly attended by the children of scientists and diplomats. The school's students were divided into different focus groups: nine concentrated on mathematics, six on physics and a couple on chemistry. It was Natasha's lot to pursue intensive studies of radio technology, although her soul soared in a quite different empyrean: literature, art, theater...

Understandably, at such schools, which were unusual for Soviet education, the teachers were also unusual. At the school, Natasha met a boy a class below her – Yasha Golfand. He told her he was the son of a theoretical physicist and that his father was a intrepid traveler and kayaker, that he loved downhill skiing and yoga, and that although an "old fogey" (far past thirty!) he was an all-around ultra-modern man, whom his son's friends couldn't get enough of.

All sorts of outings were very popular at the school – winter skiing, summer paddling and mountain expeditions. At one time all this was handled by class supervisors and teachers. Then they wearied of the extra trouble and there was a decision to shift tourism duties onto the parents' shoulders. The school made inquiries about which parents were interested in hiking and found a few enthusiasts, among whom was Yuri Abramovich.

"Then all of us inveterate tourists had a meeting with our supervisors. And then I finally saw him... You know, it's amazing, but he turned out to be exactly like I imagined... Then there was the first hike with him..."

The way she watched her idol, her enraptured gazes were impossible not to notice.

"At first I called him 'Uncle Yura,' but he pretended to get angry: 'I'm not much older than you!' (By a mere 25 years! -B.E.) I started calling him 'Yuri Abramovich.' This enraged him even more. 'Call me what everyone does – Yura.' But I, I couldn't... Then he said, 'If you keep calling me 'Uncle Yura,' I'll call you 'Grandma Natasha.'

We laughed a lot, it was even original: a fifteen-year-old 'Grandma Natasha'!..."

Basically, the girl fell head over heels in love with this handsome, petite, well-groomed man who could have been her father – married, with two children – and it was love at first sight and, as Natasha says today, "for the rest of my life"!

After finishing school, Natalia was admitted to the Moscow Institute of Steel and Alloys (MISA) in the department of the physics of metals. This was clearly chosen by her father, an engineer and physicist. Many dreamed of studying at this prestigious institute. But the prospect of becoming a great metallurgist held little appeal for college-age Koretz. She would gladly have exchanged all the crystal lattices of steel, hardening into martensites, austenites, troostites, perlites, ledeburites and other metallurgical wisdom for a rustling theater curtain or a movie camera. She was constantly dashing from lectures to movies or the theater. After the third year she broke down and left the institute.

She was in love with Efros's productions[23] at the theater on

---

[23] Anatoly Vasilievich Efros (1925 -1987; his real name was Nathan Isayevich Efros) was a famous Soviet theater director.

Malaya Bronnaya, she attended the rehearsals of Anatoly Vasilyevich. She assisted as a volunteer in the literary division at Pluchek's
Theater of Satire. She set her sights on becoming a specialist in
drama. But, alas, her attempts to enter the State Institute of Theater Arts were not crowned with success. She went to Leningrad
and in 1970 passed the entrance exams at the Leningrad Institute of
Theater, Music and Cinema. At last, she found herself in the world
that had called to her heart for so long. She graduated from the
faculty of drama studies with honors in 1975, when she and Yura
were already together.

"Yura was incredibly interested," says Natasha, "in all my theater
business. He read a lot, and more broadly than most of his colleagues.
By the way, if it hadn't been for me, he would have gotten to know
the poems of Brodsky much later than he did. Really, I introduced
him to a lot of people as 'gifts'..."

To his delighted surprise, Golfand saw before him no longer an enraptured girl but an amazingly interesting, bright, vivacious woman,
and not to fall in love with her, well, was just impossible.

"Yes, it was a real love saga that unfolded over a lifetime... And
it all happened like I'd dreamed as a fifteen-year-old – incredible!"

"You won't believe me, but I really did say to myself back in the
ninth grade, 'He'll be mine, for my whole life!' "

"Basically, you stole him!" I tease.

She laughs:

"I wasn't stealing! I worked hard to draw attention to myself and
explain that I was the only one in the world who belonged in the
picture!"

"It was stealing, stealing!" Kira enters our cheerful squabble.
"And it's lucky she stole him. Because Yurochka had a chance to
spend a wonderful part of his life with Natasha..."

Kira once came to visit me in Nazareth Illit and we unhurriedly
continued our conversations about her unforgettable older brother
Yuri Golfand.

"Of course, he had an early marriage, somehow rushed. They
lived in the dorm at the institute where Sara taught. There was a
huge room split into cubicles by plywood partitions. Then there was

FIAN, the queue for an apartment. Yura was always at the top of the list and was always left for the next time...

They finally got an apartment in Cheryomushki. And he and Sara lived there with their two children – their son Yasha, the eldest, and their daughter Natasha.

When Natasha Koretz came into his life... You know, he was absolutely honest, terribly honest. Some men are honest, but when it comes to secrets of the heart... And he didn't hide anything...

Sara suffered greatly. She visited me in Sevastopol (I worked there for a long time at a local biological station – the city feels like home to me!). She was bitter, she needed to have a cry. I understood everything: they had no love left, it had all burned out and there was no fixing it...

Our mother was a resolute person. She was genuine, she couldn't stand falseness. There was a time when Yura broke out in a nervous rash all over his face and body because of all these mental disturbances. Our mother came to Moscow and said firmly, 'That's it, you have to decide!' And she took all the heat herself..."

Namely Nina Grigoryevna insisted on divorce. Naturally, in Sara's family she was subjected to anathema.

Yura left his family. Moisei Koretz, Natasha's father, took him in. Then there was a divorce. Yuri and Natasha rented an apartment. Later they lived in a small room at Natasha's parent's place. Both their daughters were born there. The girls were four and two-and-a-half years old by the time the Golfands, through complex apartment exchanges, finally obtained decent housing on Leninsky Prospekt.

"And from Yura's first family," Kira sighs, "there's no one left. Natashenka died first, at age 27; she'd been sick since childhood, with a congenital heart defect. If it hadn't been for Yura, she'd have died as a child – he did everything he could so Natashenka would recover. She even married, but unfortunately... Then Sara herself died. And a couple of years ago Yasha was killed...

With Yasha's death I rather lost touch with the past. He was murdered by bandits... I was his favorite aunt. He asked me to write something about our family's roots, because nothing would be left. That's when I got a computer and start pecking away at something...

Yasha left behind two daughters in Moscow. I try to do the best for them that I can... Yelena, Yasha's wife, is also there in Moscow. Our children, who are now in Israel, are in touch with them..."

Life is a hard thing, and happiness exists alongside tragedy. Kira and I talked a lot about her brother's love for Natasha...an exalted, mysterious, windswept love, refined by suffering... How it all happened.

"I think he was just tired. Sarah was a good person... But I think in their last years together they lived without understanding each other..."

Natasha Koretz was charmingly sincere and direct, buoyant, tender, ethereal, and devilishly clever, erudite. And the fact that she embodied a different world, the enchanted world of art, was even more attractive. You could talk with her for hours, sometimes with all-out arguments on various topics...

When they married, he was fifty and she was twenty-six.

They had a wonderful, joyous wedding. Kira and their mother came from Leningrad, and Yura's childhood friends were there. An acquaintance of the newlyweds, the prominent critic and theater historian Yuri Rybakov, said at the time that never had he seen a happier, more compatible couple.

Many years later, Tel Aviv biologist Leonid Mittelman wrote of this as well:

"I remember I brought him something from Leningrad, from his sister, and he and Natasha met me at the station. I handed over the package, they said goodbye and left, hand in hand. I watched them from behind as they moved away: what a song that was! Such a big age difference, but they seemed like a single person walking, they were so close and dear to each other..."

Figure 3.   Natasha Koretz and Yuri Golfand, Moscow, circa 1970.

Unemployment

Their wedding took place in December 1972, when Yuri Abramovich unexpectedly found himself out of work. Some time before, Doctor of Physical and Mathematical Sciences Yuri Golfand had lost his job at FIAN.

Andrei Dmitriyevich Sakharov tells this unpleasant story in his *Memoirs*. He begins with a preamble, which one doesn't want to omit.

> In December, Lusia and I were both hospitalized... Thanks to my academic privileges we were placed together in a separate room... I worked, while Lusia corrected my text, giving valuable advice... We sometimes also had guests. Lusia's old friend, the poet and translator Konstantin Bogatyrev, came by together with another very prominent poet, Alexander Mezhirov – also a longtime acquaintance of Lusia's... I don't remember why, but I gave them something like a lecture on basic quantum mechanics. This lecture seemed to impress Mezhirov, with his penchant for clever mental constructions... Maximov dropped by several times, dressed in a brand-new checked suit, his grin warm and his blue eyes sparkling... We were delighted when Alexander Galich, Viktor Nekrasov and Lev Kopelev [24] came together to see us – a group photograph showing all of us gathered in the hospital lobby...
>
> We also had a visit from FIAN's E. L. Feinberg and V. L. Ginzburg. The latter headed the theoretical division. Ginzburg said an order had come down for all Academy institutions to cut their staffs.
>
> "The theoretical department has to downsize by one person. It's a painful but unavoidable operation. We conferred among ourselves and decided it'll have to be Yuri

---

[24]Lusia, Yelena Bonner, A. Sakharov's wife. Other individuals mentioned in this paragraph were prominent human rights activists and cultural figures in the 1970s Soviet Union.

Abramovich. He hasn't produced any scientific work at all for the last few years – he's basically just been goofing off. Besides, he has a doctorate; it'll be easier for him to get a new job than for someone without a doctoral degree."

I asked if we could somehow "fudge it" and got a dryly negative response. Unfortunately, I didn't succeed in saying anything personally in Golfand's defense. I didn't know that a few months before, at a FIAN seminar, Golfand and Likhtman had reported on a paper they had just produced, and which would become a classic – it was the first to introduce supersymmetry. (That is, in saying that Golfand "hadn't produced any scientific work at all for the last few years – he's basically just been goofing off," Ginzburg was obviously misleading Sakharov. -B.E.)

The paper hadn't come out of nowhere – the Moscow mathematician Felix Alexandrovich Berezin [25] (who met an untimely death in 1980) had already written about supersymmetry transformations. But Golfand and Likhtman were the first to examine supersymmetry as a principle in constructing a field theory. It was a momentous idea. In subsequent years, the ideas of supersymmetry would be developed in hundreds of scientific studies...

Some time later, it became clear that all the other departments at FIAN had managed to avoid layoffs, had 'fudged it' (as I'd put it in speaking with Ginzburg). As for Golfand, he failed to find work anywhere else – although he had doctorate, he was a Jew.

During his (Yu. Golfand's. -B.E.) visit to the hospital, Lusia told him, "You're being fired – you should just leave!"

A few months later, Golfand applied for emigration from the USSR to Israel, but this was denied on the unfounded pretext of his having taken part in the Tamm group's secret activities 20 years before, when in fact Golfand had done very

---

[25] A prominent Soviet mathematician (1931–1980), one of the creators of supermathematics, see M. Shifman, Ed., *Felix Berezin, The Life and Death of the Mastermind of Supermathematics*, (World Scientific, Singapore, 2007).

"abstract" work, with no knowledge of the actual devices being built; he'd never been at the Object. This issue has so far proved unresolvable.

And so, Ginzburg, the head of the Theory Department, proceeded to fire the "slacker" ... The outstanding scholar, his name forever inscribed in the history of physics (the Ginzburg-Frank theory of transition radiation, the Ginzburg-Landau theory of superconductivity, the Ginzburg-Pitaevsky theory of superfluidity, etc.), a dweller on the celestial Olympus of science, became the de facto cause of his colleague's personal crisis and bitter suffering...

FIAN had always declared itself to represent a community not only of high-level scientists but also of high morality. Ginzburg's phrase, "he has a doctorate; it'll be easier for him to get a new job than for someone without a doctoral degree," hardly seems sincere. Vitaly Lazarevich knew better than anyone that this wasn't at all the case with Golfand. Firing a Jew from any post was easy, but hiring a Jew was difficult.

Of course, there was no command to fire namely a Jew. Moreover, the recommendation had been to lay off either retirement-age employees or recent hires.

Natasha Koretz recalls:

"When we first came to Moscow, I had a chance conversation with my father while he walked with me after a parent-teacher meeting at school, where I was being scolded for skipping classes. Ginzburg, walking with us, suddenly opened up, talking about how terrible he felt winding up as a 'second class' person all the time because of being a Jew. He wasn't admitted and wasn't hired for this and that, and had gone years without being allowed to travel abroad. This 'second class' and the pitiful tone of his voice made a lasting impression on me... I didn't even know then that the person speaking was all but five minutes away from becoming an Academician. For a long time afterward, I repeated the phrase 'second class,' which amused me for some reason..."

After all these events, for the rest of his life, Yuri Abramovich demonstratively refused to shake Ginzburg's hand... In 1989, they met at Andrei Dmitriyevich Sakharov's funeral. There were many people around. Ginzburg, as if nothing had happened, extended his hand: "Hello, Yuri Abramovich!" The response he heard was unusually sharp for the intellectual, reserved Golfand: "I don't shake scoundrels' hands."

And no one of prominence stood up for the fired employee: the rumors that Golfand was aiming to make tracks for Israel spread instantaneously. Sakharov had been disgraced, and his intervention could only have had the opposite effect, causing harm. According to Natasha, "Lusia (Yelena Bonner) said that if they were to take a stand for Yura, he was certain to be put in jail."

At the Theory Department, no one dared to oppose the pressure from Ginzburg, with the exception of Efim Fradkin.

Efim Samoilovich, a future academician, was then, in 1972, the head of the sector to which Yuri Golfand formally belonged. Without the sector head's approval, the decision about the layoff was considered unofficial. Efim Samoilovich refused to sign. That didn't stop Ginzburg.

According to Boris Bolotovsky, "News of Golfand's layoff spread quickly in physics circles, first in Moscow and then beyond Moscow. The scientists had similar reactions: they sympathized with Yu. A. Golfand and disapproved of his dismissal."

Renowned physicist and department head at the Institute of Theoretical and Experimental Physics (ITEP) Professor Vladimir Borisovich Berestetsky said, "I won't shake hands with Ginzburg after this." Leading Landau school theorist Lev Pitaevsky also expressed his indignation at the measure.

For six long years, until 1980, the familiar doors of the institute would be closed to Yuri Abramovich.

In "Refusal"

As might have been expected, Golfand found no employment. "Although he had a doctorate," as Sakharov wrote, "he was a Jew." Wherever he turned, the management lowered their eyes in embarrassment. No one had the courage to offer a decent position to the disgraced doctor of sciences and major theoretician.

But even if some department head had brought himself to hire Golfand, the personnel department would have presented an insurmountable barrier. The staffing officer would have opened Golfand's work book and seen the record from his last place of employment, "laid off in downsizing." Such a record carried the stigma of leprosy. If a doctor of sciences had been fired, what a lazybones he must be! A personnel officer would only hire a "layoff" over his dead body.

True, there was one offer, but one so humiliating, so unfit for Golfand's level that he refused to accept it. He preferred ... hanging posters. Especially since most of the posters were theatrical, so now he and Natasha were in the same business!

There was no work, no money, and his "friends" rapidly vanished.

That was when they felt most acutely that they had leave. And namely to Israel. Although neither Yura nor Natalia had ever been devout Zionists, they were still Jews, and, unlike many others, weren't ashamed of this. After all, Yuri could have changed his surname and nationality in his passport long before, based on his Russian mother, Nina Grigoryevna.

He didn't snivel, didn't whine, remained outwardly calm and composed. Outwardly, that is. Yura had an extremely sensitive and, of course, vulnerable nature, so he certainly suffered – deeply, it seems – and felt seriously derailed, for several months completely unable to work, sit down at a desk and surrender himself to his calculations. Although he continued hiking, he did so more rarely, and only near Moscow – he had no money for traveling around...

Natasha, struggling, goaded all the authorities, seeking cracks in the facade, getting acquainted with the "right people." On the one hand this related to work, while on the other, she sought those who might influence the impenetrable OVIR (the Office of Visas and Registration). This infuriated Yura. If only he could avoid humiliation, humiliation before the Dragon...

The Golfands filed their first application to emigrate to Israel in December 1973, just after the conversation with Sakharov and Yelena Bonner in the hospital ward. They received their first official refusal a year later, in October 1974. A whole year in limbo, a year of uncertainty, with many friends and even professional colleagues no longer "recognizing" him on the street and no longer phoning him, for fear of implication in contact with a freshly uncovered "traitor to his country."

"Refusenik life" strengthened the Golfands as a couple and rid them of nostalgia for "mother Russia" that many "Russian" immigrants brought with them to Israel. The tyranny of the OVIR, as Natalia Moiseievna Koretz-Golfand wrote in her memoirs, was "absolutely Orwellian." She took on the humiliating, soul-destroying work of "walking on broken glass," shielding her husband from every kind of threat – including the police. Yuri Abramovich, simply physically unable to endure the OVIR officials' rudeness, would lose his temper, and that could trigger the issue of a "detention order." In their position, there was no point in providing another occasion to detain a "refusenik" for "disturbing the peace."

"In the course of my many demands to be told the reason we had received a refusal, I heard many answers, without any exceptional variety.

'It's not in the interests of the Soviet Union' was the most frequent answer.

'Divorce your husband and go wherever you please. As long as your husband's alive, there's not a chance of him being let out of here' – that was most forthright and rude one."

Of course, the most difficult test was the isolation from FIAN. People he'd worked with for twenty years now avoided his company, afraid to approach the disgraced exile...

"His former colleagues' indifference and cowardice," his sister Kira says, "painfully wounded Yura. On top of that, this came at the same time when his children from his first marriage totally severed their relationship with him (thank God, temporarily!), unable to forgive him for leaving the family."

After some time, Yura became acquainted by colleagues in misfortune, who joined together to hold informal seminars of refusenik scientists. This radically changed his entire life.

Dissent is the enemy of any dictatorial regime. In the USSR, dissent was subject to prosecution by law. After the short period of the "Khrushchev thaw," the crackdown began anew.

On August 25, 1968, seven Soviet dissidents gathered at the historical Execution Ground in Red Square to hold the USSR's first-ever sit-in demonstration, protesting the Warsaw Pact countries' invasion of Czechoslovakia.

Chronicle of Current Events, a handwritten bulletin of defenders of human rights, began to circulate. Andrei Sakharov's programmatic work "Reflections on Progress, Peaceful Coexistence and Intellectual Freedom" (discussed above) was published, and Alexander Solzhenitsyn's famous "Letter to the Leaders of the Soviet Union" appeared.

In 1970, the Committee on Human Rights in the USSR came into being.

In 1975, the USSR signed the Final Act of the Helsinki Conference on Security and Cooperation in Europe, thereby committing to respect human rights – a commitment none of the Soviet leaders intended to fulfill. A year later in Moscow, human rights activists led by Yuri Orlov [26] created the public organization "Helsinki Group," which monitored the implementation of the international human rights treaties signed in Finland's capital. The group's members faced constant harassment by the Soviet secret police. But the harsher the repression became, the movement of dissidents calling for rights and freedoms in the USSR only broadened all the more.

This was no sullen, severe gathering of people flinging themselves at bayonets. They were fighting not death but life – a life they saw as abnormal, deformed, undemocratic. They were optimistic, and responded to persecution calmly, without hysteria, even with humor.

In those years, a booklet by Vladimir Albrecht on how to behave during a KGB interrogation became very popular among the dissi-

---

[26] A prominent figure in the Soviet human rights movement. Yuri Orlov was arrested by the KGB in 1977 and sentenced to seven years in labor camp, with subsequent exile to Siberia, for the establishment of the Moscow Helsinki Watch Group. In 1986 he was stripped of his citizenship and deported to the USA in exchange for a Soviet spy arrested in America; see his autobiography: Yuri Orlov, *Dangerous Thoughts*, (William Morrow, New York, 1991).

dents. Mathematician and writer Vladimir Albrecht was secretary of the Moscow branch of Amnesty International. His "handbook" was for those whom the authorities tried to frighten and turn into informers simply by the fact of being summoned for questioning, even as witnesses, to induce them to start spreading false testimony against their friends and colleagues. The booklet's author had gone through more than one such "interview" – as both witness and accused – and was passing on his own and his acquaintances' experience of confronting the KGB machine. Written with biting irony and pride, the brochure lent strength and courage to dissidents.

Here are some quotes from the "handbook" by Vladimir Albrecht.

INVESTIGATOR. Where did you get the Gospel?
WITNESS. From Matthew.
INVESTIGATOR. Can you guess why you were summoned?
WITNESS. Yes. But that'd be better for you to say.
INVESTIGATOR. Why would it be better?
WITNESS. Otherwise, it looks like you're ashamed to say why.
WITNESS. Your intimidation forces me to confess. Which crime do you consider more serious – the one you think I committed, or the one you're committing now?
WITNESS. It's hard for me to answer your questions, since I bear no responsibility for my words.
INVESTIGATOR. No, you bear responsibility for your words.
WITNESS. Then permit me to give an affidavit of responsibility for false testimony.

Yuri Abramovich, of course, read and laughed over these witty instructions, but never used them. He also received several summons from the KGB, "invitations" to interviews. Without a moment's hesitation or fear of possible consequences, he refused to appear at such meetings and immediately hung up.

However, this didn't save him from repression, even if the measures were less brutal than applied to other dissidents. Thus, during the Moscow International Scientific Conference Yuri Abramovich spent a week under house arrest. The Golfands' home was searched, their phone tapped. The authorities tried to intimidate the scientist, threatening him with expulsion from Moscow, bringing a criminal case against him on charges of "parasitism" – much as in the case of his beloved Joseph Brodsky, who was accused of "parasitism" and exiled to the White Sea!

From the Electronic Jewish Encyclopedia:

"Golfand...was a regular and active participant in a scientific seminar that brought together Moscow refusenik scientists. The seminar was led by the physicists Alexander Voronel, Mark Azbel and Victor Brailovsky."

Yuri's appearance at the seminar wasn't accidental – in a telephone conversation, Sergei Kovalev gave him the address of an apartment where interesting people gathered. Golfand came, quietly said hello, and saw Andrei Sakharov sitting modestly in the corner. He sat down beside Sakharov, and they exchanged brief phrases.

"I'm glad to see you, Yuri Abramovich."

"Me too..." From then on, the seminars gave Yuri, as well as many others, a source of fresh air, a window on the world abroad. And most importantly: these "gatherings" of the elite of Soviet science, who'd been forcibly removed from it, gave them a sense of still being in the thick of intellectual life as before. The seminar included reports on the latest developments in various fields, along with discussions of social problems.

This was no "sedition" – everything took place in the framework of existing legislation. Such activity was not prohibited in the Soviet Union; however, without special permission from the authorities it was perceived as a challenge to the Soviet party and the government establishment. The authorities used any pretext to impede the public organization's work. The seminar participants were repeatedly arrested with no due legal process whatsoever.

Six foreign Nobel laureates expressed their support for the seminar. Its first international meeting was planned for the summer of 1974. Then the authorities decided to show "who was the boss," demanding the scheduled event's cancellation. But the KGB "comrades" suffered an unexpected fiasco. Only later did it emerge what had happened. It happened that the seminar coincided with a planned visit to the Soviet Union from U.S. President Nixon. The ban of a forum that included foreign Nobel laureates would have demonstrated the Soviet Union's complete lack of democracy.

In all the time since his dismissal from FIAN, Yuri Abramovich had almost never set foot in his own institute. The guards wouldn't admit him. He visited friends at other institutions, such as ITEP, the brainchild of Academician Abram Isaakovich Alikhanov. Incidentally, Misha Marinov, whom Golfand later met in Haifa, worked at ITEP back then.

Yuri kept working on his science. Thankfully, a mind, a table and paper suffice for a theoretician. His articles on physics' most burning problems found publication in foreign journals.

In 1976, the "refusenik" FIAN exile was elected a member of the European, and a year later, of the American Physical Society. In 1979, Yuri Abramovich Golfand became a full member of the New York Academy of Sciences.

Perhaps Golfand's significance as a scientist was finally understood in the Soviet Union only after the recognition of the theory of supersymmetry in Europe and America.

Still, though, the "American Academician" was not allowed out of the Soviet Union, whether to America or, moreover, to Israel. In 1979, a group of foreign scientists, including several Nobel laureates, appealed to the president of the USSR Academy of Sciences, A. P. Alexandrov. The letter stated:

"Golfand is an outstanding physicist. However, for many years he has been unable to find work in the Soviet Union. At the same time, he is prohibited from going abroad. Make up your minds as to whether you need Dr. Golfand or not. If he's needed, give him work. If he isn't needed, give him permission to leave."

After this letter, the heads the Academy had a talk with Zimyanin, the secretary who supervised science for the Central Committee of the Communist Party of the Soviet Union. Apparently he gave the go-ahead: so be it, let the stubborn scientist return to FIAN.

Something was changing in the air – the country stood on the brink of the perestroika boom, Communist despotism was plainly losing its power, the great Party nincompoops were moving one after the other to eternal addresses in the Kremlin wall [next to the Lenin tomb].

The year 1980 had arrived. Yura was visiting his sister in Leningrad. Suddenly the phone rang.

"Yes, he's here with us. I'll pass the phone to him."

He picks up the receiver. Listens attentively. Smiles. Then he calmly says, "No, it's I who congratulate you."

"Who was that?" Kira asks.

"Markov."

"Academician Markov?"

"Yes. Moisei Alexandrovich. From FIAN."

"And...?"

"He's inviting me to work for his department. For the same position at the same salary."

Kira was left speechless.

Markov held a place of reverence in the country. Academician-secretary of the USSR Academy of Sciences' Division of Nuclear Physics, as well as chairman of the Soviet branch of the international Pugwash movement – a confraternity of scientists around the planet who work for peace, disarmament, international security and the prevention of a world thermonuclear war.

"The rehire of a refusenik was a remarkably rare occurrence," Sakharov wrote. He knew what he was talking about. This may have been the only identifiable precedent in the history of Soviet Union, moreover in academic circles.

The scientist who returned to the institute had the same great scientific potential as before, but was now a different person – with different views on the regime they all lived under, with a new circle of friends where his FIAN colleagues no longer played a primary role. His true, abiding friendships now extended to human rights activists of lasting worldwide renown, with Yuri Orlov and Sergei Kovalev foremost among them.

In the USSR and internationally, the name of Yuri Fyodorovich Orlov – World War II veteran, doctor of physical and mathematical

Figure 4. A conference in Kharkov in 1985. Yuri Golfand is in the center of the front row. To the left of him is Dmitri Volkov, also a founding father of supersymmetry. Behind Golfand is Victor Ogievetsky, one of the pioneers.

sciences, professor, corresponding member of the Academy of Sciences of the Armenian Soviet Socialist Republic – came to symbolize the struggle for human rights in the Soviet Union. A member of the Soviet chapter of Amnesty International, the founder and first leader of the Moscow Helsinki Group, in 1953 he began working for the Academy of Sciences' Heat Technology (Teplo-Tekhnicheskaya, TTL) Laboratory, one of the top-secret laboratories of the Soviet Atomic Project. During discussion of Khrushchev's speech at the XX Congress, Orlov called Stalin and Beria "murderers in power" and advanced then-daring demands for democratic reforms in the country. For this, he was immediately expelled from the Party and ousted from his work.

Armenian Institute of Physics director Artyom Isaakovich Alikhanian (brother of Academician Abram Alikhanov, TTL's Director) gave him employment. Orlov worked in Yerevan for 16 years.

In the early seventies, two articles by Yuri Orlov appeared in underground samizdat circulation – "About the Reasons for the Intellectual Backwardness in the USSR" and "Is a Non-Totalitarian Type of Socialism Possible?" In 1976, Orlov was among the authors of a letter in defense of the writer Vladimir Bukovsky. The next year, he was stripped of the title of Corresponding Member, convicted and sent to a labor camp.

Orlov was a good friend of Golfand's. When they met, they spoke at length about the amazing idea of "wave logic," which the unbowed rights activist was passionately developing. The idea fascinated Golfand, and Orlov himself had such a magnetic personality that his every appearance at the Golfands' home was an occasion to celebrate.

During the Orlov trial, no one was admitted to the council chamber except some family members, with the remaining space occupied by "plainclothes art historians" – KGB officers in disguise. Orlov was prosecuted for crimes against the state. Yuri Golfand took part in pickets against the trial and wrote an article on Orlov and his scientific ideas, including "wave logic." Without a doubt, these publications, which saw the light abroad, helped draw the world's attention to the lawlessness at work behind the Iron Curtain.

Later, Golfand visited the imprisoned rights activist in Yakutia. He accompanied Orlov's wife Irina from Moscow to the camp and back.

Orlov was twice thrown behind bars. The first time he served seven years – from 1977 to 1984 – the second time, two years, starting in 1984, after no more than a few months at liberty. Under pressure from the international community, the Soviet elite were forced to release Orlov. The activist physicist was stripped of his citizenship and expelled from the Soviet Union in exchange for the Soviet spy Zakharov, arrested in the U.S. in the course of his employment by the USSR mission to the United Nations.

Sergei Kovalev was brought to the Golfands' home by Kira. Both biologists, Kovalev and Kira were old aquaintances. Kovalev, a candidate of biological sciences, was among those who had come out openly against the "teachings" of Lysenko as early as the 1950s.

In May 1969, Kovalev became a member of the Initiative Group for the Defense of Human Rights in the USSR – essentially the country's first independent public interest association for human rights.

In his *Memoirs*, Sakharov writes:

"I met Kovalev in 1970...he'd come to sign an appeal in defense of Zhores Medvedev. Lusia had known him somewhat earlier. At that time he was already an established biologist, who'd produced many interesting papers on neural networks and interrelated biological topics at the juncture of biology and cybernetics. He had more scientific plans as well. His published works totaled more than 60. But a blow had already been dealt to his scientific career. He was forced out of his university and bio-mathematical group because he had signed a letter in defense of Yesenin-Volpin." (Mathematician, philosopher and poet Alexander Sergeyevich Yesenin-Volpin, son of the poet Sergei Yesenin, was one of the pioneers of the dissident movement in the USSR. All told, he spent about 14 years in prisons and psychiatric hospitals. -B.E.)

"After his dismissal from the university," continues Andrei Dmitriyevich, "Kovalev found work at the Experimental Fish Hatchery, where one of the groups was headed by my cousin's husband, Vitaly Rekubratsky. They had been friends at university. At the hatchery, Kovalev studied the genetics of fish, trying to maintain some continuity with his previous work. He developed scientific ideas in some other areas too.

In recent years, my son-in-law Efrem Yankelevich worked at the same hatchery. Kovalev had a strong influence on him, and became his role model (and rightfully so)..."

In December 1974, Sergei Kovalev was arrested on charges of "anti-Soviet agitation and propaganda." The rights activist's trial was held in Vilnius. Sakharov's book includes a photo of a small group of people standing outside the courthouse – they weren't allowed in the courtroom: Andrei Dmitriyevich Sakharov, Yuri Fyodorovich Orlov, Yuri Abramovich Golfand. Interestingly, namely in the days of the Kovalev trial, the Nobel Peace Prize was awarded to Sakharov, who was not allowed to attend the Stockholm ceremony. Yelena Georgievna Bonner received the medal and read the Nobel speech on her husband's behalf.

Sergei Kovalev was sentenced to seven years in strict-regime camps and three years in exile.

He served time in Chistopol prison, then in the Perm camps, and was exiled to Kolyma.

The first correspondence that Sergei Adamovich Kovalev received from the outside world may have come from Yuri Golfand. And Kira visited Kovalev, first at the Perm camp and then at the Magadan mines.

In this biography of Yuri Golfand, I can't help but tell a bit more about his sister Kira.

When she said that she considered Sevastopol her hometown, my heart uttered a soft sigh. My life and my wife's were intertwined with this magical city for 24 years; it means more for me than a hometown, although I was born in Dnepropetrovsk.

My incurable disease.
My white city.
Morning song.
You stand guard over my memory,
To keep the pain from obscurity...
In this city, I loved.
And was loved.
And here my heart lies buried.

A large part of Kira's life is connected with Georgia. She married a Russian from Tbilisi whom she had met before the war. They soon separated. But Kira retained a lifelong love of Georgia.

Then came the Leningrad, university, and then work at the Academy of Sciences' Institute of Cytology. At the institute, a strong research team assembled – and one also marked by deeply held ideas of human rights.

Kira often met Kovalev at conferences, and they frequently turned out to be studying almost the same topics. They traveled together on biology expeditions, including in Sevastopol with Vitaly Rekubratsky, who had long worked in the Crimea.

It's a small world! I knew Vitaly and once interviewed him as he sat beside his wife, who was constantly giving her husband cues – but I had no clue that she was Sakharov's cousin!

During her trips to Sevastopol to see colleagues at IBSS (the Institute of Biology of the Southern Seas) Kira always stayed with the Korotkov family, on the Naval Side (Korabelnaya Storona). She recalls:

"Evdokia Khristoforovna's house stood on the shore of a cove where many private boats were moored. Her husband was in charge of these boats, and then when he died, 'Baba Doka' took over the boat business. She was a Greek who lived through the eviction of the Crimean Greeks to Kazakhstan. Part of the family stayed there and never returned to Sevastopol. What an amazing woman she was! Everyone loved her. And Evdokia Khristoforovna seemed to treat me like a daughter, with touching tenderness. Our mother also liked to come to vacation at this glorious home, full of the smell of seaweed... When Evdokia died, I flew to Sevastopol. Half the city was at the funeral..."

Good Lord, I remember this legendary 'Baba Doka,' a large woman with an unfading tan on her face and mighty hands! And I remember her funeral. And really, it's incredible that Kira Abramovna and I never met in Sevastopol at the time. Especially because I had a huge number of marine biologists among my friends and acquaintances; even our neighbor across the stairwell was a biological sciences candidate who worked at IBSS. And the building where we lived on Repin Street belonged to the Institute of Biology. It was actually designed by my wife Olga on an IBSS commission!

In 1989, an event occurred that was unusual for a "refusenik" : Dr. Golfand and his assistant Evgeny Likhtman were awarded the USSR Academy of Sciences' Tamm Prize for their work on supersymmetry. They were nominated for the award by the Academic Council of the theoretical physics department, going against the opinion of its head, Vitaly Lazarevich Ginzburg. This act was initiated by the prominent nuclear physicist professor Vladimir Ivanovich Ritus, a recipient of the V. I. Vavilov Gold Medal.

Ritus recalls how a few days after the assembly of the Academic Council, Ginzburg approached him and said:

"Keep this in mind, Volodya – I hold grudges."

Based on the procedure for vetting Tamm Prize candidates, the proposal was approved by FIAN's Academic Council and then conveyed to a review commission chaired by Ginzburg. Realizing that in the voting he would find himself in a position of ignominious isolation, Vitaly Lazarevich left Moscow that day...

In 1990, the Golfand family finally received permission to emigrate to Israel.

At the direction of the institute's Party committee, the Party branch of the theory department convened to voice its perspective on Golfand's "terrible" act. The Party group handed down a draft resolution that read as follows:

"The Communists of the theory department condemn this act by Yu. A. Golfand (who wasn't even a Communist! -B.E.) as treachery toward our socialist Motherland."

As it happened, though, namely Ginzburg opposed the oppressive resolution. He said, "The attitude toward people emigrating is no longer the same as under Stalin, and I don't think wanting to leave the Soviet Union necessarily equates to betraying socialism." The resolution was rejected.

A group of five left together: Yuri Abramovich and Natalia Moiseievna, their two young daughters and sister Kira. Yura's and Natasha's parents had already passed on to a better world, not living long enough to receive clearance to leave. From a letter from Academician Keldysh:

"...While experiencing...great regret at your departure from our country, I nevertheless hope that your scientific and personal relationship with our institution will not be disrupted in the future. Wherever you are, we will consider you our compatriot and colleague.

As director of the institute and head of the department of theoretical physics, I want to express to you deep and sincere regret for the harm done to you in the past, and at the same time to the institute itself, by your dismissal.

Director of FIAN Academician L. V. Keldysh"

"The Promised Land...
But is it mine?"

Many of us, leaving the Soviet Union, were ready, even in tears from the pain of parting with friends and family, to repeat to ourselves Lermontov's merciless "Farewell unwashed Russia!" Throughout their years in Israel, Natasha and Yura longed to forget the humiliation and despotism of the Soviet authorities, who accompanied them up to the last moment before their departure. To forget standing for hours in lines in the corridors of the visa and registration department. To forget how their employment records and passports were taken away. How they were forced to pay tremendous sums to renounce their citizenship. Only the Soviet government could have thought of this: forcibly stripped of Russian citizenship, you had to pay to suffer the abuse. And the Golfands longed to forget having to go several days without sleep at the airport before their flight, waiting for their luggage to be checked.

Now under the airplane's wing lay the Land of Israel. Ben-Gurion Airport. Daybreak. A car shuttles the new repatriates to Jerusalem.

...Outside the car windows, the Biblical desert.
Where cacti's prickly cascades
Cool at night amid the gloomy boulders,
Where distant hills march strictly
And palm trees melt in rosy fonts...
This is the land God swore to give,
The Promised Land. But is it mine?

"Where are you going?" fellow scientists asked in amazement. "Why Israel? It's a scientific wasteland. If you went, say, to Texas..."

What could he tell them? Of course, Yuri Abramovich knew he was heading into the unknown, and as for how things would go with finding work in Israel, he could hardly imagine. But there was a certain undercurrent, and one he felt disinclined to explain, to avoid sounding shrill or pretentious. The pain of the Holocaust. All of Natasha's relatives on her mother side were burned by the Nazis in Riga. Yura's aunt was shot by the Germans... The Holocaust cries out in the genes of Jews, even if they know little about the Holocaust... Even if Golfand said his sense of being an outcast bore no relation to being a Jew.

They rented an apartment in Jerusalem and blended in with the motley army of new Israeli citizens, the so-called "Olim Hadashim" – new repatriates. Not immigrants like in the rest of the world, but namely repatriates, returning to their homeland, the land of their pre-pre-ancestors. The joys and sorrows of absorption began.

This idiotic word, absorption, applied to people, makes the un-conditioned ear tremble. After all, the term is borrowed from the technical vocabulary for the absorption of gases by liquids. Who are the gases and who are the fluid is clear: native Israelis ("Sabra") must absorb the lightweight "gaseous fraction."

From notes by Natalia Koretz-Golfand, 1999:

> The difficulties of refusenik life gave way to the ups and downs of absorption. Of course, this wasn't at all the same thing, but it wasn't easy, especially for Yura.
>
> He couldn't get used to the hot climate and the Khamsin wind, to the differences in nature, to the small distances be-tween cities (his soul needed broader expanses! -B.E.), to the absence of any rivers like he'd loved in Russia.
>
> He didn't want and didn't try to adapt to the Levant mentality of the Israeli officials and their bureaucracy, or to the palpably provincial quality of Israeli society.
>
> But the religious Jews in their operetta costumes, contrary to all expectations, didn't annoy him. He said that maybe they, rather than the secular population, constitute the true meaning of the existence of a country such as Israel. Natu-rally, orthodox fanaticism was alien to him, as was fanaticism in any form. But he read the Torah and dreamed of reading the teachings of the Kabbalah. He kept hoping to meet some highly intelligent but not fanatical person who'd consent to

speak with him about certain non-trivial issues concerning religious views of the structure of the world. He never found anyone...

Figure 5. The Promised Land.

Any Israeli absorption begins with a unique national invention – with "Ulpan," Hebrew language courses for adults.

Yuri Abramovich had started Hebrew studies while still in Moscow. He once brought home a tutorial with an audio cassette, and started studying an hour each day. His methodical work habits paid off. Besides this, Hebrew, the brilliant offspring of an ancient people, a language devised with mathematical precision, couldn't help but win the scientist's admiration. Quite soon he was reading and writing. He clearly understood the grammatical constructions. He started listening to Israeli radio. Natasha, trying to finish institute at the time, had to bear the burden of other studies, and although she tried not to fall behind Yura, keeping up with him was of course impossible.

Golfand enrolled in the most advanced Ulpan group. Not surprisingly, he studied better than anyone. Creating a special booklet with his own charts for jotting down verbs, he developed his own unusual system of teaching "binyanim" verb groups. His former Ulpan instructor said she had preserved his notebook and continued to make use of Yura's system.

While studying in the Ulpan group, Golfand began to look for work. He sent out a list of his scientific publications and gave presentations at Tel Aviv University, the University of Jerusalem, the Weizmann Institute and the Technion. Among those who had arrived in the country before him, he had help from the Brailovskys and from Alexander Voronel. But Yuri Abramovich was older than 65 – Israeli retirement age. Here the barrier of the absurdly bureaucratic state system proved almost insurmountable. "Yes, yes, we desperately need an expert with your profile. How old are you, though?" And the employer would immediately sour...

In Golfand's case, the "age problem" was further complicated by the fact that, by and large, very few in scientific circles understood what this "Russian physicist" was studying. " 'Supersymmetry' – what's that?"

The early nineties were the peak of the "Aliyah," a time of a vigorous repatriation from the USSR (the Iron Curtain having finally collapsed) beyond what anyone who had foreseen an inevitable "Russian Aliyah" could have ever imagined. Israel was unprepared for the innumerable influx not only of musicians and teachers of Russian, but also of a huge army of scientists – including many of high caliber. Israel found this gift of fate hard to digest.

Legends circulated of some good-for-nothing bragging to others like him, "I hired a Russian Academician as a janitor!"

Other Moscow and Petersburg acquaintances who had already received solid positions proved self-absorbed, so busy bolstering their own status in their new country that they chose to ignore Yura. All niches were taken.

Fortunately, the Ministry of Science was headed at the time by the physics professor Yuval Ne'eman, an amazing man. It was thanks to his perseverance and that of Mikhail Marinov – they being among the few in the country who understood the level that Yuri Abramovich represented – that six months later, Golfand was hired as a senior researcher at the physics department of the Technion.

Yuval Ne'eman is one of the most striking figures in modern Jewish history. A prodigy who finished school at age 15, a Technion graduate, an underground fighter in Haganah combat units, a participant in the War of Independence, at age 29 a deputy intelligence chief of the Israeli Defense Forces General Staff.

Analytical work carried out under Ne'eman's supervision later became the basis for the strategic plan applied in 1967 during the Six-Day War.

In 1958, Colonel Yuval Ne'eman was sent to England as a military attaché. In London, he defended his thesis under the supervision of future Nobel laureate Abdus Salam.

In 1965, Ne'eman became a professor at the physics faculty of Tel Aviv University; in 1971, he became the university's rector.

He received the Israel Prize for science, and he became the first foreign scientist honored with the United States' prestigious Albert Einstein Award. In 1972, Yuval Ne'eman was named a member of the United States' National Academy of Sciences.

A general who had headed the Israeli Directorate of Military Intelligence, AMAN (analogous to the Soviet GRU military intelligence service), Professor Ne'eman created something akin to Mendeleev's periodic system, but in physics: he systematized all the elementary particles known at the time.

Ne'eman's study of the sources and laws of the nuclear forces acting in nature, alongside gravitational and electromagnetic forces, were confirmed when the then-largest particle accelerator, at Brookhaven (USA), obtained the omega-minus-hyperon particle. Ne'eman's theory containing the classification of elementary particles predicted this particle's existence and properties.

Concurrently with Ne'eman, an American scientist, Professor Gell-Mann, arrived the same results, and their results were published simultaneously. Alas, the Nobel Prize in Physics for this discovery

was awarded only to Gell-Mann. At the presentation of Alfred Nobel's gold medal, Murray Gell-Mann said he also saw Ne'eman as the
award's actual recipient, and that by all rights Ne'eman should be
standing beside him.

In 1982, in protest against defeatist government policies, Ne'eman
founded the right-wing Zionist revival party Tehiya. Tehiya's leadership included Geula Cohen, the legendary underground radio an-
nouncer sentenced to death by the British authorities during the
British Mandate, and the eminent writer Moshe Shamir. Many
"prisoners of Zion," repatriates from the Soviet Union, also joined
the party. To the dismay of leftists, Tehiya quickly won seats in
the Knesset and government. Professor Yuval Ne'eman was the first
minister of science and development in the history of Israel.

When Yuri Golfand arrived in Israel, the celebrated scientist was
fortunately serving his second term in the ministerial chair.

Just a few years before, Professor Ne'eman, in Moscow on business, had told Yuri Abramovich (whose publications on quantum
field theory he knew well) that he would be glad to see him in Israel,
and promised him that he would find a job there. And Ne'eman kept
his promise, obstacles and various difficulties notwithstanding.

The minister assigned care for the Golfand family to his deputy,
Dr. Eval Baruch. This man, great as a scholar and historian, and
great as a luminous soul, became not only their Virgil in a maze
of professional complications, but also simply their family's kind,
selfless, charming guardian.

Because of their daughters' conservatory studies, they didn't move
to Haifa, and Natalia entered the University of Jerusalem. The Technion leadership allotted their new employee a government apartment
where he lived during the week; on weekends, he returned home to
his family. Natasha sometimes visited her husband in Haifa.

Two weeks before Yuri started work at the Technion, he acquired
his first computer. He hadn't owned a computer in Moscow, and his
young colleagues at the Technion couldn't hide their surprise: they'd
never seen a man over forty with no PC skills. Still, he mastered
the computer quickly, and within two weeks was using the Technion

computer to type all his articles and correspondence.

Mikhail Marinov was a full professor by then, and the two began working together. Yuri Abramovich was formally listed as a senior researcher, while in the department he was referred to as a visiting professor. He was immediately given a group of young physicists as students.

Officially, due to his "age handicap," Golfand was hired for a special project implemented by the Ministry of Internal Affairs for older refusenik scientists. This also transpired with help from Eyal Baruch.

At first, Golfand's salary was paid jointly by the Ministry of Immigrant Absorption and the Technion. Then came, shall we say, an event that was extraordinary in the tight-knit ranks of the Israeli scientific community. The Scientific Council met and decided unanimously to ask the Minister to grant the "Russian doctor" the status of "full professor." This is said to have been the first such occurrence in the history of the Technion. The status was approved for Yura just before his death.

Yuri Abramovich finally found his way back to Moscow for an international physics symposium on the problem of gauge fields. But he never got to go skiing on snowy Mount Hermon – at first there was no money (with payments due on the Golfands' apartment), and then there was no free time, with too much work to be done.

Golfand drafted and used his computer to type up plans for 14 papers he planned to complete and publish in the coming years. He got through half of what he'd outlined.

Soon Yuri Abramovich turned to what he saw as his main task – developing a new idea that he spoke of as even more interesting, even more broad than the theory of supersymmetry. He'd already found an assistant, the talented mathematician Dov Ramm, with whom he planned to work out his project's mathematical apparatus.

Alas, his time ran out...

When he died, the "Hevrat Kadisha" burial society said Jewish traditions made it impossible to lay him to rest in a Jewish cemetery. After all, in Yuri Abramovich's passport (the so-called "Teudat

Zeut") the "nationality" field stated "ein rashum" – "no record." For Israel, he wasn't a Jew "according to Halacha," because his mother was Russian.

Again Dr. Eyal Baruch came to the rescue. Help also came from Fresis Salzberg, who was curator of the university where Natalia studied, and Ruth Bar On, the general director of SELAH, the Israel Crisis Management Center. They appealed to the Chief Rabbi of Jerusalem. Basically, all obstacles were overcome.

Professor Yuri Golfand lies buried in the ancient Jewish cemetery Har HaMenuchot in Israel's capital.

After her husband's death, Natalia Moiseievna faced new worries. For instance, the strictures of a "mashkanta" – the bank mortgage for buying their apartment – with interest on the loan snowballing each day. Then help came from Zionist Forum Chairman Natan Sharansky.

"Tolik," Natasha gratefully recalls, "came to our home and promised he'd solve the problem." And indeed, he arranged for help from an American science association.

In Moscow, Sharansky and Golfand weren't close acquaintances. They'd met a couple of times at the "refusenik" seminar at Alexander Yakovlevich Lerner's (Lerner, a top specialist in the field of managing large dynamical systems, waited 17 years for permission to emigrate to Israel. -B.E.). When Sharansky was imprisoned, Yuri visited his mother and regularly helped her however he could. He only got to know Natan personally after arrival in the Promised Land. It turned out that the famous Zionist prisoner was to some extent Golfand's colleague, as a graduate of the Moscow Institute of Physics and Technology.

Yuri Abramovich's final publication – on quantum mechanics – appeared only after his death.

An issue of the Technion's weekly newsletter was dedicated to Yuri Golfand – including a long article by his friend and colleague, Professor Mikhail Marinov, who unfortunately passed away a year and a half after Yura's death. The year 2000 saw the appearance Mikhail Shifman's English-language book about Golfand and his contribution to world science, *The Many Faces of the Superworld: Yuri Golfand Memorial Volume.*

Natasha and Kira continue to live in Jerusalem. Natalia Moi-seievna Koretz-Golfand works at SELAH, a national center that provides care to new repatriates who find themselves in crisis situations. It's an organization of professionals and volunteers ready at any time, day or night, anywhere in Israel, to reach out to people in distress. SELAH employs psychologists, psychiatrists and social workers. Natasha, the daughter of political prisoners, born in a labor camp, a woman who has suffered and loved, has a kind heart, capable of sharing pain, providing comfort and warmth...

"Yura and I had two daughters: the eldest is Masha and the youngest is Anya.

Yura once threatened to call me 'Grandma Natasha' if I didn't stop dignifying him with his name and patronymic. Now here I am already a grandmother: Masha has a son, named Yuri. Yura Golfand, my dear grandson – he reminds me so much of his grandfather..."

Afterword

It took me many years to prepare to tell the story of this brilliant man, whom I never met in person, whether in Russia or in Israel. He died exactly three months before my wife and I became repatriates in the Promised Land.

Before coming to Israel, I'm ashamed to say, I knew nothing about Yuri Golfand. Nonetheless, I had heard of the theory of supersymmetry, which intoxicated the imagination.

In childhood, I had an interest in theater, but also in chemistry; I filled notebooks with my poems and dreamed of becoming a circus acrobat. Yet I foolishly tried to get my foot in the door at an engineering institute, wasn't accepted, and found myself at an industrial college. I said farewell to acting and started working for a newspaper published for Black Sea fishermen, while in the evenings I studied at the Institute of Instrumentation in the faculty of shipboard electrical installations. I remember how in my freshman year my math teacher Yakov Borisovich Gutin secretly summoned his colleagues during my exam so they could see an "actor working integral equations."

I first heard about quantum field theory in physics lectures. And about the attempts to move beyond disparate hypotheses to reach something universal, conclusive, all-encompassing, irrefutable. Once an assistant professor of physics devoted almost the entire class session to the idea of "mirror worlds," a concept that was in the air then.

I reveled in the breathtaking, provocative abyss of the world's endlessness. For me, institute lectures on physics and mathematics were symphonies...

I wave my conducting baton and bury my eyes in the score. What it holds, though, instead of five lines with bass or treble clefs and dancing flourishes of notes, are completely different "sounds" : photons, quarks, antiquarks, fermions, multiplets, hadrons, baryons, mesons... The great music of modern physics!

In my multi-voiced orchestra, the "performers" are Natasha Koretz, Kira Golfand, Yura's father, mother, childhood and adolescent friends... And also Evgeny Tamm, Andrei Sakharov, Leonid Keldysh, Yuval Ne'eman, Mikhail Marinov, Evgeny Likhtman, Boris Bolotovsky, Alexander Voronel, Victor Brailovsky...

The voices of the orchestra telling the scientist's story merge into one, and it doesn't matter whether I'm hearing them in real life or in my imagination...

The first article I read about Golfand simply stunned me. Its author was the journalist Nellie Portnov. It appeared in the February 15, 1996, issue of the Russian newspaper *Vesti*. An entire column was devoted to the second anniversary of the physicist's death. The feature was called "Yuri Golfand – a Great Contemporary Scientist."

"I first saw Yuri Abramovich Golfand in the summer of 1992," wrote Portnov. "He behaved very simply and naturally, but I found it strange that he lived in the same building where I lived. And every time I had occasion to see him, I had the same sense of the uniqueness of this person who had accidentally slipped in among us..."

Then I happened to see the memoirs of the wonderful writer and translator Svetlana Schoenbrunn, a recipient of a literary prize from the Writers' Union of Israel.

"...He seems shy. Clearly an intellectual. Thoughtful and magnanimous. He listens with sincere interest to his partners in conversation and says little. He's absorbed in himself. In something known and accessible only to him. He seems somehow unsteady, brilliantly unsteady... He's like the planet Venus – surrounded by an atmosphere so dense... I have no way to look inside and, to be honest, I'm afraid to look... I always feel somewhat awkward in his presence – he's unquestionably smarter than us; he must feel like a wise elder surrounded by babbling, silly children..."

Svetlana Schoenbrunn met Yuri Abramovich's wife through her friend Hella Fisher.

"Natasha is a spark of white fire through black fire...she was born in the same labor camp where Hella did time) and her life is the theater and Yura, Yura and the theater... I haven't seen Yura yet, I don't know him yet, but I'll never be able to think of him outside Natasha..."

And here is a newspaper article by Natasha herself, written in the year of her husband's death. The newsprint has yellowed, but I've carefully saved the article all these years.

"Yelena Bonner, the wife of Andrei Sakharov, marveled at the courage he showed toward the families of dissidents and disgraced refusenik scientists. But he lacked the slightest trace of any awareness of his own significance. It was no coincidence that the people who came to say goodbye to Yura at Har HaMenuchot in Givat Shaul were former refuseniks from the Aliyah of the 1970s, and his Israeli colleagues from the Aliyah of the 1990s. There were engineers and humanities scholars, young and old, religious and secular, Yuri's friends and neighbors, everyone lucky enough to have known this remarkable man..."

Yuri Abramovich Golfand – an outstanding Russian and Israeli scientist, esteemed throughout the entire scientific world – is unfortunately known least of all to a broad public in Israel.

There was a time when every high school student in the USSR had heard something about Landau, Ioffe, Kapitsa, Kurchatov, Korolev.

It's not important whether a student knew or didn't know exactly what they were famous for; it only matters that they were known to be "outstanding," "great." Ask any Israeli student graduating high school, or even just an intellectual "Sabra," who Yuval Ne'eman was, and you're unlikely to get a clear answer. And Ne'eman's significance for the Promised Land is no less than that of Korolev or Kurchatov for Russia. Really, though, Israelis are far from the only ones unfamiliar with their great scientists. Half of those surveyed on the question "Who is Chaim Weizmann?" were unable to reply that Professor Weizmann, an outstanding chemist, was Israel's first president. To say nothing of the hero of my story – one of the key figures in modern physics, the "Russian" Yuri Golfand.

On many drives through London, on one of the streets leading to Trafalgar Square, my wife Olga and I often caught sight of a certain building's first-floor display windows, which stretch almost a full block. They feature portraits of great Englishmen: the philosopher Bacon, Isaac Newton, Shakespeare, Admiral Nelson, Lord Byron, the economist Adam Smith, Charles Dickens and Charles Darwin, the physicist Rutherford, the poet Kipling, penicillin inventor Alexander Fleming, Winston Churchill, actor and director Laurence Olivier, Liverpool foursome The Beatles, English football player Sir Bobby Charlton, and so on, up to today's celebrities.

It's not important which planetary model of the atom was invented by Ernest Rutherford or which laws of capitalism were discovered by Adam Smith. Each person in Britain may feel like a proud parent toward these native sons. If Chaim Weizmann had been an Englishman, a portrait of the chemist who saved the British army from the "gunpowder crisis" in the First World War would certainly have had a place in that long showcase on the road to Trafalgar Square...

I'd like to believe that Israelis, too, recalling names from distant centuries, will someday learn the stellar names of the outstanding scientists of their own modern history – names like Avram Hershko, Aaron Ciechanover, Israel Aumann, Ada Yonath, Dan Shechtman, Yuval Ne'eman, Yuri Golfand.

It's a pity, though, that this will happen only after I'm gone...

IN MEMORY OF YURI ABRAMOVICH GOLFAND *

BORIS BOLOTOVSKY

Theory Division
P. N. Lebedev Physical Institute of the Russian Academy of Sciences
Leninskii prospekt, 53
Moscow 119991, Russia
bolot@lpi.ru

In the late winter of 1994, Yuri Abramovich Golfand died in Israel. I had worked with him at the same department of the P. N. Lebedev Physical Institute of the USSR Academy of Sciences,[1] and I witnessed, and to some extent participated in, events related to his dramatic story. I remember when news came of his death, Ilya Isaevich Royzen and I emailed a letter expressing our condolences to Yuri Abramovich's family and science colleagues at the Technion – the world-renowned institute based in the Israeli city of Haifa. After moving from the Soviet Union to Israel, Yuri Abramovich was destined to work at this institute for only a few years. At that time, I took up a pen (I didn't have a computer yet then) and wrote down my memories of this remarkable man and the events that surrounded him. These memoirs were quite lengthy – a few dozen pages. I set these memoirs aside, hoping to return to them eventually. But when I wanted to re-read them some time later, I couldn't find them. They'd gone missing somewhere. That was four years ago, or maybe a little before. And in all these four years I never ceased to be aware of the incompleteness of this work, very important for me – my memoirs of Golfand remained unwritten. I'll try to do this now, seven years after his passing.

---

*Published in Russian in *Sem Iskusstv*, Issue 11 (36), November 2012, Ed. E. Berkovich, http://7iskusstv.com/2012/nomer11/bolotovsky1.php
[1]Lebedev Physical Institute is abbreviated in Russian as FIAN.

What gave me my impetus was the appearance of the book *The Many Faces of the Superworld*, released by the publisher World Scientific in 2000 and dedicated to Yu. A. Golfand's memory.[2] I decided to write down once more what I still remember.

***

In December 1950, I graduated from Moscow State University with a degree in theoretical physics, and at the beginning of February 1951 was sent to work at FIAN, the Physics Institute of the Academy of Sciences. I became part of the Etalon Laboratory staff. I worked at this laboratory for about six years. The laboratory's name said nothing about the work being done there. This was a time of total secrecy. The Etalon Laboratory was established for the design and construction of accelerators – complex structures for propelling charged particles to high energies. This was one side of the laboratory's work. The constructed and operational accelerators were used for conducting studies of the interaction of gamma rays with elementary particles and atomic nuclei. The laboratory was headed by Vladimir Iosifovich Veksler, a wonderful man with fine research intuition, extensive knowledge of high-energy physics, and a fantastic imagination. His proposals only seemed fantastical at first, though; later, it turned out they were quite realistic.

As a theoretical physicist, I was assigned to solve problems as needed by the Etalon Laboratory. I remember that my first work was devoted to the effect of the residual gas in the accelerator chamber and how this gas influenced the loss of accelerated particles. The accelerated particles were scattered on residual gas molecules, so some of them dropped out of acceleration mode. The loss needed assessment. After I finished this work, Vladimir Iosifovich Veksler assigned me to perform calculations related to the thick-walled ionization chamber. It was proposed that this chamber would be placed in a beam of bremsstrahlung, with the total intensity of bremsstrahlung determined based on the current that appeared in the chamber. Cali-

---

[2] *The Many Faces of the Superworld*, Ed. M. Shifman, (World Scientific, Singapore, 2000).

brating the beam of bremsstrahlung was important for experimenters studying photonuclear reactions. After performing this work, I was given another assignment. I found the work very interesting, it brought me into contact with many wonderful people, and I found discussing the problems that arose both useful and edifying.

However, while busy with tasks that, though important in the laboratory, still mainly just had local significance, I tried to follow the news, so to speak, in pure theoretical physics. At FIAN, there was every opportunity for this. When Academician Vavilov created the Physical Institute, he also provided for the Theory Department's creation. At Vavilov's invitation, the management of the department was assumed by Igor Yevgenyevich Tamm, one of the greatest physicists of the twentieth century. This was in 1934. In the first years of its existence, the Theory Department had few employees. But after World War II, the department was bolstered by younger new hires. Among the Theory Department employees in the 1950s were Igor Yevgenyevich Tamm, Evgeny Lvovich Feinberg, Vitaly Lazarevich Ginzburg [3] and Simon Zakharovich Belenky. That was, so to speak, the older generation. The younger hires arrived at the department in the late forties and early fifties. They were Geli Frolovich Zharkov, Viktor Pavlovich Silin, Dmitry Sergeevich Chernavsky, Efim Samoilovich Fradkin, Vladimir Yakovlevich Fainberg and Yury Kuzmich Khokhlov. Andrei Dmitrievich Sakharov [4] was hired by the department after defending his doctoral dissertation in 1948, but soon the will of the big bosses dispatched him to a secret institute where work was being done on building the hydrogen bomb. Soon Igor Yevgenyevich Tamm was also sent there.

---

[3] Vitaly Ginzburg (1916–2009) was a Soviet and Russian theoretical physicist, the 2003 Nobel laureate, "for pioneering contributions to the theory of superconductors and superfluids." Igor Tamm (1895–1971) was a Soviet physicist who received the 1958 Nobel Prize in Physics for the discovery of the Cherenkov radiation. Academician Evgeny Feinberg (1912–2005) was known for his profound contribution in the theory of high-energy scattering. Academician Efim Fradkin, see below, (1924–1999) was an outstanding Soviet theoretical physicist in the area of quantum field theory.

[4] Academician Andrei Sakharov (1921–1989) was an outstanding Soviet theoretical physicist, one of the principal creators of the Soviet hydrogen bomb, who later became a prominent dissident and human rights activist. Nobel Peace Prize (1975).

***

The Theory Department seminar was the scene of my initiation into pure theoretical physics. That was also where I met Yuri Abramovich Golfand. He was hired by the Theory Department in 1951, not as a physicist but as a mathematician, to perform calculations related to building nuclear weapons. But Yuri Abramovich regularly attended the department's seminar, never missing a meeting, even though the seminar was devoted not to math but to theoretical physics. He listened to reports at the seminar with obvious interest. At that time, he didn't ask questions. He was studying.

He was a cordial person. He had a cordial way of saying hello. There are people who say hello on the run, without stopping – "Hi!" – then nod and run onward. When Yuri Abramovich saw someone he knew, he would smile softly, stop, hold out his hand and slowly say, "Hello!" If he was in a hurry to get somewhere, he would put off his urgent business so he could exchange a few words with someone. I found his attention pleasant.

Yu A. Golfand didn't have his own housing in Moscow at the time. When he went to work at FIAN, Igor Yevgenyevich Tamm tracked down a room for him in the dormitory of the Moscow Engineering Physics Institute (MEPhI).[5] There Yu. A. Golfand lived with his wife and two children. It wasn't very comfortable housing, but there wasn't anything else. From time to time, the MEPhI administration would recall that a room in the dorm was occupied by someone totally unconnected with the institute. Then they'd start to evict Golfand and his family from the dormitory. Igor Yevgenyevich had to save his employee every time. Tamm would appeal to the MEPhI administration with a request to extend Golfand's period of stay at the dormitory. The rescue operation always succeeded, because MEPhI had a great respect and appreciation for Igor Yevgenyevich. For many years, he had headed MEPhI's theoretical physics department, which he had created. Golfand would be left alone, talk of eviction would cease, but a year would go by and everything would start all over again.

---

[5]Currently National Research Nuclear University MEPhI in Moscow.

***

The Theory Department seminar met on Tuesdays. Until the end of 1953, we tended not to see Igor Yevgenyevich Tamm at the seminar. He rarely came to Moscow, and his every appearance at the seminar was a cause for the participants to celebrate. After the successful testing of the first Soviet hydrogen bomb, Igor Yevgenyevich Tamm returned to Moscow. Andrei Dmitrievich Sakharov stayed on for many more years at the "Object,"[6] as the closed institution for nuclear-related work was called.

After I. Ye. Tamm's return to Moscow, the Theory Department's work on quantum field theory began to proceed at a rapid pace. Tamm organized a "likbez." The word "likbez" was a contraction of two words: "liquidation" and "bezgramotnost," or "illiteracy." This was borrowed from a name for circles where illiterate people could learn to read and write.[7] The "likbez" organized by Igor Yevgenyevich was intended to enable quantum field theory studies on the level of world science, and then to move forward on par with world science. Many theorists, including Yu. A. Golfand, attended the "likbez" classes. All the participants in the classes took turns giving presentations. Golfand was also given a topic to present on. I remember when it was Yu. A. Golfand's turn, in the middle of the presentation, Igor Yevgenyevich asked him a question – I don't remember either the presentation topic or the question. Golfand didn't give a real answer, just said complacently, "Igor Yevgenyevich, it's easy to understand."

Igor Yevgenyevich usually spoke quickly enough as was, and when he was angry, he would start speaking even faster. He sputtered, "Yuri Abramovich, I didn't understand, please explain."

Not realizing his danger, Golfand said smilingly, as if coaxing Igor Yevgenyevich, "Well, it's clear enough." And then Igor Yevgenyevich exploded. He stood up from his seat and said in the same quick

---

[6]A top secret Soviet nuclear weapon center which used to be known as Arzamas-16, a Soviet analog of Los Alamos. Currently Russian Federal Nuclear Center *Research Institute for Experimental Physics*, in the city of Sarov, Nizhny Novgorod district, 460 km to the East of Moscow.

[7]They were popular in the 1920s and early 30s.

sputtering manner, "Senior Researcher Golfand, you didn't prepare for this presentation; I deprive you of speaking rights. Next time, be prepared."

There's no such thing as a stupid question; there are only stupid answers.

At the next class, Yuri Abramovich gave a wholly adequate presentation and answered all the questions exhaustively. Igor Yevgenyevich was content.

***

A day came when the "likbez" ended. And at the next week's Tuesday seminar, Igor Yevgenyevich went up to the board and announced, "There are problems that need solving; we need volunteers!"

This related to the development of certain nuclear processes according to the Tamm-Dankov method.[8] A few people, including V. P. Silin and V. Ya. Fainberg, expressed a wish to do work on the topic. Among the volunteers was Yu. A. Golfand. Thus the mathematician Yu. A. Golfand set out on the path of a theoretical physicist. Before this, he had worked in pure mathematics. Employees involved in the nuclear project would hand him equations, and he would seek their solutions, not knowing what process they referred to, what problem the formulas given him related to, and what was the significance of the symbols they contained. And this didn't interest him. But at some point, he became interested in theoretical physics – moreover, in one of its most difficult parts, quantum field theory. This indubitably happened under the influence of Igor Yevgenyevich Tamm. His enthusiasm and creatively questing spirit had a contagious effect on many, not only on Golfand.

***

In 1956 I moved from the Etalon Laboratory to the Theory Department. I started seeing more of Golfand. Our acquaintance be-

---

[8]The Tamm-Dankov method is used in the theoretical study of the interaction of mesons with nucleons and of nucleons with each other, particularly in the deuteron theory.

came a partnership: we started work on a Russian translation of H. Bethe and F. de Hoffmann's two-volume book *Mesons and Fields*.[9] We translated the second volume. We – that is, Yu. A. Golfand, A. I. Lebedev and myself. I. Ye. Tamm served as editor for the translation. I often met with Yuri Abramovich at this time; we discussed various difficulties that he and I encountered in translating. I spent time at his home then, at the MEPhI dormitory. Golfand lived with his wife and two children – a boy and a girl – in a fairly large room, which served simultaneously as an office, a kitchen, a children's room, and a bedroom. Yuri Abramovich introduced me to his wife Sarra Yakovlevna Kogan, a nice, calm and caring woman, also a mathematician by training and also a candidate of sciences.[10] It was a warm family. In any case, several visits to them left me with that impression.

***

In 1959, Yuri Abramovich and I both took part in a symposium on theoretical physics, held in Yerevan, the capital of the Armenian SSR.[11] By this point, Yu. A. Golfand was invited to the symposium as a physicist rather than as a mathematician. We flew together from Moscow to Yerevan and back. This was my first time on an airplane. The flight to Yerevan began with an amusing incident.

At that time, IL-12 planes flew the Moscow to Yerevan route. These were small twin-engine propeller-driven airplanes – small compared to the jet liners that carry passengers now, more than forty years later. During takeoff and landing, and sometimes during the flight itself, the aircraft of that day would shake strongly, lurching from side to side, and the turbulence made some passengers nauseous. A thick paper bag was provided for such occasions. The bag was kept in a large pocket on the seatback in front of you. Yuri Abramovich and I sat together. This was my first flight, and before

---

[9]H. A. Bethe and F. de Hoffmann, *Mesons and Fields* (Row, Peterson & Co, Evanston, 1955), Vols. 1 and 2. Volume 1 was written in collaboration with S. S. Schweber.

[10]Equivalent to PhD in the US.

[11]Armenian Soviet Socialist Republic. Currently Republic of Armenia, an independent state which borders Turkey, Georgia, Iran and Azerbaijan.

takeoff I really did look at my bag and wonder about whether I'd need it or not. Then suddenly Yuri Abramovich turned to me and said, "Boris, please give me your bag."

I looked at the seatback in front of Yuri Abramovich and saw it had no bag in its pocket. I thought to myself, "If Yuri Abramovich didn't get a bag, and he's asking me to give him my bag, what am I supposed to do if I too get sick during takeoff?" Nevertheless, I immediately pulled out my bag from the seatback pocket and gave it to Yuri Abramovich. He removed one of his shoes, stuck it in my bag and put the bag under his chair. The shoe from his other foot already lay tucked in another bag under the seat. With his shoes off, Yuri Abramovich stretched his legs and smiled with bliss. All my fears immediately vanished, and I weathered both takeoff and landing easily, despite some formidable turbulence. Many years later I learned that during the war, Yuri Abramovich had worked as a technician at army airfields, and he'd had both to fly and work with military aircrafts on the ground.

In Yerevan, Yuri Abramovich and I were given a double room to share. We lived, you might say, in perfect harmony. Yuri Abramovich was a good-natured, attentive and caring roommate.

***

In my encounters with Yuri Abramovich, I realized fairly soon that his friendliness and attentiveness to people were unfeigned. When I came to him with a question, no matter what – whether about a book translation or work – he immediately dropped his own work, which may have been more important than my own, and started discussing my problems. He asked me about details, clarified nuances and, if our conversation didn't lead to a solution, kept turning over the question in his mind and, at our next meeting, went back to discussing the question on his own, not worrying about the time this took.

***

As already mentioned, Golfand's family had a tenuous position in the MEPhI dormitory. From time to time, the Golfands would face eviction, since Yuri Abramovich was an outsider at MEPhI. Igor

Yevgenyevich found it increasingly difficult to extend the Golfands' dorm stay.

FIAN occasionally received apartments for its employees, and Yuri Abramovich was put on the institute's waiting list. The line moved quite slowly, but it did move, and a day came when Yuri Abramovich was first in line for an apartment. But at the next distribution he got nothing, and the apartment went to someone who wasn't even second or third in line. At that point, Tamm went to the director of FIAN, Academician D. V. Skobeltsyn, and brought it to the director's attention that there were irregularities in the institute's housing distribution. Skobeltsyn promised to ensure that the line would move in the proper order. Yet Yuri Abramovich didn't receive an apartment the next time, either. Almost immediately after this, another attempt began to dislodge the Golfands from the MEPhI dormitory. Igor Yevgenyevich asked how things were going with issuing Golfand an apartment. Learning that Yuri Abramovich had been passed over again, Igor Yevgenyevich grew irate and, fuming, went to see the institute director. He spoke with Skobeltsyn quite curtly and ended by saying, "If Golfand doesn't get an apartment at the first distribution, I'll never shake your hand again, Dmitry Vladimirovich."

Before this conversation with I. Ye. Tamm, I don't think D. V. Skobeltsyn knew anything about what went on at the FIAN housing commission. Having learned about it from someone as respected as Igor Yevgenyevich, he made the housing commission follow the rules of precedence. In the next housing distribution, Yu. A. Golfand received an apartment.

***

In the Theory Department, Yu. A. Golfand fairly soon became a recognized expert in quantum field theory. I remember hours of heated discussions of new papers on quantum electrodynamics, on the Tamm-Dankov method, on dispersion relations, on Regge formalism, on the "Moscow zero"[12] – on everything new that had to be

---

[12]This phenomenon discovered by Landau, Abrikosov and Khalatnikov in 1954 (*Doklady*

comprehended, accepted or rejected. By then the department had become crowded; there wasn't enough room, and debaters would gather at the blackboard in whichever room had the least people.

Discussion participants included Efim Samoilovich Fradkin, Viktor Pavlovich Silin, Vladimir Yakovlevich Fainberg, and Yuri Abramovich Golfand.

Efim Fradkin had a heated, temperamental way of speaking. When done speaking, he would fall silent in order to listen to objections. While listening to objections, he would try to interrupt his opponent, take away his chalk, but this was difficult, almost impossible. And so, abandoning his efforts, he would listen to what he didn't agree with, but from time to time would still exclaim, "Level!"

This interjection meant he considered his opponent's level of development exceptionally low. Generally, discussions at the blackboard were very interesting, informative and colorful, not least of all thanks to the polemical methods employed. Vitya Silin, if someone from the respective sides in the debate disagreed with him, would appeal to the disagreeing party,

"Open your eyes!"

Or if that didn't help, he'd grimly say,

"Doldon!"

What (or who) a doldon was, I didn't know and still don't, but judging from the dynamics of the discussion at those moments, I surmised that a doldon was a thick-headed person unfamiliar with the ABCs of quantum electrodynamics. Volodya Fainberg would voice his disagreement by crying,

"You've got no tow!"

This likened the interlocutor to a defective locomotive that should tow its train, but doesn't. Yuri Abramovich mostly listened in silence. Politeness kept him from interrupting each successive speaker. He listened patiently and waited for the moment to come when he might get a word in edgewise. But the chance rarely came his way. Still, at times he would lose patience and comment on the proceedings. With an expression of mock horror on his face, he'd pronounce

---

Akademii Nauk SSSR, **95**, 497) is currently known as infrared freedom.

a single word: "Dreadful!"

Sometimes he'd couch the statement more verbosely: "Dreadful, with a gun!"

What this meant, I can't explain, dear reader. In arguments, he'd also sometimes say, "You, though, are a goose!" And then, to speak more precisely, he'd say, "Gooze!" – clearly enunciating the letter "z." What this word "gooze" meant, I can only guess.

There were also times when Yuri Abramovich, unable to express himself (that is, unable to interrupt the current speaker), listened attentively and occasionally uttered just one word, "Fantastic!" Don't think this was his way of voicing admiration for what he heard. Quite the contrary. There was an anecdote he liked about two theoretical physicists, A and B. They meet, and B asks A about his current work. A starts talking, B listens and from time to time exclaims, "Fantastic!"

After telling B about his work, A asks in turn, "And what's new with you?" "Nothing much. Except maybe that not long ago a specialist on scientific terminology spoke at our seminar. He said it's not good to use the term 'bullshit!' and it's better to say 'fantastic!'" Yuri Abramovich used the word "fantastic" in this sense.

***

We spoke to each other with the formal mode of address. True, from the beginning he called me "Borya," but I still called him "Yuri Abramovich." After all, he was six years older than me. Only late in our acquaintance, just before his departure to Israel, did I begin to call him Yura. But we kept the formal mode.

***

Time passed, and Yuri Abramovich increasingly gained a reputation as a recognized expert on field theory. His work was known and appreciated by theorists at the Institute for Physical Problems, at the Institute of Theoretical and Experimental Physics (ITEP), at the Joint Institute for Nuclear Research (JINR) in Dubna. At our Theory Department, different people had different attitudes toward him. Igor Yevgenyevich Tamm respected him, took interest in his work and often recruited him for discussing his own results and difficulties in his research. True, Igor Yevgenyevich could sometimes be heard to complain that he'd hired Golfand for the department as a mathematician and, lo and behold, he'd become a theoretical physicist, which hurt the department's math infrastructure. But it was clear that Tamm really liked more than disliked this transformation, as this "abuse" had occurred under his direct influence.

It's worth noting, by the way, how much the division between analytical and numerical computation has blurred over time. This came about as a result of the development of personal computers. It's now the rule rather than the exception that employees who receive analytical formulas can set up software themselves, fine-tune it and make the necessary calculations.

***

In the last years of his life, Igor Yevgenyevich became fascinated with the idea of constructing quantum field theory in curved momentum space. His attempt was unsuccessful. Igor Yevgenyevich worked with great enthusiasm and expended much effort on the problem, but he knew he might not be successful, and was ready for this. When the Academy of Sciences awarded I. Ye. Tamm the M. V. Lomonosov Gold Medal for 1967, he was working namely on field theory in curved momentum space. Traditionally, medals were presented at the grand general meeting of the Academy of Sciences. After receiving the medal, the laureate was expected to deliver a lecture about his work.

Igor Yevgenyevich was seriously ill at the time and couldn't attend the award ceremony, but he wrote his report, and, at I. Ye. Tamm's request, his pupil Andrei Dmitrievich Sakharov read his presentation at the general meeting of the Academy of Sciences. The paper devoted considerable space to what Tamm was working on at the time: field theory in curved momentum space. Igor Yevgenyevich noted in his presentation that the hypothesis of a curved momentum space was first proposed by the American theorist G. Snyder. He also said, "Besides two publications by Snyder himself, as far as I know, the only papers ever devoted to his hypothesis were two articles published in a very limited circulation by an American university, and those of two of our theorists: Yu. A. Golfand and V. G. Kadyshevsky. I'm very much obliged to them, because they drew my attention to Snyder's hypothesis."

Indeed, Yu. A. Golfand had published two papers on the development of Snyder's hypothesis. Tamm cited these works, which to a large extent had aroused his interest in the full range of issues posed by considering curved momentum space.

***

However, the department of theoretical physics also had employees who didn't consider Yu. A. Golfand a physicist. Among them was Vitaly Lazarevich Ginzburg, a distinguished physicist who made important contributions to many branches of physical science. Why he didn't think Yu. A. Golfand was a physicist, I don't know for certain, but I can imagine.

Modern quantum field theory is based on a very abstract and complex mathematical apparatus, which includes such branches of modern mathematics as group theory, representation theory, the theory of function spaces, operator algebra, operator analysis and much more. A person who hasn't mastered this apparatus can't glimpse physics there in the dense forest of complex mathematical techniques. Ginzburg saw no need to come to grips with this math. He may have thought that simpler methods sufficed for understanding physical phenomena, or he may not have found this branch of theoretical physics very interesting. Indeed, he did successful work in many areas, but not in quantum field theory – you might say it wasn't a division of physical science he dealt with. Beside this, he had known Golfand as a pure mathematician – which Yuri Abramovich really was when he arrived at the department. But high qualifications as a mathematician, combined with interest in field theory's physical content, helped Yu. A. Golfand quickly penetrate a range of problems in quantum field theory. When he had already acquired a name as a physicist rather than a mathematician, the following incident took place. At one of the Theory Department seminars (these were the Tuesday seminars led by I. Ye. Tamm), Ginzburg spoke on a recently published work by Freeman Dyson [13] about solid state physics (if I'm not mistaken, a work on ferromagnetism). Vitaly Lazarevich concluded with these words: "Dyson is known as the author of several works on basic problems of quantum field theory. And here, you see, he's done a fine job with solid state physics as well."

Yu. A. Golfand responded, "Vitaly Lazarevich, I don't understand what's so good about this work." Yuri Abramovich waited for clarification.

"You don't understand, because you're not a physicist," said Ginzburg.

Golfand made no reply. But something happened after the workshop: maybe Igor Yevgenyevich told V. L Ginzburg that this was no way to answer questions at the seminar, or maybe V. L. Ginzburg formed this opinion on his own, but one way or the other, at the beginning of the next seminar, V. L. Ginzburg came forward to the blackboard, faced the participants and said, "I apologize to Yuri Abramovich Golfand for my words spoken at the last seminar session." After these words, his face flushed, his hands clenched into fists, and he continued, "I apologize and I apologize, and there's nothing else I can add."

Golfand, from his seat, quietly but distinctly said, "And nothing else is needed, Vitaly Lazarevich." I saw what a great effort it took V. L. Ginzburg to restrain himself. I don't know when this mutual enmity appeared, but I think this episode displayed it clearly. On the one hand, the enmity may well have stemmed from the above-mentioned circumstance of V. L. Ginzburg not considering Yu. A. Golfand a physicist. On the other hand, Yu. A. Golfand couldn't stand being treated with contempt, and when he was, he reacted unequivocally, sometimes quite dramatically. You couldn't call his character angelic.

***

This is a good point to mention that Yu. A. Golfand began his

---

[13]Freeman Dyson (1923) is an English-born American theoretical physicist, famous for his work in quantum electrodynamics, solid-state physics, astronomy and nuclear engineering.

higher education not as a mathematician but as a physicist. In 1939, he enrolled at the faculty of physics of the University of Kharkov. The war forced him to interrupt his studies – he was drafted into the army. After the war, he continued his education at Leningrad University's math faculty and graduated with a math degree. So even if his diploma made him a mathematician, he was a mathematician seeded with physics.

***

In 1969, Andrei Dmitrievich Sakharov returned to the Theory Department after nearly twenty years of absence. On the one hand, he was at the height of his fame then – an academician, the father of the Soviet hydrogen bomb, in possession of the state's top awards. But at the same time, he was a "persona non grata," suspended from employment at the secret institute where he had worked so successfully for almost twenty years, and it cost Igor Yevgenyevich Tamm, his teacher, no small effort to secure A. D. Sakharov's return to FIAN's Theory Department. Sakharov and Golfand had a good relationship. Sakharov had long, eager discussions with Golfand on quantum field theory problems which interested them both. Sakharov held Golfand's opinion in high esteem. In turn, Yuri Abramovich admired A. D. Sakharov, both for his achievements in physics and for his purely human qualities. Sakharov was an impeccably polite, cordial and considerate person, and Golfand also liked this. Yuri Abramovich also very much sympathized with Sakharov's human rights activities.

One day after the Tuesday seminar, when most of the participants had already gone, a few people stayed behind in the conference room, surrounded A. D. Sakharov and began asking him questions, wanting to hear his opinion on the situation in the country. Andrei Dmitrievich got to talking and in particular spoke of a mathematician's recent arrest over a few banned books found during a search. Sakharov said he had written a letter to the authorities in the arrested man's defense, and read the letter aloud. Appealing to his listeners, Sakharov said, "As you can see, the letter is very restrained; it pursues just one objective – easing the plight of a man who's committed no crime. Maybe one of you will sign this letter with me?"

Golfand was among those present who signed this letter. Other signers then were David Kirzhnits and, if I'm not mistaken, Renata Kallosh – just three employees from our department. For Golfand this was the first step in his human rights activities.

The act had no visible consequences. However, there was no doubt that the competent authorities took note of the incident, especially since the letter was read aloud in a Voice of America radio broadcast, along with an announcement of all the signers' names. Igor Yevgenyevich Tamm, the head of the Theory Department, was already seriously ill at the time. When he learned that several department employees had joined Sakharov in signing a letter defending human rights, he had a talk with Sakharov specifically about this incident. The conversation took place in I. Ye. Tamm's apartment when Andrei Dmitrievich came to visit him. Igor Yevgenyevich described the conversation to me. He told A. D. Sakharov, "Andrei Dmitrievich, you're a grown man with a fairly high-ranking position; I respect your views and won't give you advice on how to act in this case or that. You bear responsibility for your actions. But the department staff who signed the letter with you may get caught in a very difficult predicament. No one will reckon with them as with you. Besides, not only they but our entire department could face punishment: there'd be talk of the Theory Department being a base for the political activities of Academician Sakharov, with all the ensuing repercussions. I'm asking you to consider all this."

V. L. Ginzburg, acting as I. Ye. Tamm's deputy at the Theory Department, had a similar talk with A. D. Sakharov. Andrei Dmitrievich understood completely, and promised to give no further cause to worry about the department's fate. He never again asked department employees to sign any of his many letters in defense of people suffering persecution by those with power. And yet he was grateful to Yu. A. Golfand for having signed one such letter.

***

At the turn of the decade from the 1960s to the 1970s, Yuri

Abramovich took an interest in a certain problem which at first seemed more mathematical than physical. Later, though, the problem's solution turned out to represent a contribution of paramount importance for quantum field theory.

Elementary particles have their own intrinsic angular momentum, called spin. And depending on what spin they have – integer or half-integer – elementary particles are divided into two classes. For example, an electron is a particle with half-integer spin; an electron's spin is equal to $\hbar/2$ – half of Planck's constant $\hbar$. A photon is a particle with integer spin; a photon's spin is equal to $\hbar$. In many respects, particles with half-integer spin behave differently than those with integer spin. In particular, two electrons cannot be in the same quantum state. Integer-spin particles are under no such restrictions. Any number of photons can be in the same quantum state. This possibility is realized in the work of lasers – devices that yield powerful beams of identical light photons. Half-integer spin particles are also called fermions, after the Italian physicist Enrico Fermi, who studied their behavior. Integer-spin particles are also called bosons, named after the Indian physicist Satyendra Bose.

Yu. A. Golfand set out to create a theoretical system in which particles with integer and half-integer spin could be considered within a unified framework, using a unified mathematical formalism. From a purely mathematical perspective, this was a matter of expanding certain transformation groups. Yuri Abramovich was familiar with this problem; his candidate thesis was devoted to issues related to group expansion.

In 1970, Moscow State University graduate Eugene Pinkhasovich Likhtman, a young, talented and educated theoretical physicist, joined the theoretical physics department's graduate program. Yuri Abramovich became his academic supervisor. And together they set out to solve this problem. Within just a few years, they published several articles offering a solution to the problem.[14] It became possible to consider fermions and bosons, despite all their differences, as

---

[14]The first publication was Yu. A. Golfand and E. P. Likhtman, *JETP Lett.*, **13**, 323, 1971.

members of a single family, and the wave functions of fermions and bosons were linked. This unified understanding was a great achievement. To me this seems analogous with the changes in space-time perception resulting from the theory of relativity. Before that theory, time and space were viewed as independent variables in describing events. But the theory of relativity showed space and time as seamlessly linked. Suppose that, in a certain coordinate system, an event occurred at coordinates $\{x, y, z\}$ and time $\{t\}$. Let's switch to another reference frame, which basically moves with reference to the first, and see the changes in the time and coordinates of the event in question. It turns out that in the new reference frame, the moment in time when the event occurred now depends not only on the time in the old coordinate system, but on the spatial coordinates too. Also, the event's spatial coordinates in the new reference system depend not only on the event's position in the old frame but also on the event's time. The theory of relativity showed the interconnection of time and space. In the same way, bosons and fermions were viewed as two completely different classes of particles, and Golfand's and Likhtman's work brought these two families into unity.

However, these articles attracted little attention at the time, and the value of the work that had been done wasn't fully comprehended in the first years after their publication. Subsequently, the connection between fermions and bosons discovered by Yu. A. Golfand and E. P. Likhtman became known as supersymmetry.

***

In April 1971, Igor Yevgenyevich Tamm died after a long illness. After his passing, Vitaly Lazarevich Ginzburg became head of the Theory Department. This fact didn't bode well for Golfand. As I've said, his relationship with V. L. Ginzburg was always troubled.

In the autumn of 1973, the Theory Department received a directorship order to implement staff cuts. The order demanded that a few employees be let go, at the department administration's discretion, in order to reduce payroll by a certain monetary sum. The sum was specified, and it was quite large. To comply with the layoff order, cutting just one employee wouldn't be enough; several positions would need elimination.

This wasn't the first layoff order I can recall. One or two such orders were handed down to the department from the institute directorship while Igor Yevgenyevich Tamm was still alive. I remember that namely when the department received the first order like this, I started having doubts that the Soviet planning system foresaw absolutely everything and excluded any possible accidents, in contrast to the capitalist system, which we were taught had no planning at all, which was why the capitalist world underwent economic crises. I couldn't understand why it made sense to hire a highly qualified specialist and then fire him a few years later.

As a rule, layoff orders contained hypocritical phrases like "For further improvements in scientific work, perform an employee appraisal and bolster the research team while achieving payroll savings of however many rubles." Igor Yevgenyevich Tamm responded calmly to such orders. On one such layoff order, I saw a resolution in Igor Yevgenyevich's hand, reading, "I see no opportunity to comply." Having written this, he sent the order back to the directorship. He believed that an employee who did bad work should be fired with no layoff order needed. Once or twice he did just that. On the other hand, if Igor Yevgenyevich was satisfied with department employees' work, he wouldn't allow the firing of any of them, even if layoffs were ordered.

***

The new department head, Vitaly Lazarevich Ginzburg, decided to comply with the layoff order. A meeting of the senior department employees was called (the department head, his deputies and the sector heads). At this meeting it was decided which employees' jobs should be cut. As it turned out, there were three: the department's oldest employee, Lidiya Viktorovna Pariyskaya; a young employee, Vladimir Volodin; and Yuri Abramovich Golfand. Lidiya Viktorovna Pariyskaya had worked as a calculationalist since back in the days when the only calculating tool was the "Felix" adding machine. This device required manual operation, like a meat grinder, by turning a handle. Jokers called this device the "Iron Felix," though they spoke

the name in cautious whispers, because that was what old communists respectfully called Felix Edmundovich Dzerzhinsky.[15] Then the
manual adding machine was replaced by mechanical ones. Unlike the
domestic Felix, these were foreign machines, the "Mercedes" and the
"Rheinmetall." They worked very noisily, and it got so loud in the
room where Lidiya Viktorovna sat that the racket was audible in
the corridor. But this didn't scare off Lidiya Viktorovna's clients
– I. Ye. Tamm, Yu. A. Romanov, A. D. Sakharov, V. I. Ritus and
many others. They brought Lidiya Viktorovna heaps of towering formulas, and she turned these formulas into tables and graphs. Lidiya
Viktorovna did remarkably conscientious, error-free and quick work,
as far as was possible with such now-antiquated technology. I never
gave Lidiya Viktorovna any assignments, but often stopped by to
visit her all the same – to discuss department business and just to
chat. D. A. Kirzhnits, V. I. Ritus and many department employees maintained friendships with her. Lidiya Viktorovna had already
reached retirement age. She was let go in the layoff, but her position was retained for her. She could work just as before the layoff.
Financially she lost a bit as a result of the layoff, because she was
transitioning to retirement and her pension paid less than her wages.
But this wasn't critically important for Lidiya Viktorovna, because
her husband, the noted astronomer Nikolai Pariysky, earned enough
that the family faced no hardship.

Vladimir Volodin was let go from his Theory Department job,
but was transferred to FIAN's computing devices department, so he
stayed at the institute and lost none of his salary.

The hardest blow was suffered by Yuri Abramovich Golfand. It
was decided to dismiss him in the staff cuts. This decision brought
Yuri Abramovich seven years of unemployment. Seven years in which
an expert with top qualifications couldn't do his actual work and had
to take any job he could get – these seven years were an extremely

---

[15]Dzerzhinsky was the first head of Cheka, a secret service dealing with political
"crimes," established shortly after the Bolshevik coup in 1917. The Soviet secret police
changed acronyms like a chameleon. It started out as the Cheka, and then became the
GPU, the OGPU, the NKVD, the NKGB, the MGB, and finally the KGB. Currently
FSB. Even now, however, people often simply refer to the secret agents as "the Chekists."

difficult test for Yu. A. Golfand and, I think, a great loss for science. He could have done a lot in seven years. As for the Theory Department, I don't think the layoff made for much of a bright spot in its history.

***

I didn't hold any kind of management position in the department; my place was that of an ordinary employee in V. L. Ginzburg's sector. Accordingly, I wasn't present at the meeting where the decision was made to lay off Yu. A. Golfand. I wasn't even at the institute that day – I was sick. A few days later I came back to work and learned about the decision. I didn't know the details then. And no one knew, if they weren't at the meeting where the decision was made. The layoff decision wasn't posted on the bulletin board and wasn't brought to the employees' attention in any other way. Considerable time passed before I learned how the discussion had transpired – not everything about it, but some details. David Kirzhnits, who took part in the discussion, told me about it.

The proposal to fire ("cut") Yuri Abramovich was made by V. L. Ginzburg. He said that Golfand was hired as a mathematician, to carry out mathematical support work for the department. He wasn't performing his duties and had turned out to be a layabout. And he hadn't done anything in theoretical physics, either. So there was every reason to dismiss him.

V. L. Ginzburg was supported by Evgeny Lvovich Feinberg. He agreed that laying off Golfand made sense, and added that Golfand's dismissal would in this case not be so much a punishment for doing bad work as much as a way for him to find work in his own field. The fact was that Yuri Abramovich had a math degree. At the moment, said Feinberg, universities in Moscow were experiencing a great shortfall in professors and doctors of sciences qualified to teach math. Without much effort, Yuri Abramovich could secure a professorship at some university's higher math department. Then he could do the work he knew best.

I think when Feinberg said it would be easy for Golfand to find a new job, he didn't picture the real situation. More on this later.

Dmitry Chernavsky also approved of the proposal to cut Golfand's position. The gist of his statements was that Golfand was the department's weakest employee and therefore ought to be cut.

As far as I know, the meeting's other participants kept silent. No one voiced any opposition. David Kirzhnits didn't have a close relationship with Golfand. Apparently he, too, thought of him at the time as not a physicist but a mathematician. That's the only explanation I can find for his tacit consent. It must be said that he later regretted the decision made back then, and agreed with me when I said the decision was wrong. But for a long time I couldn't understand why Efim Fradkin and Volodya Fainberg had kept silent during the meeting. After all, they had worked closely with Golfand namely as a physicist and not as a mathematician, and had an idea of his qualifications. I asked them about this (some years later) and got the following answers.

Efim Fradkin said that at the meeting he had indeed kept silent and said nothing against Yu. Golfand's termination. But a few days after the meeting, he had changed his mind and voiced his opposition to the layoff. Fradkin was in charge of the sector that Yu. A. Golfand belonged to. In this capacity, Efim Fradkin had to endorse the layoff by writing "I agree – Fradkin" on a sheet of paper with the text of the decision. Without his consent, the layoff decision was considered invalid. Efim refused to sign. But Golfand was still fired.

Vladimir Fainberg kept silent both at the meeting and afterward. He explained his silence by saying it was impossible to stand up to the pressure from V. L. Ginzburg.

Here I have to say that I don't know what I would have done if I'd taken part in that ill-starred meeting. Indeed, picture that you're taking part in a meeting where it has to be decided just who will be laid off. And it could easily happen that you'd be seized by fear of possible termination and overwhelmed by the thought: "anyone, just not me!" In that frame of mind, it's hard to find reasonable solutions.

It ought to be said that there was a reason for the criticism of Golfand. Over the past year, he really had neglected his duties of providing mathematical support for the work under way at the department. As mentioned, this was partly due to Yuri Abramovich's interests shifting to theoretical physics. And there was another reason.

In the past year, Yuri Abramovich had left his family, divorced his wife and remarried. Love is often not subject to rational considerations; it's hard to condemn a man for actions prompted by a wave of emotion. But it's unlikely that his abandoned children and deserted wife thought the same. For them, the family's collapse was a terrible ordeal. And for Yuri Abramovich himself, as well as for the new object of his affections, all this had its excruciatingly painful side.

Understandably, Yuri Abramovich's family upheavals had a destructive effect on his work life. Among the participants in the meeting that decided Golfand's fate, some sympathized with the abandoned family and condemned Yuri Abramovich. I think this circumstance also influenced the decision. I would note, though, that anyone who sought to penalize Golfand for abandoning his family by laying him off didn't make the best decision. By law, after a divorce, a father must provide financial assistance to his ex-wife, the mother of his children. But when left unemployed, Golfand had no chance to help his former family. So the ones who wanted to punish Yuri Abramovich wound up punishing his children.

Whatever the case, in the winter from 1973 to 1974, Yuri Abramovich was laid off from the Theory Department as a means of staff reduction.

***

Andrei Sakharov was in the hospital at the time. Vitaly Lazarevich Ginzburg and Evgeny Lvovich Feinberg visited him and informed him of Golfand's layoff. Sakharov writes in his memoirs:[16]

> We also had a visit from FIAN's E. L. Feinberg and V. L. Ginzburg, the head of the Theory Department. Ginzburg said an order had come down for all Academy institutions to cut their staffs.

---

[16]Andrei Sakharov. *Memoirs*, Vols. 1 and 2, (Human Rights Publishing, Moscow, 1996), Vol. 1, p. 570.

The Theory Department has to downsize by one person. It's a painful but unavoidable operation. We conferred among ourselves and decided it'll have to be Yuri Abramovich. He hasn't produced any scientific work at all for the last few years – he's basically just been goofing off. Besides, he has a doctorate; it'll be easier for him to get a new job than for someone without a doctoral degree.

I asked if we could somehow 'fudge it' and got a dryly negative response. Unfortunately, I didn't succeed in saying anything personally in Golfand's defense. I didn't know that a few months before, at a FIAN seminar, Golfand and Likhtman had reported on a paper they had just produced, and which would become a classic – it was the first to introduce supersymmetry.

Indeed, the discovery of supersymmetry was one of the most important achievements in elementary particle physics. So much for the "goof-off"!

This passage from A. D. Sakharov's memoirs needs clarification. By the time Yu. A. Golfand was laid off, several papers by Golfand and Likhtman had already been published (almost all of their major works), in which the goal they had set had been achieved. The introduction of the term "supersymmetry," with reference to the line of inquiry begun in Golfand's and Likhtman's works, came only later.

"Fudging" a layoff order, of course, was possible. "Fudging" meant not raising any objections to the authorities while also not carrying out their layoff orders, not cutting any employees. The heads of many FIAN laboratories did just this. Some lab heads openly refused to carry out layoffs. For example, Viktor Pavlovich Silin, who headed the plasma theory lab, upon receiving a layoff order, wrote to the directorship, "The only person who can be cut without affecting operations is me." No one who disobeyed in this way faced any subsequent punishment. I think the Theory Department management could have kept Golfand employed if they'd wanted to. They didn't want to.

***

Upon learning that he was being laid off in a staff reduction, Yuri Abramovich was outraged and offended. He considered the decision unfair, and so it was. Golfand wasn't the weakest employee. I've heard that after Yuri Abramovich was informed of his dismissal, when he met with V. L. Ginzburg, he refused to shake his hand. Ginzburg saw this as a great insult, although he could have realized that the department's staff-reduction decision had put Golfand in a desperate situation. Yu. A. Golfand's gesture was more like a form of protest (how else could he protest?) and not an insult.

The layoff left Yu. A. Golfand in a very difficult position. I remember when I heard about his layoff, I immediately thought about how hard it would be for him to find a job. But I still hoped he'd find something. I wasn't as optimistic as Feinberg, and didn't think there was someplace with open arms waiting for Yuri Abramovich. But I thought Golfand sooner or later would find a job somewhere so he could feed himself and his family. I was mistaken. No one gave Yuri Abramovich a job. The times were like that. This outcome was determined by several reasons at once, and it's hard to say which was the main one and which were secondary. And these causes were obvious. They ought to have been considered in the staff reduction.

Firstly, people who are let go in staff cuts, generally speaking, face great difficulties in finding new employment. Picture such a person coming, say, to some university's higher math department, where an opening has been announced for a vacant professor position, and offering his services. Naturally, in the very first conversation he'd have to answer the question of why he left his previous job. What can he say? That he was made redundant? That meant he was the weakest employee or an unsociable troublemaker. People like that are always the first to go, and here was someone dismissed in just that way. Hiring someone like that would be very risky, even if there were an urgent need for an employee. But let's suppose that the interview with the department head left him with a favorable impression of Golfand, that he decided to hire him, and sent him to the personnel office for processing. Yuri Abramovich would have come to the personnel office, filled out a form and relayed it, along with his workbook, to the personnel officer. The officer would have opened the workbook and seen the record about his prior job, "dismissed in staff reduction." Personnel officers dislike such entries: why hire someone expelled from another workplace? And if the personnel department resists, that's a very hard hurdle to overcome.

Another reason was that Yuri Abramovich Golfand was a Jew. At the time, this circumstance alone represented a serious obstacle to employment. At that time (the early 1970s), the relationship between the Soviet Union and the state of Israel wasn't ideal, to put it mildly. Soviet foreign policy in the Middle East was pro-Arab and anti-Israel. A vehement struggle against Zionism acquired prominence in the Soviet Union's inner life. What Zionism was, no one really knew – it was simply alleged that Zionism was a sinister doctrine directed against all advanced and progressive mankind. At the same time, it was implied that since all Zionists were Jews, all Jews were Zionists. It was very hard for a Jew to find a job – who would dare to take on a Zionist employee?

There was another reason that made it difficult to for a Jew to get a job. Those years saw the beginning of a mass emigration of Soviet Jews to Israel – as massive as the emigration authorities would allow. And the emigration authorities beset Jews wishing to emigrate to Israel with all manner of obstacles. From the perspective of the Soviet Union's dominant Marxist-Leninist ideology, it was incomprehensible and unnatural that someone would want to leave the world's most advanced state, the government of workers and peasants, and move to take up residency in a capitalist country with burgeoning exploitation of man by man, a working class that was impoverished both absolutely and relatively, and where life was growing bleaker and bleaker. In fact, of course, this perception of capitalist countries bore no relation to reality. Capitalist countries, of course, faced their own problems and difficulties, but there were no less difficult problems in the development of the Soviet state. The difference was that in the West, problems were openly discussed and gradually resolved, the difficulties were overcome, but in the Soviet Union, where we lived, talk of difficulties was suppressed and problems were compounded, which led eventually to the fall of the USSR. But this came later; at the time in question, it took some explaining to understand why someone would willingly abandon the socialist homeland, the most progressive country in the world, and move to capitalist hell. And an explanation was found. If someone decided to leave the Soviet Union, that meant this was a person with an inadequate education, who didn't understand his actions. So accountability for insufficient work on ideological education had to rest on those who were to blame. And if a person who worked at a given institution filed an application to emigrate to Israel, it often happened that the director of the institution, the head of the personnel department and the secretary of the party organization [17] would be penalized for their inadequate ideological and political work. What were the consequences of this? Suppose that in some institution a certain employee, Jewish by nationality, decided to emigrate to Israel and filed the papers for this with the emigration authorities. The institute's administration would take its share of heat for its poor ideological instruction. After this, the administration would make a point of not hiring Jews to fill any vacancies, and of getting rid of the rest of the institute's Jews, even if they worked quietly and had no plans to leave the country. I would say that this administrative vetting was in fact a hidden form of anti-Semitism.

In those years, as a rule, if a Jew made a decision to emigrate to Israel, he quit his job before applying for an exit visit, to avoid compromising anyone at his workplace.

***

And so namely this was the time when Yuri Abramovich Golfand started looking for work. His task was all but hopeless: first, he was a Jew, and second, he was a disreputable worker (dismissed in a staff reduction).

And there was yet another reason that may have hurt his chances of finding employment, although the above reasons alone were more than enough. As mentioned, Yuri Abramovich joined A. D. Sakharov in signing a letter defending a man found with banned books during a search. This act established him as an unreliable person, and quite

---

[17]Communist Party of the Soviet Union, the only legal party in the USSR.

possibly may have added to his employment troubles. Such acts were not forgotten. And it may even have been that not only this signing could have played a negative role, so much as the friendly relationship that had formed between Yu. A. Golfand and A. D. Sakharov. Sakharov was under careful, vigilant surveillance. Sakharov himself was left alone up to a certain point, but everyone who spoke with him was taken note of.

In short, a man was left jobless, with no practical chance of new prospects.

***

In those days I felt keenly aware of the situation that had arisen. I thought then and believe now that it was wrong to lay someone off like that. And this wasn't at all because of the unfairness of considering someone the weakest who really wasn't the weakest, who wasn't at all inferior to any of the rest. To be precise, of course it was shameful that Golfand was singled out as the weakest, but this wasn't the main trouble. Even the weakest should never have been laid off like he was. No one should be turned out on the street without a means of livelihood.

***

News of Golfand's layoff spread quite quickly in physics circles – first in Moscow, and then beyond Moscow. Physicists reacted similarly: they sympathized with Yu. A. Golfand and disapproved of his dismissal. My friend Pavel Yurievich Butyagin, who worked at the Institute of Chemical Physics, was a friend of the well-known theoretical physicist Vladimir Borisovich Berestetsky. Berestetsky headed the Theory Department at the Institute of Theoretical and Experimental Physics (ITEP). Butyagin told me at the time that Berestetsky resented Golfand's layoff and said that after this, he would no longer shake Ginzburg's hand. This was Berestetsky's first reaction, which may have softened later; I don't know. But I think he told Ginzburg his perspective on Golfand's layoff.

Alexander Viktorovich Gurevich, employed by our department, told me how some theorists from the Landau school (in particular,

Lev Petrovich Pitaevsky) had responded to Golfand's layoff. They said, "We used to look to the FIAN Theory Department as a model for how to treat people. When we needed some way out of a difficult situation, we tried to figure out what your department's staff would do in our place. But how could you lay off Golfand? We've never done anything like that."

About two weeks after the news broke of Yuri Abramovich Golfand's layoff, I was walking on Leninsky Prospekt on my way to work, when I ran into the ITEP theoretical physicist Boris Lazarevich Ioffe. He literally leaped on me with the words, "Why did you lay off Golfand? Did you really believe he was the weakest? Do you think you're stronger than him?" Boris Ioffe and I were on familiar terms, and his "you" referred not to me but to our entire department. I tried to find some kind of vindication, and said I didn't think Golfand was the weakest, and that I hadn't been involved in the decision about his layoff, but Boris Ioffe was seething with indignation and wouldn't listen.

A while after Golfand's layoff, a conference on high-energy physics was held in Dubna. From our department, Evgeny Lvovich Feinberg and David Abramovich Kirzhnits took part. David later told me that many of the participants had expressed disapproval of Yu. A. Golfand's layoff. While still in Dubna, David relayed this to Evgeny Lvovich. He said, "David, you can't listen to these accusations passively. Just explain that Golfand isn't a physicist but a mathematician, and that now he'll be able to find a job in his field. That won't be hard. In Moscow now there are lots of vacant professorships in higher math departments."

***

Yuri Abramovich started looking for a job. He applied to several educational institutions, one by one. Everywhere there were shortages of professor-level math teachers. And everywhere he was turned down. One institute told him plainly that the very fact of his layoff raised doubts about his qualifications. At another, the head of the math department told him he would only give Golfand a job if he brought him a recommendation from the head of the FIAN Theory

Department, Academician V. L. Ginzburg. I think this was all a sham. Even if Golfand had brought the requested recommendation, he probably wouldn't have been hired. But the relationship between Golfand and Ginzburg was such that Golfand would never have asked Ginzburg to recommend him.

At the time, I didn't imagine the gravity of the situation which Yuri Abramovich had to face. I still held out hope that he would manage to find a job as a highly qualified mathematician. I decided to help him, and turned to Viktor Iosifovich Levin, head of the mathematical physics division at the Moscow Pedagogical Institute's physics department. I had taught part-time at V. I. Levin's department for a number of years.

Viktor Iosifovich Levin was a man with an unusual destiny. He was born in India, where his father was stationed as a sales representative of the USSR. There in India, he graduated from high school. He received his higher education in England, where his father had been transferred by then. He studied math at Cambridge University and, after graduation, continued his studies under the famed English mathematician G. H. Hardy. While in England, he defended his doctoral dissertation on the theory of inequalities. Back in the USSR, he worked at the Moscow Power Engineering Institute's math department. In 1939, he became the department's head. The institute trains engineers for a variety of specialties – thermal power, hydropower, electric networks, power reactors and many other areas. All engineers need math, and each specialty entails its own set of mathematical knowledge. The department had developed comprehensive teaching courses for each specialty. During World War II, Professor Naum Ilyich Akhiezer, a distinguished mathematician and the brother of the no less renowned physicist Aleksander Ilyich Akhiezer, worked at the department. After the war, Naum Ilyich Akhiezer returned to his hometown of Kharkov.

I met Victor Iosifovich Levin in the early postwar years, when I was still a student. We vacationed together at the Centrosoyuz sanatorium near Moscow. Naum Ilyich Akhiezer visited Viktor Iosifovich quite often at the time; they strolled on paths in the park, animatedly discussed departmental business and tricky math problems, then spent hours engrossed in games of chess. Victor Iosifovich was a very strong chess player, stronger than our first category. When there were no guests, V. I. Levin would go out with a chessboard and seek partners. That was how we met.

In the late 1940s, at the height of the campaign against rootless cosmopolitanism,[18] Professor Viktor Iosifovich Levin was ousted as head of the higher math department due to "negligent work," according to the official wording. He was replaced by Moscow State University professor Nikolai Andreyevich Lednyov. I knew N. A. Lednyov; when I was a student at the MSU physics department, I took his course in calculus. He lectured very well. He knew and loved math. Also active in public life, he fell in with the reactionary contingent among the faculty, who burned with a desire to combat the symptoms of idealism and cosmopolitanism in science. This struggle in the physics department actually had nothing to do with fighting idealism or cosmopolitanism, but was directed against the most outstanding scholars and teachers. L. I. Mandelshtam, who established many areas of physics and created a powerful physics school, was forced to leave the department. His students I. Ye. Tamm and M. A. Leontovich also left the department. I was an eyewitness to the departure of Professor Simon Emmanuilovich Haykin, one of the best teachers, the co-author of the famous *Theory of Oscillations*, and the author of a wonderful textbook on mechanics. S. E. Haykin headed the department of general physics. The physics faculty's Party Committee established a special commission to examine the department. The commission was headed by Nikolai Andreyevich Lednyov. The commission produced such unjust findings that S. E. Haykin was outraged and demanded their reconsideration. He said if the committee wouldn't reconsider its findings, he would step down from the faculty. This was just what the authors of the findings wanted. The commission's findings remained in their original form, and Simon Emmanuilovich Haykin left the faculty.

In the late 1940s, Nikolai Andreyevich Lednyov took up the fight against Albert Einstein and his theory of relativity. Einstein's the-

---

[18]That's how Stalin's fierce anti-Jewish campaign was camouflaged.

ory of relativity struck N. A. Lednyov as having many deficiencies.
He created his own theory of relativity, which, in his opinion, was
free of these deficiencies. In fact, the criticism which N. A. Lednyov
leveled against the theory of relativity reflected his lack of understanding of the basics of this science. The new theory of relativity
he created didn't merit the slightest comparison with Einstein's, and
really didn't deserve to be called a theory at all. Nikolai Andreyevich expounded his "theory of relativity" at several meetings of the
physics faculty's Academic Council, and the members of the Scientific Council gave him their full attention, even though some (not
too many) had the courage to object. This event is memorialized in
lines from the wonderful poem "Eugene Stromynkin," by G. I. Kopy-
lov, a fine physicist and an extraordinary poet. The poem's hero is
a student at Moscow State University's physics faculty, and poem
describes events from the early postwar years. The poem says of
Lednyov's "theory":

> I was there when Lednyov,
> Gathering the professors' qahal
> Kicked with an intrepid toe
> At Einstein, the lion gone senile.

So this was the N. A. Lednyov who replaced V. I. Levin as head of
the higher math department at the Moscow Power Engineering Institute (MEI). Victor Iosifovich didn't immediately find a new job. He
moved to the Moscow Mining Institute (now Moscow State Mining
University), but a year later was forced out of it as well. Again he
had to spend some time looking for work. After that, he worked for
several years running the higher math department at Lipetsk Pedagogical Institute, then returned to Moscow and headed the mathematical physics department at Moscow City Pedagogical Institute's
physics faculty. In the early 1960s, he invited me to his department
to work with students and graduate students, and I took a part-time
job there, with wages set at half the usual salary.

V. I. Levin was an absolutely wonderful lecturer. At the beginning of a lecture, when it was time for mathematical expressions and
formulas, he would take chalk and write out the first formula in the

upper left corner of the board. At the end of the lecture, he would write out the last formula in the board's lower right corner. And the students could see the whole lecture there on the board at a glance.

I had an impression that he knew all of math and all the mathematicians in Moscow. He has written several good math handbooks for readers of different levels, as well as a wonderful essay on the Indian math genius Ramanujan. In those years, the faculty trained physics teachers for work in language schools. Such a teacher at a school offering an intensive English-language program could teach physics in English. The faculty had special "language" groups set up for training these teachers. Viktor Iosifovich Levin lectured on calculus and mathematical physics in three languages: in Russian for ordinary groups, in English for English groups, and in German for German ones. He lectured with complete fluency and in perfectly correct literary language.

The difficulties he faced after his expulsion from his position as a department head at the Energy Institute left Viktor Iosifovich with a deep fear of losing his job. As a result, he avoided hiring mathematicians of a "close weight class" for the department. A couple of times he called me, said the department had a vacancy, and asked me to keep an eye out for the right person. I took the request seriously and tried to do the best I could. Sometimes I would find an appropriate candidate and start to praise him to Viktor Iosifovich as a highly qualified specialist who'd already defended his candidate thesis and was finishing up his doctoral dissertation, and was a good person besides. Start off by hiring him as an assistant professor, and soon he'll make a fine full professor. Victor Iosifovich would listen to all this and say, "Maybe that's all good, but I need a junior teacher with no degree."

At first he wasn't really afraid of me, because I wasn't a full-time teacher, just a "half-timer." But a few years later I saw that he'd begun to suspect me, too, of wanting to take his place. So I left his department. This was all very sad. In about 1978, when I was still working for Viktor Iosifovich Levin's department, I was vacationing with my young daughter at the Academy of Sciences rest house near Zvenigorod, and there I met Nikolai Andreyevich Lednyov. By that time he had already retired. We got to talking. Nikolai Andreyevich asked me where I worked. I said that I worked at FIAN and taught in V. I. Levin's department.

N. A. Lednyov said, "Please let Viktor Iosifovich know how deeply I regret that I agreed to take his place. I was a reckless and ignorant person back then. I was a toy in the hands of people from the science department at the Central Committee of the [Communist] Party. They told me Levin was leaving his department in shambles and that it needed rescuing. I agreed to a transfer. I didn't understand what I was doing. Several people tried to talk me out of it, including Israel Moiseevich Gelfand (one of the greatest mathematicians of our time -B.B.). He told me, 'Nikolai Andreyevich, you're walking on living people!' But I didn't understand. Later, when I began to head the department, I saw that there had been no shambles, that everything was in perfect order. Then a few years later, this happened. I submitted an article to *Matematicheskii Sbornik (Mathematical Collection)*. They sent me a reviewer's response, a very good-natured response, matter-of-fact, with helpful comments and valuable suggestions. I made use of these suggestions. Much later I learned that the reviewer was Victor Iosifovich Levin. I'm grateful to him for that review. Please, tell that to him."

He spoke with complete sincerity. It would have been better, though, if he'd said all that not to me, but straight to Viktor Iosifovich. At the first opportunity, I relayed his words to V. I. Levin. He listened, frowned and said, "What's the use of talking about it now?"

***

I worked at Victor Iosifovich Levin's department from 1963 to 1978, with a break of several years. Yuri Abramovich's layoff happened during the time when I wasn't working at V. I. Levin's department. But I maintained a good relationship with him. I had an idea at the time that he could help Yuri Abramovich with employment. I knew Yu. A. Golfand had gotten nowhere by making the rounds of different departments. But Victor Iosifovich knew all the mathematicians, and I had hopes that one of them would help Golfand to get a job. Besides, Victor Iosifovich had wound up in the same predicament as Yu. A. Golfand before, and I thought V. I. Levin would realize the gravity of the situation better than anyone else.

I called V. I. Levin, told him about Golfand and asked for help. He silently listened to me without asking any questions (apparently I gave quite a detailed account) and asked me to call him in about ten days. Ten days later I called and asked him whether he'd been able to do something. He replied tersely, "Ginzburg acted recklessly."

I realized that Victor Iosifovich couldn't do anything either.

I didn't tell Yuri Abramovich anything about this attempt. When he would encounter Theory Department employees, myself included, he would pass by, pretending not to notice, looking away without responding to nods. This was understandable. He had been treated cruelly and disgracefully. Each such encounter left me feeling guilty. But still, after Victor Iosifovich Levin proved unable to do anything, I called Yuri Abramovich and said I disagreed with the decision to cut him from the staff and considered the decision unfair. Yuri Abramovich silently listened to my words, then silently hung up the phone. He found it hard to talk about all this, especially with a staff member from the department where he had been treated so inhumanely.

***

It was wrong to implement the layoff in the way it was done. Was it possible, though, to handle a staff reduction in a way that would cause minimal damage to the person chosen to be eliminated from the employee roster, so he wouldn't be considered the weakest and could find new work after the layoff? I tried to think of an option along those lines, and one possibility came to mind. Say the department did receive an order to cut staff. The department management meets and discusses which employee they'll have to let go this time. But the candidate for the staff reduction should in no case be laid off. If he's fired, he'll receive a "dismissed in staff cut" workbook notation and it will be very difficult for him to find a job at another workplace. But in no way is he inferior to the people staying on at the department. The candidate for reduction should be told, "We have to carry out an order to perform staff cuts. We discussed the situation and reached conclusion that we need to cut namely you. Not because your work is inferior to anyone else's, but because if we pick someone else to cut from the staff, the department's scientific work will suffer to a greater extent. But we aren't firing you. Stay at work and look for somewhere else you can go. And we'll help you find it."

How much time would finding a new job take? A few months, say, six months. But during this time, the person wouldn't be unemployed; he'd still receive his salary. The department would have enough resources to sustain one person for a few months. Then wherever hired him, he'd arrive not as the weakest employee, destined for a layoff, but as an employee of FIAN's theoretical physical department, alongside everyone else there. And the hiring at a new workplace could formally be a transfer from one institution to another.

Unfortunately, even if the course of action I'd devised had been adopted by the department leadership, it could no longer help Yuri Abramovich. Still, though, it seemed important to figure out what to do in case of subsequent staff cuts, so the employees would suffer less and the department's reputation wouldn't be marred.

I shared my thoughts with Efim Samoilovich Fradkin, a brilliant physicist and a wise man. Efim listened to me and said that my proposed course of action was of course gentler, which was good, but that on the other hand it wasn't so gentle. An employee selected for layoff would in any case have a blow dealt to his work morale for a long time. I didn't argue against this, but still felt that my proposal allowed at least some easing of the risk of unemployment.

I presented my proposal at a departmental business meeting, held about a month after Yu. A. Golfand's dismissal. The meeting was chaired by Evgeny Lvovich Feinberg. After all the scheduled issues were addressed, I asked to speak. I said that quite some time had passed since Yuri Abramovich Golfand's dismissal. It had been presumed that he'd easily find a job, but he'd still had no luck, and apparently this was no simple matter. We ought to help Yuri Abramovich to find work. And we also ought to develop an action plan for any possible future staff cuts, so no one winds up in Yuri

Abramovich's situation in the future. I explained my proposal, as set forth above.

There was no discussion, because immediately after my speech Evgeny Lvovich closed the meeting. This may have been because Vitaly Lazarevich Ginzburg was absent from this meeting, and Evgeny Lvovich felt uncomfortable discussing the issue without him there.

***

Yet my speech had some consequences. I had openly stated my point of view on Golfand's layoff. Some time after the department meeting, Dmitry Sergeevich Chernavsky walked into my little office. He had sided with those who'd supported firing Golfand. First we talked of something inconsequential; I don't remember what. And then we turned to what for me was a sensitive subject, the issue of Golfand's layoff. Dima made his perspective completely clear. He said that Golfand was first an idler, and second, the weakest employee. As such, laying him off was reasonable. So he was laid off. I argued with Dima.

"Dima," I said, "while Igor Yevgenyevich was alive, none of us was the weakest. Do you remember what Igor Yevgenyevich said when we were going to nominate candidates for election to the Academy of Sciences? He said, 'We're all about equally strong here, but let's nominate whoever has the greatest practical chances.' You see? How was it that for election to the Academy of Sciences, everyone was about equally strong, including Golfand, but for a staff reduction, Golfand came out as the weakest?"

"All the same, we have to face the truth," Dima said. "Golfand was the weakest, and laying him off was just and fair."

He spoke confidently, clearly, meaningfully, in the edifying tone of a lecturer teaching students. So we came to no agreement; each kept his own opinion.

A week later, Evgeny Lvovich Feinberg came into my office. Like Dima, he wanted to convince me that laying off Yuri Abramovich had been the right step. I tried to express my perspective: it's wrong to carry out a staff reduction in a way that obviously condemns someone to unemployment.

Like my previous conversation with Dima Chernavsky, my talk with Evgeny Lvovich produced no agreement. The conversation ended with Feinberg saying, "Golfand's an idler. He had a corrupting influence on our junior employees. His idling set a bad example. He had to be laid off. He's been laid off, and you can tell how much our junior staff's work has improved. Just look how well Ilya Royzen has started working."

"Evgeny Lvovich!" I asked him rhetorically. "To get Royzen to work well, was it really necessary to lay off Golfand?"

Feinberg fell silent, then stood up and left. I didn't want to offend him with our conversation, but I didn't agree with him. I hope he wasn't offended, and that he simply decided there was no point in further argument. He'd stated his perspective, and I'd stated mine. We each kept our own points of view.

I noticed that in our conversation, Feinberg no longer repeated the opinion he'd voiced several times before, about how easily Yuri Abramovich would find a new job. Even if he'd really thought so before, by now, two months after the staff cuts, he'd realized, as an orator once put it, that "things are in fact quite different than in reality." Feinberg also no longer talked about Golfand being a mathematician and not a physicist. I think that over the preceding two months, theorists from other Academy of Sciences institutes had told Feinberg their opinions of Golfand as a physicist.

***

The aforementioned Ilya Royzen was Ilya Isaevich Royzen, an employee of our department, and a highly qualified theoretical physicist. It shouldn't be thought that he worked badly before Golfand was fired, or that afterward he started working well. A person is not a machine, and this is particularly true of a scientist. A scientist goes through periods of creative ascent (or "creative binge," as Igor Yevgenyevich Tamm would say), with a lot that works out, and results that bring joy. There are losing streaks, when plans that initially seemed very enticing turn into fiascos. There are periods of rumination, preparatory work. All this, and much else besides, bears consideration when assessing someone. And whoever feels tempted to divide people into groups of the pure and impure runs the risk of mistakes, and often is mistaken. You don't have to look far for examples, if any are needed. It's enough to recall Yuri Abramovich's difficult fate.

Incidentally, Evgeny Lvovich's mention of Ilya Royzen in our conversation wasn't accidental. Somewhat later I learned that at the meeting leading to Golfand's dismissal, Royzen had been named as a candidate for possible reduction. I was told this by one of the participants in the meeting; I no longer remember by whom. On hearing this, I thought I should warn Ilya, so he could make sure to find a new workplace in advance. Otherwise, when the next cuts would arrive and Royzen would be laid off, he'd find getting a job much harder.

Wise Ilya took my news calmly. He said, "Golfand's layoff dealt such a blow to the department's reputation that the management won't likely ever try anything like that again."

The future's veiled in murk and mist... I agreed with Ilya, but at the same time felt very wary of a recurrence. Fortunately, the staff reduction was never to be repeated. Many years later, Ilya Royzen told me how the head of the FIAN plasma laboratory, Matvei Samsonovich Rabinovich, had reacted to Golfand's layoff. He'd predicted, "Golfand's layoff is the last one in Theory Department history."

He meant that the administration would learn its lesson from this disastrous staff cut.

***

A month passed since the day of the layoff. Yuri Abramovich spent that whole month looking for work, but found nothing. And then he was hired at FIAN again. He was offered a temporary job for two months (February and March 1974). The cosmic rays laboratory had a vacancy. The job was already intended for a specific person, but this person wasn't expected to start work there for another two months. So for the next two months the position was open. Yuri Abramovich was hired for this position. I can't say for sure, but I think the position was given to Golfand through the efforts of Evgeny Lvovich Feinberg. Seeing Yuri Abramovich's difficulties, E. L. Feinberg tried to ease his lot somehow, if only temporarily. I think by this time Feinberg already understood the department's error in laying off Golfand and sought ways to lessen the error's effects.

Yuri Abramovich Golfand was hired as a senior research fellow with a candidate of sciences degree, although he was a doctor of physical and mathematical sciences. The temporary post's salary (300 rubles per month) was a hundred rubles less than Yuri Abramovich had received before his layoff, but in those years, this lower salary still wouldn't have seemed small. Recall that the average wage in the Soviet Union in those years amounted to 120 to 130 rubles. The salary still didn't correspond to Yuri Abramovich's qualifications, but this wasn't the main problem. The problem was that the position was available for only two months.

The head of the cosmic rays laboratory, Nikolai Alexeevich Dobrotin, advised Yuri Abramovich to use the two months to look for a new job. No one required Golfand to come to FIAN every day. And indeed, throughout this time, Yuri Abramovich constantly and fruitlessly sought a new workplace. He never did find anything, and FIAN let him go again after the two months. Shortly thereafter, unable to find work in the USSR, Yu. A. Golfand applied to emigrate to Israel. With this step, he precluded any sort of employment for himself in the Soviet Union. People who applied to emigrate couldn't get jobs. At the same time, there was no guarantee of Yuri Abramovich receiving permission to emigrate.[19]

***

In his *Memoirs*, A. D. Sakharov says that Yu. A. Golfand visited him in the hospital right after the layoff. And even back then, Elena Georgievna Bonner, Sakharov's wife, advised Yuri Abramovich to leave the USSR. Elena Georgievna later recalled that Yuri Abramovich had listened to her advice with a kind of bewilderment. At the time, he was unprepared for a journey to another country. This is understandable. Many people see just simply changing jobs without changing their place of residence as an extraordinary

---

[19]See the second footnote 14 on p. 405.

event, let alone moving to another neighborhood or, all the more so, another city. Not to mention moving to another country. In the first months after his dismissal, Yuri Abramovich still held out hope for a new job in Moscow. He only decided to emigrate when all other options were exhausted.

***

Emigration case filings required character references from employers. A document from the OVIR (the Department of Visas and Permits) arrived at FIAN with a request to submit a character reference for Yu. A. Golfand. The character reference was composed and sent to the OVIR. Here is the text:

CHARACTER REFERENCE

Golfand Yuri Abramovich, born 1922, Jewish, non-Party, Doctor of Physical and Mathematical Sciences, worked at the Department of Theoretical Physics, FIAN, from 1950 to 1973. Employed as senior research fellow beginning on November 1, 1951. No disciplinary record for employment. Dismissed in staff reduction in December 1973.

Character reference issued for processing of emigration to Israel for permanent residence. Deputy Director of FIAN (N. N. Ivanov).

Chairman of the Local Trade Union Committee of FIAN (I. A. Abramenkov).

04/22/74

This brief character reference contained no praise of Golfand, but also no criticism. Apparently the reasoning was that such a character reference wouldn't attract unneeded attention to him or create further barriers to exit.

***

The Theory Department had a small Party organization, with seven communists: V. L. Ginzburg, G. F. Zharkov, O. K. Kalashnikov, V. P. Silin, V. Ya. Fainberg, E. S. Fradkin and myself. By the time in question, Viktor Pavlovich Silin no longer worked for the Theory Department; he headed the Laboratory of Plasma Theory. Yet he was still registered in the Theory Department's Party organization, perhaps due to being his lab's only communist. After Yuri Abramovich applied to emigrate, his act was discussed at a departmental Party meeting. Apparently the meeting was convened because FIAN's Party Committee wanted our Party organization to voice its perspective on Yu. A. Golfand's wish to emigrate to Israel.

At the meeting, V. P. Silin proposed the following resolution: "The Communists of the Theory Department censure Yu. A. Golfand's act as a betrayal of our socialist motherland." Opposition to this resolution was raised by V. L. Ginzburg. He said the attitude toward people emigrating was different now than under Stalin. Legal emigration could now occur for a variety of reasons: for instance, over humanitarian concerns, to reunite a family, etc. He therefore didn't see wishing to leave the USSR as necessarily a betrayal of socialism.

I remember also speaking in opposition to V. P. Silin's proposal. I said that Yuri Abramovich had been looking for a job a long time and that no one would hire him. He would never have filed to emigrate if he'd had a job.

As a result of the discussion, the Party meeting chose not to pass the resolution of censure. It was decided to acknowledge Yuri Abramovich Golfand's emigration application. The institute sent Yu. A. Golfand's character reference to the OVIR, and some time later it became known that Yuri Abramovich's request to emigrate had been denied. The reason given for the refusal was Yu. A. Golfand's role in carrying out secret thermonuclear-related work – more precisely, in nuclear weapons development. This was twenty years before. He had worked as a mathematician; that is, he sought solutions to equations obtained by theorists. He didn't understand these problems' physical aspect, and had no desire to delve into the physics involved. Much time had passed since then (over twenty years) and nonetheless he was denied an exit visa.

***

More time passed. One day an employee of our department, Svet-

lana Vasilievna Shikhmanova, told me that on the way to work she'd
seen Golfand. She'd been riding in a bus along Leninsky Prospekt.
At one of the stops Svetlana had seen Yuri Abramovich and his wife.
They were by a poster paste-up stand. Yuri Abramovich was holding
a heavy roll of posters, and his wife was carrying a bucket of glue
and a brush. They were pasting up posters. They'd been unable to
find other work. It should be noted that even such work wasn't open
to Yuri Abramovich; no one would have hired a doctor of physical
and mathematical sciences for a position in poster pasting. Natalia
Moiseievna, Yuri Abramovich's wife, had gotten the job, and he was
helping her.

***

I had an impression at the time that Yu. A. Golfand's layoff changed the moral climate of our department. People avoided
speaking of Yuri Abramovich's fate, afraid to openly express their
views about his layoff. From the outside, everything seemed to be
going well, just as before the staff cuts. But the image of Yuri
Abramovich and his unemployment lingered somewhere on the edge
of each employee's vision. Few had considered him the weakest employee. Young people especially had viewed him with great respect,
because Yuri Abramovich knew a lot and shared his knowledge, readily offering helpful advice and explanations of different subjects to
whomever needed this. Why he was fired? And if he was actually
fired, then any of us could also suffer the same fate.

Many people had thoughts like these.

***

You might say a fear of layoffs appeared in the department. And
some employees tried to use this fear for their own ends. I myself
became the object of one such attempt.

Over the years, the communists in our department would take
turns choosing Efim Fradkin and myself as Party organization secretary.[20] One year Efim would be the Party organizer and I would

---

[20] In the Soviet Union every production unit or laboratory at every enterprise or institu-

be his deputy; the next year, we would switch places and I would be Party organizer, with Efim as my deputy. And Efim and I knew all the members of FIAN's Party Committee and got along decently with them. But when Andrei Dmitrievich Sakharov returned to the department (this was in 1969), the Party Committee started treating the department differently. First, the Party Committee began holding the department's Party organization responsible for all of Sakharov's public statements. The logic here was very simple. If Sakharov opposed aspects of the existing order, this meant there was something he didn't understand. And the reason he didn't understand must be that the Theory Department's Party organization wasn't conducting outreach work with him. Later, the attitude toward the department's communists and non-partisan staff grew even worse. This happened after all the department's employees refused to sign a letter condemning A. D. Sakharov. Starting in late 1972, the Party Committee sometimes spoke of our department as a base for A. D. Sakharov's anti-Soviet activities. Going to see the Party Committee on official business felt like I was visiting a dangerous place where trouble awaited me, addressed either personally to me or to my department colleagues. And as luck would have it, in these years the department management decided that our Party organizer should be someone more politically mature than me. Vladimir Yakovlevich Fainberg fit this description. He became the Party organizer.

For several years, V. Ya. Fainberg was elected as the Theory Department's Party organizer. But in the end, he decided to extricate himself from this difficult duty. We needed to choose the next year's Party organizer at an upcoming report-and-election Party meeting. I overheard that, as before, the decision was to retain V. Fainberg as the department's Party organizer. And Fainberg himself didn't seem to mind. But before the meeting, he phoned me at home and started trying to persuade me to agree to become Party organizer.

"There are several reasons why you need to replace me," said Volodya. "First, I can't be Party organizer because I'm the depart-

---

tion had to have a communist party cell, with an "elected" leader (secretary of the party cell) who was usually referred to as *partorg*, or Party organizer.

ment's deputy director."

"Volodya," I said, "you've been both Party organizer and deputy director for several years already. That hasn't caused you any problems before now, and I don't think it will in the future." I really didn't want to be Party organizer, and decided to get myself off the hook, come what may.

"Second," Fainberg said, "I'm secretary of the FIAN methodological seminar. If I keep being a Party organizer, I can't make the seminar run smoothly."

"I'll help you with that," I said. "You can give me any of the seminar tasks. I'll do it all."

V. Fainberg paused a little, and then said, "There's another reason why you need to be Party organizer. I'll tell you, but only if you promise it will stay between us. When the department management made the decision to lay off Golfand, you were also discussed as a layoff candidate. And then Ginzburg said, 'Bolotovsky is our department's Party organizer. As long as he's Party organizer, we can't fire him.' You keep that in mind. It's in your interests to be elected Party organizer."

In order to achieve his goal, V. Ya. Fainberg had decided to scare me with the potential for my layoff. This angered me.

"Volodya," I told him, "if you want to tell me I should look for another job, I'll look for a job. But after what you've said, I won't be Party organizer under any circumstances."

"You're a slacker," Fainberg said. "You and I will talk differently from now on."

That was the end of our conversation.

At the Party meeting, when the discussion began about whom to choose for the next term, V. Ya. Fainberg still proposed my candidacy.

I refused and, turning to Vitaly Lazarevich Ginzburg, said, "Fainberg and I had a talk that was very difficult for me. He tried to persuade me to agree to election as Party organizer. He said that when Golfand was fired, my candidacy for layoff was also discussed, and that you, Vitaly Lazarevich, said: 'As long as Bolotovsky is Party organizer, we can't lay him off.' So if I don't want to get fired,

I have to become Party organizer."

Vitaly Lazarevich replied, "That's not what happened. When we were deciding on candidates for reduction, I took an alphabetical list of department employees and started reading off the names. Andreyev – we can't lay him off, he's a young specialist. Bolotovsky – can't lay him off, he's Party organizer. And so on... That's the only way you were mentioned."

"It isn't that," I said. "You can lay off anyone, including me. Just don't speculate on it." Volodya Fainberg was then elected Party organizer for another term. After the meeting, he said to me, "I told you as a friend, and you... I won't tell you anything ever again."

I don't know what really happened – whether they wanted to lay me off or not. But I strongly doubt that Fainberg was acting as a friend when told me about it. If he'd really wanted to help me as a friend, he would have told me immediately, in the first days after Golfand's layoff. Instead, he told me about it several years later, and only when it turned to his advantage.

***

For seven years Yu. A. Golfand was unemployed. He continued his scientific work or, rather, made efforts to see it continued, but this was hard for many reasons. There was the need to earn daily bread, and Yuri Abramovich seized any chance for temporary work. He no longer had scientific contact with many of those with whom he'd previously been in touch with daily and discussed scientific news and issues that interested him. He could no longer attend the Theory Department seminar – he found it difficult to associate with members of the group he'd been tossed out of in a way that had insulted him so deeply. But even if he'd voiced a wish to attend a Theory Department seminar, it's unlikely he could have gotten in. He no longer worked at FIAN, and therefore could only gain seminar admission with a one-time pass – for each visit, the Bureau of Passes would require an application to admit Yu. A. Golfand, and the application would have to specify where he worked. Where does an unemployed person work? The Bureau of Passes would never have issued a pass for someone who didn't work anywhere.

Yet a chance remained for Yuri Golfand to attend a theoretical physics seminar at ITEP (the Institute of Theoretical and Experimental Physics). The seminar leader was Professor Vladimir Borisovich Berestetsky and the secretary was Boris Lazarevich Ioffe. It was a high-level seminar, with strong physicists involved (besides V. B. Berestetsky, already mentioned, there were B. L. Ioffe, I. Ya. Pomeranchuk,[21] L. B. Okun, K. A. Ter-Martirosyan, etc.). Yu. A. Golfand greatly appreciated the chance to take part in this seminar. But of course, the seminar also benefited from such a specialist's involvement.

Admission to ITEP grounds required a pass. Before each session, seminar secretary B. L. Ioffe would bring the Bureau of Passes an application for Yuri Abramovich. As already mentioned, the application had to identify Yu. A. Golfand's workplace. Every time, B. L. Ioffe would fill in the application with the name of some mythical organization where Yu. A. Golfand allegedly worked. In so doing, the seminar director and secretary were running a huge risk. The ruse's discovery would have meant huge trouble for them. Fortunately, everything worked out.

***

In those days (the mid-1970s), people who wished to go to live in Israel but were turned down (this category even had its own name – "refuseniks") wound up in a difficult, sometimes tragic situation. These people existed in a strange limbo. They weren't yet Israeli citizens, but meanwhile were basically not considered full citizens of the USSR. Although they continued to live in the Soviet Union, constitutional guarantees either didn't apply or only partly extended to them. For example, the constitutional article by which USSR citizens had the right to work didn't apply to refuseniks. Generally they were jobless. In the case of theoretical physicists, it would seem that they could have similarly pursued their beloved science from home. Albert Einstein even believed a post as a lighthouse

---

[21] In fact, Academician Isaak Yakovlevich Pomeranchuk (1913 -1966), the founder and first head of the ITEP theory division, died in 1966, before the events narrated in this memoir.

keeper would offer the ideal conditions for doing science – no one bothers you, nothing interferes with thinking over questions that interest you. But not everyone sees things that way. Science is very hard to do on a desert island. It's incredibly important for a scientist to have scientific communication, the chance to discuss ongoing professional challenges with understanding colleagues, the chance to describe what's been done and hear advice and objections. All research teams now hold seminars. People meet regularly, say, once a week, and discuss science news, successes and challenges in how science is developing.

Refuseniks' chances for scientific communication was kept to a minimum. They generally lost access to the seminars of the scientific communities where they'd worked before applying to emigrate. Even in cases where seminar access was possible, a refusenik wouldn't necessarily make use of the opportunity, not wanting to give an excuse for the participants to be accused of talking with a traitor.

The refuseniks organized their own seminar. Famous physicists took part in the seminar's work: Benjamin Levich, Alexander Voronel, Yakov Alpert, Mark Azbel, Benjamin Fain, Yuri Golfand [22] and other refuseniks. The seminar wasn't a full-fledged replacement for the ones the refusenik physicists had taken part in before. Still, this offered a chance for scientific discussion and a way to keep the participants on a sufficiently high level in science.

Many Western physicists (in the parlance of the time, physicists from capitalist countries) knew about the refusenik seminar and tried their best to support its work. During their visits to the Soviet Union, they were involved in the seminar and made presentations.

It must be said that a foreign scientist speaking at the refusenik seminar was in a sense committing an act of civil courage. If a foreign physicist, arriving in the Soviet Union, expressed a wish to attend the refusenik seminar, officials tried to dissuade him from doing so (for

---

[22]Golfand was introduced to this seminar by Sergei Adamovich Kovalev, a prominent Soviet dissident and political prisoner. Charged with "anti-Soviet agitation and propaganda" in 1974, he served seven years in labor camps, and then three years in internal exile at Kolyma. After the demise of the USSR Sergei Kovalev continued his human rights activities in modern Russia.

instance, according to Ya. L. Alpert, Academician R. Z. Sagdeev, director of the Space Research Institute, discouraged his foreign guests from participation in the refusenik seminar); visiting the seminar was seen as unfriendly to Soviet science. If, say, an American physicist decided to go to the Soviet Union for the sole purpose of taking part in the refusenik seminar, and if he stated this goal when applying to the Soviet embassy for a visa, it's highly likely that he'd have received a refusal. Many foreign scientists took part in the refusenik seminar all the same. From time to time, the refusenik seminar even held conferences. In particular, in December 1978 a conference was held which brought together about twenty refusenik scientists and eleven Western scholars, including the president of the New York Academy of Sciences, the mathematician Joel Lebowitz. This conference could justifiably be called international.

State research institutions (the Soviet Union had no others) would never have allotted space for the refusenik scientists' seminar; the conference was held in the apartment of two refuseniks – the mathematician Irina Brailovskaya and her husband Victor Brailovsky.[23]

$$*\,*\,*$$

In 1974, the journal *Nuclear Physics* published the article "Supergauge transformations in four dimensions." The authors were two theoretical physicists: Julius Wess from Karlsruhe University in Germany, and Bruno Zumino from the European Center for Nuclear Research in Geneva. The authors independently, not knowing of Golfand's and Likhtman's results, constructed a theory featuring two types of particles – bosons and Fermi particles – with the wave functions of these particles interlinked and transforming through each other. J. Wess and B. Zumino examined specific implementations of their theory.

This work attracted many researchers' attention, and the problem began to be actively developed. In essence, Wess and Zumino

---

[23]Victor Brailovsky (b. 1935) is a computer scientist and human rights activist known for his struggle for freedom of Jewish emigration from the USSR. Irina Brailovsky is his wife, also known for her human rights activities. Both were refuseniks for 15 years, from 1972 to 1987.

had solved the same problem previously formulated and solved in the works by Golfand and Likhtman. Why didn't Yu. Golfand's and E. Likhtman's works attract notice when they appeared? It's hard to say why. Maybe the reason was that Yu. Golfand's and E. Likhtman's works emerged somewhat prematurely, when the physics community wasn't quite ready for their reception. But probably the work by J. Wess and B. Zumino aroused so much interest because it was written a little differently than the work by Yu. Golfand and E. Likhtman; one might say it was written more physically, that is, in a language more familiar to those who have studied quantum field theory. For example, the work examined an important wave-function transformation that the authors called a γ^5 transformation, thereby emphasizing the role of Dirac's γ^5 matrix. In any case, fairly soon the importance of supersymmetry in particle physics was realized, and from 1974 on there came an avalanche of publications on the research and development of supersymmetry's various aspects. In less than thirty years, tens of thousands of papers appeared on the topic.

When the significance of supersymmetry was already widely understood and accepted, I once asked Dima Chernavsky, "Well, do you still think Yura Golfand was the weakest?" Dima replied, "Who knew?"

***

Fairly soon it became clear that the pioneers in formulating and solving the problem were Yu. A. Golfand and E. P. Likhtman. FIAN received letters addressed to them from foreign physicists. Why were the letters sent to FIAN? Because published scientific articles usually indicate their authors' workplace. Golfand's and Likhtman's articles also mentioned that Yu. A. Golfand worked at FIAN. So the letters came to FIAN. But Golfand no longer worked there. When the letters' authors learned that Golfand wasn't working at FIAN, they started trying to find out where he was working currently. And it turned out that he was unemployed, wasn't working anywhere, FIAN had fired him, and he couldn't find any other work for himself.

Fine, then, the Soviet Union had no need for Yuri Golfand. But he could also have gotten a job at any foreign university, which wouldn't have had to be just any university – one of the most prestigious foreign universities would have eagerly offered him a job. But no, it turned out this wasn't possible – the Soviet Union wouldn't let him out of the country. The scientific community abroad couldn't come to grips with this strange state of affairs. Foreign physicists found all this incomprehensible. And in the Soviet Union, Golfand's predicament was by no means exceptional – many refuseniks faced the same situation, as did anyone whose views didn't conform to the official ideology.

It's interesting to note that events sometimes took different turns: a person would be called into an official agency, where it would be suggested that he write a statement requesting permission to emigrate to Israel for permanent residency, with a prompt and positive response even guaranteed. My friend Valentin Fyodorovich Turchin [24] – a famous physicist and an even more famous mathematician – found himself in this situation. He lost his job because of his human rights activities. He had to find some means of subsistence, but what can you do if you've gotten on the blacklist? No personnel department will ever let you past. Turchin at one time was forced to earn a living as follows. Imagine the end of the construction of a large apartment building. The lot where the building stands is strewn with miscellaneous construction debris – scraps of boards, reinforcing bars, chunks of concrete slabs, and so on. All

---

[24]Valentin Fyodorovich Turchin (1931- 2010) was a world-famous computer scientist. He developed the theory of metasystem transitions and the notion of supercompilation. He was one of the visionaries at the inception of the global brain idea. In the 1960s, Turchin became politically active and in the early 1970s, Turchin founded the Moscow chapter of Amnesty International. In 1974 he lost his research position in Moscow and was persecuted by the KGB. Facing almost certain imprisonment, he and his family were forced to emigrate from the Soviet Union in 1977. The Turchins moved to New York, where in 1979 Valentin Turchin joined the faculty of the City University of New York. He was also associated with the Courant Institute of Mathematical Sciences at NYU. In 1990, together with Cliff Joslyn and Francis Heylighen, he founded the Principia Cybernetica Project, a worldwide organization devoted to the collaborative development of an evolutionary-cybernetic philosophy. In 1998, he co-founded the software start-up SuperCompilers, LLC. He retired from his post of Professor of Computer Science at the City College in 1999.

this needs urgent clean-up. Workers are hired for this job. They're employed for just a few days, with the personnel department of the organization doing the construction not at all involved in the hiring. There's simply an estimate of the cleanup costs, and the foreman personally receives the money to hire and pay the workers. Valya Turchin, Doctor of Physical and Mathematical Sciences, took these kinds of jobs, with no questions asked and no applications to complete. He worked hard for the set time, at the end of the day received the money he'd earned, and went home. In his time free from work, he continued his human rights activities, spoke in defense of people facing persecution for their convictions. The authorities tracked his every step, several searches were carried out in his apartment, several of his typewriters were confiscated one after another, but all to no avail – Turchin stayed active in human rights defense.

At that point he was summoned and offered a chance to write a petition requesting for permission to emigrate to Israel. The most amazing thing about this story is that Valya Turchin wasn't a Jew. He was a native Russian. Yet Turchin wrote a petition requesting his and his family's release to Israel, because he'd gotten an explanation of what would happen to him if he disobeyed. Turchin wrote the required statement, immediately received permission to emigrate to Israel and soon departed, but turned en route and found himself in the United States.

Why the authorities, having decided to deport Turchin, demanded that he write a petition requesting permission to emigrate to Israel, I still can't quite fathom. Maybe the authorities wanted Turchin to leave the USSR but at the time a legal process for voluntary emigration had only been worked out for people wishing to go to Israel.

* * *

Soviet Jews who were denied permission to emigrate to their historical homeland behaved in different ways. Some – this was true in many cases – were already in Israel in their souls. They of course remained interested in events in the country where they still were – in the USSR. But they tried as much as possible to refrain from involvement in what was happening. They lived and acted so as not to attract a surfeit of hostile attention from the authorities. They feared that some action of theirs might worsen their situation, bad enough as it was, and undermine their hopes of emigration.

Yuri Abramovich belonged to a different category of refuseniks. He was actively involved in defending human rights. In a lawless state, this is a dangerous business. Those who spoke in defense of human rights faced trials, exiles, terms in mental hospitals. And being a refusenik while pursuing human rights work was doubly dangerous.

Yuri Abramovich chose namely this path for himself. A refusenik and unemployed, he – a mathematician and physicist of the highest caliber – didn't shy from joining the movement for human rights. I think he set out on this path under the influence of Andrei Dmitrievich Sakharov, with whom he'd become close before his layoff. Subsequently, after FIAN fired Golfand, Andrei Dmitrievich was among the few Theory Department employees he stayed in touch with, and apparently the only Theory Department employee with whom Yuri Abramovich formed an even closer relationship than before he lost his job.

In December 1975, one of A. D. Sakharov's closest associates, the prominent human rights activist Sergei Adamovich Kovalev, was put on trial in Vilnius. Sakharov traveled to Vilnius and stayed there during the days of the trial, wanting to help his comrade as much as he could. Several people traveled with Sakharov to Vilnius with the same goal of providing moral support for S. A. Kovalev. Among them were well-known physicist and human rights activists: Yuri Fyodorovich Orlov [25] – who wouldn't stay free for long – Valentin Turchin and others. Yuri Abramovich Golfand also traveled to Vilnius.

The days of the trial coincided with the award of the Nobel Peace Prize to A. D. Sakharov. Sakharov was not allowed to go to Stockholm to receive the Nobel Prize, but Elena Georgievna Bonner accepted the prize on his behalf. On the day of the prize ceremony, A. D. Sakharov and his fellow activists listened with excitement to

---

[25]See footnote 26 on p. 439.

Andrei Dmitrievich's Nobel speech, read by E. G. Bonner.

A. D. Sakharov's *Memoirs* includes a photograph showing a small group of people standing in front of the courthouse in Vilnius. These people weren't allowed in the courtroom. Among them are Andrei Dmitrievich Sakharov, Yuri Fyodorovich Orlov and Yuri Abramovich Golfand, as well as several Lithuanian activists. Golfand and Orlov, two Yuras, stand side by side. Yuri Abramovich's face is calm and thoughtful. Andrei Dmitrievich is smiling.

***

Because Yuri Abramovich was unemployed, his family – his wife, daughters and he himself – lived in poverty. There was no question of relying on aid from the state. They survived on odd jobs and help from human rights organizations, international charities, and so on. True, there was one time when the state gave Yuri Abramovich financial assistance, although not directly but through intermediaries.

In the summer of 1976, Tbilisi hosted an international conference on elementary particle physics. Andrei Dmitrievich Sakharov was among the conference attendees. He traveled to Tbilisi with Elena Georgievna. Here's what he says in his memoirs:

> Shortly before the conference closed, we had a visit from Weisskopf and Drell [Victor Weisskopf and Sidney Drell, prominent American physicists, took part in the Tbilisi conference proceedings - B.B.] Sheepishly, they said that each of them had received a package full of money (how much I don't remember). They didn't explain under what spurious pretext the money, in fact a hidden bribe, had been awarded them. Weisskopf and Drell came to us with this money and asked us to relay it to persecuted scientists and their families (which we did).

E. G. Bonner once told me about this same episode. If I understood Elena Georgievna rightly, part of the money went to help Yuri Abramovich and his family. Thus Yuri Abramovich and several other out-of-work scientists received state aid.

***

In the autumn of 1977, A. D. Sakharov wrote a letter to Jeremy Stone, who headed the Federation of American Scientists (FAS), asking Stone to speak out in defense of two refuseniks: Yuri Abramovich Golfand and Naum Natanovich Meiman.[26] Professor Naum Natanovich Meiman was a man remarkable in many ways – well-known for his work in mathematics and theoretical physics, as well as for his public activities. I hope much more will be said of him in the future by those who knew him better than I did. Like Yu. A. Golfand, in the first half of the 1950s N. N. Meiman worked on classified (secret) projects. This circumstance was the official reason for denying him permission to emigrate.

In his letter to J. Stone, Sakharov wrote that he was well aware of work performed by Golfand and Meiman, as well as of their degree of access to classified information. Both carried out calculations in idealized model representations, using techniques of no practical interest at the time of the letter's writing. Neither was familiar with actual designs. They'd never been to the "Object" – the secret site of the main work on nuclear weapons development. Given these considerations, Sakharov believed there could be no reason to bar them from leaving the USSR.

Sakharov's letter stated clearly what foreign scientists could only have guessed. Yuri Abramovich's plight attracted attention almost immediately after the recognition of his role in the discovery of supersymmetry. Foreign physicists didn't understand how such a man could be fired, deemed the weakest. They also didn't understand why such an outstanding scientist couldn't find work in his field. If this so, Golfand wasn't needed in the USSR. But why, then, wasn't he allowed to go abroad? The official answer was that he possessed information constituting a state secret. But, first, a lot of time had passed, about twenty years, since Golfand (like Meiman) had performed classified studies. And, secondly, Andrei Dmitrievich, in his

---

[26]Naum Meiman (1911 - 2001) was a Soviet mathematician and prominent dissident. He is known for his work in complex analysis, partial differential equations, and mathematical physics, as well as for his dissident activity, particularly as a member of the Moscow Helsinki Group. After emigration from the USSR in the Gorbachev era he lived in Israel.

letter to Stone, testified to the dubiousness of the barrier of secrecy in this case.

These three questions – "Why was Golfand fired?"; "Why can't he find somewhere else to give him a job?"'; and "Why not give him permission to leave?" – these three questions were asked by Western physicists repeatedly when they met with their counterparts from the Soviet Union. Whether a foreign physicist was visiting the USSR or a Soviet physicist was visiting the West on business, in either case these questions were asked and needed answering. Questions about Golfand's fate were addressed to the Soviet physicists on whom Yu. Golfand's fate might have depended, including the head of the FIAN Theory Department, Academician V. L. Ginzburg, Academician and Secretary of the Department of Nuclear Physics Moisei Alexandrovich Markov, and President of the USSR Academy of Sciences Anatoly Petrovich Alexandrov, who was also a physicist.

It bears mentioning that not only foreign physicists were concerned about Golfand's fate. Many physicists in the USSR believed that Golfand had been allowed to suffer an injustice. The man who may have had to speak with foreign physicists about Yu. A. Golfand's fate more than anyone else was Moisei Alexandrovich Markov. Based on his position – serving as Academician-Secretary of the Department of Nuclear Physics at the Presidium of the USSR Academy of Sciences – he often had to play host to foreign scientists in the Soviet Union, as well as travel abroad. But it wasn't only his position that mattered. M. A. Markov was a well-known physicist – an acknowledged expert in field theory and elementary particle physics. He was capable of assessing the value of Yu. A. Golfand's work and comprehending his miserable state. Whether Golfand got work or was allowed to leave the USSR didn't depend on Markov. Nonetheless, M. A. Markov began to take steps to give Golfand employment.

***

Vitaly Lazarevich Ginzburg, head of the FIAN Theory Department, which had fired Golfand, was also forced to discuss Golfand's fate. Both foreign and Soviet physicists expressed their disapproval of Yu. A. Golfand's layoff. Hearing these numerous objections, another person in Ginzburg's place might have been moved to doubt whether the layoff had been valid. But V. L. Ginzburg still had no doubts that Golfand's layoff was legitimate. I think his negative attitude toward Yuri Abramovich only became stronger. I remember that in my conversations with V. L. Ginzburg, whenever Golfand came up, he'd always append some abusive epithet to his name. True, once someone told me that Ginzburg, speaking I no longer remember with whom, admitted that the Theory Department had erred in laying off Golfand. But I myself never heard anything like this from him. He kept believing that firing Golfand had been right. In the late 1970s, at a meeting of the Theory Department's Academic Council, Ginzburg, who chaired the Academic Council, while speaking of the department's day-to-day business, unexpectedly started talking about Golfand. He said that the Theory Department had done absolutely the right thing in firing Golfand. Why did he start talking about this? It's hard to say. Maybe he was experiencing doubts that he'd been right, and therefore voiced his thoughts on what for him was a touchy subject, out of a wish to quell these doubts. Or maybe, convinced that he had acted rightly in arguing for Golfand's dismissal, he wanted to air his views in public yet again.

Since I had disagreed with Golfand's layoff, I decided to voice my objection. Golfand had gone without a job for many years, and my objections couldn't help him, but I felt it necessary to express my opinion. I said that Golfand hadn't been the weakest employee, that the way Golfand's layoff was handled had precluded his employment by any other institution, and that the staff reduction, if indeed needed, should have been treated officially as a transfer.

V. L. Ginzburg listened to my objections and gave me no answer. But the next meeting of the Academic Council (a month later) began with V. L. Ginzburg approaching the place where I was sitting, staring straight at me and snapping, "Firing Golfand was right!"

Having said these words, he went back to his chairman's seat and opened the meeting of the Academic Council. This time I made no objection.

***

In 1979, a group of world-renowned physicists wrote a letter to the President of the Academy of the USSR, A. P. Alexandrov. I don't remember the authors' names, but I remember that among them were several Nobel Prize winners. The gist of the letter was something like this: Dr. Yu. A. Golfand is an outstanding physicist. Yet for more than five years he's been unable to find work in the Soviet Union. At the same time, he isn't allowed to go abroad. Make up your minds whether you need Dr. Yu. A. Golfand or not. If you need him, give him work. If you don't need him, give him permission to leave.

Apparently it was after this letter that the Presidium of the USSR Academy of Sciences took steps for Yu. A. Golfand's return to FIAN. At the time, this wasn't easy to do. Doctor of Physical and Mathematical Sciences Igor Mikhailovich Zheleznykh, who worked with Markov for many years, told me that M. A. Markov went to the Central Committee of the Communist Party of the Soviet Union and saw Communist Party Secretary M. V. Zimyanin to obtain a "yes" for Golfand's reinstatement.

Apparently Markov took the key initiative in bringing up and solving the issue. He managed to convince first A. P. Alexandrov and then M. V. Zimyanin that Yu. A. Golfand should be returned to FIAN. Zimyanin gave his consent, and the matter was settled.

On one of those days I was in V. L. Ginzburg's office when V. Ya. Fainberg, our department's Party organizer, came in. He had just been at the district committee of the Party, and from there brought news of the decision to reinstate Golfand.

"We'll have to take him," he said.

"Volodya, I'll take Golfand," said Ginzburg, "but you understand our department is in a difficult position. Sakharov works for us, and now Golfand will, too. You talk to Markov. Maybe he'll take Golfand in his group. But if he can't do it, I'll take him at the Department."

Perhaps Ginzburg spoke with Markov about which FIAN lab Golfand would work in. Moisei Alexandrovich Markov led a small group of theorists in the High-Energy Electron Laboratory. He accepted Golfand in his group.

I think Yuri Abramovich probably wouldn't have agreed to return to the Theory Department. Before he was put on the FIAN employee roster, Yuri Abramovich was made a proposal to withdraw his application to emigrate to Israel. Golfand refused, but was still put on the roster. It was one of the rare, even exceedingly rare, cases where an unemployed refusenik was given employment.

***

Golfand's return to FIAN coincided almost to the day with Andrei Dmitrievich Sakharov's exile to Gorky (now Nizhny Novgorod). So the number of FIAN "deviants" didn't go up when Golfand came back.

People who don't think or act like everyone else are often called deviants. Accepting that all things in the world are relative, "deviant" can in no way be a felicitous term. Natan Agasievich Korkhmazyan, a professor at Yerevan State Pedagogical Institute, brought this to my attention.

"Boris, what does 'deviant' mean?" he once asked me.

I said, "A person who thinks differently than everyone else."

"Who is everyone else?" Korkhmazyan asked with a sly smile.

"Well, all the rest, the vast majority."

"But maybe not he but everyone else is a deviant? After all, they think differently than this lone person. What do you think?"

I agreed with him.

***

A. D. Sakharov was exiled to Gorky in the first days of 1980. Until April – from January to April – we had no official information about Sakharov, and subsisted on various rumors. It was unclear whether Sakharov would stay at FIAN or be fired. There were rumors about his possible expulsion from the Academy. Nothing definite was known about the state of his life and health. The head of FIAN's Theory Department – the department where A. D. Sakharov was a senior researcher – was summoned to meet with various governing authorities, including the Central Committee's Office of Science and the Presidium of the Academy of Sciences.

The country's leadership was developing a plan to keep Sakharov in long-term exile. Meanwhile, attempts were made to fire Sakharov from FIAN. These attempts could apparently be traced to the Presidium of the Academy of Sciences. First there was a call from the Presidium's personnel department to our department's deputy director, senior researcher Geli Frolovich Zharkov. A fantastic conversation transpired:

"Tell me please, has Academician Sakharov been coming in to work at FIAN?"

"Don't you know that he was exiled to Gorky?" Geli asked in turn.

"We know, but you tell us, has he been coming in to work at FIAN?"

"No, he hasn't," Geli had to admit.

"Write a report," the personnel officer said with satisfaction.

"A report about what?"

"What do you mean, about what? About Sakharov not coming in to work. He's violating the internal regulations of institutions of the Academy of Sciences."

At this point it became clear to Geli that the authorities wanted Sakharov fired, and moreover, at the hands of Theory Department employees. But the plan fell flat.

Geli said, "Sakharov isn't breaking any rules. The internal regulations don't say an academician is obliged to come in to work every day."

The attack was repulsed and never repeated.

Around the same time, the director of FIAN, Academician N. G. Basov, instructed his deputy Sergei Ivanovich Nikolsky to prepare an order for Sakharov's dismissal on approximately the same grounds – that Sakharov resided in the city of Gorky and was therefore unable to perform his duties at FIAN. Sergei Nikolsky didn't want to prepare this order. He phoned the Presidium of the Supreme Council and asked them to tell him the number and date of the decree exiling Sakharov to Gorky and, if possible, to send him the decree's full text. He said he was preparing an order for Sakharov's dismissal, and that the order had to reference this document. All the newspapers were reporting that Sakharov had been exiled to Gorky by decree of the Presidium of the Supreme Soviet of the USSR, but this decree wasn't published anywhere.

S. I. Nikolsky's request provoked some consternation. He was promised that he'd have all the details he was asking for, but not right away, only later. There was nothing later, though, because no such decree existed. On this basis, and, more precisely, for lack of any reason, S. I. Nikolsky never prepared an order for firing Sakharov from FIAN.

In April, an order came from the Academy of Sciences, signed by its president, Academician A. P. Alexandrov. This order put an end to the uncertainty surrounding the relationship between A. D. Sakharov and the Academy of Sciences. Sakharov was an employee of FIAN's Theory Department, and institute employees were allowed to travel to Gorky to see Sakharov for scientific discussions and exchange of scientific information. I think A. D. Sakharov's retention as a department employee and the ability to communicate with him were included in the order thanks to the efforts of Vitaly Lazarevich Ginzburg.

For Andrei Dmitrievich Sakharov, visits from FIAN physicists represented his only opportunity to discuss the problems that interested him with living human beings. Physicists from Gorky weren't allowed to see Sakharov. So Andrei Dmitrievich appreciated these not overly frequent visits. While in exile, in his letters to the Theory Department, he sometimes asked to be sent an expert on such and such a problem, and named the person he'd like to discuss it with. Several times over his seven years in Gorky, Sakharov requested that Yu. A. Golfand be sent to him. But Golfand was never sent to Gorky. I don't think the Theory Department management was to blame for this. Golfand wasn't a Theory Department employee, and really, the question of trips by this or that theorist to see Sakharov in Gorky wasn't decided in the Theory Department, or even in the institute directorship, but in some other organization – try to guess which.

***

After Yuri Abramovich started work at FIAN, I began to see him more or less regularly. This usually happened on Wednesdays.

On Wednesdays, a theoretical physics seminar led by Academician V. L. Ginzburg met in the FIAN conference room. The seminar sessions began at 10 a.m. and ended at 12 p.m. After this, a seminar led by Academician M. A. Markov started in the same conference room. I attended V. L. Ginzburg's seminar and Yuri Abramovich went to M. A. Markov's. While leaving the room after V. L. Ginzburg's seminar, I would almost always see Yuri Abramovich. He was waiting for the start of his seminar. Usually Yuri Abramovich wasn't alone, but part of a group of participants in M. A. Markov's seminar. I always said hello to him, and he replied coldly, it seemed to me, without that friendly smile so typical from him before his layoff. I understood the reason for this coldness and each time felt guilty.

Yu. A. Golfand never set foot in the hallway that housed the Theory Department. At least I never saw him there after his return to FIAN.

***

On May 21, 1981, Andrei Dmitrievich Sakharov turned 60. He spent his 60th birthday in exile in Gorky, isolated from friends and from relatives, from like-minded people and co-workers. Human rights groups decided to release a jubilee anthology in honor of the date, with the anthology including materials related to A. D. Sakharov's life and work – articles on different aspects of his multifaceted activities, congratulations from scientists and cultural figures, and other materials variously associated with the man being celebrated. The anthology was prepared in secrecy, and the authorities didn't hinder or halt its publication. The birthday book, called *Sakharov Collection*, was released abroad by the publisher Khronika Press. It includes materials provided by thirty-three authors. Among the authors are writers and poets (Lydia Chukovskaya, Vladimir Kornilov, George Vladimov, Vladimir Voinovich, Semyon Lipkin, Viktor Nekrasov, Raisa Orlov, Lev Kopelev, et al.), human rights activists (Anatoly Marchenko, Sophia Kallistratova, Larisa Bogoraz, et al.), and scientists (Boris Altshuler, Valery Soifer, et al.).

This anthology contains also an article by Yu. A. Golfand about Sakharov's work on fundamental physics problems. Writing on this was difficult because, on the one hand, A. D. Sakharov's contribution to modern physics is very significant, while on the other hand, some of Andrei Dmitrievich's articles on important physics problems weren't fully understood even by specialists. Yuri Abramovich tried to write his article in a way that would make the value of Sakharov's work clear to a wider audience, including those without science educations.

Writing a popular article about Sakharov's achievements in physics was difficult. But there were also difficulties of another kind – one might even say, not difficulties, but real dangers. It took considerable courage to be among the authors in this collection. Publication in *Sakharov Collection* could have caused the authors to lose their jobs. After all, Yuri Abramovich had only just gotten the chance to work after six years of unemployment. Really, there was no ruling out even worse consequences. Yuri Abramovich wasn't afraid. And the amazing thing was that publication in *Sakharov Collection* wasn't followed by any backlash. Then a few years later, Yuri Abramovich made another move that could have easily caused his dismissal. He traveled to Yakutia, to the rural locality of Kobyay, a few hundred kilometers from Yakutsk. The well-known human rights activist, good physicist and remarkable man Yuri Fyodorovich Orlov was serving out his exile there after seven years in a labor camp. Reaching Orlov wasn't easy. It took a flight of six thousand kilometers from Moscow to Yakutsk. Then from Yakutsk another aircraft flew a few hundred kilometers to Sangar, and then in Sangar there was a transfer to a third plane which flew to Kobyay. Sometimes there was a long wait in Yakutsk for the plane to Sangar, and in Sangar for the plane to Kobyay, so travel to Kobyay (or back) could take a week. But that wasn't the main difficulty. Everyone who visited Yuri Orlov came under the radar of the state security services, with all the ensuing consequences.

In 1974, a friend and colleague of Orlov, Doctor of Physical and Mathematical Sciences Evgeny Kupriyanovich Tarasov, came to see him in Kobyay. Zhenya Tarasov was my classmate (and my friend); we studied together at the Moscow State University Faculty of Physics. He was a highly qualified theorist specializing in charged particle acceleration. But he was a theorist namely in science. In everyday life, he was a wonderful handyman, able to weld metal, solder, lathe wood into parts of any shape, and much else besides, astounding us, who lacked manual skills. And Zhenya Tarasov was a loyal friend. He wasn't afraid to visit his friend in exile, although he worked at ITEP, the Institute of Theoretical and Experimental Physics – a classified institute in the Glavatom system. Zhenya Tarasov got in trouble because of this.

Yet nothing happened to Yura Golfand. I think, though, that all his actions immediately became known to those who were meant to keep track. Apparently there was a decision not to touch him. After all, Yura was hired at FIAN on orders from the Secretary of the Central Committee of the USSR Communist Party, Zimyanin himself.

***

In the late autumn of 1984, Efim Fradkin and I were sent to the city of Gorky to see Andrei Dmitrievich Sakharov. In the months prior to our trip, no news from Gorky about Sakharov ever reached us. To be precise, there were various rumors, but nothing definite was known. We'd heard that during the summer A. D. Sakharov had declared a hunger strike and that after this the authorities had cut off all contact with him. Nothing was known either about him or Elena Georgievna. Gaps in information are typically filled in by excessive speculation. In particular, there were rumors about the use of psychotropic drugs to influence A. D. Sakharov. This led many to worry and fear that such "treatment" could destroy his personality. Finally, in November, the travel permission was granted.

We visited Sakharov, and he spoke of what had happened in the summer months – the hunger strike, the force-feeding, Elena Georgievna's illness. It was very hard to hear all this. But the main thing that I learned from our trip was that Andrei Dmitrievich, although weakened after the hunger strike, was still the same Andrei Dmitrievich we all respected and loved.

When we said goodbye to Sakharov, he asked us to tell Golfand hello for him. Back in Moscow, I planned to find Yuri Abramovich and do as Sakharov had asked. But there was no need to look for

Golfand. I saw him in the hallway of our department. He was looking for me to ask about the trip – about Sakharov. I gave him Sakharov's hello and a detailed account of all I'd seen and heard. He listened to my story with obvious dismay, asking almost no questions.

***

It seems to me that on this day we started growing close again. His greetings became friendlier, and we sometimes exchanged a few words. Then some months later, Yuri Abramovich gave me a letter from Yuri Fyodorovich Orlov – a prominent physicist and no less prominent human rights activist. At this time Orlov had already served a full term (seven years) in a strict-regime labor camp and was in exile in Yakutia (in the little town of Kobyay). He was corresponding with Golfand and, not knowing my address, sent Golfand a letter addressed to me. Yura (Orlov) wrote about his life in exile, about his day-to-day concerns, and about how he hadn't stopped doing science. He wrote in particular that he was interested in the formulation of quantum mechanics through path integrals. I sought out books on the issues that interested him, put together a package and sent it to him. I didn't have Feynman's book on path integrals, but my friend Vladimir Pavlovich Bykov from the General Physics Institute (GPI) readily passed along the book for Yu. Orlov. A book I'd written, *Oliver Heaviside*, a biography of that remarkable scientist, also went into the package. This marked the start of our correspondence.

Some time later, a reply from Orlov arrived. With his letter, he'd enclosed his paper on multi-valued logic. It was a very interesting paper. In extremely difficult conditions, while imprisoned, first at the labor camp and then in exile, Yu. Orlov had developed a beautiful theory related to propositional logic. Two-valued logic is based on two possible answers to any question – "yes" and "no." As the Bible says, "Let your 'yes' be 'yes' and your 'no,' 'no,' for whatever is more than this comes from evil." But in real life there are not only these two answers – "yes" and "no" – but also many "intermediate" answers, such as "yes," "probably yes," "I suppose, yes", "neither yes nor no," "I guess not," "probably not," and finally, a resounding "no." So Orlov constructed a theory of systems with a continuous gradation of answers between "yes" and "no," likening them to quantum systems with a continuous spectrum. It was a very interesting paper. Yura Orlov wrote that the paper was to be conveyed to Academician Markov for review and asked me to find out from Markov whether it could be published. I think he sent the article in question to Golfand, who relayed it to Markov.

I went to Markov to see if he could help get the article published. Moisei Alexandrovich told me he would send an article to a qualified physicist for review and then, based on this review, would make a decision about publication. Indeed, he gave the article to Slava Mukhanov, one of the employees in his group. Mukhanov's review was quite positive.

I wrote to Yura Orlov about all this.

M. A. Markov was Academician-Secretary of Academy of Sciences' Department of Nuclear Physics, and I had a faint hope that he could help with the publication of Yu. Orlov's article. My message heartened Yu. Orlov. He sent me a letter where he expressed his satisfaction with the course of events. At the same time, he asked me for my opinion of his article. And then I took far from the best course of action. I wrote to Yura that I needed some time to get a better grasp of his work. Instead, my letter should have praised the article. The thing was that all Orlov's correspondence was undoubtedly perused by the local authorities. For the local authorities, Orlov was an anti-Soviet exile. Yet Yuri Fyodorovich Orlov was an outstanding physicist; it would have been good to get that across to those whose job it was to read other people's letters. Then maybe the attitude toward Orlov in Yakutia would have changed at least slightly for the better. I occasionally approached Markov and inquired how things were proceeding with the publication of Yu. Orlov's article. I would come toward the end of Markov's seminar as the participants were leaving the conference room. Usually Markov would leave the conference room accompanied by a few people with whom he would continue discussing issues raised at the seminar. I would wait patiently until Markov was alone before going up to him to learn the news about Yu. Orlov's article. Sometimes it didn't work out for me to talk with him, and I would go away empty-handed. But a few times Yuri Abramovich Golfand, seeing me patiently waiting off to one side, came up to me, took me by the hand and led me to Markov so that he noticed me, and then I could find out something to report to Yu. Orlov.

So I learned that M. A. Markov had taken Orlov's article, appended V. Mukhanov's review and given all this to the vice president of the Academy of Sciences, E. P. Velikhov, along with a cover sheet. The cover sheet contained a request to Velikhov to either authorize publication of Orlov's article or send it in to be archived (deposited) at the Institute for Scientific Information, where the article could be accessed freely. Markov told me that Orlov's article was lying on Velikhov's desk along with the accompanying documents and that he, Markov, regularly reminded Velikhov that the matter still awaited resolution.

"I'll push this thing through," M. A. Markov promised.

I wrote about this to Yura Orlov.

Soon came the Chernobyl disaster, and E. P. Velikhov left Moscow for Chernobyl to battle the disaster's consequences. Yu. Orlov's article was left lying on Velikhov's desk. Then Velikhov returned, and I again saw Markov about the situation. Moisei Alexandrovich told me that in E. P. Velikhov's absence, Orlov's article had gone missing, had vanished from the desk. Frankly, I was very disappointed and lost faith in both Markov and Velikhov. Of course, this news didn't cheer Orlov, either.

About a month later, I received a phone call from Moisei Alexandrovich Markov. He said a chance had appeared to publish Orlov's article, but that he didn't have a copy. He asked if I had one. I had one copy which the author had sent me; I immediately delivered it to Markov. But nothing came of this either. And I no longer had even one copy of the article.

Many years later, Oleg Petrovich Beguchev, the science secretary of the Department of Nuclear Physics, told me that Markov really had reached an agreement with the editorial board of the journal *Automation and Remote Control* about publishing the article. He'd given them the copy of the article he'd gotten from me, but the article hadn't passed review there either, purely because its author was living in exile.

It was amazing! M. A. Markov, a respected, well-known person, Academician-Secretary of the Department of Nuclear Physics, with access to top-ranking officials, couldn't secure the publication of a very interesting paper. Couldn't or didn't much want to, for fear of accusations of attempting to aid a man convicted under the political code.

Soon Yu. F. Orlov's exile came to an early end: he was exchanged for one of our spies who was arrested in the United States. Thus the question of publishing the article on multi-valued logic vanished from the agenda.

As the story developed, I shared all this news with Yu. Golfand. He listened, but refrained from advice and comments. I think he knew the case's details better than I did.

***

On several occasions during this period, Yuri Abramovich visited me in the tiny office I occupied in the Theory Department. He came to the Theory Department very reluctantly; his every visit required persuasion. I made tea, we sat and talked. He of course had changed considerably during his forced unemployment. His face had become sad; he smiled less than before. I had an impression that he'd become religious or at least had started learning the basics of religion. He hadn't abandoned his wish to go to Israel, hadn't withdrawn his emigration petition, and was waiting for whenever the chance to leave might arrive.

One day when we started talking about this, he told me, "Boris, you should leave for Israel, too."

I said, "Who needs me there?"

Yura replied, "God needs you."

I'd started calling him by his first name only, Yura, and he'd already started calling me by name before this time. Nonetheless, we continued to address each other formally.

I learned from him that either there were plans to nominate him as a Nobel Prize candidate for supersymmetry, or that he already had been nominated.

***

In 1989, Yu. A. Golfand and E. P. Likhtman were awarded the I. Ye. Tamm Prize for Theoretical Physics for their work on supersymmetry. This award was established by the Presidium of the USSR Academy of Sciences after the death of Igor Yegenyevich Tamm. An expert commission was created to award the prize. Academician Vitaly Lazarevich Ginzburg was appointed as chairman of the I. Ye. Tamm Prize expert commission. The prize was to be awarded once every few years (every three years, I think).

And so, at a meeting of the Academic Council of the FIAN Theory Department, Doctor of Physical and Mathematical Sciences Vladimir Ivanovich Ritus nominated Golfand's and Likhtman's works on supersymmetry for the Tamm Prize. Evgeny Lvovich Feinberg supported him. In his day, E. L. Feinberg had spoken in favor of Golfand's layoff, but fairly soon had come to see the layoff as a mistake with serious consequences. V. L. Ginzburg wasn't present at the meeting. He disliked Golfand, had a bad attitude about him; he thus considered voting in his favor impossible, but also didn't want to vote against him. Beyond a doubt, Golfand's and Likhtman's works merited such a prestigious prize.

In any case, the Scientific Council of the Theory Department unanimously nominated Golfand and Likhtman for the Tamm Prize.

Vladimir Ivanovich Ritus, who had initiated this decision, told me that a few days after the Academic Council meeting, Ginzburg approached him and said, "Keep this in mind, Volodya – I remember my grudges."

Yet for Ritus this remark bore no consequences.

After this, the decision of the Theory Department's Academic Council was approved by FIAN's Academic Council and relayed to the I. Ye. Tamm Prize expert commission. This commission's chair, as already mentioned, was V. L. Ginzburg. Golfand's and Likhtman's works were scheduled for discussion, but Ginzburg wasn't at the discussion session. Shortly before the scheduled session, he left Moscow – I don't remember exactly whether on vacation or a business trip. He preferred to stay out of the discussion. The commission unanimously awarded Golfand and Likhtman the I. Ye. Tamm Prize, and this was quite fair. The commission's decision came, of course, as a form of belated recognition, but it was still recognition.

Next, the decision needed approval from the Presidium of the Academy of Sciences. Vitaly Lazarevich Ginzburg, as chairman of the I. Ye. Tamm Prize expert commission, had to present a report on the commission's decision. He gave his report such that the decision was approved. The I. Ye. Tamm Prize was awarded ceremoniously at a general meeting of the Academy of Sciences. It was a very unusual event. The man awarded had been fired in a staff cut, spent seven years unemployed, and logged seven years as a refusenik and dissident.

***

It's interesting to note that in the early 1990s at the Joint Institute for Nuclear Research in Dubna, candidates for the best work in theoretical physics were nominated for the State Prize. It was recognized that the discovery and development of supersymmetry was one of the major achievements in recent history. The award nomination was supposed to go to several physicists, including Dmitry Vasilievich Volkov, a prominent theoretical physicist who worked at the Kharkov Physico-Technical Institute. D. V. Volkov arrived at the idea of supersymmetry at about the same time as Yu. A. Golfand, although he published his results later. There was no competition between them; Volkov maintained a friendly relationship with Golfand. I'll cite here an excerpt from Volkov's wife, Stalina Ivanovna Volkova. The passage describes the episode just mentioned:

> At the end of the 1980s, the Dubna physicists, specifically V. I. Ogievetsky, proposed to Dima [D. V. Volkov - B. B.] that works on supersymmetry should receive a prize nomination. Dima immediately asked whether the list of prize nominees included Yu. A. Golfand. The answer was negative. The thing was that Golfand by then had left for Israel; the demand for him in Moscow wasn't what it should have been. In Israel, he taught physics at the University of Jerusalem. When Dima

learned Golfand wasn't included in the list submitted for the prize, he declined to participate in the nomination.[27]

S. I. Volkova's memoirs, from which this passage is cited, were published in the book *Dmitry Volkov. Articles, sketches, memoirs*, (Kharkov, Ukrainian Academy of Sciences, Timchenko Publishing, 2007.)

Apparently after D. V. Volkov's refusal, the nomination never took place.

***

In mid-1990, Golfand received permission to leave for Israel, and a few months later flew there with his wife and two daughters. On the day of their departure, I went to Sheremetyevo Airport to say goodbye to him. I think I was the only one from FIAN. His friends and colleagues had said goodbye to him the day before. Yura introduced me to Natasha, his wife, and to his two daughters. We walked together a while in front of the airport terminal, sharing this time in silence. He was serious and thoughtful; he appeared tired. I remember someone in the departing group was taking along a parrot in a cage. The parrot sat perched with ruffled feathers and from time to time slowly, thoughtfully turned his head to the left, stayed a few minutes with head to the left, next slowly swiveled his head back to its former position and stared straight ahead, then just as slowly turned his head to the right. On the verge of departure, Yura looked a little like that parrot. He kept turning his head just as slowly and pausing, lost in thought. I wished him and the whole family a soft landing and prosperity in Israel, and we said goodbye. On the way home from Sheremetyevo I thought about how many hardships had been meted out to Yu. A. Golfand and his family, and I wished with all my heart for them to find peace and tranquility in a new place.

We met again in May 1991 in Moscow, at FIAN, which was hosting the first International Sakharov Conference on Physics. Yura

---

[27]This passage contains inaccuracies. Golfand emigrated to Israel in October 1990, and worked at the Technion – the Israel Institute of Technology – in Haifa. The Golfands' residence was indeed in Jerusalem.

Golfand was invited to this conference, and traveled to Moscow. In talking with him then, I got the impression that not everything in Israel was going as he would have liked. In particular, he still had no job. But the question of work was decided right there at the conference. One of the participants in the Sakharov Conference was the Minister of Science of Israel, the eminent theoretical physicist Professor Yuval Ne'eman. Ne'eman and Golfand met at the conference and discussed a possible job for Golfand. Yuri Golfand left Moscow with hope.

Soon he took a position at the Technion, a world-renowned research and educational institution. In autumn 1991, I was in Israel, visited the Technion and saw a strong, tanned and happy Yura Golfand. He smiled, simply shone with geniality. When I asked how he was, Yura said, "All's well, I'm making progress in my work, I like it here, and I've already started repaying my debts." Apparently he'd fallen into debt while unemployed.

Yura Golfand's office at the Technion was next to the office of Misha Marinov, also a theoretical physicist and also from Russia. Already an old-timer in Israel compared with Yura, Misha was happy to help him enter a new life. I was glad to see them both.

After my return to Moscow, we corresponded by email. Yura was preparing a major article for publication in *Proceedings of the Lebedev Physical Institute* (FIAN), and for a while I served as a liaison between him and the editors.

On February 17, 1994, Yu. A. Golfand died after a brain hemorrhage. I was told that he was alone at home when the hemorrhage occurred. His wife and daughters came home and found him lying unconscious on the floor. Soon after, he died.

His death came for me and many others as a complete surprise. It was, you might say, a death against a backdrop of well-being earned through suffering, and in speaking of well-being, I have in mind not only and not so much well-being materially (something he never chased after) but spiritually. Finally Yuri got the recognition he deserved, had the chance to work in peace, to be in touch with professional colleagues all over the world...

***

When I think about Yura Golfand, about his life, I often recall something Andrei Dmitrievich Sakharov once said. I learned about this from Boris Altshuler. A conversation with Sakharov had turned to the question of how much Andrei Dmitrievich could accomplish on the path he'd taken and how far he'd be able to move toward the goals he'd set and proclaimed. Sakharov said something like, "You have to choose a road and walk it. The distance you'll walk on this road and when you'll fall doesn't depend on you."

Yuri Abramovich Golfand chose his road and walked it. Until he fell. The road was a hard one. If he'd turned aside from it, his life might have been easier and calmer. But he didn't turn aside. He walked a chosen road as far as he did. And it was a way walked with dignity.

INDEX

Amaldi, Edoardo x, xiii, 23, 24, 43,
44, 48, 53, 57, 82, 94, 266, 278
Amaldi, Ugo xiii, 43
Ardenne (von), Manfred 54-56, 223,
224, 227, 231, 234, 289, 310
Atkinson, Robert 93, 107, 110-114,
309, 330, 333, 338

Bartz, Ilse 48, 58, 294-296, 379, 382
Becker, Richard 23, 59, 61
Berestetsky, Vladimir Borisovich
436, 490, 509
Bethe, Hans 23, 111, 114, 240, 469
Blackett, Patrick 119, 121, 125, 190,
195, 196, 198, 266, 291, 340, 342,
344, 346, 380
Bonner, Elena 433, 436, 437, 447,
460, 502, 515, 516
Bohr, Niels 20, 23, 29, 55, 100, 104,
106, 108, 149, 184-186, 188, 190-
196, 218, 227, 232, 242, 257, 267-
270, 278, 291, 332, 379
Born, Max 59, 61-63, 99, 101, 104,
261-265, 274, 291, 294, 295, 332,
338, 421
Bothe, Walther Wilhelm Georg 115,
232-234, 244, 256
Bratz, Gerda 33, 35
Bronshtein, Matvei 1, 9, 73, 77, 116,
117, 310, 348, 349, 512

Casimir, Hendrik 293, 307, 379
Chernavsky, Dmitry (Dima) 465,
484, 499, 500, 512
Cherneva, Olga xiii, 2, 347, 349
Citrine, Walter 136, 138, 140
Cockcroft, John Douglas 20, 141
Cohn-Vossen, Friedel 164-168, 361

Cooper, Edna 8, 117, 138, 142, 143,
145, 152, 158
Cybulska, Zofia 14, 371

Delbrück, Max 104, 337
Diakov, Boris 2, 53,
Dirac, Paul 9, 20, 99, 333, 336, 348,
349, 512
Dzerzhinsky, Felix xi, 482

Einstein, Albert 27, 119, 120, 122,
191, 193-195, 198, 201, 233, 293,
339, 493, 494
Elsasser, Walter 5, 7, 96, 98, 107,
114, 122, 141, 154, 307, 333, 336,
338
Esau, Robert Abraham 58

Fainberg, 465, 468, 472, 484, 503,
506-508, 520
Feinberg, Evgeny Lvovich 433, 465,
483, 485, 487, 491, 498-502, 531
Fermi, Enrico 23, 147, 239, 240, 479
Fjelstad, Giovanna (Bamsi) xii, xiii,
2, 44, 45, 47-49, 50, 102, 142, 143,
169, 170, 182, 218, 296, 310, 315,
320, 339, 345, 379, 380-382
Fock, Vladimir 20, 77, 99, 103, 348
Fomin, Valentin x, 19, 148, 149, 154,
159-162, 310, 348
Fradkin, Efim Samoilovich 407, 436,
465, 472, 484, 498, 503, 505, 526,
Frank, Ilya Mikhailovich 406, 407,
435
Franck, James 63, 100, 104, 194,
291, 309, 332, 336, 337, 338, 382
Frenkel, Victor x, xiii, xiv, 1, 2, 3,
13, 32, 45, 50, 53, 71, 194, 258,

278, 349
Frenkel, Yakov Ilyich 1, 20, 99, 149,
    322, 354
Frisch, Otto 23, 126, 127, 128, 223,
    233, 307, 343

Gamow, George 93, 101, 103, 104-
    106, 108-113, 115, 116, 119, 121,
    126, 185, 267, 270, 299, 307, 309,
    319, 339, 343, 347, 348, 351, 355
Geiss, Johannes 111, 294, 298, 307,
    316, 317
Gerlach, Walther 58, 59, 245, 289,
Ginzburg, Vitaly 80, 407, 408, 411,
    412, 434-436, 449, 465, 475, 476,
    480, 481, 483, 485, 487, 492, 497,
    499, 503, 504, 507, 518-520, 523,
    524, 531, 532
Goeppert-Mayer, Maria 47, 99, 340
Golfand, Abram Dmitriyevich 396-
    398, 401, 402
Gorman, Aglaya 273, 279, 283, 284,
    286
Gorsky, Vadim 19, 154, 310, 348
Goudsmit, Samuel 289-291

Hahn, Otto 223 , 232, 234, 245, 289,
    291
Haxel, Otto 56, 59
Heisenberg, Werner 20, 23, 56, 58,
    62, 99, 232-236, 238-242, 244-246,
    257, 258, 289, 290, 291
Hertz, Gustav Ludwig 100, 107, 119,
    234, 309, 322, 338
Hohenemser, Kurt 64, 65
Houtermans, Charlotte xi, 1, 2, 8,
    44, 45, 47-50, 53, 114, 116, 126,
    138, 142, 147, 152, 187, 194-196,
    219, 263, 284, 295, 307, 347, 350,
    355, 379-383,
Houtermans, Elsa 45, 47, 48, 95-97,
    127, 194, 219, 309, 318, 321, 322,
    340, 346

Ioffe, Abram Fedorovich (also Fyodorovich) 3, 7, 355, 399, 422
Ivanenko, Dmitri 20, 116, 141, 147,
    154, 348

Jensen, Hans 59, 268
Joliot-Curie, Frederic 20, 21, 27,
    126, 194, 195, 199, 200, 227, 261,
    344
Joliot-Curie, Irene 20, 21, 194, 195,
    200, 261, 344
Jordan, Ernst Pascual 61, 65, 299
Jungk, Robert 114, 239, 242, 332

Kalkar, Fritz 191, 192
Kanegisser, Yevgenia 116, 117, 347,
    349, 350, 352, 353
Kanegisser, Leonid 347
Kapitsa, Anna (Anya) 163
Kapitsa, Pyotr (Piotr) 6, 19, 20, 74,
    121, 125, 163, 164, 262, 263, 267,
    274, 362, 400, 408, 423, 460
Keldysh, Leonid Veniaminovich 394,
    407, 449, 450, 459
Kharlamov, Alexander 35, 37-39
Khriplovich, Iosif 82, 97, 229, 264,
    381
Kirov, Sergei 127, 151, 155, 345
Kirzhnits, David 478, 482-484, 491
Knoll, Max 46, 107, 108, 309, 339
Koestler, Arthur 7, 11-13, 15, 24, 26,
    194, 197, 200, 204
Kopfermann, Hans 58, 59, 61, 62,
    68, 268, 290
Koretz, Abram 72
Koretz, Moisei xii, 19, 71-77, 153,
    309, 310, 419, 420-425, 430
Koretz, Natasha xii, xiv, 69, 71, 72,
    74, 78, 418, 426, 427, 430-432,
    435, 438, 451, 458, 459
Kramish, Arthur 219, 253

Landau, Edmund 63
Landau, Lev 4-6, 9, 11, 19, 20, 22,
    23, 26, 29, 33, 51, 71, 73-75, 116,
    119, 127, 141, 148, 152, 163-166,

177, 195, 267, 310, 339, 348, 352, 357, 362, 400, 408, 420-425, 435, 460, 471

Lange, Friedrich (Fritz) 4, 23, 30, 31, 125, 126, 141, 267, 343-346, 362, 399

Laue (von), Max 55 , 59, 119, 120, 218-220, 223, 225, 239-241, 245, 268, 291, 339, 342, 367

Leipunsky, Alexander 6-12, 126, 127, 138, 141, 142, 147, 149, 159, 161, 177, 206, 310, 344, 349, 360, 361

Likhtman, Evgeny 68, 69, 78, 79, 393, 414, 415, 434, 448, 459, 479, 480, 486, 511, 512, 531, 532

Marinov, Michael (Mikhail, Misha) 393, 409, 411, 442, 454, 456, 457, 459, 534

Markov, Moisei 77, 404-407, 443, 518, 520, 524, 528-530

Martius (Franklin), Ursula 64, 65

Meissner, Walther 129, 132, 134, 136, 144, 151

Meitner, Lise 61, 126, 127, 223, 287, 297

Møller, Christian 185, 188-193

Müller, Lore 48, 296, 383-386

Mykalo, Anna Galina 32-36, 38, 40

Nava, Mica xii-xiv, 31, 32, 36-39, 53, 369, 377, 378

Ne'eman, Yuval 393, 394, 454, 455, 459, 461, 534

Neugebauer, Otto Eduard 185, 193

Neumann, (von) John 51, 99, 240

Obreimov, Ivan 5, 7, 75, 119, 127, 141, 154, 178, 209, 310, 340, 349, 360, 361, 363

Oppenheimer, Robert 23, 100, 192, 196, 235, 333, 336, 338

Orlov, Yuri xi, 439, 443, 444-446, 515, 516, 525, 527-529

Paul, Wolfgang 59, 59, 316

Pauli, Wolfgang xi, 48, 49, 50, 62, 99, 115, 116, 119, 122, 126, 127, 192-194, 240, 293, 303, 306, 325, 333, 339, 343 345, 354-356, 379, 382, 383

Peierls, Rudolf xi, 23, 49, 50, 115, 116, 127, 233, 347, 351, 352, 354-356,

Petrova, Nina Gregoriyevna 396-398, 401, 405, 406, 430, 437

Placzek, Georg, 23-25, 38, 141, 185, 194

Planck, Max 61, 120, 286

Planck, Marga 61, 286

Polanyi, Michael 15, 51, 119, 194, 340, 377

Polanyi-Striker, Laura 162, 383

Powers, Thomas 234, 241, 242, 290, 291

Rammer, Gerhard 54, 55, 59, 64, 65

Raniuk, Yuri xiv, 8, 25, 33, 35, 36, 42, 43, 72, 73, 148, 154, 258, 279, 280, 284

Rausch von Traubenberg, Marie 56, 266, 307

Reiche, Friedrich 239-241

Richards, Jean xii, xiv, 13, 14, 27, 35, 142, 383

Riefenstahl, Charlotte xi, 49, 114-116, 309, 354, 356

Riefenstahl, Ursula 340, 381

Rompe, Robert 56, 59, 218, 253

Rosbaud, Paul 55, 59, 219, 253

Rosenfeld, Léon 20, 99, 104, 185, 195, 269

Royzen, Ilya 463, 500, 501

Rozenkevich, Lev 19, 75, 141, 147, 153, 154, 208, 309, 349

Ruhemann, Barbara 4, 20, 23-26, 33, 34, 136, 147

Ruhemann, Martin 4, 20, 22- 28, 33, 34, 130, 136, 138, 141, 201, 357

Rumer, Yuri 20, 76, 77, 99, 163, 164, 310, 420-423

Sakharov, Andrei xi, 80, 81, 82, 393, 407, 408, 410-412, 414, 418, 433, 436, 439, 441, 443, 446-449, 465, 467, 474, 477, 478, 485, 486, 489, 502, 506, 515-517, 520-535
Szilard, Leo 51, 121, 126, 230, 232, 343, 346
Schlesinger, Charlotte (Bimbus) 50, 143, 164-168, 180, 322, 340, 343, 345
Shoenberg, Isaac 121, 125, 126, 309, 342
Shteppa, Konstantin 43, 272, 273, 278-281, 283, 285, 286
Shubnikov, Lev 4, 6, 11, 19, 24, 75, 127, 134, 141, 149, 152-154, 158, 159, 162, 208, 249, 264, 309, 333, 348, 357, 422
Sinelnikov, Kirill 8, 43, 138, 141, 142, 152, 158, 255
Sommerfeld, Arnold 49, 115, 265, 351, 356
Stalin, Iosif (Joseph) 13, 15, 17-19, 23-25, 27, 31, 37, 40-42, 127, 135, 138, 153, 159, 180, 190, 194, 195, 199, 200, 223, 253, 254, 262, 278, 350, 352, 378, 380, 395, 402, 406, 412, 422, 444, 449, 493, 504
Starostin, Igor xiv, 33, 35, 38
Striker, Éva xii, 12, 13, 19, 27, 35, 119, 151, 159, 162, 194, 309, 340; see also Zeisel, Eva

Tamm, Igor 20, 50, 77-81, 99, 119, 340, 354, 356, 406-410, 412, 413, 434, 465-469, 471, 473-475, 477-479, 481, 492, 500
Tammann, Gustav 115, 334, 336, 338
Tarasov, Evegeny (Zhenya) 525, 526
Teller, Edward 23, 28, 29, 51, 63, 99, 337
Tisza, László 4, 20, 22, 23, 28, 29, 35, 52, 141, 207, 208
Trapeznikova-Shubnikova, Olga Nikolaevna 75,

152, 158, 159, 162, 307, 348

Vavilov, Sergei 21, 77, 80, 100, 399, 406, 407, 410, 465
Vyshinsky, Andrei 13, 32, 40, 195, 197

Walter, Anton Karlovich 141
Weissberg, Alexander xiii, 4, 7-15, 17, 19, 20, 22-24, 26-28, 31-36, 38, 39, 53, 74, 98, 107, 133, 136, 138, 139, 141, 142, 147, 152, 153-156, 159, 172, 177-179, 191, 194, 195, 197-200, 207, 211, 212, 214, 217, 271, 278, 309, 338, 340, 347, 348, 351, 352, 357, 369, 376, 377, 378, 382
Weisselberg, Konrad xii, xiii, 19, 23, 31-40, 309, 369, 377
Weisskopf, Victor 22, 23, 25, 26, 112, 119, 121, 141, 193, 307, 340, 516
Weizsäcker, Carl 56, 58, 111, 230, 232, 234, 236, 242-246, 257, 289, 291, 299
Wienerberg, Alexander 16
Wigner, Eugene 51, 104, 240

Yezhov, Nikolai 40, 41, 272

Zeisel, Eva 12, 35, 159, 162, 383; see also Striker, Éva